RED PRIESTS

Indiana-Michigan Series in Russian and East European Studies

Alexander Rabinowitch and William G. Rosenberg, general editors

RED PRIESTS

Renovationism,
Russian Orthodoxy,
and Revolution,
1905–1946

Edward E. Roslof

INDIANA
University Press

Bloomington & Indianapolis

This book is a publication of

Indiana University Press
601 North Morton Street
Bloomington, IN 47404-3797 USA

http://iupress.indiana.edu

Telephone orders   800-842-6796
Fax orders   812-855-7931
Orders by e-mail   iuporder@indiana.edu

Library of Congress Cataloging-in-Publication Data

Roslof, Edward E., date
  Red priests : renovationism, Russian Orthodoxy, and revolution, 1905–1946 / Edward E. Roslof.
    p. cm. — (Indiana-Michigan series in Russian and East European studies)
Includes bibliographical references and index.
  ISBN 0-253-34128-0 (alk. paper)
  1. Communism and Christianity—Russkaia pravoslavnaia tserkov'—History—20th century. 2. Russkaia pravoslavnaia tserkov'—History—20th century. 3. Communism and Christianity—Soviet Union—History. 4. Soviet Union—Church history. I. Title. II. Series.
  BX492 .R66 2002
  261.7'0947'09041—dc21

                                        2001008456

1 2 3 4 5 07 06 05 04 03 02

CONTENTS

To Lara, Rick, and Chuck

PREFACE

"We are not particularly afraid of all these socialists, anarchists, atheists and revolutionaries. . . . But there are a few peculiar men among them who believe in God and are Christians, but at the same time are socialists. Those are the people we are most afraid of. They are terrible people! The socialist who is a Christian is more to be feared than the socialist who is an atheist."

—Fëdor Dostoevskii, *The Brothers Karamazov*

THE 1917 REVOLUTION that gave birth to Soviet Russia had a profound impact on Russian religious life. Social and political attitudes toward religion in general, and toward the Russian Orthodox Church in particular, remained confused for nearly thirty years. Orthodox clergy known as "red priests" (*krasnye popy*) banded together in an organized movement during those decades of religious uncertainty. Their organization followed a unique and controversial path in ceaseless attempts to reconcile Christianity with the goals of the Bolshevik state. By embracing the radical socialism of Lenin and his party, red priests unwittingly proved that the great nineteenth-century Russian novelist Fëdor Dostoevskii had been right. Nearly everyone—including most Orthodox believers and Bolshevik officials—feared clergymen who proclaimed themselves Christians and socialists.

Orthodox believers feared the theology and actions of red priests. Most believers were not passive observers of emerging Soviet society. They constantly sought ways to exercise their traditional faith while adapting to postrevolutionary social change. Red priests moved beyond popularly accepted limits by actively accommodating Orthodox religious beliefs and institutions to new Soviet realities. They proclaimed that accommodation was the only way to prevent the church from dying. To indicate their intention of reviving an organization that had one foot in the grave, they named their movement "renovationism" (*obnovlenchestvo*) and said they were "renovationists" (*obnovlentsy*) forming a "Living Church" (*zhivaia tserkov'*). Their opponents in the church used a pejorative term ("red priests") for renovationists. The choice of color was significant. Historically, Russian Orthodoxy described differences among clergy using only two categories that referred to the color of liturgical vestments. Married priests who served in parishes were called white clergy (*beloe dukhoven-stvo*), while those who took monastic vows were known as black clergy (*chernoe dukhovenstvo*). Although the renovationists kept traditional vest-ments—white or black, depending on their clerical rank—they lost sup-port from ordinary believers by becoming too closely identified with the country's Bolshevik ("red") leadership. Calling someone a red priest la-beled him as a traitor to Orthodoxy, an alien to Orthodox tradition, and a person who compromised his Orthodox faith to please the atheists.

Ironically, Bolsheviks feared that renovationism might compromise the party's ideology. Lenin and his allies in the party held a strict materi-alistic worldview that denied the existence of any spiritual forces. A gen-uine alliance with red priests threatened to undermine Bolshevik claims to absolute truth by saying Christianity was as acceptable as atheism among party members. Bolshevik leaders, therefore, treated the notion of red priests as a political contradiction in Soviet Russia. Early Soviet soci-ety proved more complicated, however, than political theory imagined. Believers and nonbelievers had to live together in a society filled with contradictions. Many priests, some educated lay believers, and even a few bishops initially embraced renovationist ideas in their desire to integrate Orthodoxy into the Soviet social order. Local government officials ig-nored, misunderstood, or simply remained ignorant of Bolshevik theory. They knew that the Orthodox Church would not simply disappear on command and openly protected red priests out of a practical desire to have allies in charge of Orthodox parishes. These patterns of support shifted over time, as believers, state officials, and party functionaries responded to developments in Soviet society.

This book tells the history of red priests as they repeatedly reshaped their organization and tactics in a hostile environment. For over four decades, they responded to changes in Russian politics and social expec-tations. While not ignoring evidence to the contrary, I argue that renova-tionists generally acted out of genuine religious conviction. I also argue that Bolshevik policy toward religion was complex. Party functionaries and secret policemen frequently manipulated church reformers even while publicly defending the legal fiction of separation between church and state. The history of renovationism is an important part of broader devel-opments in Russia between 1905 and 1946; it sheds valuable new light on the dynamics of society, politics, and religion in those decades.

Methodology

This study presents an institutional history of renovationism from the per-spective of the red priests and their government allies. It emphasizes the actions of organizations formed and transformed under the leadership of red priests. To describe those organizations, I draw heavily upon writings by renovationists and archival documents related to their activities. I also use contemporary published accounts and materials about the movement from a range of sources, Soviet and Western. My methods for analyzing individual and collective action by red priests come from research by American sociologists who specialize in organizational theory. I draw heavily on "neoinstitutional sociology" because of its interest in society's influence on organizational behavior.[1] Others have used neoinstitutional sociology to explain the effects of American society on American religious organizations.[2] I will not present such a detailed sociological analysis of the renovationist movement. I do, however, use two sociological tools— isomorphism and decoupling—to explain the actions of renovationist organizations.[3]

Isomorphism is a process by which organizations mimic one another. In every society, organizations experience pressure to adopt policies and practices similar to those already being used by other groups. Sometimes the government encourages organizations doing the same type of work to imitate one another. Other times an organization may simply decide to copy a successful practice used by another organization in the same field. In either case, the legitimacy of an imitated policy or practice builds as more organizations follow suit. Eventually, every organization feels pressure to adopt the same policy or practice because society expects it. The policy or practice becomes socially defined as a feature of every "good" organization. Isomorphism is evident in the history of renovationism, as the movement's various organizations mimicked other religious and political groups in a vain search for greater social legitimacy.

Decoupling explains the behavior of individuals who systematically refuse to obey the stated rules of their organization. Discrepancies between actions and rules arise because organizations are connected to their society while being dependent on the wishes of their members. Decoupling serves as a counterbalance to isomorphism by allowing organizations to ignore social pressures when conducting their internal affairs. Official policies and practices are decoupled from real actions, as seen when people disregard official policies in order to do their jobs effectively. This happens because some policies in an organization solve internal problems while others are responses to external, social pressure. By decoupling formal rules from internal practice, organizations appease both their internal constituencies (their members) and their external constituencies (their customers, clients, or society as a whole). When an organization attempts to eliminate decoupling—if its rules at all levels are "tightly coupled" or closely bound together—the organization often loses either external legitimacy or internal support. Decoupling can be seen in the behavior of red priests who professed loyalty to an atheistic government while also conducting religious services for their parishioners. Even government officials decoupled ideology from everyday practice. They professed the party line on separation of church and state but still interfered in the affairs of religious groups.

Isomorphism and decoupling help us comprehend the contradictions that surrounded the renovationist movement. Every organization faces contradictory demands for continuity and change. Change occurs when an organization yields to society's demands in order to stay in existence. Isomorphism is a mechanism for identifying and adopting necessary changes. Continuity comes from the need to maintain traditions that hold an organization together. People may give lip service to new ideas that come from the outside, but frequently they resist them at the same time. Decoupling is the means for accepting those new ideas while continuing traditional practices and policies.[4] Renovationists shaped their organizations in response to those same pressures for continuity and change. Therefore, an alternative explanation of their contradictions is possible. Instead of dismissing red priests as either religious traitors or dupes of the Bolshevik party, we can see them as being torn by demands to follow Russian Orthodox traditions on the one hand and new Bolshevik practices on the other. Instead of labeling renovationists as naive fools, we can analyze their attempt to form an organization for integrating Russia's religious past with its political future and ideological future.

Plan of the Book

This is a chronological history of the renovationist movement over the course of half a century. Previous studies have concentrated primarily on its years of greatest activity (1922–1925).[5] A study of renovationism's entire story clarifies its significance in three ways. First, the complete history of renovationism challenges traditional views that the Orthodox Church was either a hapless victim of Communism or a steadfast opponent of Bolshevism. In fact, believers and clergy from various Orthodox groups responded to Soviet policies on religion and other matters in various ways. They embraced some policies while rejecting or ignoring others. Second, the complete history gives greater insight into the impact of religious belief on Soviet politics. Whether the Orthodox masses accepted or opposed specific government policies, their actions influenced the decisions of policymakers, who could not simply ignore religious opinion. Finally, the complete history of renovationism provides insights into the process of modernization and religion. By shunning red priests, the majority of Orthodox believers defined their limits for accepting modernity. By manipulating red priests, the Bolsheviks demonstrated their contempt for Russia's religious traditions. All three groups—believers, Bolsheviks, and red priests—eventually compromised their positions for the sake of social stability in Soviet Russia.

Chapter 1 explains the emergence of those who sought regeneration within the Russian Orthodox Church between 1905 and 1921. It gives background for the Orthodox reform movement and tells how early advocates of change tried to connect their faith with revolutionary politics. The chapter also analyzes the inability of early renovationist organizations to survive in the face of opposition from both church and society.

Chapter 2 examines events from January to July 1922 that led to a renovationist revolution in the Russian Orthodox Church. It connects church revolution with Bolshevik fears of a counterrevolutionary conspiracy led by Orthodox Church bishops in Soviet Russia and abroad. The chapter describes the successful formation of a sustained renovationist organization that reflected Soviet politics by embracing social justice, promoting radical egalitarianism, promising unswerving loyalty to the Soviet state, and attacking traditional Orthodoxy. This section carefully describes state involvement in the central episode of renovationist history, when a small group of red priests took control of the church from Patriarch Tikhon of Moscow (d. 1925) in May 1922.

Revolution in the church resulted in ecclesiastical civil war. Chapter 3 documents infighting among groups for control of the Russian Orthodox Church in 1922 and 1923. It describes the fight for supremacy by different renovationist factions and the process by which church revolutionaries worked to consolidate their influence and control over the entire church. This chapter also provides details of direct Bolshevik involvement in Orthodox affairs both to limit and redirect civil war in the church.

Chapters 4 and 5 examine the history of renovationism from 1923 to 1928. Just as the Bolsheviks took a step back from Communism by adopting the New Economic Policy (NEP) after winning the political civil war between 1918–1921, so they implemented a religious NEP after the victory of renovationism in the church's internal conflict. This change affected renovationism both nationally and locally. Chapter 4 covers the religious NEP from the perspective of the renovationist response on the national level. It describes the impact of Patriarch Tikhon's reemergence as a national church leader on the organization and vision of red priests. Chapter 5 considers pressure on Orthodox believers to both accept and resist change in their parishes between 1923 and 1928. These years marked the start of a twenty-year struggle between Tikhonites (supporters of the patriarch) and renovationists for control of parish churches. The chapter also looks at renovationist responses to attacks from atheists (*bezbozhniki*), who hoped to be an avant-garde in the battle to banish all religious belief from Soviet Russia.

Chapter 6 chronicles the process of liquidating the renovationist movement as an independent organization. It was battered by a series of abrupt shifts in Russian society: collectivization of agriculture, industrialization, Stalinist terror, and a horrific war for national survival. As this chapter shows, champions of renovationism tried to adapt to social changes during the Stalinist Revolution through World War II. They clung to independence until the state dictated their reunion with the patriarchate in 1943 as part of a major shift in religious policy. Even so, some renovationists tried to hold on to parish churches until the death of their last bishop in 1946.

Although their organization ended and their name became synonymous with heresy, red priests influenced the course of Russian Orthodoxy in the twentieth century. The Russian Orthodox Church in 1946 preserved prerevolutionary doctrinal and canonical traditions. Yet it was also a Soviet organization that proclaimed unwavering loyalty to the government and unquestioning fidelity to communist ideals of social justice and progress. Red priests failed to merge Orthodox Christianity with Bolshevik ideology, but they challenged the church to confront Soviet society. They served as the hard rock upon which the Orthodox believers sharpened their identity in Soviet Russia during a process marked by suffering and confrontation.

ACKNOWLEDGMENTS

RESEARCH FOR THIS book was funded by the Fulbright-Hays Doctoral Dissertation Research Abroad program, the International Research and Exchanges Board (with funds from the National Endowment for the Humanities and the U.S. Department of State), the University of North Carolina at Chapel Hill, and United Theological Seminary in Dayton, Ohio. I thank these programs and organizations for their financial support.

I also express my gratitude to the many people who aided in the completion of this work. Donald J. Raleigh has been a friend, colleague, and mentor who guided my development as a historian in countless ways. Gregory L. Freeze provided invaluable support in all areas of Russian church history and willingly shared his vast experience with me. Time and again, Mikhail Odintsov pointed me toward archives that contained important documents on the church. Leonid Vaintraub became a valued friend as we worked to uncover the forgotten history of Orthodoxy in Soviet Russia; he and his family—Lena, Olga, and Tanya—welcomed me into their home and fed me more times than I can remember. I am indebted to Bill Husband for his extensive, insightful comments on an earlier version of this work as well as his friendship and generosity of spirit. It has been a joy and privilege to work with Janet Rabinowitch, Kate Babbitt, and Jane Lyle at Indiana University Press. Many other scholars and archivists in Russia and North America gave of their time and knowledge, so I would also thank Victoria Alexander, Fr. Vitalii Burovoi, Mark Chavez, Heather Coleman, Bill Hutchison, Mikhail Iroshnikov, Peter Kaufman, Andrei Kozarzhevskii, Daria Lomareva, Arto Luukkanen, Donald Mathews, Brenda Meehan, Dan Peris, Irina Poltavskaia, Vera Shevzov, Fr. Alexander Troitskii, Nina Tumarkin, Olga Vasileva, and Glennys Young.

This work would never have been completed without personal support from many people. In particular, I wish to acknowledge dear Russian friends (Zhenia Tsygankova; Slava Riabov; and Igor, Marina, and Katya Talashov); students, friends, and colleagues at United Theological Seminary (especially Jon Thompson, Betty Stutler, Jim Cunningham, Ty Inbody, Kathy Farmer, and Tom Dozeman); and friends from graduate school in Chapel Hill (Kate Transchel, Paula Michaels, Doris Bergen, Betsy Hemenway, Jeff Jones, and Dave Nordlander).

An earlier version of Chapter 5 appeared as "The Heresy of 'Bolshevik' Christianity: Orthodox Rejection of Religious Reform during NEP" in *Slavic Review* 55, no. 3 (Fall 1996): 614–635. I thank the American Association for the Advancement of Slavic Studies for granting me the right to publish it in this volume.

Finally, in the Russian tradition of saying the most important things last, I am grateful to Rick and Chuck for living with this project for as long as they can remember and to Lara for sharing a passion for the church in modern Russia.

ABBREVIATIONS

Agitprop	Agitation and Propaganda Department of the Central Committee, All-Russian Communist Party (Bolshevik)
ARK	Antireligious Commission of the Central Committee, All-Russian Communist Party (Bolshevik), also called the Commission for Separation of Church and State
ASSR	Autonomous Soviet Socialist Republic
Cheka	secret police, also known as VChK, (1917–1922)
GAKO	State Archive of the Kaluga Region
GARF	State Archive of the Russian Federation (formerly TsGAOR SSSR)
GPU	secret police (1922–1923)
Kadet	Constitutional Democrats (liberal political party, 1905–1917)
Komsomol	Young Communist League
NEP	era of the New Economic Policy (1921–1928)
NKIu	People's Commissariat of Justice
NKID	People's Commissariat of Foreign Affairs
NKVD	People's Commissariat of Internal Affairs
OGPU	secret police (1923–1934)
Orgburo	Organization Bureau of the Central Committee, All-Russian Communist Party (Bolshevik)
Politburo	Political Bureau of the Central Committee, All-Russian Communist Party (Bolshevik)
RGASPI	Russian State Archive for Sociopolitical History (formerly the Central Party Archive and then RTsKhIDNI, Russian Center for the Preservation and Study of Documents of Modern History)
RGIA	Russian State Historical Archive (formerly TsGIA SSSR)
RSFSR	Russian Soviet Federated Socialist Republic
SODATs	League of Communities of the Ancient Apostolic Church
SOTsDNI	Saratov Province Center for Documents of Modern History (formerly the Saratov Province Party Archive)

Sovnarkom	Council of People's Commissars
SR	Socialist Revolutionary Party
TsGAMO	Central State Archive of the Moscow Region
TsGA TASSR	Central State Archive of the Tatar Autonomous Soviet Socialist Republic
TsGAIPD	Central State Archive for the Study of Political Documents (formerly the Leningrad Party Archive)
TsGIAgM	Central State Historical Archive of the city of Moscow
TsKhIDNIT	Center for the Preservation and Study of Documents of Modern History, Tatarstan (formerly the Tatar ASSR Party Archive)
TsMAM	Central Municipal Archive of the city of Moscow
VChK	security police, also known as the Cheka (Civil War era)
VIRA	*Voprosy istorii religii i ateizma* [Questions of the History of Religion and Atheism]
VTsIK	All-Russian Central Executive Committee
VTsS	Supreme Church Soviet
VTsU	Supreme Church Administration
ZhMP	*Zhurnal Moskovskoi Patriarkhii* [Journal of the Moscow Patriarchate]

Archival abbreviations using the Russian system:

f.	*fond* [collection]
op.	*opis'* [inventory]
d.	*delo* [file]
l., ll.	*list, listy* [leaf, leaves]
ob.	*oborot* [verso]

RED PRIESTS

1.

THE PATH TO CHURCH REVOLUTION

RED PRIESTS EMERGED out of the same social turmoil that produced other revolutionary groups in late imperial Russia. After Russia's disastrous defeat in the Crimean War (1853–1856), the new emperor, Alexander II (r. 1855–1881), decided to introduce significant social changes known as the Great Reforms. Social elites from both ends of the political spectrum supported this decision, at least initially, and the Great Reforms began in 1861 with a decree that emancipated the serfs. Other reforms followed during the 1860s and 1870s. The *zemstvo*, a new body of local government, gave more power to rural local officials. Similar changes were implemented in city governments. Elementary schools for former serfs came into being along with other changes in the education system. The military was reconstructed and reorganized, as was the judicial system. Censorship was relaxed, opening the way for greater public discussion of social problems.

The Great Reforms brought unforeseen consequences, many of them negative. The government's attempts to implement gradual change at a slow pace meant that society as a whole was disturbed but not reconstructed. Nobles, bureaucrats, merchants, professionals, soldiers, and peasants alike found much to dislike in the reform legislation. They saw their privileges eroded without any compensating reward. Revolutionary groups of radical young people formed among the intelligentsia. They believed that they could construct a new kind of state in Russia and, when their ideas were ignored, turned increasingly to violence and terrorism to bring about social revolution.

The Orthodox Church as both an organization and as communities of believers was caught up in this whirlwind of political and economic change during the second half of the nineteenth century. Reform touched the institutional church with the introduction of parish councils and the modernization of ecclesiastical schools. These changes led to a reduction in the number of clerical positions and simultaneously afforded the sons of clergy an opportunity to leave church service for secular professions. Many educated men who remained in the priesthood found the ideas of the revolutionary intelligentsia appealing, especially when society as a whole began demanding a radical shift in political power at the start of the twentieth century. This chapter traces the demands for religious regeneration from 1905 through 1921 by analyzing how advocates of reform responded to the development of revolutionary Russia.

Pressures for Change within the Church Prior to 1905

X The roots of renovationism lay in a long-standing concern about the degree to which the Russian people were Christianized. From the beginning of the eighteenth century, educated Russians had concluded that the laity held a "dual faith" (*dvoeverie*) that contained as many pagan elements as Christian ones. Church leaders, working with government officials, experimented with various methods for changing popular religion throughout the imperial era. During the first half of the eighteenth century, the Orthodox episcopate relied on coercion and punishment to battle superstition among the masses. When this failed, the hierarchy switched to a more positive approach aimed at enlightening the people through various forms of religious instruction.

This emphasis on conscious Christianity from 1750 to 1850 required the active participation of the parish clergy, whom the bishops expected to educate their flocks in the course of performing other religious rituals. Competing demands on parish priests, inadequate education of minor parish clergy (deacons and sacristans), and a widening cultural gap between educated priests and simple laity all impeded this approach to rechristianization.[1] From the middle of the nineteenth century until 1917, the Orthodox Church followed a new strategy for fighting religious ignorance among the people. It expanded religious instruction outside the church by establishing a popular religious press and a system for public education. Simultaneously, church leaders explored ways to reform Orthodoxy internally by prohibiting liturgical variations that were said to promote nonbelief.[2]

While experimenting with these programs for changing popular religion, the institutional Orthodox Church had to cope with organizational transformation. Prior to the reign of Peter the Great (r. 1682–1725), the church had been a loosely structured organization, ruled by monastics and connected with the state, that dictated—or at least attempted to dictate—the rules for daily life to every Russian. Peter the Great's Ecclesiastical Regulation of 1721 restricted the church's functions to spiritual education and the supervision of moral conduct throughout the empire. He also replaced the Moscow patriarchate with a Holy Synod and mandated the establishment of an educational system for the clergy.[3] The post-Petrine state claimed prerogatives, previously within the exclusive domain of the church, in deciding the nature of the common good. Peter's reforms primarily limited the church's power by separating its structure from the government.[4]

Orthodoxy's ineffectiveness at stopping the growing wave of popular antireligious feeling led some Russian churchmen to make a different assessment of the Petrine ecclesiastical reform at the start of the twentieth century. They said that reform intentionally and successfully undermined the foundations of Russian spirituality by stripping the church of all power and transforming it into a mere governmental ministry for religious affairs.[5] In other words, these Orthodox thinkers equated the loss of ecclesiastical sovereignty with the spiritual decay they perceived in their nation. They argued that restoring the church's sovereignty—that is, giving the church leaders final legal authority over a completely independent institution—was indispensable for Russia's spiritual revitalization.[6]

The impact of this thinking on renovationism can be seen in the writings of Boris V. Titlinov, a historian who participated in the reform movement. He argued that unification of the Russian Orthodox Church and the tsarist government was incomplete. Nevertheless, their unity had become the "main feature" of church-state relations prior to 1917. In his view, the church had gradually lost both independence and legal equality when the tsarist government adopted the Byzantine model of caesaropapism. Under the Petrine innovation of synodal chief procurators, clergy became "bureaucrats (*chinovniki*) in cassocks," parishes lost their autonomy, and the church was transformed into a state bureaucracy. By the beginning of the twentieth century, the church was "already a fully depersonalized institution" with little moral authority. Believers were mired in ritualism, and secular society viewed the church with "contempt and condescension."[7]

Titlinov's damning indictment reflected a sense of disillusionment shared by his contemporaries among the Russian Orthodox clergy. They had suffered greatly in the nineteenth century's failed ecclesiastical reforms, aptly described by historian Gregory Freeze as pseudo-reform (*réforme manqué*), during which priests lost much of their influence in non-peasant society. Diocesan administration was arbitrary, chaotic, bureaucratic, and corrupt. Ecclesiastical schools were of low quality and were out of touch with developments in Russian secular culture. The intellectual level of the clergy declined; men educated in church schools often refused to serve as parish priests because of the profession's low status. In deserting, they allowed those with little or no education to fill parish staff positions. On the whole, clergy lacked a sense of their mission, purpose, and place in changing Russian society.[8]

An Orthodox priest named A. Molozhskii captured the frustration of the clergy with their country's culture when he said, "We have in Russia a score of orthodoxies that differ from each other in their fundamental beliefs."[9] He was correct, for Orthodoxy had divided into three main camps by 1905 (black clergy, white clergy, laity), and each had its own response to the continuing crisis in the faith. The black clergy, who had taken monastic vows and from whom the Orthodox episcopate was chosen, had a strong sense of group identity thanks to the Petrine ecclesiastical reforms. A new type of bishop emerged during the imperial period, when the brightest church academy graduates were offered rapid promotion into the episcopal ranks in exchange for their accepting celibate, monastic life. This system produced a class of dedicated episcopal administrators whose first loyalty lay with the church as an institution.[10] The monastic bishops opposed relinquishing their prerogatives to either state officials or the lower ranks of clergy who pushed for ecclesiastical democratization. Bishops saw the Orthodox laity as "pious" but "ignorant" and the parish clergy as corrupt, poorly educated, and greedy.[11]

In the aftermath of pseudo-reform, the episcopacy united behind a reform program of "episcopal conciliarism" (*sobornost'*). Main elements of this program included stripping power away from the Holy Synod and its chief procurator, restoring the patriarchate with limited powers, convening periodic church councils in which bishops would be preeminent, granting greater independence of local dioceses in decision-making, limiting clerical involvement in government, and permitting parishes to elect their own priests.[12] Theologically, episcopal conciliarism drew on Orthodox traditions that saw the grace of God flowing through men who were linked to Christ through apostolic succession. Their purity was maintained through monastic vows that raised them to the status of angels, in constant prayer to God. Institutionally, episcopal conciliarism aimed to restore sovereignty to the church over all its affairs. The hierarchy intended that church councils, not the state, would give direction to a revived organization that would renew the traditional foundations of Orthodox culture.

Married parish priests (the white clergy) generally opposed such proposals on the grounds that they concentrated even more ecclesiastical power in the hands of the episcopacy. These parish priests envied the status of the bishops, whose advance out of the priestly estate could not be duplicated by anyone with a wife. The parish clergy had become a distinct, closed caste in Russia by 1800.[13] While their general level of education rose dramatically as a result of the Ecclesiastical Regulation of 1721, rural parish priests felt themselves becoming increasingly impoverished and isolated. Their rising levels of education seemingly worked against them, at least until the end of the nineteenth century. Politically, they became aware of the very church structures that kept them subservient to the interests of the monastic clergy and the government. Theologically, they grew increasingly skeptical of the "superstitious" and "non-Christian" worldview of the mostly uneducated laity. Conflict with parishioners was a recurring theme for the parish clergy in the nineteenth century, centering on such issues as size of income and exceptions to church and state laws on marriage, divorce, confession, and communion.[14]

Some among the white clergy forged reform proposals that fall under the general rubric of "clerical liberalism." Clerical liberalism can be defined as a philosophy critical of both ecclesiastical and governmental authority, sympathetic to public needs, and supportive of the parish clergy's social and economic interests. Just as other liberals in Russian society among other professional groups (local officials, lawyers, doctors and university professors) aggressively agitated for constitutional reform, liberal parish clergy proposed convening a church council for the purpose of revitalizing church life and governance. They opposed, however, the increased centralization of power that stood at the heart of episcopal conciliarism. Parish clergy favored measures that would make bishops accountable to the priests and laity in their dioceses. More importantly, white clergy believed they could solve the national spiritual crisis if they had real power to dictate the church's direction, and that power would only come when they were allowed to enter the episcopate.[15]

Proposals from parish clergy for change challenged Russian Orthodox traditions. Attacks on episcopal privilege drew on a Western understanding of equality of opportunity that was alien to hierarchical Russian culture. Similarly, parish clergy who were educated in the leading theological academies of the late nineteenth century (in St. Petersburg, Moscow, Kiev, and Kazan) developed a view of pastoral work that emphasized the church's teaching role, not its ritual. They were alarmed by the success of Russian sectarians, such as Baptists, in preaching and proselytizing among the Orthodox. That success highlighted Orthodoxy's weakness among its own adherents. In response, Orthodox clergymen tried to apply effective methods from German Protestantism to their "new" mission field, the Russian Orthodox parish.[16] They approached the task of re-Christianizing the Orthodox parish as theological liberals who affirmed two underlying principles: "freedom of conscience . . . freeing people to pursue their needs and interests apart from the direct tutelage of religion or a church" and "the relative autonomy of the secular spheres of life, such as science, politics, economics and art . . . [which] is a way of recognizing the complex nature of rationality, of affirming reason's need for critical distinctions."[17]

One cannot be surprised that the lay members of the church felt estranged from clergy who held such views. The short tenure of bishops within most dioceses and nearly constant conflict between bishops and parish priests increased the laity's sense of alienation from all clergy. Ordinary believers lacked systemic proposals for church reform. They simply wanted a priest who would charge low fees and a bishop who would not interfere with their affairs by raiding the parish treasury for nonlocal needs or appointing unacceptable clergymen to their parish. Lay believers probably opposed all reform proposals, no matter how well intentioned, precisely because they did not address those very problems.

Suspicion of the institutional church reflected interests of differing segments in lay society. The intelligentsia tried to find common intellectual ground with church leaders only to be stymied by the tendency of most clergy to think exclusively in terms of Orthodox traditionalism. Government officials experienced heightened alienation from the church due to their mistrust of the clergy's intentions. Bureaucrats thought clergy were unreliable in implementing reforms dictated by the state. At the same time, clergy stopped trusting the government because of its many broken promises to provide financial assistance in the form of state salaries for churchmen.[18] Discontent simmered beneath the seemingly calm surface of church politics for decades. Mistrust and alienation permeated the Russian Orthodox Church at the start of the twentieth century. The 1905 Revolution brought all grievances to the surface.

Renovationism's First Appearance

In the late nineteenth century, the noted Orthodox philosopher and theologian Vladimir Soloviev asked, "How can we renew (*obnovit'*) our church's strength?" In posing this question, he did not merely express a general concern for ecclesiastical reform. Rather, he wanted the church to take its rightful place in the establishment of the Kingdom of God on earth.[19] Soloviev's challenge was answered during the 1905 Revolution, which loosened many of the old strictures and freed portions of Russian society to explore new options for ordering their country.

Orthodox Christianity played a key role in events that led to the first Russian Revolution of the twentieth century. Russia experienced military humiliation in its war with Japan in 1904–1905, and defeat ignited unrest among all layers of society. Fr. Georgii Gapon had organized thousands in St. Petersburg into an Assembly of Russian Factory Workers, which the government tried to contain at the end of 1904. A general strike throughout the city resulted, and Gapon decided to lead a mass march to the Winter Palace in order to present a petition for higher wages, shorter hours, and constitutional reforms to Nicholas II. The tsar refused to meet the protesters or receive their petition. Instead, soldiers were ordered to shoot at protesters, who included women and children carrying Orthodox icons and banners. The massacre of January 9, 1905—known as Bloody Sunday—sparked political revolt in Russia.

The 1905 Revolution was exceptionally volatile and complex, and Russian Orthodox clergy in general were outside the main currents that were promoting broad change. Other professional groups united with workers, peasants, and soldiers to force Nicholas to sign the October Manifesto, which promised constitutional reforms and civil rights. Some church circles issued public appeals for change, but these generally touched on purely church concerns. For example, in their annual reports for 1905 to the chief procurator of the Holy Synod, many Orthodox bishops advocated reform based on the principles of episcopal conciliarism.[20] A few radical bishops broke ranks. A central figure in the future renovationist movement, Bishop Antonin Granovskii, demanded an end to Russian autocracy.[21]

The Group of Thirty-Two, a seminal form of renovationism, published its own agenda for reform in 1905. This group of parish priests from St. Petersburg issued an open petition to the church, spelling out a program for change along the lines of clerical liberalism described earlier. For example, it opposed the restoration of the patriarchate and advocated different reforms in church administration that would allow parish clergy to elect and even become bishops.[22] The Group of Thirty-Two soon joined with lay advocates of Christian socialism to form the Union for Church Regeneration with a wider agenda for reform. The Union issued a memorandum to Metropolitan Antonii Vadkovskii of St. Petersburg that expanded on proposals by the Group of Thirty-Two. That memo demanded separation of church and state, a democratic and conciliar system for church administration, the use of the Gregorian calendar by the church, and translation of the liturgy into vernacular Russian.[23]

✻ Parish clergy on the whole were active in pursuing their version of church reform. They engaged in a wide variety of social protests during the first Russian Revolution.[24] Broad support for reform was noted in an article in *Bogoslovskii vestnik* [Theological Herald] from 1907:

> The movement for church renewal continues to live and find defenders in that stratum which, earlier, knew it mainly by hearsay. If earlier this movement found support primarily among the clergy in the two capitals, it has now penetrated into remote provinces and found there many supporters, who have openly decided to come out in defense of this movement.[25]

However, the provincial reform movement seemed less revolutionary than the reform movement in the cities. My analysis of the Iaroslavl diocesan weekly newspaper, *Iaroslavskie eparkhial'nye vedomosti* [Iaroslavl

Diocesan Gazette], from 1904 to 1906 finds remarkable growth in the number of articles dealing solely with concerns of the parish clergy. The percentage of articles per month on such issues as clergy income, education of priests' children, and clergy control over parish church councils, nearly doubled from an average of 18 percent in the first quarter of 1904 to 34 percent in the last quarter of 1906.

Repression of dissenting elements within the church accompanied political backlash in the wake of 1905. A split between moderates and radicals over accepting the October Manifesto allowed Nicholas II to claim limited victory. He maintained significant power under the Fundamental Laws of May 1906 that transformed the political system in principle. A new legislative organ, the Duma, proved unable to enforce the provisions on civil rights in the October Manifesto. Even though reform-minded clergy were not politically active in 1905, repression also befell those who advocated expansion of ecclesiastical rights. Within three years after the Revolution, the church hierarchy through the Holy Synod had joined forces with the state to end the church renewal movement. The hierarchy cracked down on protesters in the seminaries and academies and among the parish clergy. Nicholas II personally ordered 43-year-old Bishop Granovskii into "retirement" in 1908. The Holy Synod stopped considering all proposals for ecclesiastical reform and postponed indefinitely the national church council (*sobor*) that had been promised by Nicholas in 1905. Likewise, official discussions ended on topics such as changing the social status, educational system, and financial support of parish clergy.

Orthodox adoption of revolutionary rhetoric in 1905 disturbed church leaders, who viewed it as incompatible with church teaching. Sergii Bulgakov, a Russian socialist who later rejected Marxism for the Orthodox priesthood and was active in post-1917 church politics abroad, criticized Christian support for a socialist form of government. He complained that the Russian Orthodox intelligentsia had simply reoriented their revolutionary anger from the secular world to the church and sought "not only to renovate the church life, but even to create its new forms, almost a new religion" following the model of Martin Luther.[26] This charge of creating a "new religion" surfaced repeatedly in renovationist history. The militancy, impatience, and fragmentation of the political forces arrayed against autocracy in the 1905 Revolution found a voice in the Union for Church Regeneration.[27] As political power splintered, so did religious authority. Parish clergy expressed the general restlessness in society by defending and improving their own position as a caste.

The first renovationists imitated ideas from revolutionary politics as they advocated decentralization within the church. They wanted to establish a loose church structure where parish clergy, not bishops or the

Holy Synod, would lead the way to reform. Most Russians refused to support radical change in either the political or ecclesiastical arena. Fearful of the chaos that might result, Orthodox believers backed away from revolutionary propositions that would have broken state sovereignty over church affairs. The Union for Church Regeneration withered away without widespread support. Instead, the official church and its highest leaders became ever more closely identified with reactionary groups that supported the government, such as the Union of the Russian People.[28]

Early Renovationist Leaders

Frustration over the lack of church reform between 1907 and 1917 helped breed a number of future renovationist leaders. Their early enthusiasm for ideas that became the foundation for renovationism in the 1920s made them agents for change within the organized church.[29] Early renovationist agents, such as Granovskii, were creative leaders who drew upon resources in the Russian church and society to mobilize others in the attempt to change Orthodoxy. This influential group included two young parish priests: A. I. Vvedenskii and A. I. Boiarskii.

Alexander Ivanovich Vvedenskii (1889–1946) emerged as the person most identified with renovationism in the Soviet era. Before the Revolution, he was the "archetypal representation of the church's intellectual liberalism that formed in the prerevolutionary years and was sometimes caustically called 'ecclesiastical kadetism.'"[30] More important, he embodied converging desires for church reform among the religious intelligentsia and parish clergy. Vvedenskii's paternal grandfather was Jewish, but he converted to Christianity and served as a psalmist (cantor) in the diocese of Novgorod, changing his surname to Vvedenskii (from *vvedenie*, the Feast of the Presentation of the Blessed Virgin) in the process. Vvedenskii's mother was born into the provincial bourgeoisie, and his father became a nobleman and headmaster of a school in Vitebsk.

From his youth, Vvedenskii displayed both religious devotion and intellectual gifts. He studied philosophy at the university in St. Petersburg while continuing to pursue interests in music and religion. He played the piano for three to four hours every day and frequented the salon of Dmitri Merezhkovskii and Zinaida Gippius, two leading figures in the literary movement known as Russian symbolism.[31] Under their influence, he devised a plan in 1910 for identifying reasons for religious agnosticism among the Russian intelligentsia. He published a survey in the newspaper *Russkoe slovo* [Russian Word] and received thousands of replies from literary, intellectual, and political figures. The surprising volume of answers is explained by the intentional ambiguity over which A. I. Vvedenskii had requested this information; the young student of philosophy shared his name with a famous philosopher and sociologist at the University of St. Petersburg. Vvedenskii's willingness to exploit this coincidence—he was not related to his famous namesake—shows his early penchant for opportunism.

Vvedenskii reported the results of his survey in an article in the magazine *Palomnik* [Pilgrim] entitled "The Reasons for Nonbelief Among the Russian Intelligentsia." He claimed to have found two commonalties in the survey results. First, nonbelief was fed by an apparent disparity between Christian dogma and scientific knowledge. Second, respondents were repulsed by the reactionary nature of Orthodox clergy.[32] Vvedenskii's response to these results shaped his subsequent rise in the renovationist church. He chose to be an apologist for Christianity, drawing constantly on English and German models to bridge the perceived gulf between religion and science. He also decided to advocate an Orthodox reformation that would renew the church and correct the causes of clerical conservatism.

Vvedenskii's sympathies always lay with the intelligentsia—all other social groups were of lesser importance. So he addressed the problem of nonbelief among the Russian intelligentsia with a decision to become an Orthodox priest in 1912. Although neither monogamy nor celibacy fit his personality, he decided to marry and join the ranks of the parish clergy. Had he remained single, the rules for Orthodox ordination would have forced him to become a monastic priest. Nonetheless, rumors about illicit romantic encounters with various women dogged him throughout his life. Even after Vvedenskii received his university degree in 1913, the church bureaucracy blocked his ordination because of his Jewish background and suspect intellectual roots. He responded by earning a degree from the St. Petersburg Theological Academy but still could not find a bishop who would ordain him. Finally, the head chaplain of the army, Archpriest Georgii Shavel'skii, accepted Vvedenskii as a regimental chaplain in July 1914 and supported his request for ordination. Vvedenskii immediately showed the influence of "decadent" philosophy and his willingness to disregard conventional clerical behavior. While conducting the Divine Liturgy for the first time on the day after his ordination, he prayed silent portions aloud and with such emotion that the attending bishop ordered him to stop. Vvedenskii served for two years as regimental chaplain and in 1916 was made priest of the chapel at the Nikolaevskii Cavalry School in Petrograd. He gained increasing fame for his oratorical skills, in which he incorporated both philosophy and decadent poetry to evoke an emotional response from his parishioners.

Alexander Ivanovich Boiarskii, another priest from St. Petersburg, also responded to the renovationist impulse by becoming an agent of social change. Born in 1885 to a clergy family in Kholm province, he also attended the theological academy in the capital.[33] Although lacking Vvedenskii's personality and philosophical bent, Boiarskii had a genuine interest in the lives and faith of workers. Like Gapon, Boiarskii took the unusual step, for an Orthodox priest, of mingling with factory workers. After completing his degree, he became the priest of the church in Kolpino, a workers' settlement near St. Petersburg. His position on workers and church reform took an increasingly radical tone. Boiarskii was decidedly not mystical or emotional, yet he and Vvedenskii formed a strong personal relationship based on the shared desire for ecclesiastical change.[34]

Scholars debate reasons for the mutual attraction of such varied personalities as Granovskii, Boiarskii, and Vvedenski. Russian intellectual historian Georges Florovsky said that they were "full of anticipation of reforms," a negative quality that arose from "the same old and typical utopian temptation (for the intelligentsia), insensitivity to history." Historian Dimitry Pospielovsky finds more pragmatic bonds among the reformist intelligentsia, academy-educated parish clergy and lay professors at the church academies. He attributes their coalition to resentment over "the limits on their advancement opportunities within the ecclesiastical structure imposed by their marital status."[35] In other words, these educated intellectual members of the church felt capable of actively guiding the institution but were denied significant leadership positions simply because of ancient rules that placed ecclesiastical power in the hands of unmarried monastic clergy. I suggest that these reformers shared a basic dissatisfaction with religious rules governing Russian society, rules they considered outmoded. They sought new interpretations of the rules, as Florovsky notes, but were limited in pursuing their agenda by existing interpretations, according to Pospielovsky.

Churchmen such as Vvedenskii and Boiarskii also responded to "the religious voice that thrived in Russian revolutionary culture in the years before and after 1917." In the words of historian Mark Steinberg, "articulate voices of the lower classes" connected religious images and symbols with the emotions of revolution. In their writing, Russian workers used religious elements to convey the feelings and morality of their movement, which was "as much about psychological and personal needs as about material interests."[36] Vvedenskii appealed to workers because he embraced the emotional side of Christianity, albeit from within the organized church. Boiarskii focused on the moral dimensions of Christian belief as reflected in the Revolution's call for justice for workers. These two priests, like others who hoped for church reform, recognized possible links between Orthodoxy and popular support for revolution after 1905. The political changes of that year did not, however, provide sufficient basis for reform.

The earliest renovationist organization died, and the movement remained unfocused until events in 1917 provided a new impetus for its resurrection.

Renovationism Reborn: 1917

The social and political order established after 1905 displayed its fragility almost immediately after Russia entered World War I in 1914. Initial euphoria and social unity fed by a sense of divine protection gave way to domestic unrest as defeats mounted in late 1914 and throughout 1915. Mutual distrust grew between Nicholas II and leaders of society outside the imperial court. The tsar's incompetence as a military and political leader became increasingly obvious to members of the professions and captains of industry; they offered their support to the government in exchange for a greater voice in state affairs. Nicholas could not give up his belief in autocratic power as the only solution to the crisis. In late 1915, he personally assumed command of the army and left the government in the hands of chosen ministers and his wife and their dubious supporters. Ineptitude at the top and the exigencies of the war opened possibilities for the formation of public organizations dedicated to mobilizing Russia's resources for the war effort. At the same time, the war's demands on national resources fed unrest among the lower and middle classes, racial minorities, and the lower ranks of the military. The old regime sagged under the weight of social discontent and finally collapsed in a few days during the February Revolution of 1917. A new dual political structure came into being. Economic leaders and members of professions formed the Provisional Government, while soldiers, peasants, and workers formed soviets (councils) led by moderate socialists.

By 1917, the Orthodox Church had internalized that same mixture of mistrust, intolerance, and unwillingness to compromise among various elements of its supporters. The fall of the monarchy in late February drove layers of Orthodoxy farther from one another. In the words of Anton Kartashev, a journalist, professor of church history, and Minister of Confessions in the Provisional Government, both black and white clergy experienced the end of tsarism as a "psychological catastrophe." The church appeared to lose its "juridical basis for existence" in a new political order based on popular will rather than the grace of God.[37] Upon news of the tsar's abdication, Archbishop Arsenii Stadnitskii of Novgorod supposedly exclaimed, "There is no tsar, there is no church!" Archbishop Antonii Khrapovitskii of Kharkov, a known reactionary, refused public comment on that event other than to refer his questioners to a historical account of the attacks on the Catholic Church that followed the French Revolution. Some parish clergy refused to accept the change in regime and continued to offer prayers for the tsar and his family.[38] Rumors falsely claimed that clergy supported a counterrevolutionary coup to return Nicholas to the throne and permitted placing machine guns in the bell towers of Petrograd churches.[39]

Soviet publications in the 1920s used those accounts to prove that the Orthodox Church as a whole unconditionally supported autocracy and was completely hostile toward antitsarist social sentiment during the period of growing social polarization in late 1916 and early 1917.[40] That generalization does not withstand the scrutiny of history. The Holy Synod took a neutral position on events in that period and rejected a proposal by the last tsarist chief procurator, N. P. Raev, to denounce "social unrest."[41] Clergy around the country met in March to pass resolutions condemning monarchy.[42] The confusion, hesitancy, and surprise that followed the collapse of Russian autocracy came from the sudden split between politics and religion. Those who had previously challenged the connection between Orthodoxy and tsarism showed the greatest ability to adapt their religious beliefs to political change.

✷ Soon after the February Revolution, parish clergy and laity pushed their demands for a greater voice in church affairs. The first chief procurator of the Synod for the Provisional Government, Vladimir Lvov, purged the church of several conservative hierarchs, granted the academies greater autonomy, and permitted preparations for convening the church council originally promised by Nicholas II during the 1905 Revolution. At the same time, the Lvov-controlled Synod enacted a Provisional Statute for renewing parish life based on the twin ideas of self-governing parishes and dioceses. Using this statute, parishes across Russia met to vote on keeping their priests. Similarly, diocesan congresses convened to judge the fitness of local bishops. Several hundred priests and a few of the most reactionary bishops were removed from their positions. Encouraged by this ferment, parish clergy organized to express their dissatisfaction and push their own agendas for reform. These encompassed a broad spectrum of opinion, from socialist to nationalist.[43]

An example of the intellectual atmosphere in the church in early 1917 and of newly emerging leadership thriving on the air of ecclesiastical freedom is found in the establishment of *Tserkovnyi obshchestvennyi vestnik* [Herald of Church and Society]. Lvov decided to organize this new journal under the slogan "A free church in a free state." He named Titlinov, a professor of church history at the St. Petersburg Theological Academy, as editor. Titlinov was a respected scholar and possessed "a sharp, skeptical mind and cool temperament." More important, although he came from the clerical estate (*soslovie*, the closed hereditary group made of priests and their sons, who also were expected to enter church service and were educated accordingly), his outlook was secular. He approached his subject from the perspective of a modern historian, relying on archival records and contemporary documentary evidence, not as a churchman chronicling sacred events. According to Levitin and Shavrov, Titlinov was "European from head to toe. He did not display the barbaric morals of the Russian clergy from which he came. He believed in democratic and rational—not emotional—church reform."[44]

Churchmen who shared the views of Titlinov and Lvov began meeting together in Petrograd after the tsar's abdication in March 1917. Their gathering place—the apartment of Archpriest Mikhail Popov, who later became an archbishop in the renovationist church—was in many ways the "cradle of renovationism," even though similar groups were meeting throughout Russia.[45] The Petrograd group stood out, in retrospect, because of the number of its members who were prominent in the Soviet era. They attempted to influence the whole church through the formation of the Union of Democratic Clergy and Laity, whose founders included the priests Popov, Vvedenskii, Ioann Egorov, Dmitri Popov (who had served in the Fourth Duma), and A. P. Rozhdestvenskii. Scores of younger clergy in the capital, most holding academic degrees and several having taken part in the earlier Group of Thirty-Two, joined the Union. Rozhdestvenskii was elected president, and Vvedenskii was made secretary. The group began to hold a seemingly endless series of meetings and conferences. The proliferation of similar organizations at the same time meant that few paid attention to this particular group. Vvedenskii later remarked that the church hierarchy "considered [the Union] not worthy of their attention." The one exception was the Union's patron in the hierarchy, Bishop Andrei Ukhtomskii, who had also supported Lvov's March purge of the Holy Synod.[46] The goals of the Union were to support the people in opposing restoration of the monarchy, to help establish a democratic government in Russia with full civil liberties, and to reform the church and separate it from the state. Hostile to capitalism, the group also adopted a radical socialist economic policy that favored giving control over the means of production to peasants and workers.[47]

During the summer of 1917, Vvedenskii appeared to play to all sides in activities that fed later accusations of opportunism. In June, Lvov rushed Vvedenskii, Egorov, and Boiarskii to the front. They met with General M. V. Alekseev, who asked the churchmen to help stop disintegration in the army. The three priests proceeded to the battle zone and into the trenches, where Vvedenskii delivered a rousing and well-received sermon that inspired the troops and enhanced his own reputation. In August, representatives of the Russian intelligentsia asked him to speak in Moscow. The next month, he served as a representative of the democratic clergy in the Preparliament, a body formed by the Democratic State Conference as a means for dealing with Russia's political crisis until the Constituent Assembly could be convened and a permanent government structure established.[48] In the Preparliament, Vvedenskii claimed to have sided with the Bolsheviks on the debate over whether only the socialist parties should be allowed to participate in its sessions to the exclusion of the bourgeoisie. He also later said he had supported the idea of a socialist republic at the time, modeled on the Left Socialist Revolutionary program.[49]

The vitality of socialist views in 1917 among would-be church reformers such as Vvedenskii influenced their future decisions. They worked to adapt the church to public opinion. After all, 80 percent of the Russian population voted for socialist deputies to the Constituent Assembly in November 1917.[50] The support for radicalism among a small group of educated clergy could not stem the rising tide of anticlericalism in 1917. The peasants began demanding both church and gentry lands after February. In March and April, peasants engaged in peaceful forms of protest, such as vigorous negotiations with clergy on the return of land rents the peasants had previously paid. In some rare cases, as in Riazan province, priests were forcibly removed from their land. By May, local land committees began expropriating private, church, and monastic property. In response, the Holy Synod called for a delay of such activities until the convening of the Constituent Assembly. Peasants ignored that appeal and continued seizing property through the summer with raids on church lands reported in fifty-one provinces between April and October.[52] Vvedenskii associated popular anticlerical sentiment with poor attendance at church services that year, even on the great festival of Easter.[53] He concluded that many clergy, fearing the wrath of the people, had closed ranks with the episcopacy and joined forces with the liberal Kadet Party to fight the growing political threat of the Bolsheviks and the peasantry.[54]

Vvedenskii's description of church and clergy during 1917 was influenced in part by battles that were raging within the church while he was writing, in the early 1920s. Still, the Russian people did express strong disapproval of the Orthodox Church in 1917, mainly because of its continued support for the unpopular war effort.[55] In response, bishops hardened their position by condemning most revolutionary activity. In particular, many clergy came to distrust Bolshevism, seeing it as "a synonym for disaster."[56] The lack of wide support among the clergy for such radical political ideas is readily explained. The emphasis on materialism and the anticlerical bias of the Bolshevik party program repelled the churchmen. Most clergy lived in the countryside (where Bolshevik ideas had not penetrated before May 1917) and found the Bolshevik emphasis on the proletariat incomprehensible. When clergy with socialist leanings learned of

Lenin's "April Theses," published in the party newspaper *Pravda* [Truth] on April 7, 1917, they rejected his call to transform the bourgeois revolution into a socialist one based on the proletariat and poorer peasantry. Such a call was inconsistent with expectations of socialist clergy for a bourgeois democratic government before the establishment of socialism. The Soviet antireligious press of the 1920s interpreted this earlier hesitation as a sign of support for the bourgeois Provisional Government among the urban clergy, including the more leftist ones such as Vvedenskii.[57]

A national church council that began meeting in August 1917 reflected the growing mistrust of revolution by Orthodox clergy and laity. Dioceses across Russia sent mainly conservative delegates to Moscow as representatives. Also, the council's rules effectively gave the episcopacy a veto power over all proposed legislation, since three-fourths of the bishops had to agree to any proposal prior to its consideration by the far more numerous non-episcopal delegates.[58] Despite efforts by the council's leaders to keep the peace, the first sessions were stormy; questions on church property attracted special attention. Archbishop Antonii Khrapovitskii proposed an announcement to the general population forbidding the unauthorized seizure of church lands and property. Many delegates agreed this was a serious problem, since "in new conditions it [church property] serves as a guarantee of the independence of the church from many institutions of power in society."[59] This attitude of the Orthodox leadership toward church property fed Bolshevik suspicions about the church's intentions for decades to come.

By the time the Bolsheviks came to power in October 1917, the center of authority in the church, under the council's guidance, had moved away from the direction chosen by many of the non-episcopal clergy just eight months before. In the words of American historian William Fletcher,

> The chief effect of the reforms of 1917 was to restore to the episcopacy a degree of authority which had been denied it under the Petrine regulations of the Empire. Many of the white clergy, however, continued to feel themselves largely ignored in the structure of the church and were profoundly dissatisfied with the limitations or the role which they could take in church life.[60]

The fall of tsarism and convocation of the first national church council in over two centuries had removed the state from a position of sovereignty over the Orthodox Church. As long as the council remained in session, the church had a claim to legitimate authority and independence based on the fact that council delegates had been popularly elected. This undercut the functioning of independent groups such as the Union for Democratic Clergy and Laity that could not marshal opposition to the council's control. As in 1905, a group organized to promote major reforms within the Russian Orthodox Church could not find enough support to survive.

Early Bolshevik Policy on the Orthodox Church

Sustained support for organized church reform eventually came from a surprising source: the radical socialists who took control of the Russian government in late 1917. Before the October Revolution, the Bolsheviks did not dwell on their policy toward the Russian Orthodox Church. Forced to develop a policy on religion after they came to power, they first looked to their leader, Vladimir Lenin. When one considers the prolific output from Lenin's pen, one is struck by the few references to religious topics in his collected works. His attitude toward religion was formed early, remained constant, and was based on three general points. First, Lenin advocated complete freedom of conscience. He incorporated that principle in his draft program of 1902 for the Russian Social Democratic Labor Party by proposing the total separation of the church from both the state and the school system. The next year, he explained in a brochure written "To the Rural Poor" that disestablishing the church would ensure "that everyone shall have the full and unrestricted right . . . not only to profess whatever religion he pleases, *but also to spread or change his religion.*"[62] For Lenin, "everyone" did not include the Social Democrats who, as Marxists and materialists, were required to reject all forms of religious superstition. The task for party comrades was "the revelation of the true, historical, and economic roots of religious fog. Our propaganda unavoidably includes the propaganda of atheism."[63]

Lenin reconciled these two points with a third. He asserted that the battle between Marxism and religion should be fought only with ideas. As he explained, "We demand the complete separation of the church from the state so that we can fight religious fog using only ideas and ideological weapons, namely our press and our words."[64] Although not stated here, one of the Bolshevik leader's main concerns was to avoid the legal persecution of religion that led to "fanaticism" and drove believers into underground opposition to the government. As we shall see, this fear resurfaced time and again after Lenin's party gained access to the levers of power and had to make policy that promoted ideological struggle while limiting administrative excesses against organized religion.

Limiting excesses proved difficult precisely because the party's attitude toward religion was so simplistic before the October Revolution. The Bolsheviks expected to separate church and state easily. Once that was done, they believed, religion in Russia would rapidly wither away. They had no intention of imitating the tsarist policy of state sovereignty over any church,

Orthodox or otherwise. Nor did they envision an alliance with renovationist-type church reformers, as is evident from Lenin's neutral tone toward the proto-renovationists in 1905. He wrote: "The presence of a liberal reformist movement among a certain part of the young Russian clergy is beyond doubt. This movement found its exponents in the meetings of the religious-philosophical society and in church literature. This movement even has taken its own name: 'the new Orthodox movement.'"[65]

Before October 1917, radical Social Democrats had the luxury of espousing ideas without having to implement actual policy. So they had no need for church reformers. The Bolsheviks consistently supported the principles of freedom of conscience, party atheism, and solely ideological conflict with religion. They displayed a mindset that placed religious matters outside the purview of politics and vice versa. The influx of members into the party starting in 1917 included many religious believers and even some priests. Their presence would raise the necessity of cleansing the party from those still holding religious beliefs in the early 1920s.[66] The slowness of that process in the avowed atheistic organization indicated the difficulties awaiting the Bolsheviks in dealing with the persistence of religious belief.

Stalemate: October 1917 to December 1921

For the first four years after the Bolshevik Revolution, church-state relations fluctuated between hostility and negotiation, confrontation and compromise. Government and church leaders dealt with one another carefully and tried to avoid driving the obviously volatile peasant masses into the arms of the other. A stalemate resulted. Neither the Orthodox Church nor the Bolshevik party could gain the upper hand against the other, although both tried. Each side pursued goals that were incompatible and therefore unacceptable to the other. Church leaders wanted a government that would support Orthodoxy without imposing sovereignty over the church. The Bolsheviks sought to end all religious belief in Russia. Each side defended its own sphere of influence and thwarted the other's attempts to expand within that sphere. This stalemate lasted four years, during which the reformers who led the renovationist revolution of 1922 were stymied in their own efforts to affect change. They had some freedom of action but still could not form an independent organization until the stalemate was broken.

The national church council reacted strongly to the Bolshevik seizure of power on October 25, 1917. Many council members said that Lenin and his followers were usurpers and claimed that only a freely elected Constituent Assembly could express the will of the Russian people on a legal government. Some priests outside the council who questioned the legality of the new government found themselves arrested by armed workers and soldiers. In response, the council forbade expressions of political opposition in churches or its own sessions. It did not, however, keep silent about the violence against the clergy sparked by the subject, condemning, for example, the killing of Fr. John Kuchurov at Tsarskoe Selo after he made politically unacceptable remarks. Equally distressing to the council was the damage inflicted on Kremlin churches during the battle between military cadets and Bolshevik forces at the beginning of November. The delegates denounced Bolshevik disregard for "holy things" and helped spread rumors that the new government intended to attack other holy places.[67]

The church council responded immediately to the ominous political upheaval by ending two months of debate and voting to restore the office of patriarch. American historian Catherine Evtuhov notes that the long and passionate debate over the question of a return to patriarchal rule in the Russian church was not simply an administrative matter. "The council members in fact were more concerned with the deeper question of the church's status and role during the revolution and in the society that would emerge afterwards. The issues posed by the movement for church renewal in the 1900s and 1910s had become immediate."[68] Council delegates eventually approved a motion accepting the episcopal conciliar program for ecclesiastical restructuring that had been developed in the nineteenth century. Bishops would rule the church through standing committees that were responsible to periodic regional and national councils.[69]

The election of Metropolitan Tikhon Bellavin (1865–1925) as the first Russian patriarch in more than 200 years seemed to cement the bishops' victory. When the council voted on nominations for the restored patriarchate, Tikhon was the third and last candidate. A monk then drew Tikhon's name in a process that involved the random casting of lots. Aside from being "divinely chosen," Tikhon was the ideal candidate for a patriarchal throne modeled less on the papacy and more on ceremonial presidential roles. Some later regretted not having a "stronger" personality such as Metropolitan Antonii Khrapovitskii, another of the finalists chosen by the council in 1917, who might have been more effective against Bolshevik incursions into the realm of church affairs. But in November 1917, Tikhon's willingness to listen and compromise seemed to be an asset for a church hoping to maintain internal unity.

Tikhon's personal qualities and deeds were obscured first by Soviet historiography that branded him a "counterrevolutionary" who repented of his political errors when faced with the inexorable tide of history, then by the Orthodox Church, which has continued to conceal much of Tikhon's personality by promoting his martyr image (he was canonized in October 1989).[70] When one ignores historical revisionism from either direction, one finds many aspects of Tikhon's life and personality that played a role in the emergence and shape of renovationism. Tikhon personally saw life as an Orthodox bishop from a martyr's perspective even before becoming patriarch. In 1897, shortly after being consecrated bishop, he reportedly said that initially episcopal service was presented to him as "honor, worship, strength and power," but after only a few months he understood it to be primarily "administration, labor, and self sacrifice."[71] Tikhon was also a favorite of the Orthodox laity. In August 1917, he became the first popularly elected metropolitan of Moscow and, shortly thereafter, was the overwhelming choice to preside over the long-awaited national church council. Delegates perceived Tikhon as caring, compassionate, and capable.[72] He was also an accomplished leader of Orthodoxy in hostile environments, having served as bishop in Poland, North America, and Lithuania.

Tikhon represented the best qualities of Russian monastic clergy prior to the revolutions of 1917. His responses to a 1905 questionnaire on church reform squared with those of his episcopal colleagues. He expressed support for a restored patriarchate with accompanying reorganization of diocesan administrative structures to revive Orthodox missionary work, fight heresy, and revitalize pastoral leadership. He approved of the active participation of ordinary believers in parish life. Tikhon hoped to see both clergy and church involved in the sociopolitical life of the country in a way that would unite everyday existence with spiritual values, assuming, of course, that the Orthodox and their government would share those values. At the same time, he opposed the continued submission of the Orthodox Church to the state.[73]

While psychologically and emotionally ready to lead the church through the changes of early 1917, Tikhon lacked the flexibility to adapt to the new challenges, both internal and external, of the Soviet era. His own background in church leadership blinded him to the social forces that led to the October Revolution. He had little sympathy for Marxist or renovationist ideas.[74] Participants in the Union of Democratic Clergy and Laity were aware of this, which fed their displeasure less with Tikhon than with the council that had chosen to reform the church by strengthening its hierarchical structure. Writing in 1923, Vvedenskii claimed that six years earlier, the liberal clergy had opposed the restoration of the patriarchate as "an extraordinary evil" that would lead to the church's destruction unless it were abolished once again. He described a plan, organized by the former head military chaplain Shavel'skii in late 1917, to break with Tikhon. Vvedenskii wrote that the attempt was shelved because "it seemed that the time still had not arrived, and our proposition did not find mass acceptance." The opponents of patriarchal administration then decided to stay in the church, in the words of Vvedenskii, "in order to blow up the patriarchate from within."[75]

Assessing the accuracy of Vvedenskii's account of this plot is difficult, since it is not mentioned by other sources. The liberal clergy were not happy with the turn of events in the council, but they had no reason initially to blame Tikhon personally, as evidenced by their early positive relationship with him. At the end of 1917, some Petrograd clergy, including Vvedenskii, Boiarskii, and Egorov, joined by the writer Evgenii Belkov, formed the cooperative publishing company Sobornyi Razum [Conciliar Reason]. Its purpose was to express the opinions of parish clergy through brochures and journals. The contents of their journals defied simple labels such as "liberal" or "conservative." Vvedenskii wrote an article praising the recently deceased conservative priest John of Kronstadt for his pastoral skills, "liturgical creativity," and "genuine religious feeling."[76] The cooperative produced a sixteen-page brochure on "Atheism and Science," which used the assertion that all scientists were believers to prove that "it is possible to think in the spirit of materialistic and atheistic monism, but it is impossible to be happy and to live morally and socially in full consistency with this thinking."[77] Tikhon met with a delegation from the cooperative in July 1918 in Petrograd and expressed approval of their work. The publishing company's journal, also named *Sobornyi razum*, in turn voiced admiration for Tikhon's leadership.

Public expressions of reciprocal respect continued until late 1921. Tikhon showed patience toward reformers and those who expressed personal opposition toward him. Levitin and Shavrov cite five examples of Tikhon either blessing or ignoring the activities of those who pursued leftist politics or experimented with liturgical innovations, including "retired" Bishop Antonin Granovskii.[78] I have been unable to find any instances of liberal and radical parish clergy publicly expressing disapproval of Tikhon until early 1922. They had no reason to complain earlier. Tikhon's leniency toward reformers until late in 1921 was consistent with his desire to maintain church unity at any cost during the Civil War, to the point of refusing to break openly with the highly politicized émigré church. Perhaps Tikhon stressed the need for church unity to balance, if not overcome, growing Bolshevik power.

A stalemate between the Russian Orthodox Church and the Bolshevik state developed in the first year after the October Revolution. It resulted in large part from Tikhon's ability to keep the church from splintering. Yet the first months of Bolshevik rule did not unfold as the Orthodox hierarchy expected it would when they laid their hands, and hopes, on Tikhon. Finally freed from the restrictions imposed by the Petrine reforms, bishops and leading laymen of the church sought to chart a course independent from the state while refusing to relinquish the traditional privileges of an established church. These same church leaders were challenged by the inconsistency of their claims to represent the majority of the Russian people, who ignored or rejected the decisions of the hierarchy. The bulk of the lower clergy and laity pursued objectives that often were at variance with those of the council and Patriarch Tikhon. Ordinary Orthodox believers resented clerical privilege and sought a greater voice in their parishes. The latter was given to them, unintentionally, by a series of decrees from the new Soviet government.

The government refused to compromise on its principle of complete church-state separation and moved quickly to implement it. In November 1917, the state nationalized all property, including that held by the church, and abolished all laws regarding religious privileges and limits. On November 30, the Council of People's Commissars [Sovnarkom], the supreme governing body in the new Bolshevik government, first debated the question of seizing all Russian Orthodox monasteries out of a concern that they formed a strong financial base for the church. No specific decision was reached.[79] One week later, a new decree placed all church schools under the Commissariat of Enlightenment. In January 1918, the separation of the church from the state and from the school system became law. These acts soon provoked negative reactions from the masses of lay believers, including street demonstrations and riots. Yet many in the government continued to think that complete church-state separation could be accomplished quickly. Their bias against religion led them to use strong administrative measures to wipe out the influence of the church on the masses. One official, writing later to a leading Bolshevik, explained the frame of mind of those directing the early antireligious campaign.

> Many, not knowing the life and feelings of Russia, regarded the battle with the church very lightly and painted a rosy picture of victory over it. I disagreed, for I was certain that the battle would be difficult and our actions should be careful and methodical. I indicated to the commission drafting the [separation] decree that there would be outbreaks of religious excesses and that there would be bloodshed, but my words were greeted with smiles. Events have shown I was correct.[80]

Conservative churchmen who gained control of the national church council following the October Revolution likewise viewed the actions of the new regime with great alarm. While they could not arouse the general populace to support their resolutions against the Bolsheviks, they were able to tap into the popular outrage generated when the government began to expropriate church property. The authorities began with selected monasteries and churches or chapels located in government buildings, ignoring the fact that these institutions often served their surrounding communities. Believers protested the state's actions.[81] The Council responded with proposals for organizing the faithful into local brotherhoods for the protection of church property.[82]

The state countered Orthodox resistance on August 24, 1918, by describing a legal process that guaranteed control of churches to believers. A parish could form when a group of twenty people (*dvadtsatka*) signed an agreement with local authorities, who would then give the group free use of a building for "cult activities." The agreement specified in these instructions granted considerable autonomy to believers. They could govern their parishes as long as they maintained and insured the building entrusted to them for worship. New churches could be constructed, although they would become national property upon completion. The instructions reiterated the facts that the church was completely separate from the state and that no religious group had juridical status under Soviet law. A provision that nationalized all remaining church financial assets made the parish clergy totally dependent on their parishioners for support while also eliminating all sources of independent funds for the hierarchy. Although these instructions could not be implemented immediately, they threatened to undermine the financial situation and lifestyle of the clergy.[83]

An ever-dwindling number of delegates attended council sessions in 1918. They continued to represent themselves as the sovereign authority for all Russian Orthodoxy and viewed the new laws as a physical attack against the church as an institution of the Russian people. The philosophy behind the separation of church and state was beyond their comprehension. They assumed the people would force the Bolsheviks into accepting traditional church-state ties. Church leaders briefly expressed a willingness to cooperate with the Bolsheviks based on the formula of a completely free church that was simultaneously established in law as the primary religious institution of Russia.[84] The patriarchal church abandoned this position in April 1918, opting instead for political neutrality and internal unity.[85]

The church, confronted by a new social order where the values of Orthodoxy were questioned, also encountered for the first time a government that was ideologically opposed to the traditional Russian church-state relationship and refused even to engage in dialogue with an organization that dispensed ideological "poison" to the Russian people. Patriarch Tikhon became the icon for those in and outside the council who sought to reestablish Orthodoxy as the state church. The council, hoping that the multitude of believers in Russia would rally around the head of their church, feared Tikhon would fall ill, die, or suffer misfortune at the hands of the Bolsheviks. The last threat seemed very real after January 19, 1918, when Tikhon issued a message anathematizing "the confessed and secret enemies of

Christ," whom he accused of sowing "anger, hatred, and destructive accusations instead of brotherly love." The patriarch chastised those responsible for social chaos in Russia and labeled them "idiots . . . agents of Satan . . . outcasts of the human race." He ordered the faithful to have no contact with those being anathematized and to band together in defending the "Holy Mother Church" against attack. The clergy were instructed to lead the people in these "spiritual labors," despite suffering and death, because "we are firmly convinced that the enemies of the Church of Christ will be shamed and scattered by the force of the cross of Christ."[86] Though Tikhon took care not to mention the Bolsheviks by name while condemning only the violence against people and church property, the enemies of the new government clarified any ambiguity in the anathema by attempting to rally popular sentiment against the Bolsheviks.[87] Tensions between the national church council and the government ran high throughout early 1918 and increased with Tikhon's condemnation of the "shameful" Brest-Litovsk peace treaty of March 18.[88]

The council acted on January 25 to protect Tikhon and ensure the continuation of the patriarchal system by allowing him to name several *locum tenentes* (*mestobliustiteli*). These men would serve, in order of seniority, as guards to the patriarchal throne should anything happen to Tikhon. According to the memoirs of council delegate Prince Trubetskoi, on February 16 (n.s.),[89] 1918, the council held a rare closed session in which it was decided that all the powers of the patriarchate would pass to the senior *locum tenens* if Tikhon should become unable to continue serving in his position. Metropolitan Agafangel Preobrazhenskii of Iaroslavl, who later became embroiled in the many controversies over this procedure, wrote in 1926 that the council decided to allow Tikhon to name his *locum tenentes* unilaterally. To ensure their safety, the names were not even to be given to the council. Agafangel recalled two closed sessions. His description of the first matches that of Trubetskoi. At the second, according to Agafangel, Tikhon reported that he had completed his assignment without releasing the names of the *locum tenentes*.[90] On August 10, 1918, the council adopted general rules for the office of patriarchal *locum tenens*. When the throne became vacant, the Church Soviet, a representative advisory body to the patriarch established by the council, would choose the *locum tenens* by secret ballot from the members of the patriarchal Holy Synod. The person thus selected would then call and preside over a new council that would choose a new patriarch. In the interim period, all churches were to commemorate the *locum tenens* and the Holy Synod in place of the patriarch during the liturgy.[91]

Not all in the church agreed on the need for elaborate security precautions or suspected the government's motives. For example, parish priests received greater freedom under Soviet religious policy, as bishops could no longer expect government authorities to enforce punishment for breeches of canon law. Their only remaining tool was persuasion, as the government itself made clear. On April 12, 1918, the editor of the newspaper *Bednota* [The Poor] responded to a letter from a group of rural parish clergy addressed to Lenin and the All-Russian Central Executive Committee (VTsIK). The letter claimed that not all clergy were enemies of the new state and asked the government to free them from the tyranny of bishops who controlled major aspects of priests' lives. The newspaper's reply rejected the notion that the letter-writers shared a proletarian identity, although it did see a great difference between rural priests and those serving in the cities or the hierarchy. The editor then noted the separation of church and state and continued, "The church, that is, the spiritual leadership, does not now have political power. It does not command any politicians or soldiers to enforce its orders. Spiritual power is simply that and nothing more."[92]

Clergy who later led renovationism willingly embraced the same position and viewed the new government in a positive light. Decades later, Vvedenskii attempted to rewrite his personal history by claiming that the central goal of the Sobornyi Razum cooperative had been to create a true Christian-socialist political party. The publications produced by the Petrograd group offered no evidence of such overarching political goals. The series of brochures printed in 1918 concentrated more narrowly on the theme of social justice as part of "great ecumenical religious activity" and happiness for humanity. In "The Church Pastor and the Political Life of the Country," Egorov railed against neutrality in the brewing class war, protesting that the clergy must fight "for truth, for freedom of the orphans and the wretched from age-old oppression." The socialist revolution would bring the resurrection and renewal of all humankind. Boiarskii echoed these sentiments in his article on "Church and Democracy." He labeled the church "a tool of the ruling classes" in prerevolutionary Russia, isolated from the battle for the people's interests. Still, he contended that the church held great authority among the people and might have a nonpartisan political role in revolutionary society. Christian values, he argued, should be the basis for government action opposing wars of aggression, capital punishment, capitalism, the accumulation of church wealth, and land ownership; he supported women's rights, the eight-hour workday, communal property, and freedom of conscience. One must note that even these Christian radicals could not condone the violence associated with the revolutionary storm. Boiarskii advocated fighting evil only with peaceful means. In several pamphlets, Vvedenskii expressed admiration for the individualism advocated by the anarchists while condemning their methods as non-Christian. According to him, in Christian theology, "love is that dynamite which will blow up all falsehood in society."[93] Perhaps Vvedenskii addressed his comments on tactics obliquely to the purveyors of political violence, the Bolsheviks.

Even churchmen so favorably disposed toward the Soviet government found their range of political action significantly reduced after August 1918. The Bolshevik policy on church-state separation led to the church being completely forced out of politics.[94] The Bolsheviks were quite successful in denying a political voice to the institutional Orthodox Church or its leaders. Shortly after issuing his statement condemning the Brest treaty that ended Russian involvement in World War I, Tikhon resolved to move the church away from partisan politics. The reasons for this change in course are not clear. Perhaps he hoped to protect the church from retaliation for political statements. Soviet authorities dealt harshly with any organized protest against the state's religious policies by labeling the few clergy involved as "ready participants in counterrevolutionary activity."[95] Perhaps Tikhon saw that his words were being used to instigate the very violence he condemned. He might even have anticipated the approaching Civil War and voted for political neutrality in hopes of avoiding a split in the church along political lines.[96] Evidence that Tikhon had taken a new position on the church and politics came in mid-1918 when he refused to bless a leader in the White, that is, anti-Bolshevik, army in the south despite pleas from a close advisor, Prince G. I. Trubetskoi. Tikhon said he did not consider such action as possible for him, as he was refusing to engage in any politics.[97] The church felt those same pressures and willingly followed Tikhon's lead by avoiding political controversy in Soviet-controlled areas. These churchmen hoped that by staying out of politics, the church could be a force for reconciliation in Russia. That sentiment was not shared by clergy in areas controlled by White forces, where senior hierarchs such as Metropolitan Antonii Khrapovitskii took strong anti-Soviet positions.

The government remained suspicious of the church's true motives in its sudden conversion to "neutrality." The Bolsheviks explicitly rejected any possibility of compromise with what it continued to label an alien and hostile force.[98] Protestations of nonpartisanship from clergy did not limit the government's crackdown against churchmen, but opposition from believers did. Sovnarkom received many appeals in 1918 from groups of laity on behalf of priests, asking for commutation of prison sentences. The church as a whole quickly realized the significance of the separation decree and demanded that the government stay out of Russian Orthodox Church affairs, according to the letter and spirit of the new law. Harsh measures employed against the clergy in late 1918 are only partly explained by the growing Civil War that the Bolsheviks wanted and encouraged.[99] Those measures also resulted from a process, which had careened out of control, for ensuring the public good. Revolutionary tribunals often found priests guilty by association rather than on the basis of evidence of crimes. Political neutrality by Tikhon and, by extrapolation, the clergy who served under him was interpreted as an expression of support for the enemies of the Bolshevik government.[100] Even so, there is no solid evidence that the clergy were singled out for execution as a group during the Red Terror. Estimates of the number of clergy killed between 1918 and 1921 range from 1,434 to 9,000, out of a total prerevolutionary clerical estate of approximately 100,000.[101]

The conclusion that the patriarch was a secret monarchist and his church a potential counterrevolutionary organization took firm root in September 1918, aided by an assassination attempt on Lenin and the beginning of the Red Terror. The VTsIK turned its attention to Tikhon in the middle of that month and, for the first time, accepted a resolution to include churchmen under the category of counterrevolutionary forces to be sent to the secret police (the Cheka) for extra-judicial processing. Minutes from that meeting record the following:

> Tikhon composed, signed, and distributed leaflets having a clear counterrevolutionary character and calling for disobedience to Soviet power and its decrees. The Presidium of VTsIK resolves to try Patriarch Tikhon before its Revolutionary Tribunal on the charge of composing and distributing appeals inciting the populace to counterrevolutionary public acts.

Tikhon denied these and similar charges, claiming he always avoided judgment of secular authority and sent all complaints directly to the government. In his communications with the public, he only pointed out the Christian commandment to love one another. Ignoring these denials, the state acted decisively by placing the patriarch under house arrest and shutting down the national church council. Government officials also began mass arrests of Orthodox clergy, seized more monastic property, and started a campaign to discredit "holy relics." Peter Krasikov, head of the newly formed Eighth Department of the Commissariat of Justice, also known as the Liquidation Department for its eradication of religious remnants in public life, championed many of these actions. The public reacted with a flood of letters and petitions on behalf of their innocent priests. By the end of 1918, even the Bolsheviks admitted that the church still had great popular support and that religion would not disappear as quickly as they expected.[102]

During this surge of activity against the church, Lenin reiterated his support for the policy of strict noninterference in the internal affairs of all religious groups. He interpreted Tikhon's actions in early 1918 as attempts to provoke the government into action against the patriarch personally. Despite such provocation, Lenin urged restraint. He did not want to make Tikhon a martyr, nor did he desire direct conflict with the church.[103] Lenin seemed more concerned with the actions of government agencies. On November 19, 1918, he gave a speech to the First All-Russian Congress of Working Women and warned:

> We must be extremely careful in fighting religious prejudice; some people cause a lot of harm in this struggle by offending religious feelings. We must use propaganda and education. By giving too sharp an edge to the struggle we may only arouse popular resentment; such methods of struggle tend to perpetuate the division of the people along religious lines, whereas our strength lies in unity. The deepest source of religious prejudice is poverty and ignorance; and that is the evil we have to combat.[104]

Historian Michael Traina analyzes Lenin's statements on religion and the church in detail and finds no change in their content after the Revolution. Traina believes that the Soviet government verbally upheld "a policy of toleration, equality and freedom for all religions" while secretly working to undermine the church from within.[105] I would argue that this inconsistency between policy and reality resulted unintentionally from the government's miscalculation of religion's place in Russian society. The Bolsheviks did not, perhaps even could not, accept the idea that religious belief sprang from anything except "poverty and ignorance." So the party explicitly rejected "God-building," an attempt by its own members to develop a "socialist religion of humanity." Led by A. V. Lunacharskii, Leonid Krasin, and Bogdanov (A. A. Malinovskii), Bolshevik God-builders maintained that the proletariat would create a non-transcendent, earth-centered religion to complement its formation of the ultimate human society. Only this group within the party "recognized that religion's power lay in its response to people's psychic needs and argued that a revolutionary movement could not afford to ignore these."[106]

For most Bolsheviks, all religions were equally false and, unless they were supported by outside forces hostile to socialism, would collapse when their economic underpinnings were removed. Bolsheviks wanted freedom for all religions and expected that people who had such freedom would voluntarily reject "the old rubbish—the morality of slaves" taught by those religions.[107] Party leaders felt compelled to launch conspiracies against religion because its continuation implied, in their minds, the presence of outside forces working through organized religious groups to fight the new socialist order. For example, Felix Dzerzhinskii, head of the Cheka and a leader of early battles against religion, commented on the continued disloyalty of Orthodox clergy, especially bishops. In a letter to Sovnarkom, he recommended against allowing Tikhon to send representatives abroad to consult with the patriarch of Constantinople.[108]

Friction between religious believers and government officials rose during the Civil War, and the state stepped back from rigidly enforcing the separation decree. Moscow regional commissar, Emelian Iaroslavskii, who later made his reputation as a party leader on antireligious policy, denounced violations of the decree by local soviets in a letter to Lenin dated December 3, 1918. Local governing bodies in the countryside ignored the will of the people, and the implementation of church policy alienated people otherwise sympathetic to Bolshevik ideas. Even urban workers reacted similarly, as reflected in a flood of telegrams and appeals in 1918–1919 asking Sovnarkom to lift prohibitions on services, reverse church closures, and release clergy from incarceration. Opposition to the government's religious policy became more apparent in early 1919 with the emergence of strongly anti-Bolshevik church organizations in areas occupied by White forces.[109] Shortly thereafter, the Roman Catholic Church protested the oppression of Russian Orthodoxy in a telegram to Lenin.[110]

In response, the Bolshevik leadership changed its tactics on the religious question in two significant ways. First, the Eighth Party Congress in March 1919 made a fresh commitment to antireligious propaganda and scientific-atheistic education. This commitment was expressed in Article 13 of the party's new program, which promised to eradicate "religious prejudice" without "offending the religious susceptibilities of believers, which leads only to the strengthening of religious fanaticism."[111] The Congress ignored more radical suggestions, such as the ones for closing all churches and exterminating the clergy.[112] Second, the Bolsheviks began courting allies from religious groups. They first turned to sectarians, such as Baptist and Old Believer communities, hoping to find prorevolutionary sympathy among them. In its efforts to form a working relationship, the government even allowed draft exemptions on religious grounds for members of traditionally pacifist sects.[113]

Later that year, Communists began building their first bridges with Orthodox believers. In Penza, defrocked Archbishop Vladimir Putiata used political denunciation against his religious opponents in his bid to establish a separatist Free People's Church. Levitin and Shavrov claimed that Lenin had personally ordered an end to close cooperation between Putiata and local authorities in Penza.[114] This explanation is not credible in light of documents from 1921 described below, although the idea that high party officials would put an end to such active cooperation between a bishop and the local security apparatus is consistent with general policy toward the Orthodox Church in 1919. Those at the top wanted to maintain a clear dis-

tance between the government and the church, while lower-level bureaucrats found it advantageous to work with local churchmen in order to implement orders on religious policy more easily. The government also
provided support for a group known as the Executive Committee of the
Clergy (Ispolnitel'nyi komitet dukhovenstva, Ispolkomdukh), founded in
Petrograd by the layman Filippov. The choice of name alone was significant, since the Bolsheviks set up executive committees around the country to implement and monitor governmental policy. Ispolkomdukh started
in Moscow when various sectarian groups banded together as The United
Soviet of Religious Societies and Groups. With encouragement from the
secret police, Fillipov and others floated the idea of reorganizing the United Soviet into an Ispolkomdukh that would include Orthodox representation and thus form a bloc with sectarians in order to promote pro-Soviet
sentiment within the Russian Orthodox Church. After Patriarch Tikhon
refused to bless Orthodox participation in Ispolkomdukh, the government
terminated the group in December 1920 and arrested Filippov on the
charge that he had misused income from church candle factories.[115]

Such incidents illustrate the freedom of the secret police in creating
and abandoning new approaches for dealing with religious groups during
the Civil War. The Cheka had an amazing amount of autonomy in this
area; minutes from Politburo sessions lack any discussion of such secret police operations while they were being conducted. The Cheka labeled both
attempts as "fiascos" in December 1920. Putiata was castigated for having
divided loyalties and a weakness of character that blocked his ability "to
deal the church a crippling blow." The same report said, "The Executive
Committee of the Clergy took a wrong turn and began to adapt the Orthodox Church to new conditions and times; for this reason we destroyed
it."[116] The secret police were involved in internal church affairs starting
in 1919. They seemed, however, to avoid direct interference, relying instead on surrogates who were either ineffective, such as Putiata, or too
self-directing, such as Ispolkomdukh.

Activities of future renovationist leaders in 1919 were consistent with
this trend of churchmen seeking but not receiving direct governmental
support for their reform proposals. In July and August, a Petrograd priest
named Vladimir Krasnitskii wrote to the Commissariat of Justice and argued that Soviet power needed to understand and use the Orthodox
Church to achieve goals of the socialist revolution. He called the separation decree counterproductive in this regard and suggested an alternative method for building a new proletarian society in Russia through a
government-led reform of Orthodox parishes. He also argued that Orthodox "red clergy," that is, those sympathetic to the government, should be
allowed to serve in the Red Army.[117] Krasnitskii's open support for the So-

viet government and desire to help build a socialist society brought him
to the attention of Krasikov in 1919, three years before the priest came to
national prominence as the renovationist leader who advocated most
forcefully for intimate ties between the church and the Soviet state. Already known in the Petrograd diocese—a diocesan assembly had named
Krasnitskii to its Missionary Council in the summer of 1918—the young
priest served as a lecturer in the Red Army and had become the city's
plenipotentiary for Krasikov's department in the Commissariat of Justice
by the end of 1919.[118] Vvedenskii later claimed to have been a frequent
guest at Petrograd party headquarters during this same time and to have
had a long conversation with Grigorii Zinoviev, the powerful city party
secretary and member of the Politburo. To Vvedenskii's offer of a concor-
dat between the government and a reformed Orthodox Church, Zinoviev
supposedly answered, "This is impossible at the moment, but I cannot rule
it out for the future. . . . If you are able to organize something along these
lines, I think we will support you."[119] The state still wanted to keep its distance from religion.

Few changes occurred in church-state relations during 1920 and the
first half of 1921. The Soviet government grew stronger, but the Civil War
still raged. The Ninth Party Congress repeated the characterization of attacks on clergy and parishes as unwise. Both Sovnarkom and the VTsIK
continued to receive many complaints against local officials, who continued to close churches and monasteries and open reliquaries.[120] Dealing with
these actions and the general social situation took a toll on the church as
an organization. According to a British officer who interviewed the patriarch in the spring of 1920, Tikhon complained of a lack of church periodicals, a prohibition on ecclesiastical councils, and the total financial
dependence of clergy on their parishioners. He also noted a lack of candidates for the priesthood because of the closure of all the seminaries.[121] Later
that year, Tikhon was plagued by a new schismatic group in the city of
Tsaritsyn led by Iliodor Trufanov, self-proclaimed Russian patriarch and
head of a new church.[122] Even more disturbing to Tikhon, undoubtedly,
were the instances of parish-level opposition to his authority.[123]

National church leaders acted to cope with these threats to the
church's authority. On May 18, 1920, the patriarch and Holy Synod gave
diocesan bishops permission to decide all local church affairs in the event
that they found themselves cut off from the center.[124] On September 18,
the NKVD responded with a circular that instructed local officials to liquidate all local diocesan administrative councils because they were illegal under the terms of the separation decree.[125] Two months later, central
church authorities passed a new resolution on self-governing dioceses in
cases of the absence of a canonical center or the impossibility of connect-

ing with it. Local bishops were instructed to work with neighboring diocesan leaders or to rule alone if necessary. Hierarchs could divide their dioceses into smaller units headed by suffragan bishops if a break in communication with the center became prolonged or permanent. Such local adaptations were to end when contact with central ecclesiastical authorities was restored.[126]

The government was not immune from popular counterpressure to its actions in the religious arena. From August through November 1920, Sovnarkom received numerous petitions signed by thousands of believers asking that Tikhon be freed from house arrest. For masses of believers, Tikhon's arrest was connected with his opposition to the liquidation of relics and closing of monasteries, in particular the Holy Trinity Monastery founded by the revered medieval Russian St. Sergius. Tikhon's reputation as a martyr for the Orthodox faith grew. Nonetheless, the Commissariat of Justice floated proposals to try him for alleged counterrevolutionary deeds before the Central Committee, Sovnarkom, and the VTsIK. Bolshevik leaders split over the wisdom of such a course in light of the millions who supported Tikhon. Finally, they decided to free him from arrest but limit his movements in and outside of Moscow. The Cheka was assigned responsibility for watching his every move, a task it continued until his death in 1925.[127]

That decision pleased leaders of the secret police, who had lobbied for exclusive control over church policy. In his report of December 4, 1920, a Cheka department head, T. P. Samsonov, informed Dzerzhinskii of the progress being made. Samsonov agreed that communism and religion were mutually exclusive and that destroying religion was a task given exclusively to the Cheka. He reported that previous attempts at "breaking down religion from the center, using people holding the highest posts within the church hierarchy," such as Putiata and Trufanov, had proven unsuccessful. Then, Samsonov wrote of the new focus for this operation:

The lower, young, parish clergy—at least a small portion of them—are absolutely progressive, reformist, and even revolutionary in their inclination toward the reconstruction of the church. Taking this into account, the Cheka's secret department recently has concentrated all its attention on the masses of clergy in its plans for church disintegration. Only through this group will we finally be able, by means of prolonged effort and laborious work, to destroy and disintegrate the church. We have already seen some successes in this area, although truthfully not on a large scale. This path is more reliable because the elder church wolves—such as Tikhon, Vladimir Putiata, and others—can act on our behalf only to the extent that they need to save their own skins. In their hearts they see and do otherwise, whereas the lower clergy, freed from the claws of the high church wolves, sometimes work with complete sincerity for us and with us. Besides that, by working directly with the masses of believers, the lower clergy who carry out our line will also corrupt believers. And this is our goal.

Samsonov concluded his report by advocating the expansion of the Cheka's operations to include the destruction of all religious groups in the Russian Republic. Dzerzhinskii's handwritten comments dismissed that suggestion as "dangerous."[128]

Despite the work of secret policemen such as Samsonov, church and state remained in a stalemate when the Civil War ended in 1921. The Russian Orthodox Church remained powerful even after its expulsion from politics. The Bolsheviks still had to deal carefully with a religious institution that commanded strong, and possibly growing, support among the people. A U.S. State Department official watching events in Soviet Russia at this time even reported signs of a religious revival.[129] Internal Communist Party communications reflected concern over these developments. Lenin sent a telegram to Molotov in the spring and ordered him to stop all actions against the church that were alienating people from the government.[130] In the fall of that year, Lenin ordered Boiarskii's release following the priest's arrest, conviction, and sentence of a year of forced labor by the secret police.[131] Some high-ranking party officials began searching independently for ways to install more pliable leaders in positions of authority in the Orthodox hierarchy.

One revealing incident involved Lenin, Lunacharskii, Dzerzhinskii, and Bishop Putiata. On April 6, 1921, Lunacharskii wrote to Dzerzhinskii about Metropolitan Sergii Stragorodskii, who had been arrested and sat in Butyrkii Prison. Lunacharskii suggested that Sergii might be useful in Putiata's "mission" in Kazan, the details of which were not given. Dzerzhinskii forwarded this letter for comments from one of his subordinates, M. Ia. Latsis, who rejected the idea as "the recurrent enthusiasm of the 'God-seekers'" and dismissed Sergii's suitability for the task. Dzerzhinskii then sent a note to Latsis asking him to write a report on Lunacharskii's letter for Lenin, adding,

> In my opinion, the church is falling apart. We must help this process but by no means allow the church to regenerate itself and take some renewed form. Therefore, the Cheka and no one else should direct the government's policy toward church disintegration. Official or unofficial relations between the party and priests are not permitted. The party's stake is in communism and not in religion. Only the Cheka can maneuver toward the unique goal of disintegration among the priests. Any connection whatever by other agencies with priests casts a shadow on the party. This is a most dangerous matter that only our specialists will be capable of handling.[132]

This reply did not please Lunacharskii. In a telegram on May 9, 1921, he asked Lenin to meet briefly with Putiata.[133] Lenin refused to receive the archbishop and asked Lunacharskii to give him a written report on the case.[134] Lunacharskii responded quickly. He explained that Krasikov had started working with Putiata with the intention of exploring possible uses of the internal church feud begun by the archbishop. Lunacharskii became involved and communicated directly with Putiata at a time when Metropolitan Sergii was in prison.

> Archbishop Vladimir explained that (Sergii) was ready to transfer to the side of the so-called "Soviet church," i.e., of the clergy determinedly and emphatically supporting the present regime and leading the battle with the patriarch. Archbishop Vladimir insisted that if Sergii were freed, Vladimir would acquire an extremely strong assistant in the task of destroying the official church.

Lunacharskii at first did not want to interfere but was convinced by a colleague of Krasikov that Sergii would indeed join the "leftist" clergy. After being released, Sergii took up the case for restoring Putiata to his former church position, from which he had been expelled for "ecclesiastical Bolshevism." Tikhon derailed this move by Sergii by insisting on a vote by all Orthodox bishops on the question. Putiata then suggested a new strategy by which he would be installed as the head of a new Soviet Orthodox Church centered in Kazan. He claimed support for his views from many other bishops.

Lunacharskii saw great value in a meeting between Lenin and Putiata. His argument for such a meeting presaged the role that red priests would come to play in the Soviet Union.

> In fact, we are standing before an extraordinarily significant picture. A sizeable number of clergy, undoubtedly sensing the stability of the Soviet regime, wants to be reconciled with it. Of course, this renovated Orthodoxy with a Christian-socialist lining is not at all desired and, in the end, we undoubtedly will not need it. It will be eliminated and disappear. But it actively opposes the reactionary patriarch and his supporters and struggles directly with the official priesthood. As such, it can play its role since it is calculated mainly on the peasant masses, the backward merchant class, on the more backward part of the proletariat, for whom such a temporary center of clergy unity is a great shift to the left of the one that they still find in the reactionary Orthodox Church. . . . It is obvious to everyone that we cannot, of course, support the activity of Soviet Orthodoxy. It might be, however, completely advantageous to render it aid secretly, so to speak, and to create here in the religious sphere several transitional stages for the peasant masses, who generally have to make compromises.[135]

Pressure was obviously building in government circles to end the stalemate with the Orthodox Church. The famine that began in 1921 became the critical event for solidifying support to act decisively. That summer, Tikhon and his bishops looked for ways to involve their church in famine relief. They organized special collections for famine victims and asked the VTsIK for permission to form a church committee to coordinate their efforts. Tikhon also asked other nations for help for the starving in his country. The Central Committee began thinking of other ways to solve both the famine and church problems. Its accountants said that if all church valuables were seized and sold abroad, the proceeds could easily feed all who were starving.[136]

Tikhon's actions at the end of 1920 suggest he had become aware of the growing possibility of confrontation between the church and state. On November 17, the patriarch issued a decree forbidding innovations in the church's liturgical practice. Some bishops and parish clergy felt that the national church council of 1917–1918 had been disbanded before completing its work. They began to pursue their own reforms, including using folk music and vernacular Russian in parts of church services. Tikhon ordered that the liturgy be done exactly as stated in the service books to preserve its "divine beauty" and "Apostolic faithfulness." Metropolitan Veniamin Kazanskii of Petrograd had sponsored such innovations in his own cathedral, although he stopped when instructed by the patriarch. Those who continued banned practices were punished. Egorov, by this time an archpriest, was removed from his parish and was forced to use a public hall for his prayer services.[137] At the end of 1921, Tikhon wrote to Bishops Antonin Granovskii and Victor of Tomsk prohibiting them from performing the liturgy with unapproved innovations.[138] Tikhon's actions galvanized his opponents within the church. Reform-minded clergy became alienated from the patriarch's policy of preserving Orthodox unity.

Meanwhile, the government's fear of counterrevolution grew with the famine. Trotsky wrote a set of "theses" that were distributed to top Soviet government officials at the end of August 1921. He concluded that the famine was seen by Russia's international enemies as a way to attack Soviet power. According to Trotsky, the émigré White Guards planned to use this catastrophe as a pretense for staging new attacks by the White general Wrangel and to provoke new international intervention in Russia. In addition, enemies of the Soviet state hoped "to create a counterrevolutionary organization in Russia under the banner of famine relief" while actually carrying out terrorist acts against the Soviet government.[139]

Although Trotsky did not mention the Russian Orthodox Church in his theses, church activity in the fall of 1921 undoubtedly aroused his suspicions. Rumors reached the U.S. Commissioner in Riga of peasants in the central Russian provinces organizing to protect and restore the Russian Orthodox Church and fight antireligious propaganda. Local clergy and non-Communist schoolteachers supported the peasants in this expression of cultural resistance to the state. The Cheka kept careful watch over the situation and tried to transfer suspected priests, but it shunned stronger measures out of fear of a public backlash. At approximately the same time, the U.S. ambassador in Rome reported on a religious revival in Soviet Russia, particularly in the towns. He wrote, "The Bolshevik authorities are becoming genuinely alarmed at the [religious] processions which they feel themselves powerless to prevent." He also told of increased freedom of movement for the patriarch and his Synod and noted possible future negotiations between the Russian Orthodox and Roman Catholic churches.[140] In addition, a council of émigré clergy—called the Karlovtsy Synod because they met in the town of Sremski Karlovtsy in Yugoslavia—convened at the end of 1921 and adopted anti-Soviet statements, including one referring to the "bony hand of hunger" as God's instrument for breaking the power of the godless rulers of Russia. Tikhon's unwillingness to condemn and split with that group did nothing to improve his standing with the Soviet government, which was already dissatisfied with what it perceived as pathetically small amounts donated voluntarily by the church for famine relief.[141]

The stage was set for the state to break its stalemate with the Orthodox Church. The Bolsheviks had adapted their policy toward religion, as in many other areas, after being confronted with the practical challenges of governing. Their relations with the patriarch and other conservative bishops moved them toward accommodation with the so-called Soviet Orthodox during the first four years after the October Revolution. Similarly, those who hoped to reform the church found accommodation with the new political system ever more attractive as their own relations with the Orthodox hierarchy deteriorated. One should avoid, however, the trap of categorizing the motives of either church reformers or Bolsheviks as purely opportunistic or manipulative. They shared a worldview grounded in the socialist conviction that a better, more just society could be formed. At first, most party members ignored the possibility that they might disagree with the church reformers over the important issue of how religious belief would shape that society.

Renovationism began when the Revolution of 1905 unleashed forces for reform within the Orthodox Church. Support for significant change grew out of the Great Reforms from 1860–1880, as did divisions among clergy over the path that reform should follow. The split between monastic and parish clergy became clearer in their respective programs for ecclesiastical restructuring. Bishops hoped for direct rule through regular councils they would control. Parish priests wanted a voice in church affairs that they felt had long been denied them. Some sought to build upon traditions of clerical liberalism by openly combining religion and politics. They shared a conviction that the Russian Orthodox Church must change or become irrelevant in the conditions of revolutionary Russia.

Prior to 1917, renovationism encompassed a variety of programs—from mildly reformist to radically revolutionary—for political, religious, and cultural change in the Russian Church. Some advocates of reform simply wanted liturgical change, such as using vernacular Russian in Orthodox ritual or reading whispered portions of the liturgy aloud. Others pushed administrative restructuring to give the lower clergy and laity a greater voice in ecclesiastical decision-making. More revolutionary churchmen pushed for major canonical reforms that included embracing socialism, giving the laity a greater role in religious services, and lifting the age-old prohibitions against married bishops and the remarriage of parish clergy. These disparate agendas for reform arose from various sources: clerical dissatisfaction with the status quo, lay desire for parish autonomy, and the perception that secular ideas had displaced religious ones within many parts of the church.

Renovationism's critical assessment of the church's future found little support in the late imperial era among the mostly peasant and poorly educated Orthodox faithful. From the perspective of masses of believers, the Russian Orthodox Church was an enormous organization that permeated every aspect of Russian cultural life. It counted over 100 million believers out of the empire's 170 million inhabitants. Organized into sixty-seven dioceses headed by 100 bishops, the Orthodox faithful were served by 40,000 parish churches with 50,000 priests, not to mention more than 1,000 monasteries and 90,000 monks. Ties between the institutional church and government were strong, as evidenced by nearly 63 million rubles in subsidies to the church and its schools provided by the state in 1916 alone. A vibrant ecclesiastical press reached out to the educated few in nearly every diocese with weekly or biweekly publications in addition to numerous books, brochures, pamphlets, and other works.[142] To be sure, the church press frequently commented on the serious problems facing the institutional church. Still, even most critics shared the assumption that nine centuries of Russian Orthodox tradition would continue.

The revolutions of 1917 and the Civil War that followed encouraged the movement for church reform and laid the groundwork for revolution in the church by 1922. Opponents of change held on to power within the church for nearly five years after the Bolshevik Revolution. Episcopal leaders mostly rejected calls for fundamental reform, but a determined minority of educated clergy and laity continued to embrace change, hoping to transform Orthodoxy. As long as the country's new leaders were occupied with the task of consolidating political power, they gave little direct attention to religious matters and left control over such matters in the hands of the secret police. When the political climate changed in late 1921, red priests and Bolsheviks began to find common cause in promoting church revolution. Revolutionaries among parish clergy saw that they needed political support in their drive to revitalize Orthodox Christianity and bring spiritual health to the nation. Russia's new Bolshevik leaders could remove bishops who stood between red priests and those goals. For their part, the Bolsheviks had miscalculated the strength of historical forces that promised to quickly wipe away religious "superstition." Having overestimated the strength of their position, party leaders sought new allies within the church itself.

2.

RENOVATIONISTS COME TO POWER

ABORTED AFTER THE revolutions of 1905 and 1917, renovationism was born anew during the famine of 1921–1922. Several major disturbances in 1921—the Kronstadt sailors' uprising, the Green Movement in Tambov, banditry in the countryside, and the emergence of the Workers' Opposition faction within the party itself—gave the Bolsheviks reason to fear possible revolts from other sources even as they were on the verge of winning the Civil War. Leaders of the new Soviet government were no strangers to conspiratorial tactics. Perhaps that is why they became so convinced that the Orthodox hierarchy was hatching a counterrevolutionary conspiracy in connection with the famine along the Volga in late 1921. State officials could no longer accept a stalemate with the politically menacing and independent Russian Orthodox Church. They responded to the perceived threat by forging a new policy that privately abetted revolt by clergy loyal to Soviet power even as it publicly upheld the separation of church and state.

Renovationism not only revived but also thrived in the new political environment. Leaders of the movement leaned on government support while also working independently to gather the resources needed to sustain their vision of Orthodox Christianity within Soviet Russia. Success for reform now depended on both fulfilling obligations to the state and persuading other believers to embrace a restructuring of the Russian Church.

Thus, the Bolsheviks were not the primary actors in the drama that led to church revolution. They did not exercise their will over a massive religious institution through their surrogate red priests. In early 1922, government leaders led by Leon Trotsky suggested new roles for churchmen loyal to the state, but red priests chose to throw themselves into those roles because they saw how to use the state's growing interest in internal church affairs to their advantage. Following the Bolshevik script, church reformers supported the government's plan for using church valuables in famine relief and attacked church leaders such as Patriarch Tikhon who opposed that plan. Renovationist clergy also repeatedly issued general declarations of loyalty to the revolutionary socialist state. Most important, Orthodox revolutionaries followed the Bolshevik example and seized power when the opportunity arose. This chapter will explain how and why renovationists came to control the Russian Orthodox Church by the middle of 1922.

Confiscation of Church Valuables

Famine loomed as the greatest threat to the Soviet leadership at the start of 1922. Over 23 million people were starving, and some predicted the number would grow to 50 million.[1] On January 2, the presidium of the VTsIK resolved to sell valuables from churches and monasteries to buy food but stopped short of forcibly seizing all church property.[2] Such a radical step seemed unnecessary in light of a new agreement between the patriarch and state officials that allowed Tikhon to issue direct appeals to the Russian populace for aid to the starving. Other bishops also received permission to become actively involved in the collection of offerings and collections for that same purpose. The process by which the money and items donated were to be passed on to the State Commission for Famine Relief was spelled out in a special instruction approved by that body. Donations were to be brought to the churches on Sundays and holidays, when members of the parish council would collect them during the liturgy. These collections were to be preceded by the reading of the appeal from the patriarch and special prayers. Other activities for raising funds, such as processions to believers' homes or church-sponsored lectures, were prohibited.[3]

Church donations for famine relief proceeded in accordance with the VTsIK's instructions, although rumors of anti-Soviet activity by émigré church leaders cast a shadow on improved relations between church and state. Government authorities questioned Tikhon several times on his ties with the church abroad but gave no hint of the suspicions that they would hurl against him and his supporters just two months later.[4] The two sides agreed in early February that voluntary church collections were insufficient. Tikhon and his synod received state approval for a new appeal, dated February 11, that gave clergy and parish councils permission to contribute parish valuables for famine relief if parishioners as a community of believers (*obshchina veruiushchikh*) agreed and the items had no liturgical use.[5] On February 12 and 15, the government newspaper *Izvestiia* published statements by the patriarch and Archpriest Tsvetkov, the patriarchal representative to the State Commission for Famine Relief, authorizing donations of icon adornments, old or discarded items, bracelets, medallions, and even vestments with precious stones or metals that could be retrieved from the same. In many places, local officials in charge of famine relief even entrusted the work of collecting these valuables entirely to the parish councils.

Permitting religious organizations to take so much initiative did not sit well with some leading Bolsheviks, who pushed for an immediate campaign to seize all church valuables. Trotsky in particular opposed any course of action that might reinforce the church's authority among the general population. He had advocated speeding up the seizure of monastic wealth in a top-secret telegram to the Politburo on January 12.[6] Even before Tikhon's February appeal was published, Trotsky wrote a note to the department heads in charge of famine relief (P. P. Lebedev, L. S. Sosnovskii, and Krasikov) and instructed them to prepare immediately a resolution for the VTsIK presidium on the procedure for seizing and assessing church valuables.[7] Petitions from groups of citizens and believers, partially staged by the party, appeared in the Soviet press in support of seizures. The party newspaper *Pravda* carried an article complaining about resistance from Tikhon and his followers to famine relief and claiming that only a church revolution would help village clergy who wanted to give church treasures to funds for the starving but feared the patriarch.[8]

Guided by Trotsky's memo, the VTsIK and the State Commission for Famine Relief worked out detailed plans for requisitioning church valuables without soliciting any advice from Orthodox Church representatives.[9] The presidium of the VTsIK adopted a six-point resolution on February 16, although it was dated a week later in the version finally published in *Izvestiia* on February 28. The first point said,

> Within one month . . . we order local soviets to seize immediately all valuables made of gold, silver, and precious stones found in the church property used by believers. Only items that do not materially affect the interests of the cult itself are to be seized. These items are to be assigned by the Commissariat of Finance to the account of the State Commission for Famine Relief.

The presidium also established provincial commissions to take on this task and spelled out measures for assuring the public that the valuables would be used exclusively for the needs of famine relief.[10]

This unilateral decision displeased Orthodox Church leaders because it violated their understanding of the newfound working relationship between church and state. On February 25, Tikhon sent a letter of protest to VTsIK president Mikhail Kalinin. The patriarch reviewed church cooperation in famine relief, noted the state's hesitancy in accepting the church's help, and complained that VTsIK decisions made his situation "ambiguous." Tikhon feared ordinary believers would label him "some sort of deceiver or provocateur" because the VTsIK decision "implicated us in the lust for gold." Finally, he refused to allow valuables with sacred or historical significance to be taken. Tikhon's reaction reflected the displeasure of an indeterminate number of clergy, who felt their good intentions for famine relief had been betrayed and who feared that, in light of what happened to monastic property, little that they labeled as "essential to religious practice" would be immune from government seizure.[11] Tikhon reacted with a new appeal to the church on February 28. He reasserted the church's willingness to help famine victims but called the VTsIK decision of February 23 "an act of sacrilege." According to the patriarch, parishes could donate only unconsecrated items. Any layperson breaking canon law by handing over consecrated items would be excommunicated, and any clergyman would be defrocked.[12]

Tikhon acted to defend Orthodoxy against Soviet attempts to redefine its traditions. The church's legitimacy in the eyes of ordinary believers rested on the centuries-old character of the liturgy that was connected with the veneration and use of sacred objects. No church leader could relinquish such objects without the consent of the Orthodox masses. The patriarch's appeal of February 28 also sent a message to émigré church leaders openly hostile to the Soviet state and concerned that the Russian Church would be co-opted by the Bolsheviks. Bishops, clergy, and laypeople who had fled the country had little direct contact with the patriarchate, but Tikhon had to keep their views in mind when making decisions. He demonstrated his independence by refusing to capitulate to the government over acts that were clearly sacrilegious. By taking such a stand, Tikhon hoped to avoid losing authority in the church at home and abroad and thereby prevent Russian Orthodoxy's devolution into a myriad of self-governing congregations and dioceses.[13]

Émigré Orthodox leaders, however, interpreted the growing confrontation as a call to arms. Metropolitan Antonii Khrapovitskii, a leading candidate for the patriarchal throne in 1917, had emerged as the leader of Russian Orthodox clergy outside of Soviet Russia. On March 1, he sent a message to the Genoa Conference, a European economic gathering, warning of the Bolshevik threat and urging an armed struggle against Bolshevism.[14] Antonii's appeal elicited no response at Genoa but proved unfortunate for the church in Russia. The published version of this message, as contained in the émigré press, reached Russia in the middle of March.[15] The party leadership learned of it sooner, for almost immediately Krasikov referred to it in a magazine article and challenged Tikhon to excommunicate the émigré churchmen as proof that he had not been involved in their counterrevolutionary activity.[16]

Uncertainty surrounding popular reaction to Tikhon's prohibition meant that for several weeks the state seizure of church valuables proceeded cautiously. Local authorities did not pressure religious organizations for the immediate and complete transfer of valuables and often allowed parish councils to control the process. Parish leaders sought ways to fulfill the government's demands without harming their congregations.[17] Secret police reports on the public mood told of widespread resistance to taking gold and silver from churches.[18] During this same period, government leaders argued among themselves about the speed and methods for implementing the VTsIK decision of February 23. For example, Kalinin convinced Trotsky to allow believers to donate their own gold and silver, though not grain, in place of church valuables.[19] A disagreement between the secret police (now referred to as the GPU instead of the Cheka) and the Commissariat of Foreign Affairs (NKID) over how to deal with the Vatican complicated the policy issues. NKID officials wanted to normalize diplomatic relations between the Holy See and the Soviet state, while the GPU characterized the papacy as a center for worldwide religious counterrevolution. In Genoa, the NKID held discussions with the Vatican and throughout the spring advised Sovnarkom to follow a less confrontational church policy. On March 12, an official invitation for a papal mission to help feed starving Russians was issued and resulted in a program that saved some 150,000 people in 1922.[20]

Those who advocated church-state reconciliation won only a temporary victory. Events in Petrograd heightened Trotsky's sense of urgency about crushing the government's Orthodox enemies. For several years, Metropolitan Veniamin Kazanskii, the popular head of the church in the second capital, had been involved in the Society for United Orthodox Parishes, an organization devoted to distancing the church from the ideology of the new Soviet regime. After VTsIK's decision of February 23, this Society negotiated with the State Commission for Famine Relief, and the two groups developed a plan for relinquishing church valuables without conflict. On March 5, Veniamin told local party leaders that these valuables would be released voluntarily under three conditions: all other means for helping the starving had to be used, the valuables given would be used exclusively for famine relief, and only the items approved by the patriarch could be given. Veniamin also requested that representatives from the Orthodox Church control the distribution of the money realized from the sales. The government rejected Veniamin's proposal as an ultimatum and as part of a plot within the church to undermine state authority.[21]

Responding to reports of church activity in Petrograd, Trotsky submitted his own proposal to the Politburo on the role of the clergy in famine relief on the same day that the Catholic relief mission was approved (March 12). He suggested that pro-Soviet clergy be allowed to serve temporarily on famine relief committees for the following reasons:

> Our current strategy should be aimed at a schism (*raskol*) among the clergy over the issue of seizing church valuables. This is an urgent issue, so the schism should be an urgent matter. Clergy speaking for and helping with the seizures will never return to Patriarch Tikhon's clique. Therefore, I propose we form a bloc with those priests and temporarily include them in the State Commission for Famine Relief. This will also remove any possible doubts that the seized church valuables might not go for the needs of the starving.[22]

The Politburo accepted Trotsky's proposal along with a second motion for a secret commission headed by Trotsky to oversee the seizure campaign.[23] A new Commission for the Seizure of Valuables in Moscow Province held its first meeting that day and compiled a list of clergy from around the country who were to be sent to Moscow to help with the campaign.[24]

For a week after this Politburo session, tensions between church and state seemed to lessen. In an interview with *Izvestiia* published on March 15, Tikhon said he had ordered the church to cooperate with the government in turning over church valuables. He expressed his personal opinion that the sum realized from this campaign would not be as great as expected by government officials and encouraged them to be aware of the historical significance of many church treasures.[25] Tikhon planned to keep relations between the Russian Orthodox Church and the Soviet state peaceful and legally proper without allowing the seizure of essential items.[26] The Politburo responded to the patriarch's words by authorizing local delays in implementing the requisitioning campaign.[27] At this point, relations between the church and the state hung in the balance. Party leaders paused to learn Soviet society's reaction to the hard line being pushed by Trotsky and others.

Shuia: Proof of Conspiracy

The possibility, however weak, of a peaceful resolution of the seizure issue vanished on March 15 with bloody clashes in Shuia, a small industrial town not far from Moscow. On March 3, the local (*uezd*) executive committee had created a commission for seizing church valuables in accordance with VTsIK instructions. That Commission confiscated items from three churches without incident, but on March 13, when confronted by an angry mob, it decided to delay taking the main Orthodox cathedral's valuables. Two days later, a large crowd gathered in the square in front of the cathedral in order to prevent the Commission from entering the church. Attempts to disperse the crowd led to a confrontation in which four or five people were killed, including one Red Army soldier, and ten to fifteen were wounded. A telegram sent to Lenin three days after the incident blamed priests, monarchists, and other opposition groups for urging the attack on the militia and Red Army personnel, who were acting legally.[28]

This incident alarmed Lenin greatly and caused him to throw his weight behind a counterstrike against the Orthodox Church. On March 19, Lenin wrote a letter to Molotov for the members of the Politburo with explicit instructions against making copies of the letter. Anticipating that he would be unable to attend the next Politburo meeting, Lenin linked the Shuia events with reports of reactionary resistance to the seizure campaign in Petrograd and to Tikhon's "illegal appeal" of February 28.[29] The party leader concluded that reactionary clergy led by Tikhon consciously planned "to give us a decisive battle precisely at this moment." He accused those clergy of having launched a conspiracy, which was revealed in the clash at Shuia. Lenin labeled this action as badly timed and advocated a series of countermeasures against enemies in the church. The famine, he wrote, provided the necessary political cover and popular support. Confiscating church valuables would give the state a fund of hundreds of millions, if not billions, of rubles for national and international uses. Because the Russian people and international opinion would eventually oppose harsh measures against the church, Lenin laid out a plan of rapid attack against the "reactionary" clergy. These included sending an emissary to Shuia at once with instructions to arrest, try, and execute as many people as possible, especially priests and other counterrevolutionaries, for opposition to the confiscation campaign. Similar measures were envisioned for Moscow and other centers of Orthodoxy. Lenin did not want Tikhon implicated for the moment despite his clear leadership of the conspiracy, although he asked the GPU to watch the patriarch even more closely. The upcoming party congress, scheduled for March 27 to April 2 in Moscow, would take up the matter in secret. Meanwhile, a special secret commission headed by Trotsky and Kalinin would ensure the rapid confiscation of church valuables and the execution of reactionary clergy and laity. Lenin's ultimate goal was to teach reactionaries that they could not even dare to think of resisting the government for decades to come.[30]

Lenin's letter provided Trotsky with the backing he needed for his hard-line approach to the church problem. On March 20, the Politburo—with only Trotsky, Joseph Stalin, Lev Kamenev, and Viacheslav Molotov in attendance—reacted to Lenin's proposal by adopting Trotsky's seventeen-point program. It ordered Smidovich, a senior officer in the GPU, to investigate the March 15 events in Shuia and established secret confiscation commissions throughout the country, giving them detailed instructions on how to proceed with the seizure of the church's wealth. Churches in major centers were to be raided first, and the police and militia were to stand by to assist. Party members were told to avoid open involvement in the seizures, and priests who resisted were to be warned that they would be held responsible for any "excesses" that occurred. Also, requests by laity to buy valuables were to be seen as stalling tactics and not as serious proposals. Trotsky's plan directly advanced the renovationist cause with its sixth point: "Simultaneously with these [actions] encourage a schism among the clergy. Show decisive initiative in this and use governmental power to defend those priests who openly come out in favor of the seizures."[31]

The GPU, like the Politburo, wasted no time in following Trotsky's line. On March 21, the secret police reported to Lenin on "Activity of the Clergy in Connection with the Seizures of Church Wealth." According to this document, the patriarch and his synod stood at the center of opposition to the VTsIK decree of February 23. Church leaders reportedly sent thinly veiled directives to outlying areas ordering opposition to the seizures. They also held illegal meetings of believers in Moscow at which clergy preached against state policy. Furthermore, according to GPU agents, the synod had decided at its latest meeting

> not to have the clergy come out openly against the seizure of valuables from churches but to push this task on to their devoted parishioners, who allegedly ought to come out against the seizure of church valuables for their own personal reasons.
>
> GPU has learned that several local hierarchs oppose the reactionary group in the synod but they cannot oppose their superiors due to canon law and other reasons. They therefore suggest that, if the members of the synod were arrested, they could possibly organize a church council where they could elect men to the patriarchal throne and the synod who were more loyally disposed to the Soviet regime.

The GPU wanted to arrest Tikhon along with his synod and advocated allowing a church council to select replacements for those arrested. This report also recommended that all clergy and believers who opposed the seizures be sent to the starving regions and presented to the local population as "enemies of the people."[32]

Opponents confronted Tikhon both within and outside the church. Metropolitan Sergii Stragorodskii met with Tikhon on March 22 and reminded the patriarch that the three-year term of his synod, established by the 1917–1918 national church council, had expired. Sergii opined that the central church administration could be saved only by reconstituting a canonical synod. Tikhon surprised Sergii by answering that he saw no need for a synod at that time, since he simply relied on the advice of bishops who were residing in Moscow at the moment.[33] That same day, the Politburo, acting on the GPU report and another motion by Trotsky, ordered the arrest of Tikhon and his synod in two weeks. Party leaders wanted to complete seizures at major churches and then begin legal action against those who blocked the process.[34]

Tikhon and his supporters became targets of a two-pronged campaign for publicly discrediting their leadership while secretly splitting the church. Almost daily from the end of March until Tikhon's arrest in May, the Soviet press ran stories attacking leading bishops for denying food for the starving and resisting the confiscation of church treasures. Articles by priests opposing their superiors also appeared, including the "Declaration of the Petrograd Group of Progressive Clergy" signed by Vvedenskii, Krasnitskii, Belkov, Boiarskii, and eight others. This declaration appeared in *Petrogradskaia pravda* [Petrograd Truth] on March 24 and asserted that those who opposed using church valuables for the starving had been suborned by the political enemies of the government and would suffer divine judgment for their non-Christian acts. It appealed for obedience to Christ's commandments as a means of preventing divisions within the church. The authors demanded the immediate, total surrender of church wealth to the government with representatives from parishes supervising the process. The lead story in *Izvestiia* on March 28 condemned not only the crowd and local churchmen in Shuia for their actions but also the Moscow church hierarchy, who had instigated "numerous conflicts with the organs of the Soviet regime."

Simultaneous with this media barrage, the party's Commission for Agitation and Propaganda (Agitprop) organized meetings at which workers were encouraged to approve petitions in support of the government's policy toward the church. The Moscow section of Agitprop reported positive results from these sessions. During March and April, workers' collectives in three main regions of the city held 330 meetings, of which all but thirty passed motions favorable to the government. A local parish priest who otherwise supported Tikhon appeared at one such meeting at the AMO Factory and endorsed the call for believers to participate actively in the campaign to hand over church valuables. His presentation was so emotional and unexpected that the workers wondered whether he had been bribed to appear. Agitprop in Moscow denied that charge, saying that clergy and believers alike overwhelmingly backed the confiscation of church treasures, although it did report cases of "excesses" in a few areas.[35]

In reality, "excesses" such as the bloody confrontation in Shuia took place simultaneously in various Russian cities as Soviet officials attempted to seize church valuables in March 1922. Official press reports later gave a total of 1,414 incidents in which people were killed or wounded.[36] Secret police reports attributed these events to "the clergy's counterrevolutionary agitation," which led "the less conscious masses of believers to open opposition against the commissions confiscating valuables."[37] Émigré Russian Orthodox Church leaders, who hoped to destroy the Soviet regime using "the bony hand of hunger," fed the Bolsheviks' paranoia. At the beginning of April, an article by Shavel'skii published in Paris underscored the hope of churchmen abroad that the famine would cause anarchy and the fall of Bolshevism. He predicted that Tikhon would temporarily take power and transmit it, in due course, to a new and legitimate government. These émigrés expected Tikhon to use the church's wealth in the transition period to help create a new state, hearkening back to the activities of Russian saints and church leaders during Russia's political crises in the fourteenth and eighteenth centuries.[38]

That scenario misread the political and social situation in Soviet Russia. Tikhon did not have the popular support to launch a political revolt, because believers who engaged in demonstrations did not want a change in government. They merely wanted state officials to stay out of their churches. The Bolsheviks accepted the émigré scenario as a real possibility and responded with a plan to "divide and conquer" the church. On March 23, the Politburo, under Trotsky's guidance, appropriated 1 million rubles from the sale of church valuables for immediate famine relief. It also selected Kalinin to be its public spokesman and repeat the official line: the seizures were not aimed at destroying the Orthodox Church or at interfering in its affairs, the clergy disagreed on the issue, churchmen who resisted the government did so for political reasons, and the masses had initiated the idea of seizing church valuables. A 10-million-ruble expense fund financed this publicity campaign.[39]

Central party authorities labored in March and April to speed up the implementation of their new church policy. Trotsky complained to Kalinin that "in many places the seizure of church valuables is fictitious. Officials are taking only token items, leaving the major portion but claiming to have completed 'peaceful' seizures." He recommended ordering local officials to conduct a second wave of seizures that would complete the task.[40] The Central Committee agreed and sent coded telegrams to local party officials with instructions that pushed for a more militant stand in taking valuables and splitting the church. On March 28, Molotov reprimanded Bolsheviks in Saratov for erroneously targeting the lower clergy in their newspaper campaign on the seizures. He instructed secret police in the region to widen splits among the clergy, adding that the government intended to isolate the church hierarchy and thereby prevent them from "terrorizing" the lower clergy. In this regard, local authorities were told to show church leaders "the stern hand of the worker's government, since these hierarchs are daring to revolt against it." The next day, the following additional instructions for conducting the seizure campaign arrived in Saratov: use loyal priests and keep their agitation separate from the party, hold clergy opposing seizures responsible for any "excesses," begin seizures in churches headed by loyal clergy, plan carefully, and publicize the fact that people will have the ability to see that every kopeck (*kruzhinka*) collected would go for famine relief.[41] Kalinin and Molotov sent a third telegram to all local party committees one day later ordering the second wave of seizures demanded by Trotsky.[42]

These instructions coincided with the growing visibility of organized clerical resistance to Tikhon and his episcopal supporters. Soviet newspapers published the names of church hierarchs who openly approved of handing over church valuables; many of these bishops joined the renovationist movement later in the year.[43] On March 29, *Izvestiia* reprinted the "Declaration of the Petrograd Group of Progressive Clergy" and published a letter by Bishop Antonin Granovskii informing the patriarch of his decision to serve on the State Commission for Famine Relief at the government's invitation. Antonin wrote that believers opposed the seizures only because they did not think that the valuables would be used in famine relief but that he would oversee the process and help "to calm the troubled sea of believers' hearts."[44] In April, the Petrograd Group of Progressive Clergy became a force in diocesan church politics. Although some criticized the group, Metropolitan Veniamin Kazanskii used its leaders as intermediaries in new negotiations with the government. Petrograd officials agreed on April 6 to allow every church to keep certain sacramental valuables if other items of equal worth were handed over in exchange. Veniamin's Easter message approving of the offering of most church valuables, including ornamental icon covers, was reprinted in *Krasnaia gazeta* [Red Gazette]. Nonetheless, confrontations between parishioners and government authorities resumed in Petrograd later in the month.[45]

Trotsky supplied the Politburo with a strategy for splitting the church and bringing it under more direct political control. His report of March 30 acknowledged that the progressive clergy and their lay supporters could easily become a greater danger to the revolution than the patriarchal leadership. He noted, however, that this was a future danger. "Today, we must overthrow the counterrevolutionary faction of churchmen in whose hands lies the church's administration in fact." The progressive clergy would prove their loyalty by backing the seizure campaign and breaking with the patriarchate. Then they would be secretly assisted in forming a church administration, electing bishops, and even publishing "agitation material" in various areas of the country. The moment they convened their own national council in order to institutionalize "their bourgeois church reformation," the government would abort the renovationist church through a propaganda counterstrike. The Politburo adopted Trotsky's strategy and thus decided to use renovationism for its own purposes with the intention of eventually discarding it like trash.[46]

In the middle of April, Stalin joined with Trotsky to implement the new plan and push for more decisive measures to break the power of the church. Trotsky demanded the confiscation of all church valuables and reversed his earlier concession allowing substitute donations by parishioners.[47] Stalin telegraphed new instructions to regional party organizations. He ordered that the local party secretary and a representative of the provincial executive committee choose a responsible worker to oversee progress on policy toward the church. This person was expected to exacerbate the schism among the clergy and lead the loyal lower clergy in exposing and opposing hierarchs who conducted antigovernment activity. These instructions explained,

> Loyal elements among the clergy should be assured that the Soviet regime is not interfering in the church's internal affairs. Do not allow counterrevolutionary elements of the hierarchy to give short shrift to the democratic elements within the clergy. Do not urge loyal priests on with the slogan of a new national church council for the removal of the counterrevolutionary patriarch.

This telegram once again warned provincial executive committees and party organizations against openly participating in any of this activity. Initiative for change was to come only from the "democratic" priests and laity.[48]

Meanwhile, party officials continued to seek the church's wealth as much to thwart an expected coup attempt as to feed the starving, and they applied legal pressure against church leaders suspected of planning the coup. Amounts taken from churches consistently fell short of Trotsky's expectations, and he complained that the lack of accurate inventories for church property made the process difficult. He also claimed that senior Orthodox bishops had smuggled the most valuable objects abroad after 1917, and he was determined to discover the uses made of the "church capital" that had fled the country.[49] People faced criminal trials under charges that they incited revolt against the government or hid church valuables. In the Moscow trial of fifty-four churchmen, including some of Tikhon's closest advisers, the state accused the defendants of counterrevolutionary activity because they opposed the seizure of church wealth. Tikhon appeared on May 5 as the main witness at their trial and was treated in such a way as to leave little doubt that he would soon sit in the dock.[50]

Ironically, on the day of his court appearance, the patriarchal synod approved Tikhon's motion of early April that declared the émigré church organization illegal and ordered its dissolution because of its political stance. The synod also decided to collect evidence that might lead to an ecclesiastical trial of the leaders of the Orthodox Church who had left Russia. From the perspective of the state, these measures had come too late. Government officials remained convinced that Tikhon had been in communication with the émigré church organization through the aid of a foreign embassy in Moscow and had blessed their council and therefore could not excommunicate them.[51] Unknown to the public, the day before Tikhon testified, the Politburo had voted to quickly bring Tikhon to trial in a blaze of publicity. It also upheld the verdicts by tribunals in Shuia and Ivanovo-Voznesensk to execute several priests and heard a report by Trotsky once again criticizing the continued slow pace in seizing church valuables.[52]

Renovationist Revolution

Although the Politburo approved a general plan for dividing the church in March, it required several months to develop precise details for the plot. Government officials worked closely with renovationist leaders in April and May to arrange a schism. Renovationism's debut as an organization separate from the patriarchal church proved a stunning success. Leaders of the movement understood what their Bolshevik handlers expected and meticulously followed instructions. These priests were not, however, mere pawns in the hands of Communist grand masters. The educated and experienced churchmen pursued their own agenda for church revolution, and Bolshevik methods for foiling the church hierarchy's "counterrevolutionary conspiracy" fit that agenda. Renovationist leaders started their revolution by tightly linking their fledgling movement with the party's political will.

The party found an able manager for its new church policy in Evgenii Tuchkov, the uneducated but shrewd and effective head of the GPU's Fifth Department. Tuchkov's parents were Russian peasants from Vladimir province. Born in 1892, he completed a rural four-year elementary school and worked as an unskilled worker in Ivanovo-Voznesensk until 1910. After completing a secondary education course, Tuchkov worked at various factory jobs until he was drafted in September 1915 and became an army clerk on the Western front. He joined the Bolshevik party in 1917 and from March 1918 to October 1919 directed the legal division of the provincial Cheka in Ivanovo-Voznesensk. After more than two years as the organizer of a special detachment (*otriad osobnogo naznacheniia*) and then department head of the provincial Cheka office in Ufa, he moved to

Moscow as head of the Sixth Section in the Secret Department of the GPU from 1922 to 1929. Tuchkov held various positions in the secret police apparatus until October 1939, somehow surviving the political storms of the 1920s and 1930s. During World War II, Tuchkov served in the military and the League of the Militant Godless. He retired in 1947 and died a decade later.[53]

Government officials such as Tuchkov carefully coached sympathetic clergy on their parts. For example, a high-ranking secret policeman from Moscow by the name of Mikhail Shmelev received secret instructions from his superiors on organizing opposition clergy in the capital for the impending church revolution. He was ordered to prompt them to issue a statement that accused the current church leadership of leading a mutiny against the state and ignoring the needs of those who were starving. This statement would conclude that the only hope for saving the church lay in replacing its entire hierarchy.[54] In accordance with these instructions, Shmelev and a Commissariat of Justice official and former priest named Mikhail Galkin met with Bishop Granovskii and several priests in the Moscow apartment of Fr. Sergei Kalinovskii on April 19. This 36-year-old priest had a checkered past, having been associated with the reactionary church leadership of Moscow before World War I. During the war, he served as an army chaplain and after returning to Moscow in 1918 became pastor of Grebnevskii Church on Lubianka Square. In 1919, Kalinovskii attempted unsuccessfully to organize a Christian-socialist party of workers and peasants. During the famine, he directed relief efforts within his parish and supported the government's position on seizing church wealth.[55]

State officials promised Soviet support—including access to the press, resources for publishing periodicals, church offices, and the right to organize—for revolutionary clergy who gathered at Kalinovskii's home and prepared to fight against the patriarchate. The parish priests responded more positively to this offer than did Granovskii, who expressed deep reservations about whether the church revolution would succeed. Kalinovskii, too, doubted whether Soviet support for the cause would be sufficient if the movement could not attract a significant number of lay believers. The meeting ended with a four-point agreement. Granovskii would receive a cathedral from which to run the movement. A journal named *Zhivaia tserkov'* [Living Church] would be published by the conspirators. They would also make contact with Petrograd clergy and have permission to issue a general appeal to all Orthodox believers.[56]

Following this meeting, Tuchkov and officials from various state agencies recruited others to play a part in the rapidly evolving renovationist revolt. Priests favorably disposed to the revolution were summoned to Moscow. Galkin ordered Morgunov, deputy administrator of the State

Commission for Famine Relief, to help Krasnitskii when he arrived in Moscow by giving him money and a room in the Third House of Soviets. Morgunov was also instructed to send word back to officials in Petrograd that Krasnitskii was "most essential" for plans being made in the capital and therefore would be delayed in returning home.[57] Vvedenskii and Belkov traveled to Moscow at the beginning of May with the financial assistance of the secret police.[58] Then Tikhon was placed under house arrest on May 6 and informed of the Moscow Revolutionary Tribunal's decision to try him.[59] Two days later, that same court pronounced judgment on the fifty-four defendants; eleven were sentenced to be shot, thirty-three were given prison terms of one to three years, and ten were acquitted or released.[60] Granovskii immediately stepped forward with an appeal for clemency from the VTsIK for those condemned to death, thereby announcing his return to national church leadership.[61]

At the first convocation of renovationism's Moscow and Petrograd leaders on May 10, Krasnitskii, Vvedenskii, and Belkov met with Kalinovskii at his church near the Lubianka prison to discuss the next steps in their revolution. Their decisions did not stray in the smallest detail from the strategy previously laid out by the Politburo and GPU. All agreed on the threat to their church from Tikhon's policies. Vvedenskii argued that time was short because both clergy and laity were dissatisfied with the direction their church had taken. He said, "Supporters of change sense a need for creating a new organization, one that can eliminate everything obsolete and remove the rotting corpse that poisons everything living around it. If we do not come forward first, others will. We must act." Kalinovskii noted the decline of popular support for the patriarch because of his involvement in "holy counterrevolution" and observed that parish priests wanted change but lacked the leadership to achieve it. Krasnitskii proposed a meeting with the patriarch in order "to open his eyes to the situation developing around him personally and in the church." Only with reforms would the erosion of support for Orthodoxy be stemmed. Belkov cautioned that many priests in Moscow would not understand the goals of the four men at this meeting and would call them "upstarts" (*vyskochki*). In response, Vvedenskii proposed the following plan. First, they would meet with Muscovite clergy and laity in order to build support for new church leadership and a national church council. Second, they would visit individual churchmen—in particular Bishop Granovskii—and gain their backing. Third, they would recruit followers in the provinces. Only after all these pieces were in place would they meet with Tikhon.[62]

That same day, this group drafted an appeal to believers calling for an end to the Tikhon-led opposition to the Soviet government. The secret police and members of the party's Central Committee carefully reviewed

the text of this appeal. It was produced on a typewriter at the Revolutionary Military Council and certified as authentic by Trotsky's personal secretary. Stalin distributed the text to the Politburo on May 12 using special
measures to ensure its security—the discussion on the matter was purposely
omitted from the minutes of the meeting. The Politburo approved the
text, as evidenced by the fact that the only typewritten archival copy is
signed by Stalin, Kamenev, Zinoviev, Molotov, Mikhail Tomsky, and
Alexei Rykov.[63]

We can assume that Tuchkov's section was equally diligent when in-
specting the contents of material submitted for the first issue of *Zhivaia
tserkov'*. This issue was in press when the group initiating the renovationist revolution met on May 10, and 10,000 copies were distributed two or
three days later. Kalinovskii served as editor, and Vvedenskii, Krasnitskii,
and Granovskii contributed major articles. The name of the journal,
chosen by Kalinovskii to distinguish the vitality of the new movement
from the morbidity of the Tikhonite church, immediately became a label
for renovationism as a whole. Later, the term "living churchman" (*zhivo-
tserkovnik*) became a term of derision among the Orthodox masses, who applied it to anyone who tried to change Orthodox traditions.[64]

The first issue of *Zhivaia tserkov'* expressed the vision for church revolution that Trotsky presented to the Politburo on March 30. The renovationists planned to create a second church organization, run by parish
clergy and separate from the patriarch. This is evident in the memorandum
to the VTsIK in which the Initiative Group of the Orthodox Church proposed the formation of an All-Russian Committee for Orthodox Church
Affairs. An Orthodox bishop would head this committee, whose membership would include only clergy and laity who supported the ideas of the socialist revolution and were loyal to the Soviet regime. The VTsIK would
protect this new committee from the oppression of the patriarchal administration. In return, the committee would unite politically loyal Orthodox
across the nation, control the activities of the patriarchate, and promote
the peaceful observance of government decrees.[65]

When presented with an unexpected opportunity to control the
church's central administration, however, these clergy conspirators
scrapped their plans and seized power. At a meeting late on the night of
May 12, Vvedenskii, Kalinovskii, and Krasnitskii confronted Tikhon with
evidence that his anti-Soviet political activity had led to chaos in the
church. Tikhon denied any part in such activity but readily agreed to step
down from the patriarchal throne. In accordance with canon law, he gave
responsibility for the church to a senior bishop until a new national
church council could be convened. Tikhon lamented, "I never wanted
to be patriarch. The patriarchate burdens me like a cross. And you know

this well. But the church council laid this cross on me, and I am carrying it as a true son of the Russian Church should." He then dictated several letters, one of which he gave to the visiting priests, indicating his decision to abdicate temporarily. Another, addressed to Kalinin, added that either Metropolitan Agafangel Preobrazhenskii of Iaroslavl or Metropolitan Veniamin Kazanskii of Petrograd would lead the Russian Orthodox Church in the interim. A separate letter to Agafangel informed the metropolitan of Tikhon's decision. It said that the civil authorities had approved of Agafangel as temporary church head and requested he come to Moscow immediately. Tikhon wrote a final message to Fr. Nikolai Liubimov, the manager of patriarchal administration, giving similar information on the transfer of church power and ordering preparations be made to accommodate a new Orthodox leader.[66] American observer Francis McCullagh, who arrived in Moscow several months after these events, accused the renovationists of intentionally awakening Tikhon late at night in the hope that he would name Granovskii as temporary head of the church. When the patriarch refused and suggested the two other bishops, the priests backed Agafangel because they knew Veniamin was unacceptable to the Soviets.[67]

The ease with which Tikhon abdicated his position apparently surprised the renovationist conspirators. This development was not part of the original Bolshevik plot, as we can see in the appeal "To the Believing Sons of the Orthodox Church"—the very text approved by the Politburo on May 12—that appeared in *Izvestiia* on May 14. Claims made by those who signed this appeal (priests from Saratov and Moscow as well as Granovskii, Kalinovskii, Krasnitskii, Vvedenskii, and Belkov) were stunning. They said that the Soviet government had been established by the will of God to fight war, famine, and disease in Russia. The church had stood on the sidelines during these disasters, and church leaders had actually supported enemies of the people, a fact most evident in the violent opposition to requisitioning of church valuables. Then

> Churchmen tried to create a revolution against the government by refusing aid to the starving. The proclamation of Patriarch Tikhon became the banner around which the counterrevolutionaries gathered, clothed in ecclesiastical garb and emotions. But the wider masses and the majority of the common clergy did not respond to this appeal. The nation's conscience condemned those guilty of bloodshed. The death of those who have starved severely reproaches those who wanted to use the people's misfortune for their own political ends. . . . We think it is essential to convene a national church council immediately to judge those guilty of ruining the church, to decide the question of church governance, and to establish normal relations between the church and the Soviet regime. The civil war between the

church and the state, being directed by the senior hierarchy, must be stopped.[68]

No mention was made of Tikhon's abdication, undoubtedly because the text could not be altered without permission from the Politburo. The centerpiece of proposed change in the church remained convocation of a new national church council.

Even after the stunning turn of events that gave pro-Bolshevik clergy the reins of power, Trotsky worried about the ability of renovationism to sustain itself. With Lenin's full support, Trotsky's next letter to the Politburo on May 15 complained about the lack of attention by the Soviet press to the schism between the "change-of-signposters" and the "monarchist counterrevolutionaries" in the Orthodox Church.[69] Trotsky wrote that the Bolshevik goal was to support the former against the latter without "deviating one iota from our governing principle on the separation of church and state or, more importantly, from our materialist-philosophical relationship to religion." The problem, according to this letter, remained purely political because it revolved around preventing terror against the loyal renovationists by the powerful reactionary church hierarchy. He made a distinction between the government's involvement in the activities of the Russian Orthodox Church as an organization in Soviet society and state noninterference in decisions by societies of believers. Then came the passage that presaged future events.

> Elements of the clergy that are loyal, progressive, and in opposition [to the reactionary hierarchy] proceed in part from a false, formal understanding of the principle of church-state separation and in part by observing the apparently unlimited patience of the government toward the counterrevolutionary highest leadership of the church. Therefore, they do not expect that the government would give them support as citizens and as representatives of groups of believers in their fight with the machinations and material repression of church leaders.

The main task of the press, Trotsky continued, was to assure the loyal clergy that the government would protect their rights without interfering in purely religious disputes. To do this, the media was instructed to publicize the activities of Antonin and others, to inform the public of renovationism in a positive light, and to temper any criticism of the movement. At the same time, Trotsky told the newspaper editors to attempt no reconciliation between the feuding church factions and in fact to intensify it whenever possible. The mass media were to use this and other church events as a basis for planting "the seeds of atheism and materialism" in the masses.[70]

No one outside the highest echelons of the party and secret police knew these details of the state conspiracy for destroying the Orthodox Church. Renovationists learned the limits of government support only through interaction with party leaders. On May 15, Kalinin acknowledged receiving news of Tikhon's temporary abdication but refused to assist in the transfer of power to the patriarch's deputy because of the separation of church and state. The renovationists interpreted his refusal as an opportunity to act, for the next day they informed him of the creation of a new Supreme Church Administration (Vysshee tserkovnoe upravlenie, or VTsU) in response to Tikhon's decision.[71] Then Krasnitskii left for Iaroslavl to negotiate with Metropolitan Agafangel over control of the patriarchate. Before he left, Krasnitskii signed a request for clemency for the churchmen who had been sentenced to death by the Moscow Revolutionary Tribunal.[72] The Politburo responded with a decision to execute only five of those who had been condemned and to reduce sentences for the other six. Trotsky proposed this compromise as a way to support the renovationists while causing the least amount of damage to the substance of the tribunal's decisions.[73]

In Iaroslavl, negotiations between Krasnitskii and Agafangel reached an impasse, although few details of their conversations can be verified. In 1926, renovationist priest P. N. Krasotin gave an account of his conversations with Agafangel during May and June 1922. He wrote that the metropolitan had decided to wait a month in Iaroslavl before going to Moscow and that he reacted to events with the instincts of a church bureaucrat. Agafangel reportedly was sure of his position as senior hierarch in the church and called Krasotin a "traitor to Orthodoxy" for urging the metropolitan to leave immediately.[74] Krasotin appeared to have recalled events selectively. He never mentioned Krasnitskii, whose name had become an anathema to renovationism by 1926. He also neglected to mention others involved in the negotiations that played a part in Agafangel's decision. Levitin and Shavrov claimed that Agafangel and Tuchkov held secret talks during that month in Iaroslavl. In this version, Tuchkov claimed to seek a break with the new, unstable VTsU and wanted to support the metropolitan. For that support, Tuchkov demanded concessions, especially the complete renunciation of Tikhon's politics.[75]

Unsuccessful in winning Agafangel to their cause, renovationist leaders decided to take a new tack. Vvedenskii, Belkov, and Kalinovskii visited Tikhon again on May 18 to secure his signature on a written statement that would give them control of his chancery until Agafangel arrived in Moscow. During their hour-long discussion, the three priests persuaded Tikhon that continued paralysis in church affairs needed to be avoided. The patriarch agreed to sign the document after adding a paragraph stipulating that temporary control of the chancery would be supervised by Bishops Innokentii Letiaev of Klin and Leonid Skobeev of Vernensk until the arrival of Agafangel.[76] Neither the priests nor the imprisoned patriarch envisioned even a temporary break in episcopal supervision of church affairs, but Innokentii and Leonid were too weak to control the white clergymen who were determined to reform the church. Vvedenskii, Belkov, and Kalinovskii invited Bishop Granovskii to head the newly formed Supreme Church Administration immediately after their meeting with Tikhon. They claimed that Tikhon had given them the right to invite Moscow bishops to participate in that body, and Antonin accepted the invitation immediately.[77] When Krasnitskii returned from Iaroslavl on May 19, he expressed displeasure that important decisions had been made without him. His feelings were soothed when his ally Archpriest Polikarpov was included on the VTsU. Bishops Leonid and Antonin became presidents of that body, Vvedenskii and Krasnitskii vice-presidents, Kalinovskii and Belkov members-at-large.[78]

Meanwhile, the government clarified its position on the new Orthodox leadership. The Central Committee sent a coded telegram on May 19 ordering local party organizations "to show maximum but unofficial support to the renovationist movement." This communiqué advised regional leaders that although their party opposed religious belief and officially endorsed nonintervention in church affairs, they could not be indifferent toward an organization with tens of millions of followers. By helping renovationism, the majority of delegates at the forthcoming Orthodox national church council would be loyal to the Soviet regime. Yet the Central Committee also wanted local party bosses to help "sharpen the conflict" among renovationists by avoiding partisanship on the internal disagreements among churchmen over such questions as the elimination of the patriarchate and the means for ecclesiastical reform. The local press was told to present renovationism as an opponent of "ecclesiastical feudalism" without emphasizing the general fight against religion. This telegram closed with the admonition that local party leaders proceed with extreme caution and use the "unofficial plenipotentiary for church affairs," who had been selected in accordance with earlier instructions.[79]

For its part, the new Supreme Church Administration (VTsU) could not establish authority among ordinary clergy and laity by simply sending a telegram to diocesan leaders. Instead, it promoted its program at gatherings of Orthodox clergy and through the press. The first gathering was organized with clergy from a district in Moscow on May 23, but Vvedenskii and Krasnitskii could not convince those who attended to recognize the VTsU as the legal church administration.[80] The second issue of *Zhivaia tserkov'*, which was now published by the VTsU and appeared that same day, directly promoted a renovationist approach to reform. A front-page announcement of Tikhon's temporary abdication from the patriarchate was followed by commentary under the headline "What Does the Church Need?" This editorial described two major "crises" for the forthcoming national church council: an internal one sparked by Tikhon's abdication and an external one over the Church's relationship to the new political and economic order. By way of solutions, the article proposed replacing the patriarchate with "a collegial administration" and recognizing the separation of church and state while joining in the fight against economic injustice.[81]

Other major articles from that same issue revealed differences in perspective and approach among renovationist leaders. For example, Vvedenskii advised the upcoming church council to take a radically new theological approach to Christianity in Soviet Russia. He advocated the adoption of dynamic creativity as the basic principle of Christianity. Moribund traditions and the status quo were to be replaced by new Christian ethics that condemned capitalism and any other forms of economic exploitation. Vvedenskii also argued for a new understanding of the liturgy (less as something properly done and more as personal communion with the Divine) and a new basis for church administration (replacing episcopal despotism and the rule of powerful individuals with a fraternal system of married bishops and a female hierarchy of deaconesses). Finally, he urged the church to recognize the separation decree—the idea of a "Soviet Church" was unthinkable to an atheistic government—and to abandon all church involvement in political affairs. Krasnitskii's article followed Vvedenskii's and took a strikingly different tone. It ignored theological issues in favor of more practical recommendations. Krasnitskii attacked the monastic episcopacy and argued for the merger of black and white clergy. He did not offer any dogmatic basis for such a reform. Instead, he simply wrote that church renovation could advance only with the introduction of married priests into the episcopacy.[82]

Three articles by Vladimir Lvov, former chief procurator of the Holy Synod under the Provisional Government, expanded on Krasnitskii's pragmatic approach and revealed the cooperation that existed between the two men. Lvov fled Russia shortly after the Bolshevik Revolution, and details surrounding his return and early involvement in the renovationist movement remain hazy. The Politburo considered him sufficiently useful to provide him with financial assistance in March 1922 while he still lived abroad and to allow his return to Moscow shortly thereafter.[83] Two of Lvov's contributions to this edition of *Zhivaia tserkov'* counseled Orthodox believers to uphold the use of church wealth for famine relief on the basis of Christian ideals. The third, entitled "Man and Priest," took a radical position on church reform by saying that priests should not be separated from

ordinary people by dress and by rules requiring beards, long hair, and ecclesiastical garb. Lvov told priests "to throw off their cassocks, cut their
hair and thus be changed into ordinary mortals."[84]

In addition to revealing competing views among leaders, the second
issue of *Zhivaia tserkov'* presented a picture of a dynamic movement sweeping across the Orthodox Church. Different articles described the Living
Church's intellectual roots, listed quantities of food purchased by the
government using church wealth, or juxtaposed the trials of churchmen
accused of opposing the seizure of church valuables with meetings of
progressive clergy around the country. A letter from one such priest,
Fr. Alexander Blagovidov, characterized the optimistic worldview of the
movement. He asserted that all who supported the requisitioning of
church valuables and church renovation were true followers of Christ. Led
by their "all-Russian elder (*starosta*) M. I. Kalinin in the government and
Bishop Antonin in the unpretentious, conciliar Russian church," these
believers would find wide popular support.[85]

The VTsU devoted its attention to gaining such "wide popular support." Lacking success in Moscow, it focused on Petrograd as the intellectual center of Orthodoxy and the home of the majority of renovationist
leaders. Vvedenskii became the VTsU plenipotentiary in that city and
took on the task of winning its clergy to the renovationist cause. Metropolitan Veniamin, who had learned only a few days earlier that he would
be tried for opposing the seizure campaign, received Vvedenskii on May
25. The prelate was very cold to his former confidant and questioned the
right of the VTsU to name regional plenipotentiaries. He then dismissed
Vvedenskii without further comment.[86]

While reformist churchmen worked to establish their position, party
leaders continued to meet secretly and chart the further development of
the movement. At its May 26 meeting, the Politburo accepted another
proposal by Trotsky, given here in full:

> The internal battle in the church has expanded. After Tikhon's abdica-
> tion, a group with elements of "the center" (Antonin) and the left (several
> young priests) assumed the church's leadership.
> The movement proceeds mainly under the banner of a national church
> council. A new church administration might follow any of three trends:
> 1) *Preservation of the patriarchate* and the election of a loyal patriarch. 2) Eli-
> mination of the patriarchate and *the creation of a collegium* (a loyal synod).
> 3) *Complete decentralization* and the absence of any central administration
> (the church as the "ideal" aggregate of communities of believers).
> I propose that presently we do not need to become engaged with any
> one of these trends (even unofficially). *It would be much more advantageous
> if a serious battle flared up among these three tracks.* Toward this end, it is best

to delay the convocation of a church council. A definitive choice [from among the three trends] can be made later, if it becomes necessary to make a choice.

A centralized church under a loyal and *de facto* powerless patriarch has obvious advantages. Complete decentralization might be accompanied by a deepening of religion among the masses as it adapted to local conditions. Finally, *a combination is possible and even fully probable*, with part of the church preserving a loyal patriarch, who would not be recognized by other parts of the church organized in the name of a synod or under fully autonomous parishes. After all, such a combination would certainly be most satisfactory.

Are there any objections: a) against *delaying the church council for two months or longer*, b) against a temporizing policy in relation to the above-mentioned trends in the church?[87]

By accepting Trotsky's newest proposal, Bolshevik leaders changed their approach toward renovationism in light of the ease with which Tikhon was removed from the patriarchate. By preventing any chance of reconciliation through a national church council, they encouraged conflict among the factions emerging within the Living Church.

Renovationist leaders continued to follow the Politburo's lead. They learned that the council would be delayed prior to June 15, the date when the third issue of *Zhivaia tserkov'* appeared. Thus, in striking contrast with the two previous issues, only a single, brief reference to the idea of convening a national church gathering was made.[88] The churchmen gave no indication that they knew the reasons for the delay, nor would the Politburo have wanted them to know. Instead, they recognized their need for autonomy by building a base of popular support that would protect them from bishops who supported Tikhon.[89]

Vvedenskii fought to raise the VTsU's authority in Petrograd. On May 28, Metropolitan Veniamin sent a letter to all the churches in his diocese informing them that he could not recognize the VTsU without specific instructions from the patriarch. He also prohibited Vvedenskii, Belkov, Krasnitskii, and all associated with them from administering the sacraments and required they offer him repentance before they could be restored to their priestly duties. The next day, the government arrested Veniamin. Vvedenskii made the tactical error of being present at the arrest, an act that encouraged the comparison with Judas's betrayal of Christ at Gethsemane. Aleksii Simanskii, then suffragan bishop of Iamburg (later Patriarch of Moscow from 1945 to 1970), became head of the diocese. Under pressure from a GPU threat to execute Veniamin, Aleksii restored the three priests to their rights on June 4. That night, Vvedenskii addressed a large crowd of Petrograd priests and intellectuals in the Great Hall of the former

State Duma building. In a fiery speech, he attempted to convince them to support the new church administration. He was unsuccessful and was forced to flee the hall in the face of physical threats from his opponents.[90]

In Moscow, Krasnitskii pursued a new organizational path by sponsoring a Constituent Assembly which formed the Living Church Group on May 29. In writing about the decisions made at this gathering, Krasnitskii never indicated who exactly was present; he identified the founders of the Living Church Group only as "white parish priests" who decided to reexamine the core beliefs "of all sides of church life, from dogmas to parish charters."[91] These priests accepted "The Basic Principles of the Living Church Group of Orthodox Clergy and Laity," which advocated a new direction for church reform. They would not attempt to bring the old hierarchy into submission, as the VTsU originally planned. Instead, their first goal was "picking out from the general mass of Orthodox Church people those ordained clergy and laity who have openly displayed . . . their support for reform of the Russian Orthodox Church and invested their labor in this task." The Living Church Group would unite such people in each province and establish an organizational structure "for the purpose of mutual support, both moral and material." The organization would then reassess church governance, dogma, the liturgy, parish structure, ethics, and the means for adapting church life to contemporary conditions. To achieve its goals, the Living Church Group intended to rely on the press, public presentations (sermons, lectures, debates), local and national congresses, and eventually a national church council. Anyone who accepted these principles in writing could join the organization upon the recommendation of two current members.[92]

Krasnitskii modeled his organization on the most successful group in Soviet Russia, the Bolshevik party. In this, he followed the imitative process that sociologists identify as isomorphism. The Living Church Group championed rights for the white clergy, just as Lenin's party supported those of the proletariat and poorer peasantry. Like the Bolsheviks, the Living Church Group restricted its membership, although its restrictions were based on acceptance of radical church reform as opposed to radical Marxist political theory. Calling its opening meeting a Constituent Assembly evoked memories of the Bolshevik seizure of power in 1917; in both instances, the reformers argued for the necessity of establishing a fundamentally new power structure.

Formation of the Living Church Group marked an important split in the church reform movement. Renovationists had control of the national church administration and could count on some support from parish clergy and even a few bishops, including Evdokim Merezhkovskii of Nizhnii Novgorod and Amvrosii Smirnov of Briansk. Still, response from bishops and most clergy in the capitals was not encouraging, nor was Agafangel's re-jection of VTsU overtures. Lacking permission to convene a national church council, the Supreme Church Administration could not dictate changes at the diocesan and parish levels. Krasnitskii's followers decided to achieve their agenda and control the process of change by circumvent-ing the church's episcopal power structure. Decisions by the Living Church Group put it on a collision course with other renovationists.

Battling for Control

From May to July 1922, anarchy reigned in Orthodox parishes and dioce-ses across Soviet Russia. Delaying the convocation of a national church council encouraged organizational chaos among different Orthodox fac-tions and, in theory, realized the Politburo's intention for infighting among renovationist factions. In practice, the delay presented unexpected chal-lenges to church and party activists. Fissures that appeared among mem-bers of the VTsU were not always consistent with state goals. Supporters of traditional Orthodoxy did not vanish with Tikhon's arrest, and their re-sistance to reforms required ever-more-direct intervention by state officials on the side of renovationism.

State support of renovationist activities during these months oscillated between covert and open, indirect and direct. Initially, the GPU and Central Committee's Organizational Bureau (Orgburo) intended to re-main out of sight and supply secret aid to the reform movement. The Org-buro appropriated 1.8 million rubles on May 30 for a publicity campaign against Patriarch Tikhon and directed that those funds come from the GPU budget.[93] In their request for a reconsideration of that decision, the secret police argued that promoting a schism among the clergy had already consumed considerable amounts of their funds and manpower. In order to fund a new campaign against Tikhon, they would have to limit secret sup-port to the clergy who collaborated with the GPU "in the publication of printed organs, propaganda, travel around the Republic, and . . . the sup-port of a long list of newly arriving churchmen [in Moscow]."[94]

National advocates of reform used clandestine state support in their open efforts to build a following among both the clergy and laity. Classi-fied GPU reports (svodki) on political and economic conditions in the country gave a mixed assessment of renovationist success.[95] In Moscow, be-lievers reacted with hostility to trials of church leaders and spread rumors that the Communists were destroying Christianity to help the Jews. Parish clergy in Riazan province sent out an appeal to believers that called for a church council in response to Tikhon's abdication. A schism appeared among the clergy in Orenburg province, and the secret police noted a decrease of clerical influence on the populace in the Dagestan ASSR (Autonomous Soviet Socialist Republic).[96] Observers in Saratov province said that no serious problems with seizing church valuables had occurred, and the clergy, except those already favorably predisposed to Soviet authority and those who were not "religious fanatics," were still undecided about whom to obey in Moscow.[97]

GPU reports for early June indicated growing antipathy toward Tikhon's policies among the clergy and laity in Kostroma, Northern Dvinsk, and Riazan provinces. In the Crimea, however, "anti-Soviet agitation by believers" cut short a meeting of prorenovationist clergy.[98] Intelligence for the second half of that month recounted attempts at organization by both sides. Clergy were for reforms—and against Tikhon and his bishops—in the Chuvash region, Ufa province, Crimea, Voronezh, Tula, and Penza. Clergy and laity taking stands in favor of Tikhon were reported in the Tatar ASSR; in Crimea, Simbirsk, and Omsk provinces; and in Iaroslavl. Indifference to Tikhon's abdication was seen in Vladimir and Simbirsk provinces.[99]

In its summary of conditions in the Russian Soviet Federated Socialist Republic (RSFSR) for May–June 1922, the GPU assessed initial developments in renovationism. As the schism spread to the provinces, motives for change shifted from helping the government seize church valuables to reorganizing the church by replacing senior bishops loyal to Tikhon. This battle was being fought everywhere in the provinces, although renovationism was still unorganized and was under attack from powerful "reactionary" clergy. This report identified three emerging groups of clergy:

> (1) Supporters of the Living Church. In most cases, these are the petty clergy, formerly kept in total submission. They support church seizures, hold meetings, etc., and have reversed the reaction against seizures in Rybinsk, Tsaritsyn, Rostov on the Don, and elsewhere. (2) A wavering group that fears repression and is unwilling to back Tikhon openly. Individuals are working quietly against renovationism but will fold under pressure, acknowledge Soviet power and the VTsU, and pose no danger. (3) Exalted church big shots who will not reconcile with renovationism and hope to split it from the masses. They pose no special danger, despite their open activity.
>
> The whole church now waits for a church congress that will pit the first group against the third. (The second group will accept whatever is decided.)[100]

Renovationists understood that clergy were divided and worked to neutralize the third group while winning over the second. The VTsU explored the issue of how to organize renovationist activity for this purpose but by late May split internally over the approach to take.

Antonin defended VTsU supremacy over Krasnitskii's Living Church Group. The monastic bishop wanted to decouple politics from Christian morality, as seen in his advocacy of spiritual regeneration for the Russian people based on a monastic model. He suggested that monks be limited in number and that monasteries serve society by dispensing Christian charity to the poor. Moral renewal, he said, should be led not by priests but believers in general, and he opposed all reforms that might lead to the lowering of moral standards for the clergy.[101] Those promoting the Living Church Group's path for reform could find little common ground with Antonin and others who hoped to limit the power of the parish clergy. Conflict over this issue took place within the VTsU in early July, when Antonin backed a successful move to strip Krasnitskii of his membership. GPU agents intervened and reversed that decision.[102]

While renovationists argued among themselves, the government pressured them to remove "politically disloyal" members of the episcopacy. Leading Bolsheviks worried about the consequences of foreign interest in church affairs, such as a letter issued on June 1 by the Archbishop of Canterbury and other English clerics protesting against the Soviet state's repression of religion and its plans to try the patriarch for political crimes.[103] Using the literary pseudonym M. V. Gorev, Galkin issued a reply in *Izvestiia* on June 2. In an article entitled "The Last Struggle of Ecclesiastical Counterrevolution," Gorev-Galkin chided the VTsU for having only "a microscopic portion of revolutionary energy" as evidenced by the continued power of the old ruling clique of bishops. He praised the actions of both Lvov, who "acted boldly and decisively" in cleaning out the Holy Synod under the Provisional Government in 1917, and Krasnitskii, who had just uncovered "connections" between the Moscow hierarchy and English-speaking foreigners. Now the VTsU needed to go to the provinces and "cut short" the counterrevolutionary activities of bishops there. Gorev-Galkin promised that the VTsIK's decision to execute churchmen condemned by the Moscow tribunal would sober up some counterrevolutionary priests and teach the VTsU how to clean its own house in order to prevent any future episcopal political mutiny.[104]

Renovationist leaders took their cue from Gorev-Galkin and joined together in adopting a harder line toward their ecclesiastical opponents. At a second meeting between Moscow clergy and VTsU representatives, the former approved all proposals submitted by the VTsU and the Living Church.[105] Tactics used at this meeting later became the pattern for establishing renovationist control over parish clergy across Russia. Supporters of renovationism presented information on the VTsU's origins, structure, and goals at meetings for priests who served as regional superintendents (*blagochinnye*) in their dioceses. A discussion and vote of support for the

VTsU followed the presentations; those who refused to give their support faced the threat of arrest and exile by the government. Krasnitskii in particular developed a reputation for using political denunciations without regret and threatening opponents with state punishment for their alleged counterrevolutionary activity within the church.[106]

Some Orthodox laity reacted negatively to the combination of religious innovation backed by political coercion. They associated renovationism with religious Bolshevism and rejected both. The trial of Metropolitan Veniamin Kazanskii and other Petrograd clergy provides an example of how the Orthodox public soon turned against the renovationists. The government charged the defendants with counterrevolutionary activity in connection with their opposition to the decrees regarding the confiscation of church valuables. In the eyes of party officials, Veniamin's measured resistance to the seizure campaign had cleverly manipulated public opinion for the purpose of staging the church-led coup desired by Tikhon and the émigré church. Nonetheless, the state benefited from public perception that new Orthodox leaders betrayed the popular metropolitan to the government because of his opposition to renovationism.[107]

The three-week trial irreparably damaged the cause of reform. On June 12, a "fanatical woman" struck Vvedenskii in the head with a rock while he entered the court building. Although Krasnitskii hailed Vvedenskii as "the first martyr for church renovation," few shared that opinion.[108] Krasnitskii testified against Veniamin, and the Orthodox faithful decided that his actions were both treacherous and self-serving. Krasnitskii's reputation declined further when defense attorneys confronted him with anti-Semitic and anti-Bolshevik articles he had published in the prerevolutionary church press. The court sentenced Veniamin and nine others to death on July 5, and the next day the VTsU defrocked the condemned clergy and excommunicated all who had been found guilty.[109]

For years afterward, Orthodox believers in the region accused all renovationist parishioners of having Metropolitan Veniamin's blood on their hands.[110] In reality, the VTsU knew that Veniamin and the others, if executed, would be seen as martyrs in the eyes of believers. Renovationist leaders, therefore, petitioned the VTsIK for clemency and for permission to hold a church trial to discredit the Orthodoxy of the defendants. Vvedenskii sent a personal letter to the VTsIK, saying that although he still suffered from the injury inflicted by the church's enemies, he thought the government had proven its case and could show its strength by being lenient to its foes.[111] These entreaties had limited effect. The Politburo authorized that the sentences for six of the ten condemned be commuted, although not the sentences of the metropolitan and others who were "instigators and leaders . . . of counterrevolutionary policies." Party leaders saw this action as a compromise with requests made by "the loyal clergy and, in particular, the VTsU and Living Church."[112] Naturally, renovationists could not claim credit for influencing the secret process behind that decision.

Simultaneous with the Petrograd trial, renovationist leaders decided to ordain nonmonastic priests as bishops, in a dramatic break with Orthodox canon law. Only clergy with episcopal rank (bishop, archbishop, metropolitan, and patriarch) can ordain new priests and bishops in the Orthodox Church; by changing the composition of the episcopate, renovationism changed the balance of power in ecclesiastical leadership. The VTsU had a sufficient number of loyal monastic bishops to ensure a steady supply of clergy, so that was not at issue. A desire to place the most fervent supporters of major church reform in positions of power led to this significant decision, for those men could be found only among the parish clergy. This change began with Archpriest Ioann Al'binskii, a widower from Petrograd, whom Bishops Leonid, Antonin, and Ioannikii Chantsev consecrated on June 11.[113] Over the next eleven months, renovationists ordained fifty-three nonmonastic bishops, although Krasnitskii always viewed Al'binskii as special ("our first 'white' bishop") and a major step forward in church reform.[114]

Not all bishops who supported renovationism came from the ranks of the "progressive clergy." The VTsU scored a major victory on June 16 when Metropolitan Sergii Stragorodskii of Vladimir joined Archbishops Evdokim Meshcherskii of Nizhnii Novgorod and Serafim Meshcheriakov of Kostroma in signing a joint declaration that recognized the Temporary Church Administration as "the sole, canonical, highest ecclesiastical power" and advised clergy and laity to follow their example in accepting all its decrees.[115] Their declaration was published in mid-July, but it circulated in multiple copies as early as June 19 in Evdokim's diocese.[116] Prior to this declaration, Sergii and Evdokim had shown sympathy for socialism and the revolution. Serafim's participation was more surprising. After rejoining the patriarchal church in 1928, he attributed the fact that he signed the declaration to difficult personal circumstances and a hope that the general situation of the church could be saved.[117]

Increased participation by "old-ordination" bishops in the renovationist movement explains changing attitudes within the VTsU in July. Tuchkov wrote to his superior (T. P. Samsonov, head of the Secret Department of the GPU) to complain about "certain abnormalities" in the work of the VTsU. That body not only refused to accept clergy "with tainted reputations" but also displayed "an inclination toward humaneness (*uklon v storonu gumannosti*) in its relations with high-ranking anti-Soviet hierarchs and with . . . members of the Living Church Group." Lvov's presence reportedly increased solidarity within the VTsU. Krasnitskii attributed these changes to orders from Galkin—a comrade not under Tuchkov's command.[118] A better explanation is that most members of the VTsU held to Orthodox traditions that valued unity within the Church and had not yet applied the Bolshevik worldview of class warfare to the church.

Escalating conflict with Metropolitan Agafangel and other so-called Tikhonites eventually changed the perspective of the VTsU. Agafangel led the first major challenge to renovationism with a general appeal on June 18 to all true Orthodox believers. This appeal, which was printed secretly and distributed quickly, said that Agafangel had been prevented from going to Moscow to assume his new duties by the noncanonical VTsU. Admitting the need for some reforms in the church, Agafangel maintained that only a national church council could make the types of changes that the renovationists proposed. Otherwise, the introduction of such innovations would only confuse the laity and result in a schism. He instructed all diocesan leaders to run their eparchies as independent entities until the restoration of a legal central church administration. He told parish clergy to be good examples to their flocks and the laity not to allow "the new people" to confuse them. All in the church were urged to be faithful to Orthodoxy and to obey the government. A second message, undated and signed by "The Brotherhood of Adherents to Orthodoxy," appeared shortly after Agafangel's appeal and was distributed in Moscow. This leaflet minced no words, calling the renovationists "antichrists" and their leaders "usurpers and schismatics."[119]

Levitin and Shavrov's conclusion that these documents "stunned Tuchkov and the VTsU" is probably only half true.[120] Most likely, Tuchkov knew of Agafangel's appeal in advance and decided not to stop its distribution, a position entirely consistent with the Politburo's decision to watch the schism carefully while allowing it to widen. Agafangel promoted the idea of local autonomy, one of the "trends" that Trotsky had labeled desirable on May 18. Neither of these documents contained any anti-Soviet rhetoric. In fact, the church's energies were becoming consumed by internal battles as the Politburo intended, leaving nothing for political opposition.

The VTsU did not wait for its opposition to organize in accordance with Agafangel's instructions. It issued a circular reasserting its power until the next national church council and ordering "progressive clergy" to form their own diocesan administrations (*eparkhial'nye upravleniia*). These new administrative bodies were expected "to free the parish clergy from the counterrevolutionary elements of society." In the same circular, the VTsU recognized the right of the white clergy to organize themselves into groups for the purpose of exercising greater moral influence on society. The central body, now under the executive administration of Belkov, instructed provincial church leaders to inform it if these instructions were not implemented. Over the next several weeks, the VTsU removed several prominent bishops from their sees for obstructing these orders, including Aleksii Simanskii of Petrograd, Boris Lentovskii of Penza, Fëdor Pozdeevskii from Moscow, and Iuvenalii Maslovskii from Tula.[121] Renovationist sympathizers sent telegrams and delegations to the VTsU to receive guidance about implementing the growing church revolution.[122] Issues of *Zhivaia tserkov'* published during June, July, and August were filled with accounts of meetings of clergy supportive of renovationism to adopt VTsU proposals for reorganizing the church.

In the center, the task of coordinating provincial activity increasingly fell to Krasnitskii, who worked to strengthen the Living Church Group with Belkov's help. Krasnitskii gathered some Living Church members to form a Central Committee and a Moscow Committee after the initial meeting in May. On July 4, forty-two people attended another organizational meeting in Moscow and overwhelmingly adopted Krasnitskii's charter for " The Living Church: A Group of Orthodox White Clergy." This charter substantially reduced the power of monastic bishops over church administration in favor of the white clergy. It also freed parish priests from "economic dependence on the ruling classes of society" and called for the formation of a unified church treasury in every diocese.[123]

Pressures from isomorphism produced striking similarities between the Living Church Group and the All-Russian Communist Party (Bolshevik). Belkov himself wrote about those similarities. He compared relationships between the Living Church Group/VTsU and the Bolsheviks/VTsIK. The Living Church Group provided ideological guidance for the executive administration of the church (VTsU), just as the Bolshevik Party did for the government (VTsIK). The Central Committee of the Living Church Group would oversee daily operations, as in the Bolshevik Party model.[124] By copying the successful Bolshevik model, early supporters of the Living Church Group followed a more radical path for Russian Orthodoxy. They also concentrated greater power in the hands of their primary leader, Krasnitskii.

The effects of this organizational change were seen in the dealings of renovationists with their opponents before and after the July 4 meeting. In May and June, Krasnitskii guided the process for organizing renovationist circles in Moscow, Tula, Iaroslavl, and Petrograd. He met with the clergy in each of those cities and persuaded them to recognize both the VTsU as the canonical church administration and the Soviet government as the legitimate government that was implementing the socially just principles of the October Revolution. Willingness to accept the VTsU became a litmus test of loyalty to the Soviet government. In some cases, bishops who allied themselves with the new central church administration were not arrested or avoided harsh sentences for their earlier opposition to the seizure campaign. In addition, the VTsU sought to control Orthodox parishes by sending a plenipotentiary (*upolnomochennyi*) to each diocese. This new official rallied support for reform among local clergy, organized a new diocesan administration, and, if necessary, exiled the local bishop if he opposed reform.[125]

After the July 4 meeting, priests in the Living Church Group took a harder line with opponents. Accounts from Siberia provide good examples of the new approach. The bishop of Tomsk was arrested shortly after Tikhon in the beginning of May. On July 9, after news of the Living Church Group's meeting reached Tomsk, a new Siberian church administration for ten Siberian provinces was organized. Siberian renovationists wrote a new parish charter in order to dislodge the "reactionaries" who controlled parish affairs. Under the new arrangements, the parish assembly (*prikhodskoe sobranie*) held power, not the parish council (*prikhodskii sovet*). The council became merely an executive committee, and its members were denied a vote in the assembly. The assembly itself consisted of the clergy and all parishioners over eighteen years old, thus diluting the power that older parishioners (the "kulaks and bourgeoisie") formerly had over church affairs. Clergy now answered to their young parishioners, who were more likely to accept renovationist reforms. Siberian churchmen made a similar reform in diocesan administration, transferring supreme power from the local bishop and his regional superintendents to the diocesan congress. Red priests in Siberia advocated the elimination of the patriarchate and the institution of a conciliar system of administration on the national level. Hoping to set an example for the whole Orthodox Church, they made plans to hold an all-Siberian congress of progressive clergy.[126] Outside Siberia, similar moves were made to remove the most obvious opponents of reform from their episcopal sees. In a span of only fifteen days (July 6–21), the VTsU "retired" fourteen bishops, including Agafangel.[127]

Not withstanding this flurry of activity, analysts within the secret police gave a pessimistic assessment of renovationism's chances for success in late summer. They repeated that Orthodox clergy were divided into "renovationist, temporizing, and reactionary" camps; the last group was the most numerous, the most united under the old hierarchy, and the most authoritative among believers. The GPU observed that the spread of the schism had slowed throughout Russia and attributed this trend to "the drained reservoir of priests who want reform." Also, "the contingent of (renovationist) recruits includes many drunkards, aggrieved and dissatis-fied with the princes of the church [i.e., the senior bishops], a fact that aids significantly the development of antagonism between the two basic fac-tions of clergy." These analysts observed that "true defenders of Ortho-doxy" were not joining the reform movement and had discredited and pushed back renovationist groups even in early strongholds such as Cheli-abinsk and Samara. With few exceptions, "the schism among the clergy has still not affected the believing masses," who were concerned about un-folding events "but as before remain true to the old traditions."[128]

Regional reports from this period show no clear pattern of support for renovationism. The situation was fluid, and lay reactions were volatile. A gathering of clergy and laity in Kazan expressed both loyalty to the gov-ernment and a willingness to accept the VTsU as a temporary church ad-ministration. They also noted the political aspects of VTsU activity and voted that their church should be free from state interference as long as it obeyed civil law. Finally, the diocese voiced support for another national church council and decided to become autocephalous until a canonical central church administration was restored if the VTsU did not convene a council.[129] A similar gathering in Vologda province expressed a different attitude toward renovationism by rejecting mere ritualism and unthinking acceptance of tradition in favor of a less rigid approach to Orthodox ritual and moral teaching. This group also sought full separation of church and state along with a collegial church administration based on the rights of parishes and parish clergy.[130]

Confusion reigned among those who tried to guide the church for or against renovationism at the beginning of August. Petrograd reflected this uncertainty, according to local GPU operatives. Petrograd workers had not promoted the campaign to seize church valuables but had supported the renovationist schism and the trial of Metropolitan Veniamin. Women in Petrograd opposed the seizures and spread rumors that the government had forced Tikhon to abdicate and thus had promoted the church split. Significantly, peasants in the province viewed Tikhon and other church leaders as martyrs and the progressive clergy as government agents. On the whole, believers in and around the former capital were categorized as hos-tile to the schism. The majority of rural clergy formerly supported Vve-denskii and the progressive clergy but had turned against them, thanks to the ecclesiastical opposition and its successful campaign of spreading ru-mors—presumably by word of mouth—that the government and the se-cret police paid the progressive clergy. At the time of this GPU report, opponents of renovationism were attempting to prevent the nonmonastic

Bishop Nikolai Sobolov from taking control of the Petrograd diocese and progressives were working to convince the majority of clergy who refused to recognize the VTsU that they had made a mistake.[131]

Political struggle between the Orthodox Church and Bolsheviks in 1922 reflected wider social unrest within the young Soviet state. That unrest, in turn, helped spawn a sustained renovationist movement within Russian Orthodoxy. Attempting to cope with famine, the party became convinced that Orthodox leaders at home and abroad had launched an anti-Bolshevik conspiracy. The alleged plot involved bishops who intended to use church valuables to finance counterrevolution. When the state began to confiscate the church's wealth, those bishops supposedly altered their plot by igniting popular unrest through opposition to such confiscation. Violent confrontations led by believers in Shuia and elsewhere provided the Politburo with proof that their suspicions were correct. The Bolshevik high command responded by hatching a counterconspiracy for attacking so-called reactionary Orthodox leaders using clergy sympathetic to the party's social goals. These erstwhile allies were seen as only temporary, however, and the Politburo planned to discard them in the final stage of destroying the church.

Renovationists were suited to the task because they accepted Bolshevik aims of social justice, economic equality, and, most important, radical changes in traditional Orthodoxy. Church reformers particularly rejected traditions that governed the lives of Orthodox clergy, despite the fact that most ordinary Orthodox believers considered those traditions to be an essential part of their religious life. For this reason, renovationists could never have gained the necessary resources for taking administrative control of the church without the political crisis of the famine. By embracing new values—specifically one claiming that all church wealth belonged to the Soviet state—renovationists seemed to be natural allies for the Bolsheviks. These churchmen hoped to make a place for Orthodoxy in Soviet society by introducing radical changes in church structure and practice. They consciously imitated Bolshevik models when implementing such changes. Bolshevik ideology led party leaders to reject categorically any possibility of compromise with religious "superstition." In the heat of battle in early 1922, the Bolsheviks ignored this crucial difference and chose to work with politically loyal clergy. The party's secret goal aimed to divide the Orthodox clergy into three factions in order to prevent the church from becoming an influential anti-Soviet organization.

Schism unexpectedly turned into revolution when Tikhon abdicated the patriarchate. Instead of forming a distinct pro-government branch of Orthodoxy, renovationists grabbed the chance to guide the whole church in a new direction under their own Supreme Church Administration. But renovationists failed to rally support from the laity in the first months after Tikhon's abdication. Even worse, they encountered active opposition from ordinary parishioners. Clergy in the reform movement seemed stunned by the venomous reaction of the laity toward them. In an article entitled "We Believe," one red priest wrote, "Yesterday, your hands furiously applauded our strong stand for the faith. Today those same hands yank us off our pedestals. . . . You call us 'antichrist,' 'Satan,' 'impostor,' 'toady,' 'provocateur,' 'Judas-like betrayer.'" This author was particularly hurt by the lies being circulated by the opponents to renovationism and ended his article by proclaiming confidently "We believe we will win, for the truth is on our side."[132]

3.

ECCLESIASTICAL CIVIL WAR

As FACTIONS FOR and against the renovationist revolution coalesced in the summer of 1922, every group claimed that truth was on its side. No group was willing to compromise its position, so the factions continued to splinter. Red priests attacked one another with as much venom as they did anyone who continued to honor Patriarch Tikhon. Radical reformers embraced the rhetoric and methods of class warfare in the church. Others responded with more moderate agendas that advocated an equal voice for parishioners in church affairs or the reconstruction of Orthodoxy based on Christian socialism. From August 1922 to May 1923, Orthodox believers engaged in a struggle that threatened the movement for reform and Bolshevik plans for controlling religion. Conflict encouraged party officials to take direct action in preventing renovationism from self-destruction. At stake was the future of a Bolshevik Orthodox Church.

The Living Church Congress

Krasnitskii's Living Church Group sparked civil war in the church by attempting to put parish clergy in leadership positions around the country. Krasnitskii made a fiercely partisan appeal in hopes of enlisting ordinary believers for the reformist cause. He wrote, "The Orthodox white parish clergy are openly and freely speaking out (*vystupaet*) for the first time in the history of the Russian Orthodox Church. . . . Together with the laboring peasantry, the clergy gets its crust of bread by the sweat of its brow, through hard work." He further emphasized the similarities between clergy and ordinary Russians by reminding his readers that sons of clergy such as the revolutionary writer Nikolai Chernyshevskii had suffered under tsarism and had fought for a just social order. Drawing on Bolshevik revolutionary rhetoric, Krasnitskii affirmed that "the Living Church is the church of the laboring masses."

The Central Committee of the Living Church Group accepted Kras-nitskii's analysis and called on all parish clergy to join the movement. It admitted that mistakes had been made during the initial period of white clergy rule but reaffirmed that its primary goal was to enlist the support of the parish clergy, not the monks and "bourgeoisie" who formerly controlled the church. A monastic episcopacy in particular could never be trusted to help the renovationist movement because it had lost too much power and privilege under the new regime. The Central Committee pointed to Vve-denskii as an example of the fate of those who had hopes of enlisting the "free-thinking" monks in the renovationist cause, referring to Vvedenskii's temporary excommunication and the head injury he received from an irate laywoman during Veniamin's trial.[1]

In the face of continued lay and episcopal opposition, leaders of the Living Church Group advised white clergy to band together and form local Living Church cells, once again taking their inspiration from the success of the Bolsheviks. These groups were instructed to inform the center of their legislative needs for achieving control of both parish and diocesan administration. Such control would give them financial independence and the freedom to promote the renovationist program for change.[2] The Living Church Group completely adopted the view that the parish clergy were the vanguard for revolutionary change. This prompted Iaroslavskii to scribble on the front page of a later issue of *Zhivaia tserkov'*, "Priests (*popy*) of the world, unite!"[3]

Clerical unity was the goal of the First All-Russian Congress of White Clergy of the Living Church, held in Moscow from August 6–16, 1922.[4] In actuality, the Congress provoked open ecclesiastical warfare. The gathering started on an optimistic note with a grand celebration of the Divine Liturgy. Thousands attended, and Krasnitskii preached. Formal proceedings then began at the Third House of Soviets, formerly the Moscow Theological Academy, with 150 voting and 40 nonvoting delegates from twenty-four dioceses in attendance. Participants included a number of bishops (Antonin Granovskii, Evdokim Meshcherskii, Ioann Al'binskii, Ioannikii Chantsev, Vitalii Vvedenskii, and others) as well as representatives of the Eastern Orthodox patriarchs of Constantinople and Alexandria. Delegates split into six working commissions charged with preparing reports and resolutions for the plenary sessions that convened approximately every third day. Each commission worked out issues in an assigned area: legal-canonical, economic, episcopal affairs, charity and preaching, administration, drafting a charter.

The opening session on August 6 established the stance of the Congress with regard to the rights of bishops versus the rights of white clergy.

Krasnitskii started with a speech declaring that the Congress marked a new phase for renovationism. The first phase brought Tikhon's abdication and the transfer of power to the progressive clergy, who formed the Supreme Church Administration (VTsU). Now the Congress would start the second phase of expelling reactionaries from their positions of power within the church. Old counterrevolutionary monastic bishops would be replaced with new progressive ones from "the white, ordinary, working clergy." Krasnitskii reasoned that since the latter did the real work of the church, they should have real ecclesiastical power. He added that, following this transfer of power, the Living Church Group would take up its next task; namely, "to bring the laity nearer to church power, but only those who are toilers and not exploiters or oppressors of others."

Episcopal leaders in favor of church revolution spoke next, but their words of reconciliation could not stem the tide generated by Krasnitskii for ecclesiastical class warfare. Antonin reminded the delegates of his support for renovationism in 1905 and condemned conservative bishops who opposed it. He also expressed the hope that supporters of the movement would "unite not in the name of material interests but in the name of (Christian-socialist) ideas." Evdokim spoke in a similar vein, adding that the Living Church Group had made "mistakes" that needed to be corrected if they were to reach the shared goal of church renewal. His were the last moderate words spoken at the Congress. Ioann praised the gathering for overturning the domination of the monastic episcopate, which had used white clergy as "cannon fodder" during the unsuccessful attempt to overturn Soviet power. Lvov, the first layman to speak, applauded the move to rid the church of "counterrevolutionaries" and advised the gathering to purge local parish councils of reactionary elements.

The Congress convened in plenary session on August 7 and began its work of targeting enemies of the parish clergy: monastic bishops and conservative laity.[5] Delegates viewed monks as opponents of renovationism and voted to close all monasteries, converting urban ones into parish churches and rural ones into brotherhoods of workers or hospitals. Monks could renounce their vows and maintain clerical status. Monastic bishops who opposed renovationism were to be removed immediately by the Supreme Church Administration and exiled from their dioceses. The Congress requested that the VTsU order the immediate cessation of liturgical prayers for Tikhon in all churches and that the upcoming national church council strip him of all clerical rank. Those monastic bishops who accepted the new church administration were to be transferred to new dioceses, apparently a move to break their ties with the power structure. Delegates approved motions to empower VTsU plenipotentiaries in every diocese to root out and banish opponents of renovationism at all levels of church administration, including parish councils.

Turning to the rights of parish clergy, the Congress removed centuries-old restrictions related to marital status. Bishops, widowed clergy, and monks could now marry without loss of ecclesiastical rank. Related prohibitions on marriage were also abolished, including rules against a priest marrying an "honorable" widow or a layperson marrying a blood relation in the fourth degree of consanguinity or second degree of spiritual relation. When some delegates expressed the need for caution in implementing such a policy out of fear that it would provoke a backlash against the Living Church by parish church councils, the Congress abolished the rights of those councils. This was done by instructing reformers to gain control of those councils through church courts, VTsU plenipotentiaries, and even appeals to the People's Commissariat of Internal Affairs (NKVD). These decisions aimed to gain loyalty for the Living Church Group from rank-and-file parish clergy who had chafed under the old restrictions.

Soon the delegates sanctioned equally radical solutions to the financial difficulties of white clergy. The Congress set up a "unified church treasury," into which all funds from candle sales and parish offerings would flow. Diocesan and central church administrators, supervised by parish clergy, would then distribute the funds to individual clergymen. These administrators would also control all church property and receive income from chapels, cemeteries, and former monasteries. The laity would lose any control of their parish's finances and they would eventually be required to pay an annual church tax. Other motions supported the distribution of land to clergy for personal agriculture and the establishment of a social security fund for invalids, orphans, and the poor among families of clergy. Contributions from both clergy and their parishes would finance this fund.

Most Orthodox bishops did not agree with the decisions of the Congress. On August 13, the episcopal affairs commission reported on reactions to the Living Church Group by the ninety-seven active Russian Orthodox bishops. Thirty-seven approved of the group's platform, thirty-six opposed it, and twenty-four abstained. The Congress resolved to retire most of the bishops who opposed its program and to offer those who had abstained the choice of retirement or membership in the reform movement. The episcopal commission also recommended six married priests as candidates for vacant sees. Krasnitskii made a point of asking the bishops present if they would ordain those candidates the next day. Only five bishops responded in the affirmative.

The final session of the Congress on August 15 took up secondary issues, including the posthumous lifting of writer Lev Tolstoi's excommunication for heresy in 1901.[6] Delegates also elected new members for the Supreme Church Administration (five bishops, twelve priests, one deacon, and one layman) and the Living Church's Central Committee (twenty-five members, headed by Krasnitskii). At the closing celebration of the Congress in the Kremlin's Assumption Cathedral on August 16, Krasnitskii was named the first protopresbyter of the Living Church. The next day he led a delegation that asked the All-Russian Central Executive Committee for help in preventing organized ecclesiastical opposition to the Living Church. Specifically, the reformers wanted state backing to gain control of recalcitrant parish councils and to ban church convocations not approved by the VTsU. As Curtiss observes, the very nature of this meeting undermined Krasnitskii's assertion at the Congress that "no sort of bridge has been laid between the Soviet power and the church. Each will go its own road."[7]

Articles in the issue of *Zhivaia tserkov'* that included the proceedings of the Living Church Congress reflected the tone of that gathering. The first, a report proposing reforms in reading and rhetoric during the liturgy, reflects the changes envisioned by the Living Church. In it, Professor V. V. Surenskii wrote of the value of reciting prayers, reading Scripture, and preaching sermons with clear pronunciation using modern Russian.[8] His position incorporated a major concern of the parish clergy who sought creativity in liturgical forms to make Orthodoxy more comprehensible to the ordinary layperson.

Delegates to the Living Church Congress saw themselves as defenders, not destroyers, of the Orthodox faith. They did not change any Orthodox doctrines or dogma and altered only a few of the church's canons. The Congress traced the church's decline to despotic bishops and theologically ignorant laity, just as Orthodox critics had done during the tsarist era. That view lay at the heart of an article by Fr. Semenov that argued that majority rule was as unworkable in the revolutionary church as it was in Soviet politics. Both spheres need a "dictatorship" by the class who made the revolution—the white clergy in the church, the proletariat in the state—in order for the revolution to succeed. Semenov predicted renovationism's defeat if the laity and their popularly elected bishops gained control.[9] In their pursuit of acceptable reform, parish priests who joined the Living Church did not trust either monastic bishops or conservative parishioners to lead the church on the path to spiritual health.

Attitudes and actions by the Living Church Congress evoked strong reactions from monastic and parish clergy alike. Some bowed to its demands. At a trial in Smolensk for churchmen accused of opposing the seizure campaign, the central figure, Bishop Filipp Stavitskii, admitted his guilt by saying he had only been following the patriarch's orders. He then pledged loyalty to the Living Church. The court reprimanded him, although it condemned four of his co-defendants to the firing squad and imposed prison sentences on others.[10] Others abandoned the church entirely. For example, Kalinovskii resigned from the VTsU in mid-August and later announced his voluntary defrocking in the magazine *Bezbozhnik* [Atheist]. He became a professional antireligious propagandist, a profession in which he reportedly met with little success.[11] Still other clergy expressed genuine perplexity about which course to follow. Bishop Afanasii Sakharov of Kovrov wrote to Metropolitan Sergii Stragorodskii on August 24 and voiced concern over the latter's recognition of the Supreme Church Administration. Afanasii requested permission to run his diocese independently, since he knew that Sergii himself had misgivings about some of the VTsU reforms and had asked for greater autonomy in his diocese. Nonetheless, Sergii responded to Afanasii with wholehearted support for the VTsU. Afanasii did not follow Sergii's lead and was arrested and exiled to Siberia in September.[12]

As news of decisions by the Living Church Congress spread, open conflict began in the Church. Accounts circulated of believers and clergy who were standing firmly against red priests. On August 9, the parishioners of St. Daniel's Monastery in Moscow lodged a protest with the Fifth Department of the Commissariat of Justice (NKIu) against the activity of VTsU clergy. Citing Soviet law on the separation of church and state, these believers accused the VTsU of illegally usurping rights held only by groups of believers. They claimed that all who opposed the VTsU were being accused of counterrevolutionary activity and were threatened with exile and arrest. Thus, this society of believers was confused, because the VTsU appeared to be functioning with the agreement of the Soviet government. They referred to Lvov's public assertions of government support for the VTsU and asked indirectly if state policy on religion had changed. The laity worshipping at the monastery wanted to know if the government supported the VTsU, if they needed to obey VTsU orders, and if they were required to accept the appointment of a new bishop whom they did not want.[13] Other congregations in Moscow and Petrograd lodged similar complaints against Living Church activists with NKIu.[14]

Mass discontent with VTsU and Living Church actions filled secret police reports throughout August. In Vologda province, believers backed Tikhon—a "martyr" at the hands of the government—and conservative clergy preached against "progressive clergy" for being "Bolsheviks." The new church administration in Vologda lacked widespread support. In Simbirsk, clergy and believers joined together in asking the provincial executive committee to overturn the VTsU's removal of Bishop Alexander Voetskii. Clergy and laity alike in Irkutsk looked upon the new church with disfavor. GPU observers in the provinces of Pskov, Kursk, Chuvash, and Altai reported a lack of any response due to ignorance of events in Moscow. Only in Perm and Novo-Nikolaevsk were renovationists clearly on the march. As more information on decisions by the Living Church Congress reached outlying areas, opposition increased. In Orlov, "reactionary clergy" worried about bishops who had joined the Living Church and also expressed concern about a letter from local prorenovationist clergy saying that those who did not join the movement would lose their parishes. In Chuvash province, opponents of the Living Church accused parish clergy of following their selfish interests. A common thread began to emerge in these local reports: renovationism gained strength when a local bishop who opposed the movement was arrested and exiled. Such was the case in Pskov, Altai, Ekaterinburg, and Kaluga.[15]

Renovationist vs. Renovationist

The strongest reactions against decisions made by the Living Church Congress came from other renovationists. The majority of the movement's leadership felt that narrowing their base to the white clergy portended disaster, both ideologically and tactically. Individual leaders soon concluded that a counterbalance to the growing power of Krasnitskii's Living Church was required and formed new renovationist "parties." Like the Living Church, these new groups mimicked the most influential social organization in Soviet Russia (the Bolshevik Party). Unlike the Living Church, they showed greater sensitivity to Orthodox tradition when adapting the church to Soviet society.

Bishop Antonin Granovskii responded first by forming a renovationist party that intentionally appealed to the typical conservative layperson. He organized a League for Church Regeneration (Soiuz tserkovnogo vozrozhdeniia) two weeks after the Living Church Congress. The League's threefold mission was to foster solidarity between pastors and believers, limit central power, and promote a conciliar structure under the VTsU.[16] Calling for a return to primitive Christianity's democratic ideals of church life based on equality, fraternity, and freedom, the League's program advocated changes in the faith to make it free of exploitation and ritualism, spiritually creative, and morally healthy and to bring it into harmony with modern knowledge. Of course, the League maintained a position of loyalty to Soviet power. Still, the League's founding document deferred to traditional Orthodoxy. Parish clergy were forbidden to enter the episcopate, and restrictions on clerical marriage were upheld until their review by the upcoming national church council. The League's charter defended monasticism as an important aspect of Christian faith. This document also promised that the new group would run the Orthodox Church to benefit all believers, not just the caste of parish priests. To that end, the League proposed that all administrative bodies of the church have a membership that was two-thirds laity and one-third clergy.[17] On August 25, a gathering of 76 clergy and 400 laity approved the formation of this new renovationist party and elected a five-person Central Committee that imitated the Bolshevik organizational model. As Central Committee chair, Antonin sent a secret letter to all bishops of the "old order" (*staroe postavlenie*, i.e., ordained before Tikhon's abdication) and asked them to join him in countering the activities of the Living Church.[18]

Antonin's moves did not deter representatives of the Living Church, who were inspired by the militant mood of their Congress to consolidate their power in the center and the provinces. Government leaders sent messages to local officials with the reminder that "the Living Church is loyal to Soviet power" and the suggestion that they give "special attention to its needs."[19] The Kharkov newspaper *Kommunist* [Communist] recounted the tactics used. Members of the diocesan conference (an archbishop, a suffragan bishop, and three archpriests) were summoned to the local office of the Commissariat of Justice. There, the Kharkov VTsU plenipotentiary coerced them into signing a resolution expelling themselves from both church service and the boundaries of the diocese. Then, the plenipotentiary locked and sealed the doors of the building where the conference had been meeting.[20] Representatives of the Living Church used similar methods to remove another ten bishops from their positions between August 30 and September 4.[21]

The Living Church had reportedly gained momentum in the countryside by early September, despite opposition from many bishops. Officials in Viatka said that the lower clergy favored renovationism but also feared the higher clergy. In Cheliabinsk, a Living Church group successfully recruited all local clergy while their diocesan Bishop Dionisii Prozorovskii was standing trial. Although the report does not specify the charges he faced, they likely stemmed from his open summons for believers "to defend the church from desecration by apostates" in the spring. Laity and clergy alike expressed interest in the Living Church in Pskov, where the platform adopted by its Congress in August met with wide approval.[22] Resistance to Krasnitskii's group came from bishops around the country. For example, Fëdor of Kaluga instructed the clergy and laity in his jurisdiction not to join the Living Church because it was "the creation of communism." Even after his arrest, popular hostility against church reformers grew in the diocese, and anti–Living Church posters appeared.[23]

Such incidents further weakened the bonds of renovationist unity. Antonin publicly criticized the Living Church in his sermons and went so far as to shout "Christ is not among us" at Krasnitskii during the Divine Liturgy.[24] On September 12, Antonin held a mass rally in Moscow for his League for Church Regeneration and reported that Archbishop Veniamin Muratovskii had just organized the first local chapter of the League in Riazan and liquidated that city's Living Church group. Bishops in Petrograd, Tambov, Penza, Roslavl, Kostroma, and Nizhegorod responded favorably to Antonin's invitation to unite with his new organization. Metropolitan Sergii Stragorodskii joined forces with Antonin and presented a statement to the VTsU against the decisions of the Living Church Congress on the reinstatement of Tolstoi and all decisions relating to clergy marriage. Echoing these sentiments, Antonin characterized the Living Church as "a narrow, professional-estate group of white clergy inimical to the laity" that attempted to free the parish clergy's material dependence on parish councils. He demanded that the VTsU reorganize so that the number of League members would increase to eight and the number from the Living Church shrink from eleven to seven. At the same time, Antonin refused all requests to support Patriarch Tikhon's return to power.[25]

Institutional warfare between the two renovationist parties led to the formation of a third party in September. The Leftist Movement (*levoe techenie*) attempted to combine the democratic principles of the League for Church Regeneration with the reform proposals of the Living Church. This new group advocated the total separation of church and state, spiritual growth through honest labor, and theological education for clergy and laity alike. It proposed ecclesiastical administration based on consensual decision-making and full equality for all Orthodox believers—from the most esteemed bishop to the most humble layperson.[26] Little is known about the organizational structure of this group except that the Living Church's Central Committee expelled A. I. Novikov in October 1922 for being a leftist leader. During the debate over his expulsion, Novikov defended his actions, saying that he had no differences in principle with the Central Committee and had been only trying to advance the agenda for ecclesiastical change adopted by the Living Church Congress. From his perspective, the five-member presidium of the Central Committee had become too dictatorial and had shown more interest in directing VTsU activity toward the transfer or removal of bishops than in the implementation of the Living Church's program. In Novikov's mind, the leftists were loyal to the Living Church but promoted specific proposals within that organization.[27] He discovered that the Living Church also imitated the Communist Party in its ban on internal factions.

Novikov's leftist program found a home in a new renovationist party that emerged in October under the name League of Communities of the Ancient Apostolic Church (Soiuz obshchin drevle-apostol'skoi tserkvi)—

SODATs for short. Years later, when Vvedenskii recounted the origins of this group, he claimed that he broke with Antonin's League at the end of September 1922 because of personality conflicts.[28] Looking for a renovationist group of like-minded reformers, he discovered the small circle known as SODATs in Moscow. Levitin commented,

> The name was the purest fiction in that there were no "communities" nor, it follows, any league. A few religiously inclined intelligentsia simply intended to combine Christianity with the ideas of a labor cooperative. . . . Nothing came of this, and SODATs dragged out a miserable existence until fall 1922, when it found itself on the eve of dissolution. But then, unexpectedly, A. I. Vvedenskii joined it.[29]

Less than a month later, Vvedenskii took command and reinvigorated SODATs. Attracted by both its intellectual roots and its lack of "priestly elements," he decided to expand this group into a national organization and convinced the Petrograd renovationist organization headed by Boiarskii to join it. Renovationists in Moscow followed suit in November.

Vvedenskii wrote a new program for the group based on his personal theology, which merged European socialism with creative interpretations of Christian tradition. He also drew heavily upon leftist proposals rejected by the Living Church. SODATs started with theological modernization. Orthodoxy was to be purged of its pagan elements by ending veneration of holy relics and closing all monasteries. A national church council would eventually review—and presumably substantially revise—Orthodox dogma and canons. SODATs also wanted parishes to elect their clergymen, who would be rendered equal by eliminating all honorific titles and opening the episcopate to married priests. Lay believers were promised a simplification of the liturgy and a rule on purely voluntary monetary offerings to their parishes (SODATs did not support the idea of a parish tax). Like all renovationist parties, SODATs recognized the justice of the socialist revolution and professed total loyalty to the Soviet government. Vvedenskii's group became the organizational embodiment of the Leftist Movement, as evidenced by the fact that Novikov was the only layman on its six-member Central Committee, which was finally organized in January 1923.[30]

Infighting between national renovationist leaders quickly spread to the provinces, to the alarm of local clergy and state officials alike. Fr. Nikolai Pel'ts from Simbirsk submitted a report on church renovation to government authorities on September 4. Pel'ts concluded that the fight between the Living Church and the League for Church Regeneration threatened civil peace and the work of government officials in eradicating counterrevolution in Orthodox parishes. Meanwhile, he asserted, the old church, led by "fanatic monks and white clergy" with the support of 60 percent of all bishops, sought the return of the monarchy and opposed Soviet power. Pel'ts announced he was forming a new group that would unite all renovationists, although he also expressed his support for both the Living Church and the VTsU. The government official who forwarded this report to Antonin and Krasnitskii on September 5 expressed concern that conflict among renovationist groups damaged the government itself.[31]

The situation was complicated by suspicions of state officials regarding anyone attracted to Antonin's League for Church Regeneration. When the Living Church circle in Saratov splintered, the majority of its members sided with Archpriest Vostrikov, the local leader of the League. The police must have suspected his loyalty, for he was soon arrested on criminal charges. By mid-September, a SODATs organization appeared in the city.[32] Similarly, the party's Agitation and Propaganda Department (Agitprop) received accounts that Tikhonites were joining the League for Church Regeneration and so decided to assist the new group only if it displayed greater radicalism.[33] The fact that the Tikhonites looked favorably upon Antonin's faction might have led Krasnitskii to believe that the Soviet government would turn against the bishop. On September 23, the Supreme Church Administration voted to relieve Antonin of all his responsibilities and banish him from the capital, but it was unable to convince the GPU to enforce these decisions.[34]

Civil war among renovationist blocs spread to the church press. Krasnitskii penned a scathing article accusing Antonin of siding with the monks against the parish clergy and of planning to form a rival Supreme Church Administration. Krasnitskii concluded that Antonin's actions would lead to the same problems that plagued the church during the famine of 1921–1922.[35] An even more damning indictment of renovationists who refused to side with the Living Church appeared in Saratov. Archpriest Nikolai Koblov compared Krasnitskii to a majestic swan whose great work in leading renovationism was being destroyed by a monastic crawfish (Antonin), a rapacious pike (Novikov), and a treacherous "phenomenal being" (Vvedenskii).[36]

Titlinov published a vigorous and lengthy defense of Antonin's decision to form the League for Church Regeneration. He applauded the church revolution that deposed Tikhon and formed both the Living Church and the Supreme Church Administration. The split in renovationism came with the August Congress, which had adopted "radical tactics" and a "class-oriented" approach toward church reform. Extremists in the Living Church placed their own interests above those of the church by using compulsion to achieve their goals and thereby pushing the lay masses away from the new church. Renovationists more inclined to idealism and conciliatory tactics witnessed the results of the Living Church's intolerance. To save the movement and correct the one-sided decisions of the Congress, these reformers chose to follow the program offered by Antonin. The wisdom of that move was seen in "many clergy and thousands of laity" who joined the League for Church Regeneration, first in Moscow, then in Petrograd, then around the country. Titlinov refused to attack the Living Church as an opponent of renovationism. Rather, he labeled it as the first phase of innovation that, without mass support, had to be bypassed in order to launch a genuine church revolution "from below."[37]

The Living Church spurned overtures for reconciliation from renovationist fellow travelers. At its Central Committee's plenum on October 3–5, the organization expelled Novikov and heard reports on Antonin's attempts to gain control of the VTsU.[38] In the provinces, the struggle was not limited to words. Divisions among the reformers confused local authorities and added to the disruption of renovationism. In Penza at the beginning of October, the local GPU wrote that all openly reactionary clergy had joined the League for Church Regeneration and that local officials had responded by arresting that group's diocesan committee for holding two "illegal meetings." This naturally led to the local League unit's disintegration.[39] In Tsaritsyn, the scene was repeated when authorities arrested League leaders at the instigation of the local Living Church cell.[40] In its summary report on events in the Orthodox Church for October, the GPU found that internal disputes among VTsU members weakened that body and caused it to sever nearly all its connections with the provinces. In the provinces, the clergy divided among the various groups and did not join any one decisively. The secret police also reported a heightening of conflict between renovationists and Tikhonites at the local level.[41]

This running battle among advocates of renovationism stemmed from serious disagreements about the direction of and rationale for ecclesiastical reform. Each group was guided by a different aspect of the Bolshevik Revolution and sought support from a different segment of the church. The Living Church courted parish clergy exclusively and showed a deep mistrust of ordinary believers. This group was most faithful to Bolshevism as a political movement, adopting the party's organizational structure and model of class warfare. The League for Church Regeneration looked to the masses of lay believers for its support, just as the party looked to the poorer peasantry. Antonin's League hoped to heal the rift between parishioners and clergy by renouncing the Living Church's language of caste division. Service to the whole church was the League's populist rallying cry. Clergy would not be the masters, laity would maintain the rights they won through the national church council of 1917–1918, and bishops would continue to be drawn from the ranks of monks. The League also promised radical reform of the liturgy for the purpose of making religious ritual more comprehensible to ordinary believers. Under Vvedenskii, SODATs strove to win intellectual elements in and outside the church by embracing socialism as the foundation for postrevolutionary Christian morality. Its appeal to the earliest Christian traditions—solidly influenced by Renaissance humanism from the West—crossed the boundaries of the two other renovationist groups. SODATs supported the rights of all layers of the church except the traditional episcopate. It promised both liturgical reform and canonical change that would allow parish clergy to remarry and enter the episcopacy. It also offered women a place in the church's clerical leadership as deaconesses.

Destructive competition among groups of reformers brought open civil war and raised a major new problem. The party encouraged the growth of factions among renovationists out of fear that reformed Orthodoxy might successfully adapt to Soviet society. This strategy weakened renovationism, however, and opened it to attacks from those who defended traditional Orthodoxy. With the arrested patriarch as the rallying point, those attacks were so strong and sustained that they came to be known collectively as the "Tikhonite terror" (*Tikhonovshchina*). Sustained popular opposition within the church proved the greatest obstacle to renovationist success in the 1920s and forced the government to act.[42]

The Antireligious Commission

Tikhonite attacks and internal splits threatened renovationism with disintegration just months after it had taken control of the church's national administration. The government responded to this threat by shifting from open confrontation in the pursuit of church wealth to a more clandestine manipulation of the complicated church schism. Party leaders decided to exercise greater control over Cheka implementation of church policy. The Central Committee consolidated various committees already handling parts of this task into a single Antireligious Commission (Antireligioznaia kommissiia, or ARK) comprised of powerful party bureaucrats and high-ranking officers from the secret police.[43]

The party organized ARK first for the purpose of overseeing publications by loyal clergy. Prior to the Living Church Congress in August, renovationists had produced only five issues of their national magazine *Zhivaia tserkov'*. Delegates at the Congress received encouragement to produce local renovationist periodicals. These began to appear in various dioceses at the beginning of September as bimonthly or monthly publications of twelve to sixteen pages with press runs of 500 to 1,500 copies. Invariably, the front page of the first issue contained an indictment of the horrible situation inherited from the old church and a promise that a new day had dawned under the restructured diocesan administration. Stories on renovationism's local and national progress filled these periodicals, which were secretly subsidized by the government.[44]

Although party leaders encouraged renovationist propaganda against the Tikhonites, they worried when the flood of new renovationist periodicals also proclaimed the convergence of Orthodox Christianity and revolutionary ideals. In September, the Central Committee set up a special Commission for Antireligious Propaganda to oversee all religious publications.[45] Two weeks later, when the editors of *Pravda* requested permission to print articles against renovationist ideology, Agitprop advised them to be critical of reformist Orthodox groups and to seek approval from the new Commission for Antireligious Propaganda for all articles on religion before they were published. Not all felt this was the best course to take, however. One of Agitprop's experts on antireligious propaganda, N. N. Popov, worried that criticizing renovationist attempts in order to form a unified central administration was "unprofitable" because only a powerful VTsU could "liquidate the reactionary bishops in the provinces. Without the VTsU, the job of cleansing the church will become gravely complicated."[46]

Precisely those complexities in directing renovationism provided Bolsheviks in charge of implementing religious policy with a second reason for ARK. A special body called the Commission on the Church Movement, which was composed of GPU officers and Krasikov, met on September 27 to discuss factionalization in the VTsU. These officials were not shy about making decisions that directly interfered in renovationist affairs. They ordered that Archbishop Evdokim Meshcherskii become a member of the VTsU, and they advocated a strengthening of the Leftist Movement and an end to discussions about merging the Living Church and League for Church Regeneration.[47]

The Politburo soon combined work of the two Commissions (Church Movement and Antireligious Propaganda) into ARK as a new body with "authority to implement church policy . . . in both the center and the provinces." The new group replaced all other bodies responsible for that policy. It was expected to carry out directives on written and oral propaganda and agitation, working closely with the GPU, the Fifth Department of the Commissariat of Justice, and Agitprop, all of which were represented on it. At Trotsky's recommendation, the Politburo named Popov as ARK's presiding officer and ordered him to report every two weeks.[48]

Addressing threats to renovationism from the ongoing Orthodox civil war became the Antireligious Commission's top priority. ARK repeatedly intervened in the affairs of red priests throughout the 1920s and always saw problems in political terms, not ecclesiastical ones.[49] At its first meeting on

October 23, 1922, ARK decided to back the GPU's program for "liquidating Tikhonite supporters" and to examine "the impact on the VTsU of the active battle among its three factions (League for Church Regeneration, Living Church, and Leftist)." The Commission assigned Tuchkov the task of preparing a report on the *Tikhonovshchina* and gave a leading antireligious writer named I. I. Skvortsov-Stepanov the job of writing a set of theses to guide the Central Committee's work in antireligious agitation and propaganda.[50]

These two documents set the limits ARK expected to impose on its dealings with the church, including red priests. Skvortsov-Stepanov's theses condemned the medieval worldview and economic self-interest of all Orthodox clergy; some hoped to gain a privileged position by taking on "a socialist tint" but found these hopes dashed. The document warned against preferring any group of clergy because of their professed ideology. The Russian Communist Party considered them all the same but would not repress them—as long as they did not engage in counterrevolutionary activity. Orthodoxy's future would bring more factions and continued ideological criticism from the party. Communism's goals remained suppression of religious counterrevolution and leading the masses out of religious superstition to the truth of the modern scientific worldview.[51]

Tuchkov's report took a pragmatic and positive view of renovationism as the means for rooting out reactionary bishops, clergy, and lay activists in the Russian Orthodox Church. He summarized the "fight against the Tikhonite reactionary clergy" as follows:

> To win [this fight], the so-called Living Church group was formed, consisting primarily of white priests. It provided us with the means to cause a quarrel between priests and bishops similar to a fight between soldiers and generals. Hostility between the white and black clergy existed long before now, since the latter had great privileges in the church and used canon law to protect themselves against competition from white priests for the highest positions in the hierarchy.

Tuchkov explained how the secret police used these circumstances to the party's advantage. Parish priests backed by the government worked through the VTsU to replace the most reactionary Tikhonite bishops with men loyal to the Soviet government. As of the end of October 1922, the task was over half completed: nearly 100 bishops in sixty-eight dioceses had been replaced. Tuchkov concluded that finishing the job of "destroying the Tikhonite and semi-Tikhonite episcopate and depriving it of ecclesiastical authority" required uniting the church under an episcopate of married priests. Only then could the government be sure that the bishops stood against Tikhon and his policies. Once troublesome bishops were removed, the GPU would begin a campaign to drive Tikhon's supporters out of the parish councils. Tuchkov advised use of proven methods "by setting one part of believers against the other" through the formation of lay groups known as Advocates of the Renovationist Movement (Revniteli obnovlencheskogo dvizheniia). After the *Tikhonovshchina* was destroyed, the unity of the loyalist church could be broken by means of a national church council where renovationism would once again splinter over differing programs for reform.[52]

Based on the recommendations in these two reports, ARK decided to end civil war among renovationist groups at the end of October. Antireligious Commission members concluded that the sixty-five Tikhonite bishops who still controlled dioceses around the country were taking advantage of conflict among red priests. These bishops took advantage of confusion among renovationists "to organize in various places—although not under an obvious Tikhonite banner, and to expel renovationists from diocesan administrations. They are not submitting to the VTsU." ARK stopped renovationist squabbling by ordering the Leftists and the Living Church to form a coalition, implying that Antonin's League for Church Regeneration could not be trusted to attack the remaining Tikhonite bishops with sufficient vigor. The Commission also approved measures to strengthen renovationism through state action that would remove Tikhonites from positions of authority at the national, diocesan and parish levels.[53] Shortly afterward, Tuchkov informed the Politburo that substantial progress had been made. The VTsU had united its three renovationist factions to fight the *Tikhonovshchina*, replaced fifty Tikhonite bishops, instructed churches in the provinces on methods for driving Tikhonites out of parish councils, and issued a decree ordering priests and bishops to recognize Soviet power.[54]

ARK continued to face the problem of proliferating renovationist organizations. For example, red priests in Siberia formed a separate organization led by Peter Blinov in October 1922. A council of representatives from Siberian churches elected Blinov president and then unanimously named him bishop of Tomsk and Siberia. He became the first married bishop in the Russian Orthodox Church and soon assumed the title of Metropolitan of All Siberia. A series of similar ordinations occurred in the weeks that followed, to the consternation of Antonin, who quipped, "All Siberia has been covered by a network of archbishops who have flown into archbishoprics directly from the ranks of drunken *d'iachki* [minor, unordained parish clergymen]." The Siberian renovationists finally came under control of the VTsU in December.[55] Another new renovationist faction appeared in Moscow in October 1922 under the name the Free Workers' Church (Svobodno-trudovaia tserkov'). This group had no connection

with the VTsU, although it intended to demand the right to send representatives to the forthcoming national church council. ARK seemed in-
trigued by the group's slogan, which called for driving all bourgeoisie out of
Orthodox churches. The Free Workers' Church program denied all sacraments, rites, dogma, and canons. It said that the old forms of Christianity
must be replaced by a religion based on science, for soon science would
bring personal immortality to all people. The program also suggested that
church buildings be converted into meteorological stations. In one of its
reports, ARK expressed pleasure over the group's ability to shock émigré
newspapers and indicated that the Moscow Soviet was deciding whether
to permit their use of a vacant church.[56]

Government officials ended strife within the VTsU but did not call a
complete halt to rivalry among renovationist factions. The state's long-
term plans included splitting the loyal church, so some tension among
groups was desirable. Lively clashes between the Living Church and SO-
DATs frequently occurred in Petrograd. Krasnitskii visited that city at the
end of November to resuscitate the local chapter and had some success in
convincing some priests who had quit the organization to rejoin. However,
Boiarskii managed to keep control of the diocesan administration.[57] On
January 2, 1923, the Living Church Archbishop of Petrograd, Nikolai
Sobolev, resigned due to clerical opposition, and Artemii Il'inskii was
elected.[58] A major confrontation raged in March 1923 when Archpriest
N. A. Koblov arrived in Petrograd with documents naming him as the
new VTsU plenipotentiary and head of a special commission for liquidating autocephaly. Koblov vigorously attacked autocephalous churches and
alienated his fellow renovationists. He took the senior clerical position at
Kazan Cathedral, thereby displacing Archpriest L. M. Teodorovich. Teodorovich refused to surrender his post and even made a public declaration
of his ties with the secret police. Koblov ordered Artemii, Boiarskii, and
Gremiachevskii, the former plenipotentiary, go to Moscow. These three
complained that Krasnitskii had sent Koblov to eliminate rival renovationist groups in the city. Leaders in the Petrograd diocesan administration
accused Koblov of forcing priests to join the Living Church, instructing
laity and clergy alike to ignore Artemii and the diocesan administration
and refusing to obey VTsU orders not signed by Krasnitskii. Because these
actions weakened and confused Petrograd renovationists, diocesan officials
asked for Koblov's recall and limitations on Krasnitskii's activities. Krasikov forwarded this complaint to Tuchkov, who responded laconically,
"Koblov is a 'living churchman' and fully loyal to Soviet power."[59]

Accounts from Petrograd and elsewhere show that the Bolsheviks preferred the Living Church to SODATs and the League for Church Regen-

eration. The reasons for this are clear. Krasnitskii's group closely followed the Bolshevik model and put the least amount of emphasis on theological debate. The Living Church stood for the rights of parish clergy and loyalty to the Soviet state. Vvedenskii pushed SODATs toward theological innovation in Christian socialism and attributed his group's growth to its appeal among clergy and laity who disliked the Living Church. A more likely explanation is that government officials allowed SODATs to expand despite its Christian socialism as a substitute for Antonin's League for Church Regeneration. For parish priests, membership in SODATs offered greater security against arrest than the League for Church Regeneration and greater autonomy to its local units than the more disciplined and centralized Living Church. The League remained a problem because of its appeal to Orthodox traditions and its ability to attract members still loyal to Tikhon. For example, a local League leader in Saratov province was arrested in late October for distributing Agafangel's June appeal. Likewise, active "reactionary" clergy in Kostroma were supposedly connected to Antonin's group.[60]

State-imposed unity among renovationist groups shifted the focus of the church's internal conflict. Reformers faced off against Tikhonites and continued to have difficulty building support among the Orthodox masses. Secret police reports repeatedly acknowledged this point in October and November. "The Living Church group has no authority. Tikhon's supporters are the most active," was the message from Orlov. The clergy in the rural areas surrounding Simbirsk remained hostile to church reform. A general meeting of clergy in Kostroma elected a majority of "reactionary" clergy, Tikhonites, and even two "monarchists" to their new diocesan administration.[61] In Saratov province, Living Church agitation at public lectures failed to win nonrenovationist clergy.[62] With few exceptions, assessments of local church activity indicated indifference or hostility to renovationism.[63]

Despite this continuing problem, ARK produced reports filled with appreciation for renovationism's usefulness in the closing months of 1922. The VTsU was praised for removing dozens of Tikhonite bishops from their dioceses and issuing resolutions of loyalty to the government that included declaring the fifth anniversary of the October Revolution a church holiday. Four bishops and twenty priests led a celebratory liturgy on November 7 in Tambov's main cathedral with 2,000 people in attendance. Popov emphasized how all these developments deepened the church schism and commended the VTsU for following all of ARK's directives without question. ARK concluded that until the Tikhonite church was completely destroyed, it was premature to begin fighting renovationism.[64]

Also, the Commission reported it had banned public debates between renovationists and party activists because such events distracted the former from their main task of fighting Tikhonites.[65]

Bolshevik appreciation for renovationism had limits. As red priests stopped fighting among themselves, they returned to their mission of combining their Christian faith with Bolshevik goals for Russian social transformation. In November and December, ARK placed provincial church publications came under special scrutiny because they substituted "mysticism and greater church education for the fight against church counterrevolution." ARK planned to stop the publication of many renovationist journals simply by removing their secret state subsidies. Funding continued, however, for newspapers and magazines in major urban centers with the understanding that "the strictest censorship" would ensure that those publications "carry out an active battle with Tikhonite counterrevolutionaries. The supervisory organs will ensure these journals include articles and notices that attack magical and supernatural elements in the Orthodox cult." State policymakers advocated renewal of government funding for the VTsU press organ (*Zhivaia tserkov'*) provided that its contents also be "strictly monitored."[66]

Tuchkov personally took charge of redirecting the energies of red priests toward battling anti-Soviet elements in the church. He pushed for the reorganization of parish councils and the elimination of autocephalous groups. Even after many Tikhonite bishops had been removed, enemies of reform worked for "the complete independence of their parishes" until a church council met and replaced the VTsU with a legitimate church government. When parish church councils refused to send funds to the center, ARK bolstered VTsU finances by placing lucrative chapels in Moscow under its jurisdiction. It also agreed to find funds to help VTsU prepare for a national church council with the understanding that the party's Central Committee would limit preconciliar activities in the provinces and control the council's agenda.[67]

Events in Petrozavodsk illustrate the process used to purge parish councils. In August, the council controlling that city's episcopal cathedral asked Bishop Evfimii Lapin to remain in his position until a general meeting of the parish could be held. It also decided to stop praying for the renovationist archbishop of the region and removed five clergymen from the cathedral's staff because they were members of the Living Church. Fr. Gumilev organized a public religious procession "in support of the old church." Evfimii, Gumilev, and another priest were soon arrested, but the cathedral's parish council was not disbanded until December 31. The council protested to the Commissariat of Justice on January 14, 1923, asserting that Evfimii was not a counterrevolutionary and had been arrested only because he opposed Archpriest Dmitriev, the VTsU plenipotentiary. The Commissariat of Justice solicited Tuchkov's advice on this matter; he replied much later that the bishop and dissident priests all had been sentenced to three years of internal exile for anti-Soviet activity.[68]

Open resistance like that shown in Petrozavodsk was easily subdued. ARK showed greater concern about subterfuge by parishioners opposed to renovationism. Discovering such disguised opposition proved troublesome. In Kursk province, "reactionary" laity and clergy tried to join groups dominated by "progressive clergy," presumably to camouflage their true position.[69] Administrators in Novgorod had difficulty deciding which regional central church bodies should be allowed to register after a politically dubious diocesan council claimed to recognize the VTsU.[70] ARK countered these schemes by directing the VTsU to discipline bishops and priests who had joined renovationist groups but still followed Tikhonite policies.[71] Deciding how to treat parishes that identified themselves as "apolitical" or autocephalous was not as easy; these congregations vowed to stay out of politics but refused to recognize the VTsU's authority. Petrograd's autocephalous movement convinced city officials to recognize its rights to organize and to compete freely with renovationists for parishes. As a result, renovationism in the former capital soon found itself diminished and surrounded. ARK concluded that autocephaly was a cover for Tikhonites and instructed the secret police to arrest and interrogate all parish leaders claiming this status. Tuchkov personally investigated and quickly suppressed Petrograd's autocephalous movement.[72]

Even during such turmoil within the Orthodox Church, general levels of popular observation of religious rites remained too high for government leaders. According to a published survey of Altai province, the overwhelming majority of citizens continued to baptize their children, pay for religious funerals, and organize church weddings. Over 90 percent of the population reported some connection with the church. This figure held for all subgroups except members of the Russian Communist Party, and even one-third of that group admitted "reverting" to the church on occasion.[73] ARK's assistance to renovationism edged toward a strategy for suppressing popular religion while it rooted out the last vestiges of counterrevolution in the church. Initial movement in this direction began in November, when ARK reported that "soon the VTsU will implement resolutions on a new-style calendar that will shift all church holidays." Two months later, the Commission discussed laws to prevent minors from participating in church services.[74]

Caught between a desire to strengthen anti-Tikhonite forces in Orthodoxy and an ideology that promised that all religious belief would disappear, Bolshevik leaders expected ARK to reconcile the irreconcilable.

ARK fulfilled this impossible task by decoupling party rules from its practical decision-making. Its reports reflected the party line on church-state
separation and the basic untrustworthiness of clergy. ARK repeatedly re-
assured the Politburo with plans for the future destruction of all religious
organizations, including renovationism. ARK officials, however, acted in
accordance with a different set of rules, which demanded their coordina-
tion and cooperation with clergy. Tuchkov exerted great control over the
VTsU and purely religious matters. Krasikov's department in the Commissariat of Justice served as a cover for ARK's secret meddling in the
church.[75] For example, Krasikov wrote to the Commissariat for Foreign Affairs in December 1922 regarding church property located abroad. He
claimed the VTsU had initiated a plan for gaining control of the same, but
in reality ARK wanted to deprive "White-Guardist counterrevolutionaries" of the property and had instructed the church to send representatives
abroad to take legal ownership.[76] Decoupling became more pronounced
when the famous atheist Emelian Iaroslavskii became president of ARK in
January 1923.[77] In the years that followed, Iaroslavskii publicly promoted
atheism and church-state separation but secretly oversaw plans to direct
activities of the Orthodox Church.

While ARK looked for subtle ways to bolster renovationist fortunes,
other governmental organs aggressively closed nonrenovationist churches
throughout the country. Local officials interpreted the order to cleanse
parish councils of elements hostile to Soviet power as a license to use harsh
administrative methods against the Church. Soviet records do not give statistics on numbers of churches closed during the winter and spring of
1922–1923 but refer to this process as massive. Officials closed the churches using criminal indictments, administrative decrees, and exorbitant taxes
on both clergy and parishes. The state also began charging rent on church
buildings and imposing fees for the production of church-related items
such as candles.[78]

Financial pressure on the church had an unintended negative impact
on renovationism. A conference of regional VTsU plenipotentiaries discussed the financial crisis these charges caused renovationist parishes.[79]
Antonin boldly protested directly to the All-Russian Central Executive
Committee. He acknowledged the state's ideological desire to isolate the
church and eliminate it but pointed out that the separation decree had led
to instructions about believers' use of churches without charge. Antonin
called the new policy requiring church payments to the state exploitative
and wrong, legally and morally. He asked that they be changed in the spirit
of the "church NEP" and "the new church justice." VTsIK temporarily re-
scinded all church taxes in February 1923 pending its review of the policy.[80] Local officials apparently refused to act on this change, so Antonin

sent a second protest on April 8 asking the Commissariat of Justice to enforce the VTsIK's decision as complaints from the provinces continued to
arrive.[81]

The government-imposed cessation on renovationist infighting forced
red priests to face opposition from outside their movement. They recognized that most Orthodox parishioners did not accept proposed reforms
and tried to ameliorate conflict with the broader church. A congress of
VTsU plenipotentiaries voted in December 1922 to "prepare for a church
council . . . widen renovationist activity . . . and work for church unity."[82]
Renovationists decoupled local action from the general rules of their
movement in their effort to halt attacks from their opponents.

Indications of a willingness to temper renovationist militancy first appeared in the church press at the beginning of 1923. This shift in attitude
was most apparent in renovationist publications. When *Tserkovnaia zaria*
[Church Dawn] appeared in Vologda in September 1922, its lead article
took a hard reformist stance. The journal promised strong support for
parish clergy as the conscious elements of Orthodoxy who were required
to educate illiterate masses on the inevitability of the Living Church reforms in light of the Bolshevik Revolution. In contrast, the premier issue
of *Slovo zhizni* [Word of Life], which was published in Viatka on January 5,
opened with a promise to print only the truth. That article was followed
by a pledge from the new diocesan VTsU plenipotentiary that he would
not use repression against his opponents.[83]

Discussions within the Moscow and Petrograd diocesan administrations in early 1923 displayed a similar spirit of openness and cooperation.
Believers did not, however, respond as expected. The Moscow diocese
sought ways to increase authority in its churches and asked the VTsU not
to issue announcements to Moscow parishes without its consent. Nonetheless, its control over diocesan clergy was tenuous, and it often reverted to
expelling those who refused to toe the renovationist line.[84] In Petrograd,
the renovationist administration asserted its autonomy by rejecting innovations in ritual. Nonetheless, a contemporary observer commented that
most of the city's Orthodox believers recognized Bishop Nikolai Iarushevich, a leader of the autocephalous movement, as the legitimate head of
their diocese. This anonymous source also explained that renovationist
clergy and bishops served in mostly empty churches that they had taken
over by force.[85]

Renovationist publicists also tried to attract believers with the argument that the government would tolerate Orthodoxy only if it renounced
any opposition to the new political order and replaced religious superstition with genuine service to the Soviet people.[86] The "join or be crushed"
argument convinced some churchmen, such as Archpriest F. I. Nikol'skii

from Ulianovsk. A popular, energetic, and educated priest, he surprised many in his city by joining the Living Church. When an elderly parishioner asked why, Nikol'skii responded, "Thanks to this, I know the bell on my church will ring and my ancient cathedral will rise above the city sixty and one hundred years from now."[87]

Tuchkov's department in the GPU kept a careful watch over the spread of renovationism and continued to produce periodic reports on the church for ARK. A report covering events between December 15, 1922, and February 15, 1923, assessed the movement's strengths and weaknesses by regions within the country.[88] Renovationism attracted the most followers in the center, the southwest (Ukraine and Black Sea), Kirgizia, the Urals, and Siberia. Its weakest regions were the north, northwest, and west, as well as provinces in the Volga River basin. Within almost every region, however, support or opposition was not uniform. These geographic patterns remained unchanged through May 1923. GPU daily reports for the first five months of the year gave little additional information about Orthodox Church activity, and the items that were included generally reinforced the picture painted by Tuchkov's survey of mid-February.[89] Two items from these reports touched on developments that proved important later. Laity from the Crimea invited renovationist clergy to serve in their churches because so many reactionary priests had been exiled for anti-Soviet activity. This was precisely the result red priests and ARK officials wanted. On the other hand, an alarming trend appeared in Tiumen province in the Urals where, in response to the schism among Orthodox believers, part of the peasantry had joined Old Believer congregations.[90] The flight from Orthodoxy to sectarianism, agnosticism, or atheism alarmed renovationist leaders as early as January 1923.[91]

Dress Rehearsals

From the schism's inception, the church's first priority had been to convene a national council to decide questions raised by Tikhon's abdication. The state's primary goal had been to eradicate counterrevolutionary potential within the Orthodox Church by removing reactionary bishops. An important part of the plan was to have a public trial of Patriarch Tikhon in which he would be found guilty and sentenced to be executed. Difficulties in achieving either of these goals led to their becoming intertwined during the first half of 1923. ARK intended to use its extensive influence over the VTsU and its constituent renovationist groups to orchestrate a council that promised to help solve the Tikhon problem. Along the way, the government organized dress rehearsals for the two events, using surrogates to test the waters.

Trying Tikhon for counterrevolutionary activity initially seemed easy for the government. ARK discussed the process on November 14, 1922, and gave the GPU a month to finish its investigation.[92] At that point, the Commission intended to permit a national church council only after the trial ended.[93] Two weeks later, the Central Committee's secretariat took up the matter of the investigation for the "great church trial" and temporarily assigned Comrade Lunin, the vice-president of Moscow's Council of People's Courts, to the investigation.[94] These measures were to no avail; the GPU had trouble limiting the investigation and deciding the extent of Tikhon's criminal activity. On January 30, 1923, at its first meeting with Iaroslavskii presiding, ARK again discussed Tikhon's trial and issued a new date for its completion (March 25). It also dictated specific charges that would be pressed against him; namely, fighting the separation decree and the unsealing of relics, opposition to the confiscation of church wealth, and "systematic counterrevolutionary activity." It ordered the Supreme Court "to place the necessary resources for conducting this trial at the disposal of the GPU" while keeping "the charges and defendants to the minimum." At this same meeting, ARK approved VTsU plans to prepare for a national church council. Its preparations included sixty-seven theses drawn up by the VTsU as the basis for a church-wide discussion of reform prior to the council. ARK eliminated specific theses that required prospective council delegates to recognize the socialist revolution and voice support for the proletariat. It also vetoed a proposal inviting retired bishops to attend the council. The Communists further stipulated that elections for parish councils must be held before selecting delegates to the national council.[95]

VTsU officials and secret police cooperated to ensure that the council's agenda and membership would not undo the renovation revolution. The official announcement of the upcoming council denounced Tikhon as an enemy of Soviet power and argued for the abolition of the patriarchate. Issued on February 1, this notice indicated that the council would convene on April 15 and gave detailed rules for the election of delegates. The process described three levels of assemblies—parish, district, and diocesan—for narrowing down the field of candidates. Superficially democratic, the rules in reality greatly reduced the possibility that Tikhon's supporters would be represented in any number. Other rules for the council stacked its final membership roster with a large number of delegates drawn from the VTsU and its regional plenipotentiaries.[96] During the electoral campaign, the Living Church moderated its stand in the hope of winning support for its candidates. It issued a new version of its platform that rejected class consciousness in parish affairs, promoted lay participation in the Eucharist without the requirement of repentance, and advocated the concept of purely voluntary gifts to the clergy from their parishioners. The group's Moscow committee chimed in with a series of slogans for the upcoming council that promised no changes in either the liturgy or fundamental Orthodox dogma on Mary, the Trinity, and the nature of Christ.[97]

As the renovationists organized, the state investigated Roman Catholic clergy in the country. Still casting around for conspiracies, the GPU suspected a plot between Tikhonite Orthodox believers and Catholics led by Archbishop Ian Tsepliak to unite the two Churches. On February 6, ARK decided the evidence was sufficient to find Tsepliak guilty but delayed the trial until Tikhon's case was also ready. The Commission instructed the Supreme Court to start the patriarch's trial no later than March. To allow the elections for the Orthodox national council to proceed, the Commission decided to halt the implementation of a secret order from the NKVD that liquidated all diocesan administrations.[98]

Discussion of possible church reforms accompanied the election of council delegates in Orthodox assemblies across the nation with few disruptions. In the Kazan diocese, the published VTsU theses received limited support from delegates at the regional assemblies. Believers agreed that the national church council should decide the fate of reforms while defending the essentials of Orthodoxy. In practical terms, they dismissed ideas for translating the liturgy into modern Russian, allowing priests to wear secular garb, eliminating the patriarchate, or ordaining married bishops. One regional gathering expressed approval for giving parish priests the right to remarry out of sympathy for the plight of widowed priests with young families.[99] Tambov's diocesan congress was favorably disposed to the general idea of church reform yet still expressed opinions very similar to those of Orthodox believers in Kazan. Nonetheless, it upheld the right of both national and ecumenical church councils to legislate on the most important areas of Orthodox life.[100]

The separation of official ideology from everyday implementation of church policy continued. By late February, ARK found that it still was unable to resolve the Tikhon affair. It delayed the start of his trial yet again and reminded State Prosecutor N. V. Krylenko to finish Tsepliak's case first. ARK assigned Popov to guide a pretrial agitation campaign against Tikhon in the provinces. Tuchkov continued to supervise preparations for the council, and the Commission finally decided to quash the Free Workers' Church out of fear that it would harm state policy on renovationism. While ARK stated that the national church council had to fully comply with the laws separating church and state, it also ordered the GPU to take "the most decisive measures" when dealing with churchmen and laity who "make up parish councils and actively oppose the implementation of preparations for the council."[101]

Conflict between the party's broad directives and daily management of religious policy unexpectedly became obvious after ARK decided that the council would fully implement the decree separating church and state by abolishing all Orthodox national and regional administrative bodies, including the VTsU. Tuchkov sent a memorandum to Iaroslavskii expressing concern that this decision would give Tikhonites free reign in fully independent parish churches. As a result, the renovationist allies of the Soviet state would lose their positions of authority in the church. The Politburo overrode ARK's decision at Iaroslavskii's request because it "recognized the continued existence of the VTsU was essential." ARK was instructed "to take steps to ensure that the national church council's acceptance of the decree separating the church from the state be in sufficiently elastic form to preserve the rights of the VTsU."[102]

Intervention by ARK in Orthodox Church affairs increased in March when it set strict limits for the national council's actions. The national council would allow the VTsU to continue administrating the church but would not decide "the question of ecclesiastical reform, because the VTsU and renovationist groups still have not prepared believers for reform." Instead, council delegates would only hear "an informational report" on reform proposals. Immediately after the council ended, various renovationist groups would be allowed to hold individual congresses in Moscow to debate questions on ecclesiastical reform. ARK intended once again to widen the splits within renovationism throughout the country. The Commission also decided that the council would replace the old-style calendar with the new-style one, adding both a prohibition against including religious figures or events on state calendars and permission for privately printed religious calendars that followed the new Gregorian style. ARK also dictated the VTsU's composition after the council. The VTsU's membership would remain a coalition of representatives from various church groups, but its presiding officer would not be named by the council. The task of selecting a president would be done by the new VTsU after the council adjourned; ARK intended for Krasnitskii to fill the position.[103]

At this same meeting, discussion of the upcoming trials for Tikhon and Tsepliak led ARK to set the patriarch's court dates as March 25–30. Guilty verdicts in both trials were assumed, and ARK asked that the Politburo "give precise instructions to the court about the extent of punishment, taking into account the international situation."[104] Tikhon's trial was tied to the final destruction of his ecclesiastical network and the victory of renovationism. On March 7, the Party's Central Committee authorized a secret circular to all provincial party committees, informing them that the Supreme Court would receive Tikhon's case at the end of March and instructing them to use the process to discredit the nonrenovationist Orthodox Church as a counterrevolutionary organization. Local officials were told to organize clergy and believers in public condemnations of Tikhon's anti-Soviet past in order to justify the repression against him and his supporters in the present.[105]

Concrete decisions on the fate of the national church council and Tikhon had finally been made. The stage was set for the first dress rehearsal—a two-part trial run for the council. In the first stage, the Living Church convened a preconciliar session on March 11 with representatives from across the country. They met in Moscow and, according to a glowing account in *Izvestiia*, displayed order, propriety, and genuine religiosity.[106] The second stage took place at a SODATs congress in the Second House of Soviets from March 15–18. Both *Izvestiia* and *Bezbozhnik* printed detailed accounts of the proceedings, in which Vvedenskii, Boiarskii, Novikov, and Antonin figured prominently. The theme for this gathering was the link between Christianity's social role and the policies of the Soviet government. Boiarskii emphasized the need for Christian teaching to be independent from Marxist doctrine, saying "Christianity . . . should be more socialist than all the socialists and communists put together." He responded to Vvedenskii's argument for union with "the ship of Soviet statehood" by saying, "The church has no need to sail on any ship since it can walk on water." Antonin also stressed the need to spread Christian truth rather than engage in apologetics with the political structure. After this show of independence, the congress resolved to oppose capitalism and Tikhonites but to support labor. It also moved to reorganize parish councils immediately in order to remove parish leaders who exploited the labor of others. After a leader of the Russian Evangelical Christians addressed the delegates, Boiarskii stepped forward to affirm the Orthodoxy of SODATs and to reject any form of union with sectarianism. On this point, the congress overwhelmingly agreed.[107]

Both preconciliar meetings had gone smoothly from the perspective of Bolsheviks and renovationists. Delegates addressed parish concerns by asserting their independence from the government in religious matters and their commitment to Orthodoxy. They pleased the government by affirming their political loyalty to the state and repudiating Tikhon's misguided decisions. Despite the success of these meetings, ARK reluctantly accepted a delay in the start of Tikhon's trial and, still believing that it must precede the national church council, decided that the council could begin no earlier than April 30.[108]

Preparation for Tikhon's trial involved another dress rehearsal, which began the day after the SODATs conference ended. The trial of Tsepliak and thirteen other Catholic priests did not, however, achieve the desired result of convincing the international community to accept criminal prosecutions of church leaders. Even before the trial began, the British Minister of Foreign Affairs made a speech in Parliament in which he surmised correctly that the Tsepliak trial was nothing less than a tool for preparing the ground for Tikhon's case. Events in the courtroom followed the script with no surprises; on March 26, the highest-ranking defendants (Tsepliak and his assistant Butkevich) were condemned to death. The remaining priests were given prison terms. International reaction was so swift and negative that VTsIK hesitated for several days before carrying out the executions and then reduced Tsepliak's death sentence but confirmed Butkevich's. In a diplomatic note to the Commissariat for Foreign Affairs on March 30, the British government threatened Russia's material interests if Butkevich were to be executed. Nonetheless, he was shot on the following night, provoking a storm of protest abroad throughout April.[109]

Against the background of mounting international pressure, ARK continued planning for a show trial with Tikhon in the starring role. On April 3, ARK suggested to the prosecutor that Metropolitans Sergii Stragorodskii and Mikhail Ermakov be considered as possible co-defendants with the patriarch. The seriousness of these discussions was obvious from ARK's attention to minor related issues, such as the distribution of tickets, naming of the main prosecutor (Krasikov) and essential witnesses (Krasnitskii and Vvedenskii), and assuming responsibility for finances (Popov). Even so, ARK could not ignore the need to maintain a semblance of distance between the state and renovationism. It instructed Krasikov to respond to ongoing complaints from Tikhonites about VTsU behavior with verbal answers, not written ones, "in order to preserve the moral authority of the renovationists." Along the same lines, Tuchkov was asked to ensure that all laws were followed when renovationists expelled Tikhonites from their parish churches.[110]

Repeated delays confused those anticipating or dreading the start of Tikhon's trial. On April 6, *Izvestiia* wrote that Tikhon's trial would begin on April 11. This was a bad choice because it fell in the week just before Orthodox Easter, so the newspaper reported in its next issue that his trial date had been changed to April 24.[111] Even this proved unacceptable, since the Twelfth Party Congress was scheduled in Moscow from April 17 to 25.[112] On April 12, the Politburo rejected a NKID proposal requesting reconsideration of the decision to try and execute Tikhon. G. V. Chicherin, Commissar for Foreign Affairs, argued that prosecuting Tikhon would harm the Soviet Union's international interests and alienate its friends abroad. The Politburo not only rejected Chicherin's proposal but also adopted a top-secret motion that ordered the country's Supreme

Court to punish Tikhon for his "colossal crimes." Party leaders also instructed the foreign ministry and press to depict Tikhon as the head of a counterrevolution among churchmen *and* "gentry-landowners." Iaroslavskii was given oversight of this press campaign to ensure that it "does not reveal secrets of the preliminary investigation."[113] With these actions, Tikhon seemingly moved ever closer to trial. On April 12, Popov submitted a budget of 280,000 rubles for a seven-day trial and a sixteen-person staff to orchestrate publicity in the Soviet Union and abroad.[114] The patriarch was taken to the Lubianka prison for repeated interrogations. On one occasion, Tikhon was allowed to read the file compiled against him; in response, he asked what the date was for his trial. His interrogating officer responded that it had not been set and would depend on the patriarch. The secret policeman mentioned international ramifications and said the church was waiting for the patriarch to recognize the government. Tikhon refused this peace overture.[115]

During the Twelfth Party Congress, the Politburo decided to delay Tikhon's trial yet again. A single-sentence motion by Dzerzhinskii proved sufficient to cause that body to reverse its earlier rejection of Chicherin's argument and consider international reaction. Dzerzhinskii's motion passed on a voice vote by Politburo members during the congress, and the records do not indicate that they changed their minds.[116] When Iaroslavskii learned of this decision, he wrote to the Politburo to present ARK's arguments for not delaying the national church council any longer. ARK thought the council would help the case against Tikhon by condemning his counterrevolutionary activity. The trial could then take place later in May, giving the state extra time to publicize details of Tikhon's crimes abroad and "his relationship with the ordinary clergy and church council." Iaroslavskii also wrote, "Intensive agitation in connection with Tikhon's trial is undesirable."[117] In making this point, Iaroslavskii may have wished to avoid the possibility of disturbances during the spring planting season.[118] Postponement of the trial was decided so late and with such secrecy that a newspaper in Kaluga ran a story in its April 25 edition saying, quite mistakenly but in accordance with the earlier plan, that Tikhon's trial had begun the previous day.[119]

At the end of April, public demonstrations against the VTsU took place in Moscow's suburbs. At the diocesan congress on April 23–24, delegates supporting Tikhon disrupted the proceedings every fifteen minutes by singing prayers. When the motion to condemn the patriarch's anti-Soviet activity came up for discussion, these same delegates made such a loud disturbance that Krasnitskii was forced to interrupt the session. The congress discussed and approved the motion only after the Tikhonites walked out in protest that evening.[120]

During the closing days of April, government plans for the church unraveled. Practice sessions for the national church council and Tikhon's trial had gone as planned. Participants in the renovationist congresses and the trials of Tsepliak and Butkevich followed their scripts. But the audiences for these events refused to sit and watch quietly. The international community showed unexpected interest in the trials of churchmen in general and Tikhon in particular, while domestically Tikhonites resisted the rush toward a national church council dominated by renovationists. The Politburo decided on a last-minute delay of Tikhon's trial, but Iaroslavskii successfully argued for holding the council as planned.

The National Church Council of May 1923

The second Russian Orthodox council of the twentieth century represented the apex of renovationist power and the end of civil war in the church. Council delegates met in Moscow from April 29 to May 9 and numbered somewhere between 350 and 476, representing all seventy-six dioceses of the church.[121] Official protocols of the gathering were published immediately after the sessions, but Tuchkov's report from 1924 told of the government's behind-the-scenes control of the council's actions.

Tuchkov gave a stark picture of manipulation and infighting during the council. He wrote that nearly 500 delegates attended the council from four groups—the Living Church, the League for Church Regeneration, SODATs, and Tikhonites; 75 percent of the total came from the first two groups alone. He admitted that a majority of those present were renovationists because of governmental assistance in the selection process. Tikhonites intended to use the council to condemn the reform movement and place Agafangel at the head of the church. Renovationists, on the other hand, planned to finally consolidate their position in the church by giving the VTsU a canonical basis, condemning Tikhon and the émigré clergy, establishing the church's political loyalty to Soviet power, and introducing liturgical innovations. In a powerful declaration of GPU influence over the gathering, Tuchkov reported:

> The council might have collapsed if we had not secretly intervened, since the groups were disinclined to any reconciliation among themselves. Krasnitskii's group in particular laid claim to the leadership of the council and the church and rejected any coalition in the council or the future Supreme Church Administration to be elected by the council. He wanted to expel all opponents to his Living Church group from the council and to reserve it only for Living Church members. Krasnitskii made peace with the other groups only when he sensed that his supporters, for reasons incomprehensible to him, were beginning to be unfaithful to him and support a coalition.

The reason his supporters were unfaithful was that about fifty percent of the council's delegates were our informants, so we could turn the council in any direction.[122]

Lvov provided a different perspective on the thinking of the Living Church leadership at the council. Writing to VTsIK vice-president Smidovich, he assessed the situation in Russian Orthodoxy on the eve of the council. He recalled the golden days of the movement from May to August 1922, when renovationism was united and organized under the Living Church in its fight to rid Orthodoxy of counterrevolution. Lvov claimed that Antonin blocked implementation of the program adopted by the August Living Church Congress and surrounded himself with "reactionary elements from parishioners," thereby showing once again why the monastic clergy could not be trusted to spearhead lay renovationist activity. After the VTsU prohibited the introduction of married bishops, renovationism weakened further by splitting into rival parties.

Unity and strength would return to the movement, according to Lvov, with the Living Church's return to supremacy. The League for Church Regeneration was old church, and SODATs embraced sectarianism. Only his group was truly revolutionary and could reconcile the church with the Russian socialist revolution. He rejected proposed church reforms in dogma and liturgy because they were divorced from revolutionary Russia's real social issues. He explained, "The reformationist element sinks into sectarianism. The elements desiring faith according to immemorial tradition remain in Orthodoxy. By taking on the tint of reformation, renovationism is not becoming a movement of any kind among the population of Orthodox believers. The Living Church wants to drive all elements of the old order out of the church and unite the church's ideology with revolutionary socialism." That goal would only be achieved through unity within the Living Church: "Only with unity will the council be successful. Otherwise, it will turn into anarchy."

Lvov ended his report by revealing its main purpose: to express support for Krasnitskii. While he approved of the actions of the Living Church in Siberia, he could not support Metropolitan Peter Blinov as presiding officer at the council. Blinov had too little authority in the church as a whole, and his ordination was questionable. To avoid chaos at the council, the only logical choice for its president was the talented leader of the Living Church, Krasnitskii. In Lvov's words, "If we recall that the council will conduct the trial of Patriarch Tikhon, then 'who will preside over the council' is not a neutral question for the regime." Lvov made a convincing political case for Krasnitskii as the only renovationist leader able to guide the council in trying and removing Tikhon from office.[123]

Conflicts among renovationists or between them and the Tikhonites never surfaced in official accounts of the council. On the contrary, church and state press alike stressed the overwhelming unity of the gathering in conducting its business. The reports acknowledged the presence of Tikhonites at the council but always presented them as small in number and weak in arguing their case. The gathering followed its program without a single publicized hitch. After an opening day filled with speeches that praised renovationism and condemned Tikhon and his followers, the council got down to business. On May 2, it elected Blinov as president and decided other organizational matters. The only foreign representative on hand, Bishop Edgar Blake of the Methodist Episcopal Church in America, praised the renovationists for being involved in Russian society and pledged 5,000 dollars for theological education.[124]

The next day, Tikhon was accused, tried, and convicted in absentia of aiding and abetting counterrevolution, capitalism, and foreign intervention. As Curtiss noted, "Properly speaking, there was no trial, for the accused was neither present nor represented, and no evidence was furnished for the charges made."[125] Charges against Tikhon fell under such vague categories as breaking Christ's commandments and allowing the church to fall into ruin. The council defrocked Tikhon and replaced patriarchal administration with a ruling body composed of bishops, priests, and laymen. Tikhon's removal required the approval of the bishops, who were meeting in a separate assembly. The record of their "unanimous" vote of approval included the signatures of only fifty-four of the sixty-six bishops present, and three signatures were completely illegible.[126]

The council's deliberations then moved to issues of the marital status of clergy. At the evening session following Tikhon's removal from office, the council considered the question of a married episcopate. Voices raised for and against this proposal were mainly those of bishops ordained before 1917, although Boiarskii stepped forward at a crucial juncture in the debate. As expected, both the council and its episcopal assembly approved a resolution for "the implementation of a white, married episcopate equal in rights with those who are not married." On May 4, the discussion broadened to remarriage of clergy and ended with the expected results. All clergy except bishops could remarry with the permission of diocesan authorities. Any clergyman who had been defrocked because he had remarried could be reinstated to his previous clerical rank. Clergy could now marry widows or divorcees. Antonin proposed an amendment that prohibited the remarriage of bishops and was supported, somewhat unexpectedly, by Boiarskii.[127]

These two unlikely allies broke ranks on the issue of relics. Boiarskii gave his views during a presentation on cases of forgery and falsification of holy relics in Russia. He advocated the careful examination of all relics. In the ensuing debate, the council asked Antonin to express his thoughts on the issue. He requested time to consult with other bishops. At the evening session, Antonin argued persuasively that relics should be preserved for moral and religious reasons. The council responded with a resolution to recognize genuine relics and to eliminate any secrecy in their preservation and display. In a similar vein, the convocation approved a motion that closed all monasteries except those that embodied the concept of Christian brotherhood based on communal labor.[128]

Behind the scenes, party functionaries controlled events and headed off any public confrontations. On May 4, ARK responded to Tuchkov's account of the council's actions by deciding that

> Krasnitskii might attempt to make a scene at the council . . . in order to discredit its President Blinov. Therefore we order comrade Tuchkov to take measures for preventing this and involving Krasnitskii in the active, coordinated work of the council. . . . We have no objection to the Supreme Church Administration's receiving the $5,000 promised by Bishop Blake under the condition that the money should be placed in institutions under the State Committee of Finance. . . .We will allow a deputation from the council for defrocking Tikhon and assign the GPU to implement this.[129]

Clearly, ARK wanted to control the church council and was willing to act quickly and decisively when the unexpected happened.

Tikhon's response to the "deputation from the council" was not unexpected. During the break between the morning and evening sessions of May 4, five delegates called on the former patriarch. One of them, Bishop Vitalii Vvedenskii—who was not related to the SODATs leader and later became a major renovationist leader—recalled that meeting twenty years later. Vitalii, Blinov, Krasnitskii, and two other clergymen were driven in a Ford automobile to the Donskoi Monastery, where Tuchkov awaited them. As they entered Tikhon's apartment, Blinov presented him with a written copy of the council's resolution. Without showing any emotion, Tikhon sat down at a table, donned his eyeglasses, read the document, and wrote the following words upon it: "I have read this. The council did not call for me, I do not know its competence, and therefore I am unable to recognize its decision as legal. Patriarch Tikhon /Vasilii Bellavin/."[130] The council never reacted to Tikhon's response and probably never officially learned of it.

Lvov wrote a second report to the government on May 5, halfway through the council, and concluded that renovationism had been strengthened by the national council. Nonetheless, he felt that the VTsU had lost

respect due to Blinov's "unexpected decision" to call for a vote on Vvedenskii's elevation into the episcopate. In private, Blinov claimed to be
following the wishes of "the government." Lvov could not resist mention-
ing his earlier warning to VTsIK of the danger of having Blinov and not
Krasnitskii preside over the council. This event dealt "a great public blow
to the council's authority."[131] At least one high official outside ARK agreed
with Lvov's assessment, but for different reasons. On May 6, Chicherin
wrote to Iaroslavskii on behalf of NKID to explain how American and
English journalists viewed the story. He said that so far, the council had
been a "winning phenomenon in the highest degree" for the government,
because "it demonstrated to the whole world that freedom of conscience
exists in Russia." Still, Chicherin had two concerns. The first centered on
rumors that Krasnitskii's group had been prevented from caucusing by
"some circumstances beyond its control." The second resulted from the
arrest of a Salvation Army representative in Moscow. Chicherin asked
Iaroslavskii to send him more information on how things actually stood so
that the rumors could be squelched.[132]

The national church council ended peacefully. The assembly approved
the switch to the new-style calendar, effective June 12, 1923, and excommunicated émigré clergy associated with the Karlovtsy Synod. Vvedenskii
made an impassioned plea for church reform, but the council decided that
his comments reflected his personal agenda and refused his invitation to
make immediate reforms. Krasnitskii rebutted Vvedenskii's arguments, saying the crucial matter was "village clergy . . . their living conditions and
material Christianity." Finally, the council resolved "not to introduce any
universally required reform of dogma or liturgy" and asked "all who worked
for church renovation to preserve the unity of the church with all the
means at their disposal." At the closing session on May 8, delegates voted
to keep the VTsU as the governing body of the church under a new name,
the Supreme Church Council (Vysshii tserkovnyi sovet, or VTsS). After a
recess, the body offered to make Krasnitskii the archbishop of Petrograd.
He refused this honor but did accept the title of protopresbyter.

Elections to the new VTsS followed, based on the principle of propor-
tional representation by renovationist groups. The Living Church received
ten seats on the new body, SODATs six, and the League for Church Regeneration only two. Leaders from each group sat on the new VTsS, and
all were elected unanimously. In its final decision, the council agreed that
it could not recognize autocephaly for the Ukrainian church and referred
the matter to the next council for further consideration.[133] The council
officially ended with a prayer service of thanksgiving in the Cathedral
of Christ the Savior on May 9. Supporters of ecclesiastical reform had

weathered a year of civil war in the church and emerged with a unified organization.

Transformation of the Orthodox Church proved more difficult than red
priests imagined after Tikhon abdicated in May 1922. They sought a genuine ecclesiastical revolution that would replace traditional Orthodoxy
with a modern form better suited to the Soviet era. Replicating a political
revolution within the church required more than simply replacing a patriarch or his bishops. Advocates for reform recognized the need for a program that would attract wider support from Orthodox constituents. They
also had to counter opposition from opponents within the church and fulfill demands imposed by political leaders outside the church.

Shaping a revolutionary program for Russian Orthodoxy nearly destroyed renovationism. Krasnitskii hijacked the term "Living Church" and
applied it to his personal vision of a church revolution led by parish priests,
the Orthodox "proletariat." Renovationism first split into two connected
bodies: the Supreme Church Administration, which served as the um-
brella for all renovationists, and Krasnitskii's Living Church Group of
parish clergy, which combined ecclesiastical Bolshevism with nineteenth-
century clerical liberalism. But clerical liberalism in the Soviet era proved
extremely unpopular among the Orthodox masses, particularly the peasantry. Soviet laws on separation of church and state granted a large degree
of autonomy to parishes, and parishioners were unwilling to hand their
power to parish clergy. In addition, living churchmen discredited themselves by modeling their capture of ecclesiastical power on the success of
the Bolsheviks. Renovationists adopted the ruthlessness toward their enemies, the language of class struggle, and the organizational features of the
Communist Party. In each of these areas, red priests compromised Orthodox traditions that many Russians held as sacred.

Renovationism's failure to attract masses of ordinary believers led to
the formation of competing reformist groups and encouraged additional
government action. Krasnitskii once again took the lead by rallying parish
clergy with promises of ecclesiastical power and economic security. Antonin reacted with a program for Orthodox regeneration aimed at at-
tracting laity and more conservative clergy. Vvedenskii appealed to the
intelligentsia and priests who wanted theological freedom. As these groups
fought among themselves, enemies of reform attacked all living churchmen. Soviet officials grew impatient and decided to force desired out-
comes. The party responded by forming ARK and implementing legal
action against hostile Catholic and Orthodox leaders. Government agents
also redirected inter-renovationist rivalries into more desirable assaults on

Tikhonites. Red priests were to destroy the old church before being turned on one another.

Reformers responded to mass alienation by decoupling revolutionary rhetoric from everyday Orthodoxy. To maintain state support, they continued to hold essential positions on loyalty to Soviet power and repudiation of patriarchal church structures. To keep parish clergy in their camp, they validated new rules on marriage, finances, and episcopal power. But to attract ordinary Orthodox believers, renovationists staged a traditional national council that rejected radical innovation "for the time being." Imitation of Bolshevism faded as the embrace of religious traditionalism increased. Red priests seemingly found a workable balance for bringing their church into Soviet society. By the end of the national council, in the words of historian John Curtiss, "the Renovationists seem to have believed that they had finally established their regime and that, in spite of the continuing opposition of the Tikhonites, its success was assured. These hopes were to be rudely disappointed."[134]

4.

THE RELIGIOUS NEP

IN AUGUST 1923, Emelian Iaroslavskii told a group of Moscow party workers that the situation in Soviet Russia had become more complex and,
therefore, they must attempt to conduct a dialogue with the church. He
informed his audience that the party had decided to turn away from the
politics of War Communism in relation to religious leaders and show
greater toleration of organized religion in the area of "social-political practice." ARK's president and Russia's leading atheist publicly denied that the
government had a plan for a "religious NEP," but his words signaled a
change in religious policy that helped reshape renovationism for the rest
of the decade.[1]

Iaroslavskii's speech connected religious policy with Soviet Russia's new
political direction during the era known as the New Economic Policy
(NEP), from 1921 to 1928. The Tenth Party Congress adopted NEP in
March 1921 as a reaction against both the failure of War Communism and
the multiple threats to Soviet power seen in civil disturbances in Tambov,
Kronstadt, the Volga region, the Caucasus, and Siberia. NEP was envisioned as the means by which the government could quell popular discontent with its economic policies (especially grain requisitioning) without
making major concessions in the political sphere. A grain tax, payable in
kind, replaced the forced confiscation of agricultural products. The government lifted restrictions on small manufacturing, shops, and service in-
dustries but maintained control of heavy industry, finance, and foreign
trade. An idea of peaceful cooperation (*smychka*) between the town and the
countryside guided the new policy. The Bolsheviks hoped that the proletariat and the peasantry would work together during this time of retreat and
recovery in the drive toward a communist society in Russia. Controversy
raged within the party over the wisdom of NEP throughout the 1920s. The
Bolsheviks finally abandoned NEP in favor of collectivized agriculture and
rapid industrialization, the hallmarks of the Stalin Revolution.

Historian William G. Rosenberg calls NEP Russia a society in the process of "transition," one turning "on the broad social and cultural axes connecting what tsarist Russia had been to what Soviet Russia was about to become." He explains that NEP not only marked a transition "from an essentially preindustrial order to a powerful, autonomous state" but also helped create "the fundamental elements of a new Soviet social order, culture, and national identity." Part of this process included the selection of methods appropriate for creating that new order. He feels that historians now need to leave questions about "struggles for power" aside and instead look at "the complex and consequential interactions between social and cultural components of resistance and change."[2] During the religious NEP, which lasted from the middle of 1923 through 1928, renovationism stood at the center of the controversy over whether to embrace or resist change within the Orthodox Church.

The application of NEP principles to organized Orthodox Christianity was delayed for two years by the fight against "Tikhonite counterrevolution" in the church—the fight that had seen red priests seize control of the national church administration and fight a civil war inside Orthodoxy. By 1923, the agricultural crisis had passed, crop yields were rising, and the overall standard of living had started to improve. The state no longer sensed danger from a church-led coup d'état and so pursued a new policy toward religion modeled on institutions from the economic and social arenas. Parish communities were given considerable autonomy while the upper levels of church administration remained under strict supervision by the secret police. The government encouraged and often actively promoted competition among rival Orthodox groups for the loyalties of the faithful. Its goals were to weaken the church as an organization, lessen the influence of religious "superstition" in Russian culture, and strengthen the underlying premise of Bolshevik antireligious propaganda that religion was false science propagated by clergy whose only goal was to line their own pockets. Organized religion itself was used as a tool against the very worldview it promoted.

This chapter will examine renovationism's reactions to the religious NEP on a macro level, that is, as an ecclesiastical organization responding to a new political environment. It will consider the structural ramifications of the government's new policy toward the Orthodox Church between June 1923 and December 1928. My purpose is to explain the impact of changed national policy on renovationism as an organization. The next chapter will analyze renovationism at the micro level during this same period and describe pressures on the movement from popular religion as practiced in Orthodox dioceses and parishes throughout Russia.

A New Ecclesiastical Policy

The Soviet government's new policy toward the Orthodox Church in mid-1923 was a variation on the one adopted by the Politburo the previous year. As described earlier, party leaders intended to use the emerging three-way split in the church (a loyal patriarchate, a conciliar national administration, and a movement toward complete decentralization) to drive "counterrevolutionary" Tikhonites out of the hierarchy and then out of parish councils. On Trotsky's recommendation, the Politburo in 1922 voted not to favor any one of the three factions so that none of them could become dominant. At the beginning of 1923, Iaroslavskii and Tuchkov had taken charge of the day-to-day implementation of religious policy through the Antireligious Commission (ARK). Mid-year, ARK reassessed the original policy and convinced the Politburo that revisions should be made to allow competition between Tikhon and the renovationists. Renovationist successes and concerns by foreign governments for Patriarch Tikhon's fate forced this course correction.

International confrontation about Tikhon initiated the policy change. On May 8, 1923, with renovationists showing exceptional unity in the closing days of their national church council, the British Foreign Minister, Lord George Curzon, submitted an official note to the Soviet government. The "Curzon Ultimatum" demanded that Soviet representatives immediately cease all Communist—and therefore anti-British—propaganda in Asia; this same demand had been part of the March 16, 1921, trade agreement between the two countries. Curzon did not trust the Bolsheviks to keep that agreement and was worried that rebellion might ensue if Soviet agents continued their activities in Iraq, Persia, Afghanistan, and India. He also expressed moral outrage over other Soviet actions, particularly the insolence with which the Bolsheviks responded to European complaints about their treatment of Russian religious leaders.[3] Point twenty-one of Curzon's ultimatum referred explicitly to the repression of senior clergy in Russia, recalling the fate of Veniamin, Butkevich, and Tsepliak. It mentioned the arrest of Tikhon and his imminent trial for "counterrevolutionary activity," condemning such an open attack on religion as an affront to the moral sensibilities of the civilized world.[4] Curzon's ultimatum gave the Soviet government ten days to give a satisfactory reply or face the consequences; namely, a suspension of the trade agreement.

Government leaders, who were not very sensitive to diplomatic nuance, responded to the ultimatum as if it threatened invasion and war. They arranged public demonstrations in Russia against the British, although Chicherin and Trotsky also instructed the city soviet of Moscow to avoid any action that might provoke international action. At the same time, the Soviet government attempted to extend the time for a reply and to appease the British with several notes that offered partial solutions to the grievances. Curzon stood firm, and the Soviet government relented to all his demands by June 13. That day, Curzon wrote, "I think that I may claim to have won a considerable victory over the Soviet Government, and I expect them to behave with more circumspection for some time to come."[5]

Curzon's victory had unexpected consequences for the Russian Orthodox Church. Renovationism's new national administrative body, the Supreme Church Soviet (VTsS), immediately denied Curzon's charge of religious persecution by the Soviet government in a message on May 12 to the Archbishop of Canterbury. During the Soviet government's initial response to the crisis in the second half of May, ARK continued its previous strategy for battling ecclesiastical "counterrevolution." In accordance with earlier plans, the Commission transferred the patriarch from house arrest to the Lubianka prison on May 23. Tuchkov informed renovationist leaders that the patriarch's criminal trial would soon begin, and believers in the provinces believed that Tikhon would soon be executed.[6] When fears of the Curzon "threat" intensified at the beginning of June, ARK changed its treatment of the old church by ordering the GPU to punish those responsible for closing Tikhonite churches illegally and to suggest how the process could be reversed. The patriarch was allowed to write articles on "his current relationship to Soviet power and the conditions of his imprisonment." Tuchkov visited the cities of Vladimir and Murom to gain firsthand information on massive church closures in those areas. After this trip, he convinced the Commission to sanction the voluntary surrender of church valuables with the understanding that those who did so would not be prosecuted. In addition, the Commission gave provincial executive committees the power to approve public processions of venerated icons.[7] The most dramatic evidence of the shift in state policy, however, came in a public announcement that Tikhon would be released from prison.

Curzon's action alone did not force the Soviet government's reassessment of its policy toward the Tikhonite church. Two documents written by Iaroslavskii for Stalin and the Politburo presented other reasons for the change. The first, a proposal dated June 11, 1923, stated:

We must immediately implement the following resolution concerning Tikhon's case:

1) Continue the investigation of Tikhon indefinitely.

2) Inform Tikhon that it might be possible to release him from prison if:

a) he writes a special statement in which he repents fully of his crimes against Soviet power and the masses of workers and peasants and expresses his present loyalty to Soviet power; b) he acknowledges the government's right to bring him to justice for these crimes; c) he breaks openly and decisively with all counterrevolutionary organizations, secular or religious, especially those associated with the Whites and monarchists; d) he clearly expresses a negative attitude toward the new Karlovtsy council and its participants;[8] e) he announces his negative opinion of the machinations of the Catholic clergy (through the pope), the Archbishop of Canterbury, and the Ecumenical Patriarch Meletius; f) he expresses agreement with some church reforms (for example, the Gregorian calendar).

If he agrees, he will be freed, transferred to Valaam Monastery, and not be prohibited from religious activity.[9]

These conditions pointed to a government campaign to neutralize Tikhon as an icon around which opponents of the regime, at home or abroad, might rally. The concessions demanded from the patriarch would signal a change in his attitude toward the new order in Soviet Russia, and his statements would defuse the time bomb of international intervention on his behalf and alienate those who had taken up his cause abroad. The first point in Iaroslavskii's proposal kept the stick of future criminal prosecution in view while the last paragraph proffered the carrot of freedom and return to church leadership in exchange for Tikhon's acquiescence to state demands.

Iaroslavskii's second document contained arguments that convinced the Politburo to follow the new path. This document played such a fundamental role in renovationism's history that it is included in full.

A Brief Justification for the Proposal Concerning Tikhon

1) Such a step is essential. It would vindicate our delaying Tikhon's trial. Otherwise, we would give the impression that we fear the White Guards' threats.

2) Conversations with Tikhon have revealed that, using some pressure and promises, he will agree to this proposal.

3) If he does agree, his statements will have enormous political significance. They will completely trump the plays of all émigrés. They will be a blow to all organizations centered on Tikhon. Tikhon will prevent the strengthening of VTsU influence, while his own personal influence will be compromised by his connection with the GPU and his public statements. His attacks against the Archbishop of Canterbury, Meletius, Antonii [Khrapovitskii], and the pope will be primarily a slap in the face to the British government. In European circles, this will remove any pretext for any action by England in defense of Tikhon. Finally, his agreement to any reform (he agrees to recognize the new Gregorian calendar) makes him a "heretic" or innovator in the eyes of the true Orthodox.

Through this action, the VTsU will return to its earlier position with a significant lessening of its influence.[10]

These documents show that the strength of renovationism weighed heavily on the minds of state policymakers. They did not see the church reform movement as weak, although historians have often assumed the opposite.[11] The Soviet government freed Tikhon partially because of international pressure, in particular in response to the Curzon ultimatum. In addition, party leaders worried that they not be seen as having caved in to that pressure by freeing Tikhon without first compromising his integrity in the eyes of his supporters. However, Iaroslavskii twice mentioned reducing the power of the renovationist Supreme Church Administration in his arguments for freeing Tikhon. As noted earlier, ARK intended to weaken renovationism immediately after the close of the national church council by splitting the movement once again on the issue of specific reforms. The Commission never executed this plan; perhaps it tried and failed, perhaps the Curzon crisis forced it to abandon the plan. In either case, Iaroslavskii's rationale for freeing Tikhon included a clear statement of the threat renovationism posed after its successful national council.

Tuchkov shared Iaroslavskii's view that the national church council strengthened renovationism and attributed this to the formation of a coalition in its new VTsS. Recalling the first steps for enacting the new policy in a report written for the Thirteenth Bolshevik Party Congress in May 1924, he listed the positive effects of that council in splitting the Orthodox Church, the émigré press, and leaders of other religious groups over the issue of supporting Tikhon. It also unified renovationism. On the negative side, the chief bureaucrat for religious policy noted that the council lacked influence among ordinary believers because it mistreated Tikhon and accepted radical reforms. Tikhon's release increased the "squabbling" among the churchmen since he alone had played the martyr who refused to compromise with the Bolsheviks and who stood firm for the faith. Tuchkov recalled:

We had the problem of winning over Tikhon, so that he would not only apologize to Soviet power but also repent of his crimes, thereby putting the monarchists in a ridiculous position. I must say that this work with Tikhon was extraordinarily difficult. He understood perfectly that his involvement would not end with just one act of repentance, that afterward he must obey and act on the orders of the GPU. This fact bothered him most of all. But, thanks to the circumstances and conditions under which Tikhon was imprisoned and to the way we approached him, we successfully convinced him. He wrote the statement of repentance with his own hand, a document that divided him from those who just three days earlier thought he was steadfast and undaunted.[12]

Above all else, these documents from Tuchkov and Iaroslavskii defined the aims of the religious NEP; namely, secretly nurturing internal church rivalries and thereby preventing any group from becoming strong enough to reunite Orthodoxy.[13] The evidence conclusively shows how ARK incessantly worked behind the scenes—its very existence was never mentioned in published accounts until 1991—bestowing favors on any group whose activities furthered factionalism within the church without compromising the appearance of state neutrality. The GPU encouraged the main Orthodox groups to compete against one another. Secret policemen under Tuchkov's supervision also watched these groups closely for any hint of anti-Soviet activity, punishing individuals, not whole factions, for such activity. Ironically, while the Tikhonite church saw itself as standing firm against the united anti-Orthodox front of Bolshevism and renovationism, the renovationists thought the government was neutral in Orthodox affairs and repeatedly argued for abandoning neutrality in their favor. Their arguments centered on the proposition that renovationist loyalty was genuine and the patriarchal church's was feigned.

The government played a public role as referee in fights among Orthodox factions. That policy took effect immediately after the Politburo accepted Iaroslavskii's plan. Tikhon submitted a statement of guilt and repentance to the Supreme Court of the RSFSR on June 16. The Commissariats of Justice and Internal Affairs soon released a new set of instructions on how to implement the decree separating church and state. Churches that engaged in "counterrevolutionary" activity could be stripped of their registration, and governmental organs were prohibited from interfering administratively in church affairs through such tactics as exiling clergy and closing churches. The new instructions also forbade religious groups from meddling in the internal affairs of their rivals in a provision clearly aimed at both renovationists and Tikhonites. Parish affairs were placed squarely in the hands of the citizens who had reached agreements with local soviet officials to use church buildings, not in the hands of the church hierarchy.[14]

Behind the scenes, party functionaries did not confuse public neutrality with indifference as they pursued two distinct goals: deflecting international opinion sympathetic to Tikhon's plight and weakening renovationism. Guided by the first goal, on June 19 ARK demanded that Tikhon revise his written appeal to Orthodox believers before he could be freed from prison. Furthermore, the Commission ordered the patriarch to write a new statement within five days that made no reference to the renovationists but acknowledged his own guilt and condemned the activities of foreign ecclesiastical leaders.[15] These conditions explain the eleven-day delay between Tikhon's recantation before the Supreme Court and his actual discharge from prison. Tikhon's release was announced on June 27, and his statement to the church—the one ARK demanded on June 19—appeared in *Pravda* the following day. Publicity surrounding Tikhon's release produced the expected dissipation of international furor over the state's mistreatment of the patriarch. Representatives of the international press watched Tikhon emerge from the Lubianka prison on June 27 and learned that he would be living at the Donskoi Monastery even before church leaders heard the news. Soon after, the state produced and released a short film entitled *Tikhon after His Repentance* that was shown in Russia and abroad.[16]

Tikhon's repentance figured prominently in the government's strategy to weaken renovationism's influence by promoting natural antagonism between old and new churchmen. ARK dictated the procedures by which the patriarch's condemnation of renovationism was distributed on July 1 as a separate leaflet addressed to the Orthodox faithful.[17] In the year that followed, Tuchkov's department within the GPU felt that its primary accomplishment was to "deepen and shape the schism in the Orthodox Church," now comprised of three parts: the Tikhonite church (now further divided over the issue of cooperating with the government), the renovationist church, and autocephalous dioceses. The secret police claimed credit for deepening the schism through operatives who participated in a multitude of national and diocesan church congresses held by the renovationists in 1923–1924 and who advocated measures "to keep renovationists in the position of nonreconciliation with Tikhon." Tuchkov did not report the nature of these measures, although they seemed to have been related to the unmasking of former tsarist officials among the Tikhonite clergy, attacking monarchists on parish church councils, uncovering illegal Tikhonite church organizations, and splintering the Orthodox Church abroad.[18]

The government's policy worked. Tikhon's freedom to rally his followers promoted Orthodox disunity. In the three months after his release, Tikhon received written statements of support from hundreds of clergymen and congregations across Russia, statements that earlier would have resulted in governmental prosecution of the authors. Most claimed that their allegiance to the patriarch had never died despite having submitted in writing to the VTsU. The clergy repented of their activities during the renovationist interregnum and begged Tikhon to pardon them for wavering during his imprisonment. Many priests often explained their lapses in terms of financial coercion by Living Church officials. Others pointed to the actions of church hierarchs, such as Metropolitans Sergii and Leonid, to justify their recognition of the VTsU. All recognized Tikhon as the true head of the church and petitioned him to receive them back into canonical relationship, which he did.[19] The freedom to back the patriarch without fear of state retribution extended to the episcopacy. Fourteen bishops residing in Moscow drafted a special decree immediately after his release asking him to return to the patriarchal throne. Within a year, 100 bishops—a substantial percentage of the pre-renovationist episcopate—had signed that decree without experiencing any retaliation from the state.[20]

Finding that his liturgical activities were relatively unhindered within Moscow, the patriarch began the process of "cleansing" Orthodoxy of renovationism. Tikhon announced in an interview published on June 29 by *Izvestiia* that he would serve the liturgy at different churches and invited the Orthodox to pray with him. The public responded enthusiastically. At his first service on July 1, a great crowd gathered, spilling out into the streets around the building. The first reconsecration of a former renovationist church took place in July during a festive ceremony that included public repentance by clergy and ritualistic acts emphasizing the idea of renovationism as a heresy, akin to atheism, that had desecrated holy objects. The greatest act of penance and pardon came at the end of August when Metropolitan Sergii Stragorodskii bowed before the patriarch in a humiliating public ceremony of expiation for his ruling on the canonicity of the renovationist revolt. These acts encouraged Tikhonites around the country to physically expel their enemies from the churches.[21]

Tikhon's freedom to appear in public also served governmental policy by disarming his foreign and domestic backers. The anti-Soviet press abroad initially insisted that Tikhon's repentance was a fraud and subsequently, when forced to admit that that was not the case, questioned close connections between the patriarchal leadership and the GPU. Reactionary bishops in the Soviet Union abandoned the Tikhonite camp because Tikhon had shown such weakness, thus causing a new split in the Orthodox hierarchy.[22] ARK acted to widen that split in July by pressing Tikhon to issue new public statements of loyalty and antagonistic messages to foreign church leaders. In return, the Commission rewarded Tikhon. The state postponed his trial indefinitely and allowed the formation of patriarchal diocesan administrative committees in areas where the renovationists were not ensconced. ARK also approved the release of repentant Tikhonite bishops and consented to a second antirenovationist message from Tikhon to Orthodox believers.[23] ARK's ability to offer such incentives reflected its broad discretionary powers from June 1923 until late 1929.

Lower-level officials who deviated from official church policy aroused ARK's wrath, but it was hard pressed to give clearer instructions because of the secrecy that cloaked that policy.[24] The ARK did not have an independent bureaucratic apparatus and relied on local officials from the GPU and the Commissariat for Internal Affairs (NKVD) to carry out its decisions.

Many provincial government officials either misunderstood or ignored instructions that ordered them to stop helping red priests defeat Tikhonites and to start preserving a balance of ecclesiastical power. These local officials in effect decoupled the center's orders from their local practice. They preferred to use administrative methods, such as transferring parish churches from one group to another or exiling troublesome clergy, instead of the more subtle agitation and propaganda methods pushed by party leaders.[25] At times, local officials expressed confusion over contradictory instructions from the center. For example, they asked for clarification after being told to arrest clergy opposed to renovationism despite earlier orders to avoid showing favoritism toward any one Orthodox group.[26] Such cases encouraged local authorities to adapt official policy statements on the church to local conditions.[27]

Believers and clergy also refused to follow the rules laid out by the Politburo and ARK. Immediately after Tikhon's release, the Soviet press painted a picture of the Orthodox Church as divided into three parts: a patriarchate headed by Tikhon, a synod led by Krasnitskii, and a movement for independent parishes championed by Antonin.[28] In public, the government disavowed any intention of interfering in the affairs of any church group. In private, ARK worked to balance the three groups against one another. At the end of 1923, however, Antonin's group suffered a near-total collapse. ARK responded by attempting to create "a third VTsU" that would maintain the model of three-way competition between the patriarchate and renovationism.[29] Similarly, when the old churchmen threatened to extinguish renovationism completely in Petrograd in early 1924, ARK moved to replace that city's "completely self-discredited renovationist leaders" with "more authoritative figures for opposing the Tikhonites." Bishop Manuil Lemeshevskii, the patriarch's point man, was arrested, although only after he had won back the majority of parishes in the city now named Leningrad.[30]

ARK overcame confusion and disobedience of its policies by devising new strategies for tightly coupling local actions and national plans. The center continued its attempt to maintain the appearance of state impartiality while ensuring destructive competition among Orthodox factions. In early 1924, the Commissariat of Justice enacted an ARK decision to allocate contested church buildings according to the numerical strength of each Orthodox faction in a given area. This method proved effective both for encouraging Orthodox rivalry and in its ready adoption by local officials. Instructions for resolving a conflict in Ulan-Ute indicate how this strategy emerged. City officials asked for the commissariat's guidance in dealing with their four Orthodox churches and warring factions of believers, who threw "various exaggerated accusations" against one another but had avoided criminal activity and had not "disturbed public order." Krasikov replied that the officials should end quarrels over church buildings by assigning them according to the number of believers in each group. If only one church building was available, it should be physically divided in two by a barrier so that each group was isolated from the other. Taxes, insurance premiums, and other payments should then be assessed in line with the size of each group. These instructions soon became codified in a circular from the commissariat to its regional representatives.[31] Neither renovationists nor Tikhonites were happy when they lost a church building to the other group. When this happened they blamed one another and not the government, thanks to the new, seemingly evenhanded, guidelines and the state's traditional role as the defender of equality and homogeneity.

The government also increased antagonism among Orthodox groups by playing on their distrust of one another's motives. While ARK toiled to prevent genuine reconciliation within the church, Tuchkov insincerely pressured Tikhonite bishops to reunite with their renovationist counterparts. As expected, the old churchmen refused this proposal because they were convinced that renovationism had fallen from true Orthodoxy and had become an atheistic weapon for destroying the church from within. State pressure for reunification made Tikhonites even surer of this assessment. For their part, the renovationists asserted their Orthodox credentials and welcomed state support for unity among all true believers. Renovationists blamed reactionary Tikhonite leaders for continued disarray and the social impotence of Orthodoxy in Soviet Russia. With these new tactics, Tuchkov boasted of his department's success in church affairs, writing, "We have secured secret control over both Orthodox churchmen and sectarians."[32]

In reality, the Politburo's policy had limitations that the most ingenious bureaucrats could not overcome. By rejecting open coercive and administrative measures against believers, the party leadership made it impossible for local government officials to control or even stifle reactions by the Orthodox masses. The public reaction to Tikhon's discharge from prison illustrated the limits of the new ecclesiastical policy. The Communists expected the patriarch to be discredited in the eyes of the faithful; instead the Orthodox public received him ecstatically. In the popular mind, he had suffered at the hands of the godless but had remained faithful to God. His release had an element of the miraculous, an understandable conclusion given the seeming certainty of his execution until the day he walked out of the Lubianka prison. This "miracle" lent itself to the explanation of divine intervention and led logically to the acceptance of Tikhon as the recipient of divine favor. Those who opposed him therefore opposed God. In the eyes of the laity, Tikhon had not been compromised by his declarations of loyalty to the state, even though renovationists were condemned by the masses for that very act.[33]

Another example of the limits to the religious NEP is found in the refusal by the Orthodox masses to use the civil calendar despite the passion with which they accepted Tikhon back as patriarch. Both Tikhon and the renovationist council agreed to switch from the old-style church calendar to the new-style civil one. In September 1923, Tikhon began to observe the liturgy following the civil calendar, until widespread resistance in the church caused him to abandon this experiment by the end of the year. Renovationists stopped trying to enforce the order on calendar reform even earlier, although scattered parishes used the new calendar as late as 1929.[34] Despite this lack of success, the government continued to press for the calendar change out of a desire to increase labor discipline by reducing the number of religious holidays observed by workers. ARK discussed the matter no fewer than fourteen times during its regular sessions between 1923 and 1928. On November 13, 1923, it decided that church holidays would be celebrated according to the new style in 1924 with the exception of Easter, although the Commission made clear that it hoped clergy would also observe Easter according to the Gregorian calendar.[35] The minutes of a special party subcommittee on the calendar illustrate the surreal nature of the discussions. When that subcommittee met on November 17, 1923, the atheists Krasikov and Tuchkov chose a date for Easter 1924 in consultation with a representative from the renovationist synod.[36] Soon after this meeting, ARK reversed its position and instructed the GPU not to repress opponents of the calendar change if their opposition was not an expression of "counterrevolution."[37] Tikhon informed the Commissariat of Justice on February 5, 1924, that his church was unable to switch to the new calendar. A week later, ARK angrily responded by affirming the calendar change and ordering Tuchkov to reactivate the investigation into Tikhon's counterrevolutionary activity.[38]

Calendrical reform remained a contentious issue for the government for the rest of the decade. It flared up again in November 1924 when ARK decided to fix all holidays in 1925 except Easter according to the civil calendar and expressed its intention to end the exemption for Easter in 1926. The uniform use of a single calendar was viewed as especially important in the cities and industrial areas, and ARK entrusted the GPU with the responsibility of working "tactfully" to enlist clergy support. At the same time, the Commission forbade the printing, sale, or distribution of old-style calendars for 1925.[39] In early 1925, the Politburo entered the debate. It vetoed an attempt to substitute holidays commemorating revolutionary events for church ones in Moscow province and gave trade unions the right to decide whether church holidays would be observed according to the old or new style. The trade unions equivocated by supporting the new calendar but authorizing local authorities to use the old one if workers in the locality so desired.[40] Thereafter, the calendar issue simmered without resolution. Periodically, ARK would devise a new solution that then would be blocked by opposition from the Orthodox laity.[41]

A letter to Mikhail Tomsky, head of the trade unions, voiced the deep dissatisfaction of leading government officials with the effectiveness of religious opposition against the civil calendar. On December 29, 1927, D. Sverchkov of the Commissariat of Transportation wrote to Tomsky and protested the continued celebration of church holidays "in total contradiction to all our policies." He noted that only Orthodox holidays, not Jewish or Muslim ones, received such preferential treatment, adding, "I understand the reasons that force our state to be conciliatory with [the Orthodox]." Sverchkov also pointed out that the proletariat had been freed from religious superstition but used the holidays "to spend their time recklessly." For example, production in some large Moscow factories dropped 40 percent immediately after Christmas that year. To make matters worse, workers celebrated the holidays according to both the old- and new-style calendars, resulting in the loss of millions of rubles in manufacturing. The author proposed a change to a holiday schedule that included only days with "historical significance," at least in the cities. Sverchkov acknowledged that the peasantry would not change their ways, but at least if they came into the cities on Easter and Christmas, they would discover everyone at work. He ended by requesting Tomsky's support for this proposal before trade union and party committees. Tomsky declined on pragmatic grounds by arguing that if the government tried to introduce new holidays on days of historical significance, "then the people will celebrate the old, the new, and the 'newest' holidays."[42]

Uncontrollable religious reactions by the masses on issues such as Tikhon's popularity and resistance to calendrical reform became unexpected constraints on the government's new policy for the Orthodox Church. These limitations eventually brought changes in the state's attitude toward renovationism. In 1924–1925, ARK tried unsuccessfully to stabilize the movement by allowing it to publish periodicals and hold another national church council. By late 1925, the Commission responded more coolly toward the reformers, although it still found them useful for such tasks as gaining control of Orthodox Church property abroad and leading attacks against either sectarians or reactionary Orthodox bishops. As renovationist groups continued to lose popular support, their value to the government waned. Soon, the movement stopped being a factor in ARK's calculations for promoting Orthodox factionalism. Party officials shifted their attention to stirring up dissent among the aspirants to the patriarchal throne, which became vacant after Tikhon's death in April 1925. Renovationism increasingly became a marginal player in state policy.

From Soviet to Synod

The renovationist leadership responded to the religious NEP with rapid shifts in course and personnel. Tikhon's reemergence in June 1923, coupled with evaporating state support for renovationism and popular dissatisfaction with reforms instituted by the national church council, caused parishes to desert the Supreme Church Soviet in droves. The movement contracted as quickly as it had expanded, with wrenching consequences. New leaders stepped forward with a new agenda for preserving renovationism's legitimacy. Organizational preservation replaced aggressive expansion. This section will explain the effects of the religious NEP on the national renovationist organization.

Relations between the new VTsS and ARK remained unchanged in May and June 1923. State officials backed the VTsS decision to prevent a weakening of its authority by blocking the creation of a separate Ukrainian renovationist organization. ARK helped maintain renovationist supremacy over its Orthodox rivals by banning Tikhon from appealing to believers in response to his involuntary removal from all church positions. ARK also responded favorably to various renovationist requests to transfer Metropolitan Evdokim to Odessa, to allow the Living Church's Central Committee to buy a stenograph, and to grant Vvedenskii permission to teach at state universities.[43]

Unknown to the renovationists, national leaders worried about the consolidation of renovationist power as much as the Tikhonites did. Old and new churchmen competed directly for the same resources (believers, parishes, donations, and buildings). Tikhon's fear that renovationists would remain in control of the Orthodox Church and gain complete control of its resources was the decisive factor in his decision to acquiesce to the state's demands.[44] The state's concerns centered on its ideological competition with renovationism. As noted earlier, ARK shut down or restricted renovationist periodicals for promoting Christian beliefs. Tuchkov purged theses for the national church council to remove references to Christian socialism. Particularly troublesome from the government's perspective was the renovationist proclivity for framing its beliefs in the Bolshevik language of class conflict, social justice, and opposition to economic exploitation.

Tikhon's release redirected renovationism's energies even as it reopened splits in the ranks of red priests. The Soviet press exposed the differing concerns of top renovationist leaders. A story published on June 29 reported that Antonin demanded that the former patriarch repent before the church, Novikov denied that Tikhon had the right to perform the sacraments, Krasnitskii voiced fear over Tikhon's future actions, and Lvov expressed his hope that Tikhon would join the reform movement. After the patriarch's condemnation of renovationism appeared, Krasnitskii called an emergency joint meeting of the central committees for the Living Church and SODATs. Agreeing to form a "single, tactical renovationist front" and combat the new *Tikhonovshchina,* those present resolved to end all infighting, both public and private, and to unify their organizations at all levels.[45] That plan never became a reality because of the personal conflicts that wracked the national church administration even before Tikhon's release became known. The national church council revealed personal animosity among Krasnitskii, Vvedenskii, Blinov, Boiarskii, Antonin, and Lvov. In June, the situation worsened. On the 20th, Vvedenskii suddenly and quietly disappeared from Moscow; he may have learned in advance of Tikhon's imminent release and sought to avoid the fallout that he correctly guessed would follow. Antonin and Krasnitskii openly engaged in a struggle for power within the central church administration, trading accusations of incompetence and toadyism. When Antonin threatened to break with the highest renovationist body, Krasnitskii staged a preemptive strike by convincing the VTsS to expel Antonin and strip him of all his posts.[46] At the same time, Krasnitskii attempted an unsuccessful coup at a church in Moscow by installing his own people in the parish leadership. Moscow authorities refused to back him in yet another sign that the state had developed new rules for its dealings with the Orthodox Church.[47] His complaints about this treatment reportedly met with a tactful but unequivocal rebuff from Tuchkov.[48]

Thus, even before the full effects of the Politburo's decision to free Tikhon were known, the central renovationist administration found its forward momentum dissipated by hostility from both the party and the church, by administrative difficulties, and by conflict among individual leaders. Then, the organization lost its primary political function—preventing any possibility for a church-led counterrevolution—when the patriarch declared his loyalty to the Soviet regime. Seriously weakened, renovationism lacked the resources to prevent a rapid loss of its parishes to the resurrected patriarchate.[49]

Statistics on shifts in parish allegiance indicate the magnitude of renovationism's decline after June 1923. According to historian and renovationist activist Nikolai Platonov, the VTsU exercised some form of control over perhaps 70 percent of Orthodox churches in the RSFSR at the height of its influence in May 1923.[50] Although archival records do not indicate the total number of churches open in 1923, Soviet officials counted approximately 32,000 functioning parish churches within the boundaries of the RSFSR, excluding the autonomous republics, on January 1, 1928.[51] Because there is no evidence of massive church openings or closures for the four years and six months prior to that date, the same number also seems to be a reasonable estimate for 1923. So, according to Platonov's estimate, as many as 22,400 churches (70 percent of 32,000) may have joined the movement by the time of the national church council.

Table 4.1 indicates the downward trend in the number of renovationist churches between 1923 and 1927. Assuming that the April 1924 figures collected by Tuchkov's GPU department were a representative sample, the number of renovationist parishes in the RSFSR declined to approximately 15,000 (47 percent of 32,000) within ten months of Tikhon's release.[52] The renovationists lost 7,000 parishes to the patriarchate, a decline of 32 percent. In his 1924 report, Tuchkov repeatedly commented on the shaky commitment to renovationism among the parishes that remained in the movement. His observation is consistent with the defection of an additional 5,000 parishes in the RSFSR from renovationism by January 1925 (one-third of the previous total). Defections slowed over the next ten months with a reported loss of 9 percent of renovationist parishes in the RSFSR, but even church officials questioned the accuracy of the figures for October 1925. A summary report issued in January 1927 showed 6,248 renovationist parishes (20 percent of all Orthodox churches in the Russian republic).[53] By October 1927, only 5,181 of those churches remained (16 percent of the Orthodox total). The Russian Federation's NKVD counted 3,364 functioning renovationist churches as of January 1, 1928, but not all regions of the RSFSR were included.[54]

Assessing the relative strength of Orthodox groups by counting the parishes they controlled begs the question of their real health in terms of mass support. Without a census that gives numbers of laity who were Tikhonite or renovationist, we must rely on anecdotal evidence. Tuchkov wrote in September 1923 that "the Tikhonites are everywhere and always in greater numbers than the renovationists."[55] Tikhonites often claimed in their petitions and statements to the government that renovationist churches were very poorly attended and used this fact to argue for the transfer of church property to patriarchal parish councils. Decline in total renovationist parishes over time undoubtedly was fed by the government's policy of dividing churches by the number of parishioners in a given region. Tikhonites claimed that renovationists held on to a disproportionate number of church buildings in relation to their support among believers. If true, this buttressed renovationist authority among both laity and clergy. Church buildings themselves were holy places—even if con-

Table 4.1. Renovationist Parishes 1924–1927 (by region)

Region	April 1924				January 1925 Renovationist Parishes	October 1925 Renovationist Parishes	October 1927 Renovationist Parishes
	Renovationist	Tikhonite	Neutral	TOTAL			
Altai*	178	196	55	429	127	127	32
Arkhangelsk*					85	110	32
Astrakhan*	15	8		23	44	25	
Baku*					16	16	28
Bashkiria-Ufa*					124	159	67
Belorussia						500	100
Biisk and Oirat*					77	45	63
Blagoveshchensk*						86	
Briansk*					103	103	112
Cheliabinsk*					212	212	42
Cherepovets*					106	106	70
Cheringov	400	300	128	828			
Chita*						133	86
Chuvash*	220	8		228	159	76	43
Crimea*						55	13
Don*					312	162	83
Donetsk	190	260		450			
Dzhetysui*					119	119	110
Ekaterinburg/Sverdlovsk*					163	110	28
Ekaterinoslav	180	370	12	562			
Enisei*	254	20	36	310			
Gomel				800			
Iaroslavl*					7	9	26
Irbit*						115	66
Irkutsk*	142	112		254	101	103	48
Ishim*					77	77	48

Ivanovo-Voznesensk*	99	342	441	86	233	54
Kaluga*				83	83	65
Kamensk*				56	25	64
Karelia-Olonets*				110	110	111
Kargat-Kain*				68	67	
Kargat-Kainsk*						42
Kazan'*	102			320	353	126
Khabarovsk*					15	
Kharkov	246	4	650	400		
Kiev	600	500	1,200	100		
Komi-Permiatskii*				15	19	1
Kostroma*				263	263	15
Krasnoiarsk*					27	24
Krasnokokshaisk*						26
Kuban-Chernomor*	431	57	488	482	482	446
Kungur*				115	115	12
Kurgan*				323	120	75
Kursk*					38	55
Kustanai*					56	55
Leningrad*	163	260	423			53
Minusinsk*				74		115
Moscow*		1,245	1,322	95	107	
Nizhnii Novgorod*	77	20		61	33	21
Novgorod*	30	25		20	35	13
Novocherkassk*	180	40	220		150	
Novonikolaevsk/Sibirsk*	700	400	1,120	91	66	56
Odessa	292	82	399			
Omsk*				111	122	66
Orenburg*				74	88	85
Orel*	425	173	598	388	230	119
Penza*	11	3	14	78	73	51
Perm*				200	200	58

Table 4.1. Renovationist Parishes 1924–1927 (by region) *continued*

Region	April 1924 Renovationist	April 1924 Tikhonite	April 1924 Neutral	April 1924 TOTAL	January 1925 Renovationist Parishes	October 1925 Renovationist Parishes	October 1927 Renovationist Parishes
Petropavlovsk*					81	43	59
Podol'sk	250	550	298	1,098			
Poltava	50	750	81	881			
Pskov*	57	336		393			23
Riazan*					15	15	
Rostov-na-Donu*					49	15	58
Samara*					56	55	
Sarapul*					190	100	18
Saratov*					224	224	
Semipalatinsk*					142	103	81
Shadrinsk*							16
Smolensk*					386	352	245
Stavropol*				225	55	55	58
Sysola-Vym*							50
Taganrog*					36	36	15
Tagil*							47
Tambov*	320	520		840	200	156	91
Tashkent*						107	91
Tavrika*					55		
Tersk*							14
Tiflis					40		
Tiumen*					17		12
Tobol'sk*					10	10	6
Tomsk*					227	176	
Troitskoe*							28
Tsaritsyn/Stalingrad*					299	307	261

Region							
Tula*	732			787	709	627	455
Turkestan*		49		6	111	6	22
Tver*					16		37
Ukraine						3,000	
Ul'ianovsk*					309	170	
Ural'sk*	174	46		220	35	58	
Urbitsk-Turin*					115		
Usol'e*						139	37
Velikii Ustiug*				555	139		
Viatka*	304	251		421	137	166	72
Vitebsk	143	44	234				
Vladikavkaz*					85	79	64
Vladimir*	193	207	206	606	390	224	
Vladivostok*						58	32
Vologda*	69	335	275	679	167	141	128
Volyna	80	700	18	798		200	
Voronezh*					746	616	353
Zlatoust*							3
Totals	6,961	8,510	1,898	18,262	9,986	12,796	5,281
Percentage of total	38%	47%	10%	100%			
*RSFSR only	4,468	4,290	603	9,454	9,946	9,096	5,181
*Percentage of RSFSR total	47%	45%	6%	100%			

Sources: The figures for April 1924 draw on incomplete data compiled by Tuchkov in preparation for the Thirteenth Party Congress (RGASPI, f. 17, op. 60, d. 509, ll. 100–126). Those for January 1925, October 1925, and October 1927 are taken from *Vestnik Sv. Sinoda*, 1925, no. 1 (March): 15–16; 1926, no. 7 (3): 2; and 1928, no. 2 (25): 8, respectively. Further analysis of these statistics is found in Dmitri A. Sidorov, "Orthodoxy, Difference, and Scale: The Evolving Geopolitics of Russian Orthodox Church(es) in the 20th Century" (Ph.D. dissertation, University of Minnesota, 1998), 265–67, 271–72. Sidorov's Table A4.1 (p. 265) mistakenly counts the Kuban'-Chernomor province twice.

trolled by red priests—and the Orthodox faithful would not stay away. Intra-Orthodox fights over property rights played an important role in parish life during NEP, as we will see in the next chapter.

The sudden shift from expansion to contraction destroyed opportunities for rapid advancement by clergy within the church. During Tikhon's imprisonment, renovationism attracted churchmen eager for reform or hoping for rapid promotion. These men were rewarded with greater responsibilities in dioceses across Soviet Russia when bishops and clergy who were unacceptable to the government were arrested and exiled. By sanctioning marriage for bishops and remarriage for clergy, the national church council promised continued upward mobility for those willing to innovate. New leaders accelerated the rate of growth of renovationism that, in turn, allowed them to reward supporters with an abundance of high-level positions in the organization.[56] When renovationism began its decline, the most adventurous leaders either abandoned the movement or were pushed aside by conservatives within the renovationist movement who sacrificed radical reforms in favor of organizational preservation.

Tuchkov noticed this phenomenon and explained it in one of his 1924 reports. He concluded that the authority of the renovationist leadership had been "compromised" even more than Tikhon's after his repentance. While the "less strict" renovationists returned to the patriarchal camp in the second half of 1923, the remainder criticized the program for reform and demanded a change of course. Unpopular leaders were replaced with more acceptable ones, the factions united, and the Supreme Church Soviet became the Holy Synod, with Metropolitan Evdokim Meshcherskii of Odessa at its head. Evdokim understood his main task to be fighting Tikhon and the *Tikhonovshchina* by trying to win back Tikhonite bishops, priests, and laity. Tuchkov added, "Of course, Evdokim's ability to attract such hierarchs and priests would have been completely unsuccessful without our secret support. Thanks to that support, more than 200 bishops joined his cause."[57] Tuchkov did not elaborate on the content of that "support," but on the basis of previous GPU campaigns within the church we might assume that it included incentives (promotions, suppression of enemies, money) for those who followed the GPU's wishes and punishment (harassment, arrest, exile) for those who refused.

The religious NEP altered the church's political environment but did not change it completely, as evidenced by Tuchkov's report. In mid-1923, Evdokim emerged as the leading figure in the adaptation of renovationism to that altered environment. Krasnitskii invited Evdokim to take Antonin's place on the VTsS at the beginning of July. The metropolitan of Odessa did not arrive in Moscow until July 20, and Vvedenskii later attributed the delay to Tuchkov's behind-the-scenes maneuvers to gain control over Evdokim. The new renovationist leader swiftly found support for restoring traditional forms of Orthodox governance. Evdokim's backers purged the movement of organizational forms modeled on the Communist Party. Renovationist central committees, *gubkoms* (provincial committees), and *raikoms* (regional committees) were eliminated. The national church administration reclaimed the traditional name of "Holy Synod" and drove discredited individuals from its ranks. Krasnitskii was the first to go because of his notorious reputation within the church and his radical temperament that was ill suited to consensus or conservatism.[58]

Under Evdokim's firm hand, the first and only plenum of the VTsS ratified these changes on August 8, 1923. That body expanded its membership to include six bishops of nonrenovationist ordination and three of renovationist ordination. The most surprising addition was the highly respected archbishop of Riazan, Veniamin Muratovskii. The plenum adopted a series of recommendations by Evdokim to improve relations with the masses of Russian believers. It restored ties with the Eastern Orthodox patriarchs and ratified the VTsS decision to rename itself as the Holy Synod. All renovationist activities were placed under the Holy Synod's control with the abolition of all parties and factions. The plenum also voted to pursue Orthodox unity by avoiding schism, to publish a biweekly newspaper, and to restore retired bishops to their posts. Krasnitskii and Vvedenskii were excluded from membership in the new synod, although the latter was "co-opted" into that body immediately after his return to Moscow.[59]

The new leadership needed to discover resources for renovationism's continued existence and organizational stability under the rules of the religious NEP. Renovationists learned that they could no longer count on immediate and unwavering state support in fighting their ecclesiastical rivals. The government did make decisions favoring renovationism when renovationists fell in line with state interests. One such decision provided sorely needed financial stability for parishes and clergy loyal to the Holy Synod. Regulating activities of cemetery chapels proved bothersome for local officials, perhaps because of their inability to prevent public funeral rites. ARK and the Commissariat of Justice agreed in mid-1923 that cemetery chapels held by "reactionaries" should be transferred to renovationist congregations.[60] This policy remained in force at least until 1925, according to correspondence between the Commissariat of Justice and Moscow officials, and resulted in renovationist control of cemetery chapels across the country.[61] Consequently, some renovationist parish clergy received a steady source of income from requiem masses even after other donations from the laity had all but disappeared.

Another example of government officials helping renovationism in order to further state policy goals is found in the debate over registration procedures for regional and national ecclesiastical bodies. In October 1923, ARK concluded that the rules for registering religious groups needed to be revised in order to give the Holy Synod and its diocesan administrators control over parish councils. The reasons for this change were not given in the motion but seemed linked to the GPU's earlier concerns that anti-Soviet elements plotted together in those councils. ARK forwarded its motion to the Politburo and asked for quick action to prevent "catastrophic consequences for the so-called church-renovationist movement that would bring to naught all work by ARK and the GPU over the previous year." The Politburo approved ARK's request and assigned Kamenev to work on preparing the necessary legislation, which was approved on February 26, 1924. The new registration procedure forbade those being investigated or convicted of crimes from participating in the organization of religious communities. It also made changes of registration complicated. These provisions armed renovationists with new weapons with which to control their own parishes and harass the parishes of their opponents.[62]

The Holy Synod learned the limits to state assistance in fighting its enemies but not the impediments that the government placed in the path toward church reunification. Renovationist leaders never publicly acknowledged the futility of its drive to bring Orthodoxy together under a single organization. Perhaps they misunderstood the goal of ARK policy on unifying various factions. The Commission played a role in pulling renovationist groups together, starting with its first discussion about the possibility of uniting all renovationist factions into a single group on July 24, 1923.[63] The incompatibility of this decision with Antonin's expulsion from the Supreme Church Soviet was ignored; his League for Church Regeneration existed independently of both the patriarchate and Holy Synod until shortly after his death in early 1927.[64] ARK perpetuated the fiction that it supported even wider church unity while actually considering whether a separate renovationist organization would be the best counterweight to the growing strength of the Tikhonites.

By August 1923, rivalry between Tikhonites and unified renovationists turned into a competition to show "who is more harmful or beneficial to Soviet power."[65] Tuchkov gave details on the ever-sharpening fight between the two groups. Each engaged in denunciations of the other, allowing the GPU to uncover more than 100 priests who were former tsarist officers or other reactionaries. Tikhon himself succumbed to the hope that the secret police could help him eliminate his ecclesiastical enemies, according to Tuchkov. He wrote, "Generally these hostile groups are making an effort to win the trust of Soviet power and be in its favor. For example, Tikhon said to me several times that 'you [that is, the GPU] treat us like stepsons and the renovationists like sons.'" Tikhon then asked the GPU "to destroy the nest" of Orthodox bishops who controlled St. Daniel's Monastery in Moscow and opposed the patriarchate. Tikhon added that he would prefer to not be on friendly terms with the GPU but had no choice as patriarch.[66]

Since it was in the government's interests to keep the two groups at each other's throats, any discussion of reconciliation was only a ruse to increase their animosity. Not that the Holy Synod faked its interest in Orthodox reunification. Most of its members sincerely desired to see the church unified and actively involved in Soviet society, not realizing that their interest in unity helped party officials deepen the chasm between the Orthodox. The first attempt at reunification took place in the summer of 1923, when the new Holy Synod led by Evdokim entered into negotiations with leading Tikhonite bishops. They agreed on a plan by which Tikhon would retire and the united church would then convene a national church council to decide the fate of the patriarchate. This agreement collapsed when Tikhon refused to step down and threatened to break with his own bishops if they continued to negotiate with the renovationists.[67]

A second, most dramatic, attempt occurred in May 1924. Krasnitskii announced that Tikhon had agreed not only to receive living churchmen back into the patriarchal fold but also to give its representatives six seats on the new patriarchal soviet. Tikhon accepted these terms in exchange for government promises to close his criminal investigation, to permit the formation of a central church administration, and to allow the patriarchate to convene a national church council. The press made no secret of these conditions or of Krasnitskii's obvious delight at regaining ecclesiastical power. The agreement collapsed when parishioners and bishops expressed overwhelming disgust at accepting the leader of the despised Living Church. Tikhon's willingness to acquiesce diluted his influence among the senior hierarchs of his own faction but did not affect his popularity among the laity.[68]

A final push for reunification came after Tikhon's death in 1925, when the Holy Synod began organizing a joint national church council for the purpose of resolving all issues disputed by the two camps. In May, a group of patriarchal clergy attempted to reconcile with the synodal organization in Leningrad but ended all contacts with the renovationists at the order of the local Tikhonite bishop.[69] This idea of a combined renovationist and Tikhonite national convocation met with opposition from the patriarchal *locum tenens*, Metropolitan Peter Polianskii, who despised renovationism as much as Tikhon had. The metropolitan met with Archdeacon Dobrov, a member of the Holy Synod, in July to discuss the terms for participating in the upcoming church council. Peter denied having the authority to make a decision and said he needed the advice of all his bishops, including those who were imprisoned or exiled. Dobrov replied by saying that the synod could not influence the release of Tikhonite bishops, which caused Peter to respond with a promise to let the synod know his decision.[70] Peter's response came in the form of a message to the whole church in which he condemned the planned "false council" (*lzhesobor*) and characterized renovationists as the worst enemies of Orthodoxy because they were trying to destroy the church from within.[71]

Peter's rejection of renovationist overtures ended unification talks for twenty years. The Soviet government became convinced in late 1925 that Peter was hatching an anti-Soviet conspiracy within the church. GPU sources supplied Vvedenskii with a letter of dubious authenticity that "proved" that Peter had contacts with monarchists living abroad. Vvedenskii enthusiastically read this letter to the renovationist national church council in October. When the government arrested Peter in December, the synodal church took the blame for having uncovered the evidence that destroyed him.[72] Peter was imprisoned in solitary confinement until the government had him shot in 1936.[73]

Renovationism reorganized into a more conventional church structure led by the Holy Synod and signaled the movement's turn away from radical reforms by purging its leadership. These moves could neither stem the loss of renovationist parishes nor give a basis for reunion with the patriarchal church in a way that would preserve the reform movement. Government support appeared unpredictable; at times state officials clamped down on Tikhonite parishes and bishops, while at other times they provided invaluable assistance to renovationist parishes and organizations. To stay viable in the national arena, the renovationists needed to find a new institutional strategy for surviving in Soviet society.

Orthodoxy, Sobornost', Loyalty

The renovationist national administration developed a plan to strengthen its position based on Orthodoxy, conciliarity (*sobornost'*), and political loyalty. The Holy Synod aimed each of the program's three prongs at a specific constituency in Russian society. It hoped to gain support from masses of believers because of its genuine Orthodox faith, from clergy because of its collective decision-making, and from the Soviet regime because of its unwavering loyalty. This emerged as renovationism's organized response to the changed social and political environment of NEP.

Boosting its Orthodox credentials became renovationism's first priority. In a statement issued after its August 1923 plenum, the Holy Synod challenged Tikhon's Orthodoxy by laying the blame for schism at his feet. The synod, however, accepted its obligation to end the church's suffering and bring internal peace to the church. It would be the responsible party by preserving Orthodox purity while also supervising transformations in the church required by Soviet society.[74] Simultaneous with this message to Orthodox believers in Russia, the Holy Synod began communicating with the Orthodox patriarchs of Constantinople, Alexandria, and Jerusalem. The synod's official greetings to these eastern patriarchs in August 1923 included an explanation of how Tikhon's misguided leadership had led the Russian church to ruin. By mid-September, the Eastern Orthodox patriarchates had recognized the Holy Synod as the legitimate head of the Russian church.

The synod found foreign recognition of its authority to be a powerful weapon against the Tikhonites throughout NEP and even into the early 1930s. The first issue of the synod's new publication, *Vestnik Sviashchennego Sinoda* [Herald of the Holy Synod] devoted over 10 percent of its space to descriptions of solid ecclesiastical ties between the renovationist synod and foreign Orthodox hierarchs.[75] After a two-year hiatus, that publication reappeared in 1925 and continued irregularly thereafter until 1931, with every issue featuring articles that highlighted international Orthodox recognition of the renovationist church administration. Soviet foreign policy objectives helped the renovationists in this part of the campaign to establish their Orthodox credentials. By recognizing the Holy Synod, the Eastern Orthodox patriarchs strained their ties with the Russian émigré church. For their part, the patriarchs hoped that good relations with the Holy Synod would bring diplomatic payoffs. They calculated that the Soviet government's expanding relations with the Islamic governments of Turkey and Egypt would result in assistance for Orthodox minorities in those countries.

The Soviet government assisted the renovationist drive to shore up its domestic Orthodox credentials by undermining Tikhon's authority. This move served state interests as well as renovationist ones. On July 31, the public prosecutor for Petrograd province prohibited Orthodox churches from commemorating Tikhon in the Divine Liturgy. The rationale for this decision, supported by Novgorod's public procurator, was that Tikhon had not been cleared of criminal wrongdoing but had merely been freed from prison through the mercy of the court. The All-Russian Central Executive Committee's (VTsIK) ruling of August 18, 1922, still applied: those who commemorated counterrevolutionaries such as Tikhon in church services could be sentenced to three years in prison. In a related matter, the Commissariat of Justice replied to an inquiry from Boiarskii that a patriarchal synod did not exist and could be formed only as a result of an all-Russian congress of religious societies. The Commissariat of Justice issued a bulletin on December 8, 1923, prohibiting the liturgical commemoration of

Tikhon as a "public demonstration against the government of workers and peasants" and repeated this point in a second bulletin after Tikhon's case was officially closed in March 1924.[76]

State regulation of liturgical practice worked against renovationist claims of true Orthodoxy. Neither the government nor the Holy Synod wanted Tikhon to organize a potentially dangerous national church administration, but the consequences of their collaboration hurt the church reformers. Ordinary believers blamed living churchmen when government officials repressed anyone who prayed openly for Tikhon in the liturgy. Renovationists apparently never perceived the advantage to the state when it shifted the blame on to them.[77]

Local officials often encouraged ties between Orthodoxy and Soviet goals for society. This fact strengthened ARK's determination to avoid any public links between the state and the Holy Synod. The Commission even launched an investigation after the synod released a church-wide statement "indicating its ties with and support from Soviet power." The GPU was told "to take appropriate measures forbidding similar statements" in the future.[78] By July 1924, ARK had moved against provincial bureaucrats who ignored official rules on church-state separation and accepted political activity within churches. The Commission's protocols record the following instructions for evenhanded treatment of Orthodox groups:

> We see great danger in open support of renovationists by government organs and in limitations on Tikhonites. Therefore, we assign the OGPU to guide local officials in ceasing repression employed against Tikhonites for the tactical purpose of strengthening the renovationists. At the same time, these officials are not to relax their fight against ecclesiastical counterrevolution but should check all denunciations by renovationists against the old churchmen (Tikhonites) before arresting them. We also assign the OGPU and Smidovich to issue directives so that the distribution of church buildings proceeds in such a manner that the old churchmen are not left without any such buildings.

Furthermore, ARK instructed local officials not to close churches illegally and decided to allow Tikhon's commemoration in the Orthodox liturgy if he agreed to change his title from "Patriarch of all Russia" to "Patriarch of all the USSR."[79]

The Holy Synod did not rely on state power alone in the drive to solidify its Orthodox credentials. Borrowing an idea from its old-church rivals, the synod petitioned the VTsIK to reopen the church housing the relics of St. Sergius, which was located at the famous Holy Trinity Monastery outside Moscow. This petition (dated October 21, 1924) explained that the requested action would prove that the Soviet government did not persecute religion and also would help preserve an important historical monument.[80] Had this petition been granted, the synod would have controlled a cultural landmark highly revered by the Orthodox masses. In February 1925, the synod issued a bulletin to all diocesan administrative groups informing them that the church's new slogan was "Renovationism Is Orthodoxy." The synod aimed this campaign against the Tikhonite charge that changes by the "new church" endangered the eternal salvation of Orthodox souls.[81]

The synodal church's adjustment to popular Orthodox sentiment in the NEP era was encapsulated in "A Program for Church Renovationists." A group of living churchmen in Leningrad laid out eighteen theses and commentary in this nineteen-page pamphlet. The program included progressive but nonradical principles for Orthodox renewal based on the twin goals of realizing moral perfection in individuals and Christian ideals in society. Its authors argued that the historical church had often strayed from these goals and only renovationism could return the church to the correct path. Strong elements of Christian socialism remained in the theology of the group: it condemned human exploitation and advocated brotherhood, equality, and love of neighbor. The program also incorporated mild reformist themes by advocating the compatibility of faith and science, downplaying the role of monasticism, and reexamining canon law. The authors did not push a radical agenda. They upheld the decisions of the Seven Ecumenical Councils as models of conciliar decision-making processes in the church. For that reason, the Orthodox liturgy was immutable. In matters relating to clergy, the pamphlet defended the propriety of married bishops and remarried priests but added, "As long as the church masses have insufficiently accepted the idea of equality of some clergy, the appointment of bishops and other clerics should conform with the opinion of the parishioners in any individual church." These Leningrad reformers hoped to mollify popular opposition to renovationist clergy by combining this compromise with greater "clergy discipline." Priests were advised to avoid drunkenness and smoking as well as to conduct daily liturgical services and observe traditional rules on fasting.[82]

While the Holy Synod targeted lay believers with its emphasis on renovationism's Orthodoxy, it promoted the principle of *sobornost'* (conciliarity) to stem the flow of clergy out of its camp. Theologically, renovationists considered the principle of collective decision-making to be the source of free and creative church life.[83] One of the synod's first acts after taking control of the church in August 1923 was to limit the role of the old VTsU plenipotentiaries. Most of these had been Living Church loyalists whose high-handed tactics offended local church leaders. The synod's representatives to diocesan administrative bodies were liaison officers rather than all-powerful surrogate bishops. In 1925, the synod stripped plenipotentiaries of all authority, thereby increasing the power and autonomy of the diocesan councils. Bowing to local wishes, the synod later offered dioceses the option of eliminating the position of local plenipotentiary.[84]

The centerpiece of the conciliar principle remained periodic conferences of clergy and laity. Regular diocesan congresses gave parish priests in particular a voice in local affairs while limiting the possibility for arbitrary episcopal action. Two national church gatherings in 1924–1925, along with the promise of more national church councils in the future, rallied the clergy around the banner of *sobornost'*. Each one served as an occasion for the Holy Synod to regroup, reorganize, and highlight the place of conciliarity in the reformed but still Orthodox church. The synod found its first opportunity to hold a national gathering when the Ecumenical Patriarch announced his intention to hold the first Ecumenical Council in over 1,000 years in Jerusalem during 1925. In preparation, the synod convened a preconciliar conference in Moscow from June 10–18, 1924.

Because the conference's agenda included only items of concern to the Russian church, it became in fact, if not in name, another renovationist national church council. Four hundred delegates, including eighty-three bishops, heard opening speeches by Evdokim vilifying Tikhon and by Vvedenskii arguing against compromise with the old church. These positions encountered no opposition from the delegates in attendance, who voted to uphold the 1923 national church council's decision against Tikhon. Yet the gathering spent most of its energy in deciding on a new direction for the synodal church. The conference resolved to attempt reconciliation with the Old Belief (the remnants of the seventeenth-century schism in the Russian Orthodox Church). It also affirmed the Holy Synod as the supreme church administration. Another important decision by the conference limited the rights of individual priests to implement liturgical reforms until a special commission studied the issue, although diocesan administrative bodies could allow such reform unilaterally. Delegates also adopted motions to improve clerical education and promote greater conciliarity by increasing the power and responsibilities of the synodal church's highest-ranking bishops (metropolitans). The conference approved a petition to Sovnarkom asking for fewer restrictions on the public actions of believers as well as a lowering of taxes on the church.[85]

The impact of these decisions has often been ignored, undoubtedly because the proposed ecumenical council for which the conference prepared was repeatedly postponed until it was finally abandoned in 1928. Nonetheless, the preconciliar conference proved important for renovationism because it continued the shift in ecclesiastical power away from the center and toward the dioceses and regional metropolitanates. The synodal church began moving from a centralized episcopal federation to a confederation of independent regions governed by metropolitans. This change reflected both renovationist rejection of patriarchal administration and principles of NEP that allowed freedom for organizations as long as they did not threaten the Soviet state.

In the year between the preconciliar conference and the second renovationist national church council of 1925, patriarchal and synodal church leaders engaged in a vigorous campaign for the allegiance of Orthodox clergy across Russia. Both Tikhon's death and Metropolitan Evdokim's resignation as head of the Holy Synod inspired the renovationists to press for peace with the old church on terms that would not require their total abdication of principles.[86] Remaining true to the memory of the late patriarch and undoubtedly sensing the flow of the masses in their favor, old churchmen refused to compromise their conditions for reunification. Tikhonites turned down an invitation to participate in a Ukrainian church council in May 1925, even though the Ukrainian renovationists were willing to accept a prohibition on married bishops and remarried priests.[87] In Russia, the patriarchal church still demanded that all renovationists publicly repent of heresy. Tikhonites refused to recognize any renovationist ordination and set strict rules for accepting living churchmen who had been ordained in contradiction with Orthodox tradition. Married bishops were demoted to the status of parish clergy, and priests who had remarried were received only as laymen. For the second group, this meant a complete loss of vocation and impoverishment because of the difficulties former priests had finding employment in Soviet Russia. The Holy Synod copied this tactic by ordering public repentance of clergy who left renovationism and later decided to return, but this directive seems to have been ignored.[88]

The Holy Synod promised that the 1925 national church council—also known as the second renovationist *sobor*—would bring peace and unity to Orthodoxy.[89] It did not. Tikhonites boycotted the gathering, which meant that the council and its 300 delegates (equally divided among bishops, parish clergy, and laity) resembled earlier, purely renovationist gatherings. Long debates among council delegates over the means for reaching a rapprochement with Metropolitan Peter were interrupted by impassioned speeches against any deviation from the original course of reform. The renovationist historian Titlinov explained to the council that the internal divisions in the church dated back for centuries and would be healed only after a long process of reconciliation. The 1923 national church council, in his view, revealed antagonisms within the church known to its leaders but not to the masses.[90] Later, he elaborated on these views:

> For the mass of believers, renovation of the church means a change in old ecclesiastical customs—a white episcopate, the remarriage of clerics, and the like. In our popular ritualistic faith, the external forms are easily confused with the essence of the church—a fact that is skillfully used by those who are looking for an excuse to cut themselves off from any movement that threatens their conservatism. The 1925 national church council, by trying to blunt the edge of the decisions by the 1923 national church council, sought to tear this weapon out of the hands of our antagonists, to attract the masses, and to reveal the true reasons for divisions in the church.

Titlinov defended this strategic withdrawal and declared it was not a betrayal of principles. "We did not enter into conflict with the old churchmen over questions of marriage or monasticism but for the rebirth of living Christianity and to capture a world escaping from the influence of the church."[91]

In reality, the council of 1925 merely gave retroactive approval to "concessions in tactics, not in principle" made earlier by the Holy Synod. Faced with popular displeasure over innovations in the church, the synod slowed the introduction of married bishops and limited the remarriage of parish clergy before the council even convened. The synod also ruled that adoption of the new-style calendar was voluntary. The national church council confirmed these decisions of the Holy Synod. Delegates also affirmed the equality of married and unmarried bishops while requiring "circumspection" in assigning married bishops and in permitting clergy to remarry. For the first group, the "merits of episcopal candidates" were to be considered; for the second, local parish consent was required as part of an examination of the special circumstances of the widowed clergyman. Parish officials were given permission to decide which calendar to follow. In debating these reforms, the Russian national gathering admitted that only the upcoming ecumenical council could make final decisions that would be binding on all Orthodox believers.[92]

The church council of 1925 achieved mixed results. On the negative side, it accelerated the decline in renovationism's fortunes. Parishes deserted the Holy Synod in droves because the council failed to end the rift with the patriarchate.[93] Consequently, the state stopped including the shrinking renovationist faction in its plans to divide the Orthodox in Russia. On the positive side, the council chose a moderate reform policy that appealed to advocates of change without further alienating those who found comfort in more traditional Orthodoxy. These decisions solidified renovationism's core of support and energized the church in the provinces.[94] Following the council, the synod took on features of a confederated council. In 1928, it changed the name of its press organ to *Vestnik Sviashchennego Sinoda Pravoslavnykh Tserkvei v SSSR* [Herald of the Holy Synod of Orthodox *Churches* in the USSR].[95] Finally, ARK apparently concluded that the Tikhonites had achieved victory over renovationism and it turned to other matters, as evidenced by its decision to sow dissension in the ranks of bishops loyal to the patriarchate without involving the Holy Synod.[96]

Just as the campaigns based on Orthodoxy and conciliarity met with limited success, the synodal church's insistence on its political loyalty to the state yielded fewer benefits as NEP progressed. From the time of Tikhon's release, renovationists counted on the value of their unswerving loyalty to keep the state on their side. Initially, the government whipped Tikhon and his associates in line with the threat of renewed assistance for the reformers. For example, ARK repeatedly threatened to reopen the investigation of Tikhon's counterrevolutionary activity, a move that would have strengthened the renovationist hand considerably.[97] In response, Tikhon issued multiple statements that proclaimed his loyalty, including a "testament" (*zaveshchanie*) that he signed on his deathbed.[98] Tikhon also verbally acceded to some church reforms, although he later refused to impose them.[99]

Most important, the Bolsheviks tried to manipulate the loyalty issue to press for an acceptable national administrative body within the patriarchal church. They wanted "dependable" people in positions of power surrounding the patriarch, while Tikhon needed a central administration to fight renovationism effectively. In December 1923, ARK discussed and tabled a motion to bring Krasnitskii and Tikhon together. By February 1924, the Commission agreed that Tikhon could organize his own synod if it included "a set of people well-known to the OGPU," although Krasnitskii still was not included. The investigation into Tikhon's illegal activities during the famine was closed in March, and soon afterward the GPU accepted the task of gathering a "semiofficial" Tikhonite synod of "selected" churchmen, including Krasnitskii. As recounted earlier in this chapter, ARK pressed the patriarch to accept Krasnitskii on that synod. The Commission considered this step so "politically useful" that it told Tuchkov to use verbal persuasion followed by "other measures" as needed to convince Tikhon and his circle of bishops to accept the head of the Living Church.[100]

Tikhon did not accept Tuchkov's proposal immediately. First, he issued a prohibition on all former patriarchal bishops who had gone into schism, including Evdokim and Antonin, and invalidated all ordinations by those bishops after April 15, 1924.[101] Tikhon complained to Sovnarkom president Rykov on May 8 about the obstacles he had encountered in trying to form a synod and identified the source of difficulties as his refusal to recognize the renovationists. He requested that the government review all cases of his arrested bishops and asked for an easing of the taxes imposed on his churches. Soon afterward, Tikhon visited Rykov to ask why he could not organize a national church congress. Rykov sought a ruling from the Commissariat of Justice on the matter and was told that Tikhon had not followed the legal procedure of calling a national congress to elect an administrative organ. The Commissariat further advised giving permission for free competition between Tikhonites and renovationists.[102] Only after meeting with Rykov did Tikhon agree to accept Krasnitskii into the patriarchal synod, although he withdrew the offer on July 1. The patriarch may never have known that on June 17, ARK began preparations to allow a Tikhonite national church council along with the registration of their national church organs "in light of reconciliation with the Living Church." Permission was also going to be given for regional Tikhonite administrative bodies, an end to the repression and imprisonment of Tikhonites, and commemoration of the patriarch in the liturgy.[103]

Tikhon's wavering over state demands increased the value of the renovationists' staunchly pro-Soviet principle. The Holy Synod pointedly reminded the government of this. In an October 1924 letter to Soviet president Kalinin, the synod said that Tikhon and his monarchist supporters attacked renovationists on the basis of their loyalty to Soviet power. The letter suggested that Tikhon be treated as a criminal and locked up in a monastery outside Moscow in order to bring peace to and stop counterrevolution within the Russian Orthodox Church.[104] By the spring of 1925, some in the OGPU agreed that such action was necessary. The secret police interrogated Tikhon on March 21 about the appearance of a list of repressed Russian Orthodox bishops sent from the patriarch's inner circle to the émigré press. Tikhon denied any role in the matter, although he did acknowledge receiving copies of the list. Tikhon's interrogator recommended arresting the patriarch for discrediting Soviet power, but the case was dropped when Tikhon died on April 7.[105]

With Tikhon's passing, the synodal church lost the advantage of having sole, unquestioned loyalty to the government's decisions. ARK encouraged divisions within the Tikhonite camp and identified dependable leaders in the old church.[106] With the appearance of multiple patriarchal *locum tenentes*, ARK extended privileges to those it considered most loyal. Such privileges included convening national conferences, awarding control of church buildings, and allowing access to the public through debates and publications.[107] Renovationists rejoiced at the splintering of the Tikhonite opposition after 1925 without realizing its negative consequences for their own future.

Despite renovationism's steadfast loyalty, Soviet officials treated the movement with contempt in the late 1920s. This interesting historical twist has come to light only through access to party documents. After 1925, ARK never again referred to renovationism as a useful tool against the Tikhonites. The Holy Synod lacked credibility and support in the center, and its strength on the periphery did not impress Moscow-based policymakers. The state's derisive attitude toward the movement brought further restrictions on reformist ideological activity, although ARK's leaders continued to use the synodal church to fight sectarians and gain control of church property abroad. The first hint of this change in attitude came in February 1925, when ARK approved a series of restrictions on renovationist ideological activity. The theological school in Leningrad was forbidden to teach courses on politics. "Discussions" on religious topics could only be held during church services. Dioceses in Smolensk and Tambov were prohibited from holding theological courses or publishing periodicals. Even Vvedenskii, whose willingness to follow Soviet orders never wavered, was informed that his public lectures had to be limited to purely religious themes. Over the next three years, ARK passed more restrictions. Renovationist publications were told to print only official announcements and news. Vvedenskii's lectures were limited solely to the counterrevolutionary role of the old church and the *Tikhonovshchina*. Later, all his lectures had to receive state approval prior to being presented. The synod's periodical could no longer print articles of an "ideological-philosophical character"—the only acceptable items were official pronouncements from the Holy Synod and pieces that disparaged other religious groups. ARK tabled indefinitely the synod's request for permission to publish a translation of the liturgy in modern Russian.[108]

Many of the harsher restrictions appeared after Metropolitan Sergii Stragorodskii issued a declaration of loyalty to the government on July 29, 1927. When Sergii came out unequivocally in favor of Soviet power, open resistance to renovationism increased. Old-church bishops, finally free to return to their former dioceses thanks to Sergii's declaration, received a martyr's welcome from local believers, who feared that war would result from the continuing turmoil in the party and the growing economic crisis. They became convinced that it was "dangerous to be red" and avoided all contact with "the red church."[109] The renovationist press depicted Sergii's declaration as a tactic for realizing the metropolitan's ecclesiastical ambition. In this effort, renovationists took unusual risks out of desperation because of Sergii's move toward political accommodation. They implied that

Sergii had sabotaged a secret process by Tikhonite bishops in the fall of 1926 to elect a new patriarch. Metropolitan Kirill Smirnov of Kazan had amassed the most votes until the GPU stopped the election after learning of the process from one of its participants. In the renovationist version of events, Sergii had denounced his fellow bishops to the secret police in order to stay in power. A renovationist periodical in Kazan even accused Sergii of being a Communist because his declaration equated the joys of atheists with those of believers.[110]

This controversy should not be viewed as mere personal animosity among competing church leaders. It touched on the central question for the church in NEP; namely, the relationship of religion to politics and society. Sergii chose the path of political neutrality and social isolation in exchange for governmental noninterference in the areas of Orthodox dogma and practice. In those two areas, the future patriarch was very conservative and most at odds with those who advocated change.[111] The degree to which a desire for self-preservation and personal advancement influenced his actions is still a subject of debate. Disregarding his possible personal shortcomings, Sergii's policy of defending the perceived center of Orthodox purity stood in stark contrast to renovationist hopes for keeping Orthodoxy actively engaged with Soviet society.

The state's new contempt for renovationists did not prevent it from using them for some tasks. When Soviet officials became concerned about the spread of sectarianism, they enlisted the synod's help in fighting non-Orthodox groups. Anxiety in this area surfaced in December 1924 after the Orgburo heard Iaroslavskii report on the success of sectarian groups with Soviet youth and decided to study the troubling phenomenon.[112] A year and a half later, unable to stop the sectarian tide, ARK approved Tuchkov's recommendation to use Orthodox priests to battle sectarians with the proviso that "this battle should be conducted only in the area of dogma and should not cross that line."[113] In April 1927, the Politburo itself discussed the increase in sectarian activity and the role of "kulaks and other anti-Soviet elements" within it.[114] The following month, ARK voted neither to help nor to hinder antisectarian endeavors by Orthodox missionaries. Eventually, the Commission even sanctioned Vvedenskii's antisectarian public lectures as long as he received permission in advance of every appearance.[115]

The government also feared the use of church property abroad by anti-Soviet groups and pushed renovationists, whose loyalty it continued to trust, to get that property under their control. ARK took up this issue in November 1924 and subsequently encouraged the formation of renovationist groups in France, Palestine, and the United States for the sole purpose of gaining legal title to parish churches in those countries. ARK pressured the renovationist synod to act on this matter with repeated requests through June 1926. In return, the Commission allowed new church publications (with severe editorial restrictions) and public meetings by renovationist groups. One time the government even provided funds for loyal church groups abroad.[116]

Tikhon's release in mid-1923 dramatically altered the position of renovationism in Soviet society. Movement toward a single, centralized Orthodox organization ended with the shattered hope of the VTsU that it would become the state church of Soviet Russia. Renovationists lost their monopoly on legal legitimacy among all Orthodox groups and could no longer draw on militant Bolshevik models to attack ecclesiastical enemies. The church's revolution and civil war ended; the religious NEP began.

In accordance with their theology and politics, national renovationist leaders chose adaptation and not resistance to the government's new ecclesiastical policy. This choice shaped their response to pressure from a variety of sources, including traditional Orthodoxy. Bishops who remained in the movement forced moderation in the composition and tactics of its central leadership, as seen first in the shift from a Bolshevik-style Supreme Church Soviet to a more traditional Holy Synod and later in the devolution of power from the center to regional metropolitanates. Aggressive champions of church reform and revolution such as Antonin left the movement. Some who wished to stay, such as Krasnitskii, were forced out, while others, such as Vvedenskii, remained by compromising with the new leadership.

That leadership moved to preserve renovationism by accommodating demands from parish clergy, parishioners, and the state. The resulting program incorporated three themes: conciliarity, Orthodoxy, and political loyalty. NEP renovationism promised parish clergy a role in the church's decision-making process through local, regional, and national councils. Parishioners had representation in all councils and were repeatedly assured that renovationism was truly Orthodox. This new program offered the state continued and unwavering political loyalty. None of these steps proved successful in preventing the mass exodus of believers from renovationism.

Renovationism's influence declined as its popular support dwindled. Patriarchal church leaders focused on internal disputes, and government officials in charge of Orthodox policy lost interest in the movement. Soviet officials applied their own standards to renovationism and disparaged it for being unable to maintain its hold on power. The Holy Synod accepted a more limited political and social function as a state surrogate for fighting sectarians at home and controlling Orthodox property abroad.

From a broader perspective, the Soviet state's eagerness to pull the plug on renovationism just when it seemed to be on the verge of self-sufficiency after the 1923 church council boded ill for the future prospects of the Russian Orthodox Church. Soviet leaders assumed that traditional Russian religion was worthless, but Bolsheviks still had to interact with religious groups in the Orthodox Church that were strongly defended by masses of believers. In that interaction, party leaders and bureaucrats exhibited complete disrespect for those groups and a callous willingness to manipulate them for political ends. To the renovationists' credit, they did not give up their attempts to reverse those assumptions and integrate Orthodoxy in Soviet society. They may not have recognized the duplicity of the state toward the church, although one suspects that prominent leaders such as Krasnitskii, Granovskii, Evdokim, Boiarskii, and Vvedenskii understood more than they admitted in public. Even if they knew the true goals of Bolshevik religious policy, red priests continued to work for a synthesis of Bolshevism and Christianity. Of all the obstacles placed before them, church reformers could not overcome rejection of that synthesis by both ordinary believers and party activists.

5.

RENOVATIONISM IN THE PARISH

THE NEW ECCLESIASTICAL policy of the 1920s made a significant impact on Orthodox organizations throughout Russia by giving believers the freedom to choose among church factions vying for their loyalty. Soviet and church records provide detailed accounts of the struggle between red priests and Tikhonites at the local level. The sharp conflict that gripped the Orthodox Church offers insight into social and political processes churning through Russian society. This chapter will analyze pressures on renovationism at the micro level to explain Orthodox behavior in dioceses and parishes.

"Bolshevik" Orthodoxy as Heresy

Most clergy and laypeople who remained in the Russian Orthodox Church during NEP rejected renovationism entirely. For them, it was a more than simply a schism in the church; it was a heresy created by the Bolsheviks. Orthodox believers framed the issue as a matter of doctrine, not as a matter of internal church politics. Secret police from Leningrad captured the essence of this attitude in a report on a church in Benitskaia district (*volost'*) in July 1925:

> Members of the parish council in the village of Begunitsa vigorously agitated against the renovationist movement, saying: "Renovationist priests are commissars in cassocks. They support Soviet power because it pays them. They betray the people. They don't believe in God; they burn icons and rob churches. God has sent Soviet power to punish us for our sins. If people will pray as they did in the past, then the Lord God will deliver us all from this evil."[1]

This attitude extended to the renovationist episcopate. During a procession from Ustiuga to Kotovalo led by a bishop loyal to the Holy Synod, "the Tikhonites sent monks ahead who told the populace not to receive this bishop because he was a communist impostor [*samozvanets-kommunist*] and a servant of Soviet power."[2]

The characterization of renovationism as a break with true Orthodox faith began immediately after the VTsU took power in mid-1922. It spread throughout the patriarchal church and became the norm for Orthodox laity who supported the "true faith." They readily rejected as "traitors and heretics" formerly trusted parishioners and even priests. Supporters of the patriarchate narrowly defined community as isolated from and opposed to others, as "we versus they," and the homogeneous Tikhonite "we" were openly hostile toward the renovationist "they."

Orthodox groups spelled out the reasons for this attitude in different terms for different audiences. When addressing the government, parishioners based their protests on the law that required the separation of church and state. Time and again, they complained about renovationist motives and activities to state officials in written appeals that landed in the files of the Commissariat of Justice. Congregations resented governmental interference in their internal affairs and the alliance between renovationists and the state. They fought attempts to change Orthodox practice and challenged local officials who helped reformist clergy by arresting their opponents. They resented the new alliance being forged by the renovationists and the state—an alliance that allowed some parish clergy to usurp power for crass material motives.[3]

Protests from parish councils capture the essence of charges made against renovationists. In December 1923, believers from Olonets province argued that the living churchmen had violated the separation decree and broken the law by insisting on the new calendar and prohibiting commemorations of Tikhon in the liturgy. The new leaders had also taken away the right of parishes to select their own clergy, usurped church power, and repressed their opponents by replacing bishops against the will of believers. Furthermore, the petitioners condemned both the procedures for selecting delegates to the 1923 national church council and that body's decisions, citing in particular those allowing married bishops and the remarriage of priests. They summarized their discontent with these words:

> After one and one-half years of renovationist activity, it is clear to us that the renovationists have not the slightest intention of renewing Orthodox Church life according to the ideals of Christ our Savior. Renovationism is only the struggle by clergy for ecclesiastical power and does not take into account the wishes of believers or the laws on freedom of conscience. These clergy only want to reach the rank of bishop and archbishop, to wear a bishop's miter, and to sit in an episcopal see to rule the church.[4]

In a similar vein, believers in Kaluga province objected strenuously to renovationist calls for the city's executive committee (*gorispolkom*) to prosecute Tikhonites. Their complaints centered on a monastic priest named Vladimir who opposed renovationism at first and was sent to Moscow to investigate the VTsU. Upon his return, Vladimir announced that the new church authorities had appointed him to run the Kaluga diocesan administration. At the time, according to Vladimir's former allies, "renovationists in the town totaled only 50 to 100 people, of which five or six were clergymen," and no other Orthodox laity or clergy would have relations with the "renegades." Disregarding his lack of popular support, Vladimir committed "sacrilege" by taking control of the local cathedral with help from state officials and over the objections of its nonrenovationist congregation. Vladimir then set up his own administrative council and convinced the government not to allow anyone to work as an Orthodox clergyman without approval from the diocese. Approval was given only to clergymen in Kaluga who pledged obedience to Vladimir and the VTsU.

Sudden conversions to renovationism by local church leaders heightened believers' suspicions. Trustworthy local representatives, such as Kaluga's Vladimir, left for Moscow opposed to the VTsU but returned as willing, active supporters of reform. A similar case was reported in Ekaterinburg, when a delegation came back from the capital with orders to remove the old bishop and take charge of the diocese.[5] Some renovationist opponents did not need to travel farther than the local GPU office to change their views. For example, Archpriest Nikolai Platonov of Petrograd convened a meeting of clergy in his district in order to speak out against VTsU decisions. His actions led to his arrest and interrogation by the secret police, after which Platonov emerged a free man and an energetic missionary for renovationism. A few years later, he rose to the rank of metropolitan of Leningrad.[6] Naturally, those who continued to oppose the new movement felt betrayed and, in their attempt to explain what happened, questioned the integrity of their former allies. Threats by renovationists to deprive their clerical opponents of their livelihoods and denounce them to the authorities exacerbated that sense of betrayal.[7]

Across Soviet Russia, Orthodox believers concluded that their diocesan administration had become an arm of the government. Priests and bishops who refused to submit to the VTsU lost their right to serve in dioceses under renovationist control and became targets of "unjustified criminal prosecution." Parish councils in Kaluga received a list of priests who were prohibited from serving in Orthodox churches. If anyone on the list was allowed to continue in his duties, the diocese threatened the parish's leaders with criminal prosecution "as accomplices of professional clergy who have lost their rights because they are counterrevolutionaries and do not recognize the Supreme Church Administration of the Russian Orthodox Church."[8] Tikhonites in Kaluga somehow obtained a copy of secret instructions from the city's executive committee that told local officials to require a certificate (*udostoverenie*) from Bishop Vladimir before registering any clergyman. The Moscow office of the Commissariat of Justice condemned these instructions as a violation of the decree separating church and state.[9]

Such violations increased after the VTsIK issued new instructions for religious societies on August 2, 1922. These instructions required societies to register with the central state administration or a provincial executive committee, both of which had the right to refuse registration to groups engaging in any activity contrary to the laws and constitution of the RSFSR. Unregistered societies were given three months to comply with these instructions, while registered societies were rewarded with permission to hold provincial and all-Russian congresses for the purpose of setting up church administrative organs.[10] By early 1923, clergy who refused to register with the local authorities were being fined and, if they refused to pay, sentenced to several months forced labor.[11] On April 27, 1923, *Izvestiia* indicated that the state would use the registration requirement against local parishes that continued to oppose the Living Church.[12] In many places, officials in charge of registration required the prior approval of the local renovationist diocesan administration before completing the process. Renovationist dioceses, in turn, often withheld or withdrew that approval from congregations that refused to make "contributions" to maintain the diocesan and central church bodies. Parishes protested against paying these "taxes" against their will.[13]

Although the government repeatedly denied that it supported renovationism, Orthodox parishioners knew the truth. A layman from Tver boldly asked the head of the Commissariat of Justice, "Is the VTsU an organ of state power?" He wanted to learn whether he and his fellow believers in the area were required to obey VTsU orders and register their congregations. A commissariat official replied that the government regarded the VTsU "as the representative of the Orthodox groups that join it. . . . But it is not an organ of government power . . . and following its resolutions is purely voluntary." According to this statement, the government supervised the VTsU and all similar organizations for the sole purpose of ensuring state security. Therefore, all religious groups indeed needed to register with the administrative department of their local soviet.[14] Confronted with such obvious lies, the ordinary layperson suspected correctly that the government had a plan to destroy Orthodoxy from within, using the renovationists.

Insidious methods used by the government behind a facade of legality to close down churches controlled by "reactionaries" reinforced that perception. In Petrograd, a parish council wrote to the Commissariat of Justice that the diocesan administration wanted to close the church illegally. The commissariat told the diocesan body that the government upheld the rights of the independent parish council. It also explained that if a parish "disturbs legal and social order, infringes the rights of citizens of Soviet Russia, or displays counterrevolutionary activity under a religious flag," it could be prosecuted under criminal law, and its right to use the church building could be revoked. Soon afterward, the Petrograd diocese falsely accused the recalcitrant parish council of anti-Soviet activity and gained jurisdiction over the church building.[15] In effect, the Commissariat of Justice both reprimanded local officials for their actions and tutored them on proper methods for ousting the troublesome congregation.

Rank-and-file believers felt besieged by blatantly repressive measures and the obvious cooperation between Bolsheviks and renovationists. A complaint from Tikhonites in the city of Tver indicated the depths of their frustration. They read the newspaper *Zhivaia tserkov'* and concluded "that the Living Church group is not based on the purity of Orthodox teaching." As proof, they cited the sectarian qualities of the group; namely, its intention to violate the canons and writings of the church fathers. Their petition to the Commissariat of Justice accused the VTsU of illegally appointing clergy in the diocese and meddling in the affairs of independent Orthodox congregations in order to promote the "rights and privileges . . . of the narrow white clergy estate." Furthermore, the local Living Church plenipotentiary acted egregiously by asking government officials to enforce his decision to remove Tikhonite bishop Gavriil Abolymov from his see. Believers in Tver received support from some of their clergy who also refused to accept either the innovations or authority of the Living Church.[16]

Opponents of renovationism took a different tone in their correspondence with the church's patriarchal hierarchy. Many who wrote rejected renovationism in ecclesiastical terms and explained how they were forced to obey the VTsU. They condemned as heresy decisions by reformers to change the liturgy, the calendar, and rules for the dress and behavior of clergy. The heretics had compounded their "sin" by pressuring parishes to accept these changes. This theme of duress figured prominently in petitions asking the patriarch to accept parishes back into canonical relationship with him. These statements flooded Tikhon's chancery in 1923–1924. They frequently claimed that the parish accepted only the minimum amount of renovationist control necessary to keep its church open and functioning. Some clergy acknowledged renovationist authority in 1922–1923, for example, but refused to allow the renovationist liturgy to be performed in their church. Or the liturgy was performed but the local clergy themselves did not participate or join any renovationist group. Some defended their actions by claiming that the VTsU seemed canonical because senior hierarchs recognized it.[17]

Other letters proclaimed their authors' unwavering faithfulness to the patriarchate in the face of renovationist pressure. Believers from Serpugov wrote to Tikhon in June 1924 and trumpeted the fact that they had resisted the snare of "innovations" and held to "true Orthodoxy." They attributed their steadfastness to the patriarch's example of remaining true to Christ despite persecution. They also admitted that while he was imprisoned they had been afraid that "the anti-canonical trend of church life would weaken and destroy the church." His release confirmed that their choice had been correct. In a similar vein, a Leningrad priest named Zhemchuzhin sent a letter to his Tikhonite bishop and explained the reasons behind popular opposition to renovationism. Fr. Zhemchuzhin wrote that he never joined renovationism because he was truly Orthodox and it was not. The synodal diocesan administration failed to understand that the laity, in particular less educated members, "held to the faith of their ancestors, however poorly understood" and therefore would never agree to any of the changes proposed by the "church revolutionaries."[18]

Parishes across Russia most frequently expressed opposition to renovationism because it was alien and non-Orthodox. Its "red priests" were Bolshevik functionaries out to destroy Orthodox religion by teaching that the altar was unnecessary, the canons were not relevant, marriage was not required, baptism was not useful, the saints were not effective, and icons were not needed.[19] Just after Tikhon's release, a Moscow priest named Kotov combined these ideas in a sermon that denounced the members of the VTsU as "impostors" in a sermon. He later proclaimed, "Our church has two sworn enemies. The first is Soviet power, the second—the VTsU."[20] Such attitudes were fostered by periodic rumors that the government planned to close all the churches and forbid priests from administering the sacraments.[21] In October 1925, Tikhonite church officials told a visiting papal representative in Moscow that "the renovationists are not Orthodox—they are not even Russian because they use the new calendar and destroy the divine order by cutting their hair and beards."[22]

Betrayed by those they trusted and worried by the strange ideas of the reformers, the Orthodox masses became convinced that renovationism was alien to their faith. Some decided it was the religion of the antichrist and looked for "signs" that would prove it.[23] The number on the license plate (999) of Vvedenskii's car was interpreted as one such sign, since it was the number of the antichrist, 666, upside down.[24] In Lipetsk province, most Orthodox believers refused even to enter renovationist churches "for fear of receiving the mark of the antichrist."[25] One Orthodox believer wrote to another in 1927 and complained that the close union of the renovationist church and the Soviet state in Russia would destroy religion and therefore stood as the first sign of the apocalypse.[26] Others simply rejected the VTsU's claim to be the authoritative governing body for Russian Orthodoxy. In a petition to the Commissariat of Justice from January 1923, parishioners from Moscow's Valaam Monastery argued against transferring its property to the VTsU because it was "a completely different organization in religious spirit."[27] Most of the masses steeped in Orthodox tradition branded the Living Church a "new faith." One priest serving in a remote rural area outside Kazan reported that his parishioners spread rumors of a "new faith" in Moscow that did not recognize icons or keep the fasts and, most important, was "being supported by Soviet power and has just become the state religion of the RSFSR." As proof, they said that all priests must join the new faith or be replaced by those who would.[28]

After Tikhon reclaimed the patriarchal throne in June 1923, renovationists formulated a new strategy for preserving their movement on the basis of Orthodoxy, conciliarity, and political loyalty. On this basis, renovationist priests sought to change the minds of their parishioners. Examples of their new strategy are seen in two articles from the October 1923 issue of the church periodical *Drug pravoslavnogo naroda* [Friend of the Orthodox People]. The first, "Soviet Power and the Living Church," categorically denied rumors that the government controlled the Living Church with the goal of transforming Orthodoxy into "a red Bolshevik faith." This accusation, according to the author, ignored the facts that the Communists opposed all religions and that, thanks to the decree separating church and state, "Orthodoxy will be neither white nor red but free." In the second article, Fr. V. Beliaev, a student at the Kazan Theological Academy, recounted his personal investigation into changes made in Saratov churches. He, too, had heard that the Bolsheviks wanted to destroy the Russian Orthodox Church, that all priests had become Communists and wanted to eliminate the holy sacraments and church altars, and that the One Holy Apostolic Church had become the false Living Church. Arriving in the city, he was told that the living churchmen were heretics who forced the government to jail their opponents. On the street, two elderly strangers approached Beliaev and asked, "Father, are you a Communist, too?" At the cathedral, he saw a renovationist priest reviled and insulted by a mostly female crowd for being "a heretic, traitor, betrayer, Judas, etc." Yet, in observing the liturgy, he saw no changes in the sacraments or innovations in the service. Based on these observations, the author called for peace and revival within the church, along with patience until a new national council could be held.[29]

Despite the change in renovationist tactics, the Orthodox masses remained convinced that renovationism was heresy. By leveling this accusation, supporters of traditionalism used one of Christianity's most powerful weapons against their opponents. Heresy itself, however, is difficult to identify precisely at the level of popular belief. Historians of Christianity often encounter charges of heresy but find the accusation vague because those so accused invariably refute it. Often, those denounced for heresy respond that their accusers are the real heretics, although seldom is the heretical label applied to all sides in the judgment of history. That judgment is itself a reflection of organizational concerns by history's winners, who record their interpretation of internal church disputes.

George Zito's research on heresy as a sociological phenomenon offers an alternative method for analyzing the Tikhonite charge of renovationism as heresy. Zito explains that "heresy threatens established power relations" by posing "a threat . . . to the presumed connection between *belief* and *action*." People assume that anyone sharing similar beliefs will act a certain way; heretics challenge that assumption because their actions seem incongruous with those beliefs. Zito argues, "Heresy plays with the cognitive base upon which beliefs and meanings are erected and from which action is presumed to flow." Heretics use the same words as "true believers" and, by acting differently, cause those believers to experience "cognitive dissonance, imbalance or incongruity."[30]

Renovationism's lack of congruence with Orthodox tradition initially provoked resistance from the Orthodox population. The government interpreted their resistance as anti-Soviet and, therefore, politically counterrevolutionary because it was seemingly against the intent of the religious reforms themselves. Renovationists said that they were Orthodox Christians who supported the divinely ordained political order and upheld the church's traditional beliefs. Old church believers, the supporters of Tikhon, decided that the renovationists acted in ways that were not consistent with such beliefs. Specifically, they changed the liturgy, altered the calendar, attacked episcopal power, denigrated relics, and worked with the Communists.[31] Such actions were inconsistent in the popular religious mind with true Orthodoxy. Ordinary Orthodox believers branded the renovationists as heretics precisely because the would-be reformers attempted to enforce an unacceptable reinterpretation of Orthodox belief.

A key element in renovationism's reinterpretation of Orthodoxy lay in its emphasis on the divine's transcendence over the world, as opposed to its immanence in the world. Guy Swanson, a sociologist of religion, has defined divine immanence as the belief that spirits are "actually incorporated in particular times, places and things" and that people possessing a strong sense of immanence feel they have a "direct, palpable contact with ultimate things, with spirits and spiritual powers."[32] Renovationist innovations threatened to diminish the sense of divine immanence for most parishioners, and, in the process, to undo the social, political, and cultural relationships founded on Orthodox religious culture.

In the social sphere, adoption of the civil calendar had important implications. The countryside in particular followed a "cycle of holy days and holidays" that was intimately linked with the traditional calendar.[33] When renovationists pushed the new calendar, rural Orthodox believers experienced a direct attack on their network of social relations. They never forgave the living churchmen for this assault, although they ignored Tikhon's temporary support of calendrical change. The patriarch's short-lived advocacy of the Gregorian calendar from June to December 1923 was outweighed by his defense of traditional Orthodox practice based on divine immanence. Tikhon especially benefited from his discharge from prison, an event perceived by the masses as a miraculous deliverance from Bolshevik oppression and as proof of God's favor. A renovationist periodical in the Piatigorsk diocese published an article on the beginning of this phenomenon in February 1923. Under the title "The Tikhonite Crisis," an anonymous author described the "contagion of the 'Tikhonite terror' (*Tikhonovshchina*)," that is, the fight against church reform. He explained that Tikhon had not been commemorated in the diocesan liturgies for ten months, "yet in choked whispers many secretly invoke the name of 'Most Holy Tikhon.'" The author admitted he could not explain how Tikhon had taken on a mystical quality as head of the church, especially since believers knew little about the personality of Tikhon. He concluded with a political analysis, saying that the former patriarch had become a figurehead that was being used by others for anti-Soviet purposes.[34]

In the political realm, Orthodox laity wanted to keep renovationists and other agents of the atheistic state out of parish affairs. The reformers were no different from the Soviet officials who ignored the 1918 decree that separated church and state. Both groups threatened the world described by historian Helmut Altrichter as marked by "the actions and practices, institutions and customs" of everyday Orthodox believers, who were overwhelmingly members "of a precapitalist peasant society, subsistence-oriented and averse to running risks." In describing this society in Tver province, Altrichter finds "insoluble conflicts" between everyday Orthodox life and the new society emerging under Bolshevism. He writes about religion's "deep embeddedness" in that society and Bolshevism's misunderstanding of the nature of popular belief.[35] He does not mention popular reactions to renovationism, although they complement his argument because living churchmen launched an internal assault on lay authority within the parish. Parishioners responded to this threat by driving the movement from holy ground, that is, out of the parish church building. Denouncing renovationism as a heresy that threatened to defile the holy faith, they did not stop after liberating a specific church from renovationist apostasy. Their goal was nothing less than reclaiming *every* parcel of Orthodox ground from these traitors to the faith.

Renovationist liturgical alterations gave opponents of reform final proof that the devil controlled the movement. The Orthodox Eucharist is a series of manifestations of divine immanence through the performance of ritualistic acts. Salvation in this tradition comes not from grace dispensed by the true church, as in Catholicism, or from belief evoked by preaching the Word of God, as in Protestantism. Rather, Orthodox believers are saved by the proper and corporate completion of liturgical acts in which God is present. Renovationist clergy performed salvific rites but behaved in ways that showed they did not believe in the immanence of those rites. They changed the words, the actions, and even the time—the calendar—that helped undergird the laity's understanding of sacred immanence.[36] By causing such cognitive dissonance during the most sacred moments in Russian religious culture, renovationists drove away Orthodox believers en masse.[37]

Thus, calendrical, theological, and liturgical reforms all worked against renovationism in the popular mind. Serious issues of ultimate importance relating to social networks, political forms, and the salvation of one's very soul were at stake. Most believers agreed that the reforms were incompatible with genuine Orthodoxy no matter what renovationism claimed. The Orthodox population resolved the contradictions within those claims by categorizing renovationism as the work of the antichrist and, consequently, as heresy.

Tikhonovshchina

Having demonized the proponents of this new, non-Orthodox faith, many laity fought renovationism with every means at their disposal. The government referred to their actions as the *Tikhonovshchina* ("Tikhonite terror"). Believers threw insults, and occasionally even rocks, at clergy who supported the Living Church. Priests threatened with physical injury sought police protection, for they could not perform the liturgy in peace or appear on the street without fear of attack. Parish churches became battlegrounds for opposing forces, and even religious processions could spark conflict.[38]

The rising popularity of Tikhon's cultic status fed physical violence against renovationism. In September 1922, the GPU fretted over rumors from Pskov that the patriarch had been shot. Secret policemen also kept careful watch over a large crowd that gathered outside at the Donskoi Monastery in Moscow in hopes of catching a glimpse of the patriarch during a major church feast.[39] A forged document supposedly signed by Tikhon circulated in Moscow in December 1922. It anathematized the VTsU for being the "body of the antichrist" and was read from the pulpits of churches in that city on the popular feast day of St. Nicholas (December 19). Following his release from prison in July 1923, Tikhon categorically denied having ever signed such a document and called it an attempt by émigré enemies of Soviet power to use his name for their political purposes.[40] This disavowal seems plausible in light of the close guard the GPU had posted around the patriarch. Tikhon could have released the document only with government permission, and such permission would never have been given for a statement that fed the *Tikhonovshchina.*

Violent demonstrations against renovationism led, however, to retaliation by the state against the Tikhonite church leaders. For this reason, parishioners more often relied on the power of the purse in pressing their clergy to disobey the VTsU or, later, the Holy Synod. In Tatarstan, parish priests experienced this economic pressure and expressed concern about how they would care for their families in the face of lay opposition to the renovationist movement. When a village priest read the gospel in vernacular Russian instead of Old Church Slavonic, some in his congregation threatened to cut off donations of food.[41] The parish councils of urban churches in the same region devised a new slogan as winter approached: "Let the Living Church give firewood to the priests if they decide to join it."[42]

Economic coercion may have prevented many parish priests from breaking with traditional Orthodox theology and practice. The evidence suggests that their decision to stay with the patriarchal church may also have been linked to their level of education. Renovationism tended to appeal to priests with seminary or academy degrees. Gregory Freeze has shown that a nineteenth-century reform allowing students to transfer from ecclesiastical schools to secular schools caused a steep reduction in the percentage of parish clergy with seminary degrees by the end of the century. In 1890, 88 percent of parish priests and 40 percent of all parish clergy (priests, deacons, and sacristans) had a seminary education. By 1902, those statistics had fallen to 64 percent for priests and 29 percent overall. In 1911, three out of every four seminary graduates pursued careers outside the church.[43] Statistics are unavailable for later years. In light of the closing of all church schools and the flight of clergy abroad after the Revolution, the general level of education for parish clergy must have continued to fall. A small item in Kazan's renovationist diocesan journal pointed to this change. The article bemoaned reports that new priests came from the peasantry and differed from the educated clergy of the past. Unlike their predecessors, these peasant priests were indistinguishable from their parishioners. "Among these new pastors, superstition widely blooms and has deep roots. The law of reversion to type holds even in the realm of spirituality."[44]

After Tikhon's release and the cessation of state administrative pressure to recognize national renovationist church organs, parish clergy and their congregations joined together in asserting their opposition to renovationism. Those who earlier felt themselves victimized by the heavy hand of the Living Church now exacted revenge by launching unrelenting attacks based on a rising sense of parish autonomy and alienation from Soviet culture. Most parishes endeavored to preserve holy time and space within the walls of their churches. In practical terms, this meant keeping the old calendar, the traditional liturgical forms, and the continued reverence of icons and saints. The Tikhonites also wanted a pure (unmarried) episcopate without any power to interfere in parish affairs.[45]

Reaction against renovationism was not limited to supporters of the patriarchate. The reform movement never became a way station on the path to atheism as Lunacharskii had hoped in 1923. It did, however, push many believers out of the Orthodox camp while consuming the energies of those who remained within it. Russians who sought a religion that combined Christian teachings and revolutionary socialism apparently joined non-Orthodox religious groups. Russian Baptists and Evangelical Christians in particular "consciously emulated Bolshevik codes and rituals" in reconciling socialist ideas of economics and teachings associated with primitive Christianity. These sectarians captured the "genuine emotion and commitment" that Bolshevism sought and renovationism needed, thus arousing the enmity of both the Communist Party and the Holy Synod.[46]

Our knowledge of the growth of sectarian religious groups in the 1920s is still fragmentary, so it is not possible to make definitive statements about who joined those groups. Logic dictates that the new converts had previously been counted among the Orthodox and that they left the church out of dissatisfaction with its form of religious expression. Renovationism could have provided the new home for believers alienated from Orthodoxy except for the fact that by the time sectarianism expanded in the middle of the decade, the Holy Synod had already altered its course to attract mainstream Orthodox believers. By abandoning reforms that might open them up to the charge of being "sectarian," renovationists lost the opportunity to attract Orthodox believers who wanted a religion more congruous with Soviet political culture.

The real reason the Communists encouraged Orthodox infighting was to drive people away from religious organizations altogether.[47] Party policies were successful in doing this. Large numbers of former believers abandoned religion entirely in the 1920s, and their exodus probably was the greatest blow to renovationism. Only a small percentage of Soviet citizens became active atheists. The majority simply became nonreligious in a process of acculturation to a new social norm that demanded that all references to God be eliminated from public and private life. Nonreligion became the new standard in Soviet culture, and many people—wishing to advance socially or simply bowing to social pressure—chose to adhere to it. The new group of agnostics may have numbered 46.5 million out of the country's 130 million population in 1928. This change struck renovationism hardest, because the new nonreligious might have moved to the movement's middle religious ground if Russia's Communist leaders had tolerated a compromise between religion and Soviet society.[48]

Bolshevik Orthodoxy in the Parish

As NEP progressed, the renovationists found themselves in a figurative no-man's-land, under siege by the old church on one side and the Soviet government on the other. The government included priests in the category of the disenfranchised (*lishentsy*) that included all from the "privileged classes" under the old regime, such as nobles and military officers. These disenfranchised individuals lost all their political rights in the Soviet system and were subject to discriminatory policies in housing, taxation, and education. Being deprived of a place in society weighed particularly on the renovationist clergy, who sought to be involved in the political process but found their access denied. Although attacked by their co-religionists for being Bolsheviks, the renovationists were excluded from emerging Soviet society because of their religious beliefs and class identity. The Twelfth Bolshevik Party Congress in 1923 had called for systematic antireligious propaganda and agitation with the goal of ending all religious belief among workers and peasants. This was part of a broader plan for ridding the party itself of all believers.[49] The atheists who directed the League of the Godless did not target their attacks against just one branch of Orthodoxy, and the Commissariat of Justice looked on the renovationists' proclamations of loyalty to the government as merely a ploy for strengthening its organization throughout Russia.[50]

Priests, who were the backbone of renovationist support, were especially vulnerable to the growing intolerance of "alien elements" in the Soviet Union. No one has analyzed them as a distinct group during this period, but stories about priests and their families appear frequently in other studies. For example, Sheila Fitzpatrick's work on class identity in NEP society gives several illustrations of how the Soviet definition of class placed clergy in the enemy camp. Party members were chastised for marrying the daughters of priests, while the children of priests attempted to get relatives to adopt them and thereby hide their "non-Soviet" roots. In some cases, children formally broke "all ties with the clerical estate" or attempted to convince their fathers to voluntarily defrock themselves.[51] Throughout the 1920s, the political climate grew increasingly hostile to those promoting non-Bolshevik socialism, such as the renovationists.

Caught in the crossfire between Tikhonites and atheists and finding little room to maneuver in the developing Soviet system, the embattled renovationists faced constant challenges as they strove to maintain their organization at the local level. Active diocesan committees, the remnant of governmental support during 1922–1923, could not parlay their strength into popular support because they had bishops, priests, and churches but no money.[52] Pinched for cash, diocesan leaders continually cut back on their obligations. In October 1925, a cathedral in Northern Dvina had had an income of only 32 rubles for the previous three months, and even that money was seized to pay the cathedral's debts. The church could no longer pay its "starving" deacon or psalmist, nor could it afford to send money to its bishop for his return trip from the second renovationist church council in Moscow.[53]

Erosion of support from local government officials exacerbated this loss of financial clout. Originally, those officials preferred to deal with the renovationists who were politically trustworthy and willing to please the state. Such favoritism was consistent with secret instructions issued by Moscow before May 1923. After that date, the center sometimes overturned local officials' decisions that showed favoritism to any Orthodox faction. In reality, party leaders in charge of church policy wanted to avoid open support by the GPU and local officials for the renovationists. As late as September 1924, ARK directed the secret police as follows, "In strengthening the renovationist movement work more tactfully and conspiratorially so that its Tikhonite opponents cannot gain the impression that the Soviet government supports renovationists against Tikhonites." Yet at that same meeting the commission prohibited the GPU from enforcing sanctions imposed by one group of believers against another against administering religious sacraments. This decision weakened renovationism.[54]

Once again, we see contradictions inherent in the Communist Party's policies toward religion. Regional representatives for the party, the government, and the secret police needed to disengage the general rule of church-state separation from their specific duty of ensuring Soviet social order in their local areas. This seemed impossible to do when central authorities imposed the general rule at will. During the second half of 1923, the Commissariat of Justice supported the majority of appeals by Tikhonite congregations against local executive committees that had upheld decisions by renovationist diocesan administrations. The Commissariat of Justice returned control of parish churches and freed priests falsely accused of counterrevolutionary activity in Semipalatinsk, Vladivostok, Iaroslavl, Poltava, Riazan, Khabarovsk, Nizhnii Novgorod, Perm, and Siberia.[55] The fact that local decisions were not overturned in all cases added to the confusion of local officials. For example, the Commissariats of Justice and Internal Affairs defended the actions of the Samara provincial executive committee in prohibiting the Tikhonites from organizing a rival diocesan administration and supporting the actions of the renovationist bishop against his old-church opponents.[56]

Ironically, a weakened renovationist diocese sometimes turned to a charismatic bishop to hold it together. In the fall of 1923, the renovationists in Saratov experienced a miniature revival of activity with the arrival of their new archbishop, Kornilii Popov. Even he could not improve the material situation of synodal clergy who, according to the local GPU, had abandoned the reform movement at the beginning of winter for economic reasons.[57] On the other hand, the departure of a strong bishop could lead to a marked decline in the strength of a diocese. Such was the case in Rostov when Bishop Nazarii Andreev left the movement in 1925.[58] Archbishop Mikhail Trubin succeeded during his brief tenure in Arkhangelsk from October 1925 to June 1926; he published a new local newspaper and vigorously defended both renovationist reforms and his commitment to Orthodox purity. But his transfer to the Baikal region dissipated the momentum he had built in the diocese.[59]

While the Holy Synod noted the connection between strong bishops and thriving dioceses, it also found the growth of episcopal power troublesome. Renovationists could not forget that the fight against despotic bishops initially rallied the reformers. In addition, powerful bishops often clashed with parish clergy, a side effect the synod sought to ameliorate by frequently transferring the former.[60] Yet this solution brought new problems. Over time, most renovationist dioceses became loose confederations of independent parishes. Occasionally, a diocesan administration tried to impose its will, but parishes and priests obeyed only when it suited them. When the local administration proved too bothersome, the offended party ignored its orders or transferred loyalty to the Tikhonite church. The Moscow diocese began a running battle in 1928 with Archbishop Georgii Zhuk when he refused to give up control over the Vaganov Cemetery church in which he served as priest. The diocese responded to complaints by some parishioners that the archbishop ran the parish without consulting the laity. Georgii responded to the diocesan administration's threat of sanctions by claiming that only the parish had the right to hire or fire him under Soviet law.[61]

This incident is interesting because it was one of the few cases where the Moscow diocese prevented a parish from transferring to the patriarchate.[62] The vast majority of churches in that diocese nominally fell under renovationist jurisdiction in May 1923. By February 1926, only three bishops and forty clergy remained in thirty-seven churches; the diocese had included over 1,000 churches before 1917. The number of renovationist parishes declined to twenty-six by October 1, 1927, with a mere twelve churches in the city of Moscow itself.[63] The superintendent of the city called his parishes "small islands in the midst of a hostile sea of other church groups." The solution to this problem, according to him, was for all renovationist parishes to see themselves as interconnected, like a family, and thus resist further erosion of support.[64]

Faced with such deterioration, diocesan administrations experimented with several tactics for improving its position. Often, diocesan officials had no other option than propaganda. For example, when a Tikhonite congregation switched to the synodal camp, the move was heralded as "a mighty success" and a sign that the tide had turned in favor of the renovationists.[65] Such good news was rare, at least in Moscow. Other dioceses were able to bring new parishes into the renovationist fold even after 1923. The Holy Synod reported that in the eight months prior to October 1, 1927, it had lost 154 parishes to the Tikhonites but had accepted 212 from the enemy camp, for a net gain of 48 parishes in this period.[66] Kazan diocese also seemed to attract new parishes at this time, according to statistics compiled in 1932 (see Table 5.1).

Table 5.1. Renovationist Parishes in Kazan Diocese, 1923–1928

Year	Parishes Added	Parishes Lost	Total	Notes
1923			100	Estimated*
1924	100		200	Registered parishes
1925	100		300	Registered parishes
1926		100	200	Loss followed the 1925 council
1927		50	150	Loss resulting from the council
1928	51	21	179	One parish church was closed. Situation in diocese stabilized.

*This low initial number resulted from strong protests after the 1923 council's decision to implement the new calendar. TsGA TASSR, f. 1172, op. 3, d. 1209, l. 71 ob.

Source: TsGA TASSR, f. 1172, op. 3, d. 1209, l. 80.

Inspired to take the offensive by their gains (however small), renovationists displayed a spurt of creative activity that promoted unity at the diocesan level based on the ideas of Orthodoxy and conciliarity. Bishop Nikolai Polikarpov of Klin was especially active in courting Tikhonite clergy using those methods. When clergy from both Orthodox factions expressed an interest in joint services following Tikhon's death, Nikolai gave his blessing. Learning of this afterward, the Tikhonite hierarchy in Klin squashed further contact, fearing de facto unity and reconciliation in the diocese.[67] Around the country, renovationist clergy met on a regular basis in miniature informal councils to discuss common concerns. One small band of Moscow clergy held several sessions in late 1926 for the purpose of unifying local renovationist activity. The participants recommended that educational workshops for clergy be held in all parishes. They also arranged for the printing and distribution of a renovationist liturgy used throughout the diocese. That group later expanded its discussions to include methods for helping clergy respond effectively to protests from the laity, although these proposals died for lack of wider clerical support.[68]

The Moscow diocese continued to display a distinctive characteristic of renovationism; namely, a willingness to innovate. It adopted a new set of guidelines for renewal based on suggestions made by the church's "evangelist" (*blagovestnik*), Metropolitan Alexander Vvedenskii, to the Holy Synod in April 1927. He suggested an eight-point program for eliminating the *Tikhonovshchina* in and around Moscow, starting with a study of counterrevolutionary activities of the old church and renovationist differences with Tikhonites. Using the "facts" found in this study, the reformers could convince the old-church laity that renovationism was true Orthodoxy. Vvedenskii explained, "They must see not only our political loyalty but also our religious activity. *Tikhonovshchina* is defeated in those dioceses and parishes where the pastor is the spirit of the parish and not a bureaucratic dispenser of rituals, where the bishop is not an ecclesiastical general in the old-regime fashion but an apostle." The remaining points of Vvedenskii's program stressed eliminating bureaucratic mores among the leaders of the diocese by finding new "activists and cadres" who would engage in pastoral work and pull in the masses. These fresh troops would come from the "unused capital of renovationist forces," especially students in the theological schools.[69]

This plan for revitalization had achieved little by the end of 1927, according to the minutes of a Moscow diocesan congress held in December. Although Metropolitan Veniamin Muratovskii noted improvements in the diocese, he also voiced concern about the "lack of discipline" among the clergy under his supervision. This concern apparently referred to the willingness of renovationist clergy to flout the traditional rules on dress, hair, and sexual conduct. The parish clergy at the congress attributed the low morale among their colleagues—a condition that was related to the problem of discipline—to disorder in the church, over which they had no control. Symptoms of that disorder included passivity among the laity and defections of clergy to the patriarchal church. In response, the congress called for "strict fraternal discipline," clerical solidarity, activation of the laity, better episcopal supervision of parishes using more suffragan bishops, and financial aid for poorer parishes.[70]

Most renovationist difficulties in the dioceses and parishes resulted from Tikhonite economic attacks. All religious organizations suffered from government policy aimed at reducing their economic base through high mandatory fees and exorbitant taxation. This policy had a greater impact on the renovationists, who were already financially weakened by the agitation of their religious rivals.[71] At first, Tikhonites used economic pressure to prevent clergy from implementing VTsU-mandated reforms. In 1923, Saratov priests refused to join the Living Church mainly because of their material dependence on the people; these clergymen realized that they would not receive money to pay their rent if they attacked traditional Orthodox practice.[72] By 1925, the patriarchal church had fully appropriated the power of lay loyalty and economic clout in the battle to gain control of parish churches. A telling example comes from a meeting at the main cathedral in Kazan, where Tikhonites and renovationists debated the issue of joint liturgical services. One Tikhonite reportedly said that he permitted the poor to receive sacraments in synodal churches but not the rich—the point being that the poor could not make the customary payments to priests in exchange for sacramental rites.[73] Similarly, outside Bogoliubskii Cathedral in Moscow, Tikhon's supporters agitated openly against believers giving any material support for the church, urging believers not to enter the church, light candles, or give offerings to the Communist, satanic clergy who served there.[74]

The laity's willingness to boycott renovationist churches, even in places where there was no Tikhonite alternative, led many synodal clergy to poverty or unemployment or both.[75] At the close of the 1925 renovationist national church council, Vvedenskii expressed sympathy for bishops who had a real meal only one day in three and priests who lived on a mere 10 rubles a month. On another occasion, he praised Deacon Ivanov, who had been driven out of his parish by Tikhonites and been left with only a shirt and one potato. A woman took pity on the deacon and gave him a second shirt, but he still had to walk around in the dead of winter in his sandals (*v laptiakh*). Despite his poverty, the metropolitan continued, Ivanov refused the Tikhonite offer of "a shirt, boots, and a hunk of bread" if he joined them, for he was "armed with the truth of our renovationism."[76] Vvedenskii's melodramatic comments are substantiated by petitions for financial assistance submitted to the Moscow diocesan administration. One priest asked for money and a transfer because the parish in which he served had six clergy and the senior priest claimed 45 percent of the offerings.[77] Fr. G. Bogoslovskii asked for help from either the Moscow body or the synod, citing his need to care for his sick wife and three young children and the fact he had been out of work for three months after his parish church reduced its clerical staff. The diocese refused his request because it had no money to give.[78] Clergy who lost their positions and could not locate another generally had difficulty finding work in the secular economy. The chronic high unemployment during NEP made life difficult for citizens with untainted pasts,[79] let alone those who were "alien" to Soviet society.[80]

Parishes reacted to the old church's economic siege by shedding excess clergy, thereby adding to the financial woes of renovationist churchmen. For example, the laity from the church in Semenov Cemetery requested a reduction in the number of its assigned clergy, saying they could not support a staff of six priests, a deacon, and a psalmist. Even before the Revolution, the church had paid only two priests and two psalmists. By 1925, sources of prerevolutionary funds had disappeared, the church had apartment space for only three clergy families, taxes were high, and both Tikhonite and synodal clergy were offering unauthorized requiem masses in the parish cemetery. Therefore, the number of such masses conducted within the church itself had been cut in half. This fact compounded parish financial difficulties arising from fewer services being held in a church empty of parishioners.[81] In addition to quarrels with their parishioners, renovationist clergy began fighting among themselves as the Darwinian struggle for survival resurrected century-old rivalries in the clerical ranks. Priests feared their own sacristans and deacons and often accused these lower clergymen of undermining their superiors through plots to turn parishes over to the patriarchate. Renovationists in the strong Kuban-Chernomor diocese charged that local Tikhonites promised rapid promotion to psalmists and deacons who switched their allegiance.[82]

Some clear cases of such fifth-column activity among clergy appear in the records. A typical ambiguous case comes from Moscow in early 1925, when the diocese removed the Deacon N. P. Vozdvizhenskii from his position in the wake of a complaint by the archpriest of the parish, I. I. Sokolev. Sokolev complained that Vozdvizhenskii had repented before the Tikhonites and was plotting to gain control of the parish for his new masters. The deacon protested that charge and countered with the claim that the archpriest was an atheist in league with the Communists because he denied central Christian doctrines and thereby destroyed the faith of his parishioners. After conducting an independent investigation, the diocesan administration found that the deacon and laity opposed Sokolev but were not Tikhonites. Therefore, the diocese decided to replace both clergymen in order to keep the parish in the renovationist fold.[83] A similar case appeared in a Moscow Tikhonite church when an archpriest lodged an appeal against his renovationist deacon—a former Tikhonite psalmist who had married a widow and therefore could not be promoted in the patriarchal church. In a petition for help from his archbishop, the archpriest accused his deacon of agitating against Tikhon in the parish and using renovationist liturgical forms.[84]

During NEP, renovationists proved as ineffective in countering claims that God had abandoned them as they were in raising funds from their parishioners or in keeping the peace among their clergy. The charge that they "lacked divine grace" (*bezblagodatnye*) stuck like glue. The Tikhonites never relented in their denial of the immanence and efficacy of the divine within churches controlled by the synod. Their creativity and tenacity knew no bounds in this campaign. In May 1925, the Tikhonite clergy tried to paralyze renovationist activity among the masses by using icons that "rejuvenated"—became brighter—when placed in patriarchal churches but darkened again as soon as they were carried into synodal ones.[85] Tikhonites in Kazan said they would need to reconsecrate their churches with holy water if they allowed renovationist priests to serve the liturgy there.[86] A particularly zealous Tikhonite pastor from the Kuban region instructed his flock, "If renovationists give you the Easter greeting 'Christ is risen!' you reply, 'The Lord is risen indeed, only not for you." Another Tikhonite from the same area asserted, "I would sooner exchange the Paschal kiss with a dog than with you renovationists!"[87] All these acts were in addition to cases of public assaults, rock-throwing, insults, and rumors against those who sided with the Holy Synod.

Four newspaper reports from Tambov province in the summer and fall of 1926 illustrated the fronts where the synod's supporters fought their battles during NEP. Clerical rivalry was the theme of the first article, in which Fr. N. Larin contended, "The renovationist pastor is fortunate if his colleagues—the deacon and psalmist—share his beliefs. But this is very rare. In most cases the lower clergy are hostilely inclined toward their own renovationist priest." Larin then gave examples of how that hostility had been channeled into action against the priest. The deacon spread rumors about his superior, hoping to turn the parish over to the old church and be rewarded with the priest's job. Believing the rumors, parishioners collected money for the deacon's trip to Moscow where he could be "reconsecrated" (i.e., reordained in accordance with Tikhonite rites). A local archpriest promoted similar insurrection among deacons and psalmists, leaving priests without any means to support their families. From these observations, Larin concluded, "Renovationist priesthood is voluntary martyrdom." Synodal clergy saw priests in neighboring villages living well because they served "in the old style" and refused to have "*any* social contact with renovationist priests."

Sowing discontent among the laity was another tactic used by the old church to gain control of parishes, according to the second account. This variation began with the people being satisfied with their synodal priest until a kulak, "Vasilii Andreevich," suddenly appeared in the parish. "Vasilii" indicated he was neither renovationist nor Tikhonite. However, he constantly reminisced about the "good old days" when young and old alike showed respect toward him and others. This kulak then started pushing the parish to join with the patriarchate not because of Tikhonite pressure but from a desire to return to the old ways. He also impugned the local renovationist bishop by calling him a Communist, refusing to receive him at home, and pointing out the good fortune of nearby parishes run by old-church bishops.

The third report from the same region castigated infighting among the clergy that led believers to abandon the church or flee to sects. Such anti-Christian infighting was explained in part by the fact that seminary-trained parish clergy were "now as rare as stalks standing in a mown cornfield." Their places had been taken by men motivated to be priests out of self-interest or monks fleeing closed monasteries. Renovationism appealed mainly to priests with higher levels of education and showed a bias against clergy who did not display adequate "consciousness" of their role in leading the Orthodox out of the darkness of religious superstition and into the light of more rational Christianity. The final article announced that while not a single synodal church was left in the region, the Baptists enjoyed great success there. The Tikhonites, however, still were not satisfied. They refused to allow a deceased renovationist clergyman to be buried in priestly vestments because they considered him only a deacon; the patriarchal archpriest and regional superintendent (*blagochinnyi*) who performed the funeral was relieved of his post. The article closed with the charge that the Tikhonites would not even let the dead rest in peace. They were so concerned with renovationism, as rare as it was, that the local Orthodox had no one to defend them from the true dangers they faced.[88]

These accounts show that renovationist reformers could never remove the black mark of heresy on their records. They certainly tried to defend their program for change as a valid interpretation of Orthodox tradition, never understanding that their opponents could not be swayed by even the most sophisticated theological arguments. The lay believers who received permission from the Soviet government to conduct services on nationalized church property knew that the culture outside the church's walls was in transition. They responded by refusing to allow Soviet culture, represented by renovationism, within those walls.

Despite their lack of success, renovationists saw the direction in which Soviet society was moving and shaped an Orthodox response to their new environment. NEP stirred up a vigorous social struggle outside the church; that struggle was reflected within the church by the battle between the two main Orthodox factions. The ecclesiastical schism resulted from social pressure that encouraged the millions of Soviet citizens to abandon Orthodoxy for religious sects, atheism, or agnosticism. The old church responded to these rules by attacking the Holy Synod, and the majority of laity who remained loyal to Orthodoxy rejected the renovationist movement because it represented a "Bolshevik" approach to faith. It was rational, modern, and extremely political. The predominantly rural masses had no empathy with such changes in their faith, for it simply did not correspond to their everyday experience of life with its nonrational mysterious relationships made comprehensible through encounters with divine immanence. Political elites and the emerging red intelligentsia also had no use for the church reform movement. These segments of society accepted the absence of religion in their Soviet construction of reality, just as they later rejected arguments for delaying implementation of their plan for a modern industrialized country. Priests and Orthodox intellectuals who supported renovationism tried to integrate religion into the Soviet social structure. They failed because their proposal for building socialism in all of Soviet Russia, including the church, violated deeply held requirements of both Communist Party leaders and ordinary parishioners that socialism might be realized everywhere *except* in the church.

6.

LIQUIDATION

IN RELIGION, AS in all aspects of Soviet society, 1929 was the year of the Great Turn. The religious NEP was abandoned when the state "substituted itself for society, to become the sole initiator of action and controller of all important spheres of life."[1] Stalinist zeal for building "socialism in one country" resulted in a policy guided by the slogan "the struggle against religion is a struggle for socialism."[2] The state imposed tighter restrictions on the practice of religion as it pushed the country into rapid industrialization and the collectivization of agriculture. A new campaign by the party-state to form a godless country transformed into a campaign of terror against religious leaders in the second half of the 1930s. Political activists branded all religious organizations as anti-Soviet, therefore making them targets for liquidation. The secret police apparatus crushed all forms of organized religion, and national leaders publicly claimed victory over religious superstition by 1940. The situation changed dramatically immediately after the Germans invaded in June 1941. Orthodox Christianity in particular became a major source of support for a Russian government that faced annihilation. Churches reopened by the thousands on both sides of the front, forcing Soviet leaders to formulate a new modus vivendi for working with organized religion.

Red priests repeatedly attempted to adapt to all these changes. They never gave up on their ultimate goal of blending Orthodoxy with Soviet Communism, even when the definition of Soviet communism continued to change. This chapter will explore the twists and turns of history between 1929 and 1946 as advocates of church renovation tried to reconcile their vision of Orthodoxy with a state that actively worked for their liquidation.

"A state of lawlessness"

Backers of the Stalinist cultural revolution showed growing disdain for legal propriety toward religion in 1929–1930 and sealed off possible avenues for the resurgence of renovationism. The People's Commissariat of Internal Affairs (NKVD) led the charge for administrative ways to close parish churches out of a growing irritation with the tenacity of religious belief. Russian historian M. I. Odintsov chronicles attempts during NEP to draft national legislation for regulating activities of "religious cults." He attributes the failure in drafting such laws to an attitude within the NKVD that "what was needed were not laws but a state of lawlessness" for the complete eradication of religion. The commissariat blocked general legislation that would restrict its activities; instead, it favored departmental instructions and secret circulars that prevented believers from hiding behind their supposed legal rights. Those tactics complemented the government's overall strategy for making the parish church a religious "reservation," that is, a place where unacceptable religious practices could be contained and limited.[3]

That approach fit perfectly with the rules of class warfare in a country that saw itself in a state of emergency. Popular sensibilities were already under attack from a war scare and street demonstrations in 1927. The procurements crisis threatened supplies of food for the cities. Show trials for Shakhtyites and other "bourgeois" specialists from the old technical intelligentsia fed fears that enemies were hiding within the country.[4] NKVD statements that all religious believers were politically disloyal resonated with the frenzy of 1928–1929. At a critical juncture in debate about policy options, the NKVD produced a report to prove the treachery of religious groups. This document claimed that believers everywhere were joining forces against Soviet power and preparing antigovernment demonstrations. Believers purportedly pressured local officials during the election campaign for local soviets, set up underground counterrevolutionary organizations, distributed anti-Soviet leaflets, used terror against activists in the campaign for atheism, and joined together to block church closings or build new churches.[5]

Similar claims of political subversion by Orthodox groups figured prominently in the agitation and propaganda campaigns of the late 1920s. The Soviet press frequently published accounts that depicted widespread efforts by Orthodox clergy and laity to use village soviets in defense of their religious interests.[6] Officials interpreted church activity as an organized, conscious attempt to undermine religious policy at the local level. Rural believers were seen in dualistic Soviet terms, that is, as older, mostly female, wealthy, uneducated peasants who stood opposed to younger, mostly male, poor, educated, atheistic, urban workers. Such dichotomies lay at the foundation of Soviet ideological interpretations surrounding the dialectical struggle that gripped the nation beginning in the late 1920s.

The charge of Orthodox political subversion is suspect in light of the government's own archival records. Evidence collected by state officials on counterrevolutionary activity by bishops, priests, and lay believers misrepresented the fervent desire by the majority of Orthodox believers to keep Soviet culture and politics out of their parish churches. Such misrepresentations began during the campaign to confiscate church valuables in 1922 and continued to appear in official reports. For example, Tuchkov cited specific examples of activity by "anti-Soviet elements" in the Orthodox Church in his report for November 1924. A religious procession protested against arbitrary limitations on singing during the event. Believers taking part in a prayer service held in an open-air bazaar made personal threats against the policeman who tried to stop them. Parishioners opposed high taxes on their churches and spoke against red priests when state officials tried to give renovationists control of patriarchal parishes. Former tsarist military officers and Orthodox clergy continued to associate with each other. For Tuchkov, these scattered reports pointed to the formation of an antigovernment conspiracy, although the examples he provided hardly constituted proof.[7]

Odintsov examined the primary evidence behind the NKVD's reports and offered an explanation of actions by Orthodox believers that is more consistent with their antipathy toward the political process. He argues that state officials collected fragmentary accounts and carefully selected petty details to paint a scene that would allow the use of extralegal means to eradicate religion. Occasional activities of individual clergy and lay activists became conclusive proof of organized religious opposition, while every demand that the government obey its own laws on religion became transformed in the perverse logic of Communist Party governance to "anti-Soviet activity."[8]

Historian Sheila Fitzpatrick came to similar conclusions in her analysis of religion among the peasantry before and after the collectivization of Soviet agriculture. Fitzpatrick noted that the peasants neither strongly approved nor disapproved of the Soviet government during NEP; they had lost interest in politics. Religion became "a key issue," however, in the cultural clash between generations over Soviet cultural norms. Wearing crosses and being married in the church signified allegiance to traditional rules, just as using makeup and dancing the tango indicated that Soviet behavior had become accepted. Fitzpatrick argues that although Russians frequently expressed their opposition to the regime in religious terms, this reflected long-standing hostility toward the government in general, not the Communists in particular. She stated, "At the time of collectivization, the Russian peasantry drew on the symbolism of Orthodoxy to express their protest."[9]

Nonetheless, in the early months of 1929, party leaders acted on their interpretation that organized religion was the enemy. Although Stalin's circle backed the patriarchal faction of the church in the mid-1920s because of Metropolitan Sergii's influence among the peasantry, the procurements crisis fed a more negative attitude by government leaders toward both the Orthodox Church and kulaks. In the words of historian Alekseev, "That crisis revealed the true relationship of the highest government and party officials to the peasantry, its way of life and spirituality." By April 1928, Stalin was telling meetings of party officials and activists that the reactionary clergy were playing a role in the state's difficulties in securing grain. He reminded the Moscow party organization of the similarities between the current situation and the events of 1921–1922, when the government seized church valuables. Affirming that many religious organizations supported the kulak opposition, the general secretary supported moving against them all.[10] Central party organs responsible for religious policymaking proceeded cautiously. They made a verbal distinction at first between attacking anti-Soviet actions and attacking religious behavior. Such a distinction posed a major problem: in Stalinist Russia, all religious belief was defined as anti-Soviet. Party leaders considered the behavior of believers to be a result of "the slow tempo of the development of socialist construction" and thought leaders of religious groups used belief to mask anti-Soviet sentiments. ARK and the Orgburo agreed in January 1929 that administrative measures were counterproductive in attempts to prevent the growth of religious groups.

Shortly thereafter, the Politburo adopted a new fifteen-point program for strengthening antireligious activity. This landmark document replaced the religious NEP with a Stalinist religious policy. Vigorous antireligious propaganda stood at the heart of the new plan for "reducing the influence of religious leaders and building socialism." Ten of the plan's provisions ordered more propaganda by the Commissariat of Enlightenment, trade unions, the press, the artistic media, the army, voluntary organizations, and, most important, the League of the Godless. The remaining five points signaled the end of toleration for lax local implementation of national rules on religious groups. The party intended to rally the masses in the fight against religion, especially in areas surrounding former monasteries. Meanwhile, the NKVD and OGPU were directed to take schools, courts, and the registration of civil acts totally out of the clergy's hands. Cooperatives and collective farms (*kolkhozy*) were told to be vigilant in uncovering secret religious societies, while all Soviet and agricultural organizations were ordered to eliminate (*izzhit'*) the observances of religious holidays.[11] These provisions reveal that the clergy continued to perform civil and educa-

tional functions at the end of the decade, despite numerous directives prohibiting such activity since January 1918.

Communists believed that religious organizations joined with kulaks,
members of the bourgeoisie, and nepmen to mobilize the unenlightened
masses against the government and the party. The Stalinist goal of con-
structing "socialism in one country" required intensification of class struggle, and class struggle in the Soviet context included eradication of religion. The government rationalized the dissonance between freedom of
conscience and religious oppression using a campaign that condemned believers' counterrevolutionary acts and not their mistaken ideas about the
existence of a spiritual realm. That distinction guided two significant decisions by the presidium of the VTsIK on April 8, 1929. First, the presidium passed a resolution "On Religious Associations" that deprived religious organizations of the right to perform any activities except purely religious ceremonies within the walls of their "houses of prayer." It then
formed the Central Standing Commission on Religious Questions, headed
by P. G. Smidovich, a prominent Chekist. The new Commission included
representatives from the secret police, trade unions, and Commissariats of
Internal Affairs, Justice, and Enlightenment.[12] It had responsibility for implementing religious policy in the RSFSR and, after 1935, throughout the
USSR.[13]

Further hardening of the political stance on religion came in May,
when the Fourteenth All-Russian Congress of Soviets changed the constitution of the RSFSR. The wording of the fourth article of that charter
was amended to allow "the freedom of religious confession and of antireligious propaganda." This change altered earlier wording that had allowed
religious propaganda and intended "to limit the dissemination of religious
prejudice by means of propaganda frequently used for counterrevolutionary purposes." Within a month, the Second Congress of the League of the
Militant Godless had adopted a platform for the active struggle against religious superstitions as part of class warfare.[14]

Soviet leaders unleashed the social forces of a class war that spun out
of their control in religion just as it did in factories, classrooms, and professional groups.[15] The fervor of this new revolutionary movement buried
any attempt at an orderly imposition of restrictions on religion in public
life, a fact bemoaned by ARK on May 18, 1929. That body heard reports
on "excesses" in many areas of the country connected with closing churches. Believers resisted these actions, and the process itself interfered with
grain collection. ARK decided to review cases of closures and instructed
local officials to avoid excesses that incited opposition from the peasantry.[16]
In June, the Orgburo weighed in with a bulletin that was signed by Molo-

tov and addressed to all local party committees. This document said that the process of church closures "has taken a mass character that is an intolerable distortion of the party line in the area of the battle against religion." Party organizations were chastised for underestimating the strength of religious belief while overstating the growth of antireligious fervor among the masses. Such mistaken analysis had led to "armed confrontations in the last four to five months." The bulletin forbade the illegal closure of churches by local officials without the authorization of regional or central bodies. It also ordered an end to arrests of clergy for purely religious reasons.[17]

Molotov's instructions were ignored. Enthusiastic supporters of the Komsomol and antireligious organizations refused to back off in the countryside. Some zealous atheists threatened to arrest those who voted against closing churches at local meetings. On December 29, 1929, the OGPU informed the Central Committee of the Communist Party that the reelection campaign for delegates to local soviets had become the pretense for closing churches. "During [the elections], almost every meeting adopted a resolution on the need to close some religious building." Molotov's bulletin had briefly curtailed such excessive behavior, but "the wave of church closures swelled anew" in the fall grain seizure and collectivization campaigns. The regions began to compete to see who could close churches most quickly, a game led by the local plenipotentiaries in charge of grain collection. In the central black-earth regions, nearly all the churches were shut down, but religious feeling continued unabated. The OGPU recommended that "the Central Committee reaffirm its earlier disobeyed directive by holding the secretaries of party committees personally responsibile for its implementation." The secret police promised to issue similar instructions to its local agents.[18]

As in the campaign against Tikhonites in 1922–1923, the center thought that its instructions were not being properly understood in the provinces. National leaders feared social unrest among the masses and reprimanded provincial officials for actions that fed unrest. Local officials thought they had faithfully obeyed instructions and were showing their loyalty to Soviet ideals by promoting class struggle. Contradictory messages continued to flow out of Moscow. The Central Standing Commission on Religious Questions condemned local excesses in January 1930 and simultaneously granted provincial and regional executive committees the power to close churches. It also banned all religious congresses on the basis of the new constitution. Shortly afterward, Sovnarkom and the VTsIK ordered a renewal of "the struggle against counterrevolutionary elements in the leading organs of religious associations" by instructing the governments of all the union republics to eliminate those organs.[19] Central authorities expected regional officials to use effective agitation and propaganda, not force, to eliminate religious organizations.

Genuine commitment among red priests to the accommodation of Orthodoxy to communism provided no protection from the political storm. Odintsov notes that 1929 gave birth to a new view of the connection between political opposition and the clergy (called "servants of the cult" in Soviet documents):

> At this time the proposition took hold that servants of the cult should be held accountable for "anti-Soviet activity." Theological interpretations concerning the "affinity" of communist ideas and religion began to be reevaluated as political "accommodation" and double-dealing, as a "cover" for "church types trying to conduct their subversive work against socialism."[20]

This change hit renovationists hard. The first quarter of 1929 saw the last decisions by ARK favorable to the Holy Synod. The Commission permitted Vvedenskii to engage in the final debates of his career and did not object to the publication of a prayer book in vernacular Russian, although a paper shortage prevented it from ever going to press. By the end of the year, ARK had restricted public religious activities as well as anything that smacked of church-state cooperation. It upheld the closure of a financially important synodal chapel in Moscow and refused to allow the publication of church calendars and the use of land for agricultural purposes by the clergy.[21]

Closures of parish churches devastated renovationists as zealous officials worked to drive all varieties of Orthodox "superstition" out of the countryside. Statistics on Orthodox churches that were closed throughout the RSFSR in 1929–1930 are not available. In the Moscow region, however, 696 out of some 4,120 churches were closed that winter.[22] Records from Tatarstan provide an indication of the antireligious campaign's impact on renovationist parishes in a specific diocese. Reporting on the situation of Orthodox believers in 1929, Tatar party officials echoed national sentiments that Orthodox clergy were "counterrevolutionary," that the church fed peasant backwardness, and that parishes depended on financial help from kulaks and the urban bourgeoisie. Within the Tatar Republic, 397 active Christian churches were served by nearly 800 clergy, approximately 100 of whom lived in Kazan. This report attributed renovationism's failure in the republic to the fact that "the ecclesiastical reformist movement is devoid of roots in the local soil and is a weak trend among the intelligentsia. The *Tikhonovshchina* has already won." Increasing numbers of parishes were transferring to the Tikhonite faction in the city and countryside. Clergy who supported that faction were considered "monarchists, despite Sergii's 1927 declaration."[23]

The Kazan diocese offered a different appraisal of renovationism in the region. On July 1, 1929, diocesan officials told the Holy Synod that the situation was quiet. Some parishes had left the movement but others had joined, so the overall numbers remained constant. Indeed, the report described the relationship between renovationists and old churchmen as "calm" (*spokoinyi*); some of the latter even attended services at synodal parishes. The situation was unchanged, according to the next quarterly report, written in October. By December 15, the Stalinist Revolution hit Kazan. The diocese chose its words carefully in reporting what happened: "Influenced by the general trend in civic life and by heavy taxes, several churches in the diocese have closed. Also, many priests were unemployed, although now they are returning to their positions." The diocesan administration appealed to local officials regarding excessive taxes on clerical incomes. Meanwhile, one district in the diocese reported that a lack of priests had caused several villages to unite and form a single parish.

The next report from Kazan, dated April 1, 1930, indicated the futility of earlier efforts. The diocese now told of massive church closures and numerous unemployed clergy. By January, fifty-seven parishes had been shut down. Between January and March, church closures were "uncontrolled." Only a single church remained open in several regions. Many renovationist clergy succumbed to political pressure and renounced not only their ordination vows but also their belief in God. The only sign of hope in the report was a line on government announcements that collectivization and dekulakization would ease. This, the report said, should calm some "fallen clergy" and allow many of the unemployed to return to their parish duties. Indeed, by June, renovationists on the Volga felt an easing of political pressure. They told the synod of their renewed activity throughout the region, "thanks to state prohibitions on distortions in collectivization and the administrative closure of churches." Local officials tried to correct mistakes by returning parish buildings. The number of functioning churches in three cantons jumped from seventeen on April 1 to sixty by June 1.[24]

Reopening of parish churches that had been closed by extralegal means took place soon after publication of Stalin's "Dizzy with Success" article in *Pravda* on March 2, 1930. The Central Committee quickly engaged in political backtracking and ordered churches to be reopened. The NKVD informed state and party leaders that a halt in "the excessively rapid rate of collectivization of agriculture" coincided with a decrease in antireligious activity:

In the fall and winter of 1929, our analysis was filled with reports of large numbers of resolutions passed at general meetings of citizens to eliminate religious communities, close church buildings, and forbid the tolling of bells. Beginning in February and March of this year the situation has become exactly opposite. Reports from many places tell of middle peasants fleeing from the collective farms along with a serious movement to open churches, return bells that were taken down, and return clergy from exile. Up until this time a great many petitions came in to administrative departments requesting legal approval for the closure of churches. Now the flow of requests for opening churches and for permission to hold religious processions has increased.

In the Moscow region alone, 545 out of 696 closed churches were reopened by June 1930.[25]

If the Kazan diocese was typical of the whole synodal church in the winter of 1929–1930, renovationism suffered an enormous shock during the lawlessness that accompanied mass collectivization. True, the effects were ameliorated by the strategic withdrawal in the spring. Nonetheless, the synodal church did not have any social standing or purpose by the middle of 1930. Government officials had no use for its services and little concern for its welfare. So when the Holy Synod pleaded for the return of the Mother of God icon to its cathedral in Kazan, the VTsIK instead transferred it to the Main Administration for Science.[26] In late 1929, the synodal newspaper published its last article that referred to the social mission of the church in Soviet Russia[27] and Vvedenskii engaged in his last public debate.[28] Proponents of the new revolution in Soviet culture saw no place for churchmen, especially those who still believed in the possibility of linking communism and Christianity.

A Godless Decade

Red priests did not share the assessment that Christianity had no place in Soviet Russia, even in the "godless" 1930s. This is the most striking aspect of the movement that emerges from archival records. The limited information available for the period admittedly allows only an impressionistic picture rather than a detailed portrait.[29] Details now available show that during the 1930s, renovationists continued to profess unwavering loyalty to the political system and hostility toward the perceived reactionary politics of the patriarchal church. Leaders of the movement tried to maintain the allegiance of their clergy despite continued closures of parish churches and even the Holy Synod itself.

Renovationism's main problem in the 1930s was the public campaign against religion. That campaign pressed Soviet citizens to embrace atheism or at least stop expressing religious belief openly. After the party ended illegal church closures in 1930, Iaroslavskii and other leaders in the League of the Militant Godless demanded greater vigilance, atheistic education, and agitation to gain new members. The League's success in these areas varied, although the organization generally moved toward a concept of Soviet society that was nonreligious as opposed to antireligious. According to historian John Curtiss, committed atheists emphasized "attaining the economic and social goals of the [First Five-Year Plan], with the antireligious struggle relegated to a minor place." He notes that in the countryside, the push was for "freeing the peasants from a petty-bourgeois world outlook, of freeing them from all religion."[30]

Antireligious work was impeded in the 1930s by popular attitudes. The masses tired of confrontation between religion and atheism, especially when atheists continued to force the issue. Deprivations and famine accompanied breakneck collectivization and industrialization, raising fears about the future. Those fears were reflected in apocalyptic speeches of homeless monks and parishless priests, who were new martyrs in Orthodox eyes. Repression of the clergy also fed people's fears and contributed to religious extremism. On the whole, a large portion of the Russian population held to religious belief but moved farther away from traditional Orthodox practice.[31]

In the struggle for the allegiance of parishioners, the patriarchal church maintained the upper hand, thanks to both its aggressive attacks on the renovationists and state support for its leader, Metropolitan Sergii Stragorodskii. Even during the trauma of collectivization, Sergii's supporters expressed hostility toward the renovationist heresy. Sergii issued a decree in August 1929 stating that the only valid renovationist sacrament was baptism. Infants confirmed in the synodal church had to be re-chrismed (reanointed with holy oil), before being recognized as Orthodox by the patriarchal church. Sergii also permitted only limited recognition of marriage rites performed by renovationist clergy and imposed restrictions on funeral ceremonies for renovationist believers. The Holy Synod responded that Sergii had been guided by economic motives in issuing these rules. It pointed out that old-church clergy charged large fees for marriages and funerals and that Sergii had said nothing about the sacraments of repentance and communion, for which the laity paid nothing to priests.[32] A few months later, Sergii and his patriarchal synod clarified the rules for receiving clergy and laity back into the Orthodox Church. The new guidelines, adopted on April 10, 1930, stressed the need for those seeking admittance to have "a clear awareness of their sinfulness outside the church and sincerely repent of their sin by being in the schism."[33] In interviews with representatives of the foreign and Soviet press at this time, Sergii denied all allegations of government persecution of clergy or believers and linked such allegations with a Catholic plot to attack the Soviet Union.[34] In the midst of persecution, Tikhonites pressed their attack against the only enemy target they could safely engage, the renovationists.

The antireligious fervor connected with early collectivization soon eased, but Sergii and his synod continued to move against red priests. A new periodical, *Zhurnal Moskovskoi Patriarkhii* [Journal of the Moscow Patriarchate] published resolutions that said that clergy obedient to the renovationist Holy Synod had lost divine sanction and desecrated the sanctified objects they touched. For example, when asked about the possibility of conducting joint Tikhonite and renovationist liturgies in the same church and on the same altar, the patriarchal church expressed disapproval. An exception could be made in extreme circumstances, but even then the Tikhonites were told to insist on using a separate altar.[35]

The old-church hierarchy upheld the rule that renovationist ordinations were invalid and, through several contested cases, defined clear regulations for ensuring that former living churchmen were properly vetted before being readmitted into the "Orthodox" priesthood. Without exception, remarried parish clergy and married bishops were unacceptable. Two cases indicated the limits of Tikhonite toleration. In the first, a deacon who had twice abandoned renovationism for the old church was defrocked because his first repentance was judged "insincere." In another case, a Moscow church had accepted a former renovationist deacon on its parish staff after requiring that he confess to a local priest rather than to the diocesan bishop. This heretic had then defiled his church's altar by serving the Eucharist but was judged the least guilty of the parties involved. Sergii's synod considered the clergy of the parish, especially the senior priest, to be most guilty because they had violated canonical order. Those clergymen were forgiven because of "the lack of canonical consciousness and church discipline" at that time. The senior priest had to repent personally before Sergii and was warned that any similar defiance of canon law would result in his defrocking.[36]

Sergii's central church administration was aided in its fight against renovationism by preferential treatment from high government officials between 1931 and 1935. That preference possibly arose from the belief by party leaders (specifically Stalin) that Sergii's influence among the peasantry could help calm the feelings inflamed by collectivization.[37] The extent of this assistance is still unknown, but evidence that it existed is clear in church publications. The Holy Synod found it increasingly difficult to publish its periodical after 1928 and stopped producing it entirely after April 1931. This would not be surprising in light of the growth of antireligious sentiment during the First Five-Year Plan were it not for the fact that at this same time Sergii received permission to issue the *Zhurnal Moskovskoi Patriarkhii* (See Table 6.1).

Table 6.1. National Orthodox Publications, 1925–1935

	Renovationist *Vestnik Sv. Sinoda*		Patriarchal *Zhurnal Moskovskoi Patriarkhii*
YEAR	Number of issues	Average Press Run	Number of Issues
1925	4	4,000	—
1926	7	4,000	—
1927	7	4,000	—
1928	8	3,500	—
1929	5	3,000	—
1930	2	2,000	—
1931	3	2,000	6
1932	—		3
1933	—		3
1934	—		3
1935	—		1

Note: Neither faction published anything between 1936 and 1942.
Sources: Publication data from issues of the periodicals.

If party leaders backed Sergii over the Holy Synod, provincial officials expressed the opposite preference. They liked the unquestionably pro-Soviet—and therefore politically less troublesome—renovationist parishioners and not the Sergiites. This trend is evident in statistics compiled by the Central Standing Commission on Religious Questions after mid-1930 and the mass reopening of parish churches for both groups. At the beginning of 1931, the Commission counted 23,213 Tikhonite and 4,159 renovationist churches in the RSFSR. Over the next three years, 537 Tikhonite and only 2 renovationist churches were closed through a legal process that required VTsIK approval for decisions made by local officials.[38] These figures must be read carefully for two reasons. First, they reflect reports grudgingly submitted to the Commission by provincial officials, who resisted a full accounting of their handling of church matters. Second, the number of churches closed included only those cases where parishioners appealed decisions by local officials within fifteen days. Nonetheless, cases involving the closure of a parish church and its transfer to another group indicate that renovationists often had the upper hand. In twenty-three contested cases that came to the Commission's attention between 1930–1937, six were decided in the favor of the Tikhonites, four of them in 1930. In the remaining seventeen cases, the Commission or the VTsIK upheld the renovationists thirteen times, ordered a division of the church building three times, and (in one case) decided to close the church completely.[39]

Cases involving church closures and transfers can be placed in the larger pattern of the Standing Commission's deliberations. By late summer

Table 6.2. Cases of Church Closures Reviewed by the Central Standing Commission on Religious Questions, February–August 1931

Meeting Date	Total Cases Reviewed	Building Returned to Believers	Building Closed	Cases Undecided
February 6, 1931	42	37	5	—
April 6, 1931	17	14	3	—
April 16, 1931	45	15	24	6
June 16, 1931	61	21	38	2
July 26, 1931	19	1	18	—
August 6, 1931	10	0	10	—

Source: GARF, f. 5263, op. 1, d. 9, ll. 3–32.

of 1931, that body had stopped overruling provincial executive committee decisions on closing churches, and the number of cases it reviewed had declined significantly. The trend is evident in Table 6.2.

For two years, beginning in late 1932, state officials flirted once again with the idea of using renovationism against a perceived threat from Tikhonites. Arguments in favor of helping renovationist parishes resurfaced in the Standing Commission, although the reasons for returning to this old policy were not explained. The Commission may have believed that the patriarchal church was planning concerted action against both the government and its renovationist "allies." This charge appeared in the explanation by a local executive committee in the Crimean ASSR for its decision to restrict the activities of a bishop loyal to Metropolitan Sergii.[40] Soon afterward, the Commission received a secret report on "Religious Organizations, the Breeding Grounds for Counterrevolutionary Activity," which hinted at possible clerical influence over workers. The Commission responded with a motion to permit publication of the Holy Synod's periodical—a motion forwarded to "responsible organs," which apparently vetoed the idea.[41]

The synod did receive permission in late 1934 to print a brochure that outlined a plan for aggressively combating the old church. This new plan of attack borrowed tactics directly from renovationism's opponents in a clear example of isomorphism. The Holy Synod proclaimed its unwavering commitment to Orthodox canons, just as the Tikhonites did. It resolved to use such Tikhonite techniques as repentance and strict rules for recognizing the ordination of clergy who transferred into the renovationist church. Laity were warned that they endangered their souls by adhering to the old church in words identical with those of Tikhon's supporters a decade earlier. The synod even accepted a proposal to make diocesan bishops and their councils the central players in this renovationist counter-attack—thus placing the episcopacy in control. Strikingly absent from this brochure was any reference to political disloyalty by the old church. One suspects that the synod had decided that proclamations of solidarity with the Soviet regime were futile in gaining support from either the authorities or the Orthodox laity.[42]

Central authorities showed renewed interest in promoting renovationism by permitting the publication of this document. Local officials found ways to express a similar preference. During the spring 1933 campaign to issue internal passports to the population of Leningrad, a representative of the secret police instructed regional inspectors from the Standing Commission on new rules for clergy. Passport offices were prohibited from issuing documents to clergy; that duty belonged to a *troika* from the regional soviet. Passports would not be issued to men with degrees from theological seminaries or academies, to priests associated with the Josephite schism, or to conductors of church choirs (even if they were amateurs). Parish churches could have no more than two clergy, and chapels could have no more than one. And officials were ordered to treat Sergiite clergy "especially firmly" (*osobenno krepko*) and renovationists "gently" (*miako*).[43]

Even such covert assistance could not address the greatest difficulty in renovationist parish life—the lack of priests. Many parish churches were open in name only after 1929 because of this shortage of clergy. The Holy Synod recognized the problem of "fallen clergy" as early as 1929 and tried but could not develop methods for maintaining their loyalty. The most serious problem was clergy who defected to the patriarchal camp. Remarried priests and married bishops could not leave renovationism without loss of status. To preempt defections by those who had not broken traditional rules on marriage, the synod promoted clerical loyalty to renovationism with honorific titles and rapid promotions.[44] That practice led to an expansion in the number of bishoprics within the church and the rapid promotion of clergy into newly created sees.[45] In a related development, the Holy Synod chose a monastic bishop, Metropolitan Vitalii Vvedenskii of Tula, as its presiding bishop on the death of Metropolitan Veniamin Muratovskii in 1930. By purposely passing over the more zealous and scandalous Metropolitan Alexander Vvedenskii, the synod affirmed its commitment to avoiding controversy and the loss of clergy that might have resulted.[46]

Another vexing problem for synodal church leaders was whether to readmit those who had voluntarily given up holy orders either by renouncing their clerical rank or publicly denouncing faith in God. Some in the synod sought ways to accept clergy back in either case, while others argued for harsher treatment of those who denied Orthodoxy. Throughout the early 1930s, the Soviet government encouraged clergy to abandon their profession by publicizing stories of men with long careers in the priesthood who gave up the cloth. In a 1931 speech, Iaroslavskii announced that literally thousands of priests had voluntarily defrocked themselves.[47] Diocesan records show the extent of the shortage of clergy in the Holy Synod. Of the 137 parishes under renovationist control in Kazan diocese as of September 1, 1930, thirty-three (24 percent) had no priest. Reports submitted for the next year told of increases in parish clergy vacancies due to arrests, summons to forced labor, and fear of high taxes. By July 1931, only 115 of the 152 parishes in that diocese could offer regular liturgical services, although the situation remained stable through 1932.[48] Regional commissioners for religious affairs in Saratov province reported in late 1936 that renovationism had been completely discredited and the believing population had returned to the old church. They explained this phenomenon by saying that many renovationist priests had either voluntarily defrocked themselves or had been arrested.[49]

Synodal clergy voluntarily left the profession because of the legal restrictions and burdens placed on all clergy. During the First Five-Year Plan (1929–1932), their taxes increased an average of 32 percent. They also had to pay more for housing and the education of their children. In the mid-1930s, the tax rate on income earned by "servants of the cult" was approximately 500 percent higher than the tax rate for workers.[50] Parishioners also experienced the financial strain as they struggled to fund clerical salaries and various fees and taxes connected with the use of their church building. For example, Sovnarkom set electricity rates in Moscow and Leningrad at 30 kopecks per kilowatt-hour for factories, but churches had to pay 4 rubles per kilowatt-hour plus a 30 percent fine for excess usage.[51] Such exorbitant tariffs, combined with the general poor economic conditions for individuals in Soviet Russia during the First and Second Five-Year Plans, impoverished the clergy and encouraged their defection from the priesthood.

Although priests were often in economic distress, not all of them chose to pursue other careers. Nor did they blame the government for their woes. Renovationists in Kazan adopted a series of theses about the political path of their movement. They stated that while the church should stay out of politics, it still had a responsibility to judge the bases of social and political life using Christian teachings.[52] Similarly, newspaper and magazine articles told of Orthodox clergy who had accepted and promoted the changes of the 1930s. Renovationist and Tikhonite clergy alike argued that religion was in harmony with communism and upheld the policies of industrialization and collectivization. Such sentiments were surprising not because clergy looked favorably on socialist ideas (this was obvious when renovationism emerged in the early 1920s) but because of the anti-Soviet reaction in the villages to the policies in question. Some priests tried to purge their parish soviets of kulaks and replace these undesirable elements with workers or poorer peasants. Other clergy refused the sacraments to any peasant who did not join a collective farm. Still others backed governmental cultural and economic campaigns by helping to sell government bonds, urging tractor payments, or giving up church bells. Occasionally, a priest would take this to the extreme, as in the case of a crucifix adorned with a hammer, a sickle, and the slogan, "Workers of the world, unite."[53]

Efforts to combine Orthodox Christianity and communism became futile when Soviet society unraveled in the terror unleashed after the assassination of the Leningrad party boss Sergei Kirov on December 1, 1934. Churches, clergy, and lay activists were easy targets in the witch-hunt for enemies within the country. Although all Orthodox believers eventually experienced tremendous suffering during the Great Terror, red priests found temporary shelter in their sincere and consistent pro-Soviet stance.

After the assassination, Soviet society moved quickly to clamp down on even the limited freedoms that church organizations had enjoyed. This new campaign against the church was motivated less by ideology and more by the fear of denunciation for allowing enemies of the people to operate unhindered. In February 1935, the Central Standing Commission for Religious Affairs shut down the private printer that had produced church literature, including the *Zhurnal Moskovskoi Patriarkhii* and the Holy Synod's plan for attacking the old church.[54] Diocesan administrative bodies stopped functioning throughout the country. The Holy Synod "voluntarily" dissolved itself, and Metropolitan Vitalii took the title of Primate of Moscow and of All Orthodox Churches in the USSR. The synod defended its decision "to abandon the collective decision-making process in dioceses" by saying that that model of leadership was ineffective in fighting the old "monk-led" church. The Holy Synod also defended the diocesan episcopal model as canonical.[55] The political climate did not tolerate groups of churchmen, even those loyal to the government, to meet together and possibly plot against the state. To survive, renovationism dropped one of its core principles (conciliar decision-making) in light of Soviet society's new paranoia about religious meetings. Meanwhile, the Standing Commission—headed by Krasikov after Smidovich's death in 1934—protested to the Procurator of the USSR about the sudden surge of cases in which the laws about religious societies had been broken. Once again, administrative pressure was being used against believers as church buildings were closed without approval of local or central executive committees. Abuses cited by Krasikov included the imposition of punitive taxes on churches and unwarranted harassment of parish clergy.[56] This time, however, the Standing Commission's protests were completely ignored.

Fragmentary information on renovationism between 1935 and the Nazi invasion of the USSR in June 1941 paints a picture of steady decline. The Standing Commission made its last detailed description of the movement in a top-secret "Report on the State of Religious Organizations in the USSR, their Relation to the Proposed New Constitution, the Work of the Commission on Religious Affairs of the Central Executive Committee of the USSR, and the Practices of Implementing Legislation on Religious Cults (compiled from Religious Affairs Commission files for January 1 to September 1, 1936)." This 62-page document began with a summary of the "mistakes and administrative distortions" of government officials in the process of enforcing Soviet laws on religious organizations.[57] The biggest problem was that religious buildings (churches and chapels) continued to be closed in violation of proper procedures. Table 6.3 shows the results of those closures.

Table 6.3. Status of Religious Buildings in the USSR, April 1, 1936

	Buildings Open before 1917	Closed Legally	Not Closed	% Not Closed	Of Buildings Not Closed		
					Active	% Active	Inactive
RSFSR	39,530	20,318	19,212	48.6%	14,090	73.3%	5,122
Ukraine	12,380	7,341	4,487	36.2%	1,116	24.9%	3,371
Caucasus	3,965	3,310	655	16.5%	390	59.5%	265
Belorussia	2,183	1,706	477	21.9%	239	50.1%	238
Uzbekistan	15,905	9,193	5,712	35.9%	4,830	76.7%	882
USSR	73,963	41,868	30,543	41.3%	20,665	67.7%	9,878

Sources: GARF, f. 5263, op. 1, d. 32, l. 3. The figures for open buildings prior to 1917 do not include those in the areas of the former Russian empire that were not part of the USSR in 1936 (Poland, Finland, Lithuania, Latvia, Estonia). The 1936 totals did not include information from the Kazakh and Buriat ASSRs or the following regions (*oblasti*): Eastern Siberia, Cheliabinsk, Omsk, and Orenburg.

According to the report, only 28 percent of churches and chapels open before 1917 continued to serve an active religious role in 1936, although 41 percent of these buildings had never been legally closed. The Standing Commission attributed the dramatic rate of illegal church closures to local officials who did not see religion as a matter of political significance. According to those officials, "Everything has already been settled with religion. . . . We don't have to waste our time with it. . . . Only old men and women believe in religion any more." Therefore, local executive committees assigned all problems related to religious groups to the NKVD or Financial Department. These bodies, in turn, did not worry about working with the masses of believers and simply seized church buildings for grain storage or condemned them because of incomplete repairs. Parish churches were also closed when they refused to register clergy or because of the threat of "epidemics," that is, on the pretense of preventing the spread of disease by parishioners who gathered together for worship.[58]

Local officials illegally favored renovationists and used them to interfere in church affairs, according to the Standing Commission. Its report cited many examples of such favoritism arising from the "erroneous" assumption that the renovationists were the most loyal of the Orthodox factions. The Commission concluded, "There is actually no principle difference between the two groups." Nonetheless, it received numerous complaints from parishioners whose churches were transferred from old-church to renovationist control and subsequently closed with the help of the renovationists. The general pattern in these cases was that parishioners refused to recognize the "red, Soviet priests" or attend services conducted by them. When the parish could no longer meet its financial obligations, the renovationist priest turned over the keys for the building to local government officials, who then declared the church closed.[59]

Several examples of such behavior and its unexpected consequences were included in the Standing Commission's report. The presidium of the city soviet in Ivanovo defended the renovationists as "revolutionaries" in front of old-church representatives. In many areas of the country, only renovationist parishes remained open, a fact that gave the "oppressed" old-church clergy "a halo of sanctity" among believers and thus contributed to popular unrest. Such favoritism at the local level also fed the emergence of new, uncontrolled factions within Orthodoxy. In the village of Novaia Sotnia, a strange phenomenon had been observed in 1936, when a group of fifteen to twenty laypeople regularly visited parish churches there. These people gathered on the church grounds and entered the building only after the service began. They attended the services until the time for communion, and then organized their departure in order to show that the renovationist parishes lacked divine grace. This group used symbolic action to warn other Orthodox believers not to attend or support such parishes.[60]

During the growing political terror that followed on the heels of this report, information on the state of renovationism stopped flowing into the Standing Commission's files. Leaders of every Orthodox faction became targets for political repression. The Stalin Constitution of 1936 gave civil rights to the clergy, but Iaroslavskii led the charge to ensure that priests did not stand as candidates for elections to the soviets in 1937.[61] In May, a new party slogan was adopted: "Orthodox churchmen and sectarians are trying to poison our children with religion. Let's repulse the hostile attacks by churchmen and sectarians."[62] By the end of 1937, even Krasikov's expressions of concern about illegal closures of church buildings reflected the mood of the times. While he still opposed such actions because "sufficiently large numbers of workers are still religious," he also categorized religious organizations as sources of substantial anti-Soviet activity. He suggested that the government find ways to liquidate the leadership of parish groups who led such activity.[63] Krasikov's position was consistent with the movement among other government leaders at the time to revise or eliminate all existing legislation on religion. Georgii Malenkov told Stalin that the 1929 decision by the VTsIK and Sovnarkom on religious associations had given "legal protection to the most active portion of churchmen and sectarians to form a complex network of legal organizations hostile to the Soviet state." He proposed a solution that eliminated all ecclesiastical administrative bodies and banned the church's episcopate.[64]

That impatience with organized religion's resiliency manifested itself in a new drive by local authorities to close the functioning churches in their areas after 1937. While their parishes were being "finished off," believers seemingly accepted the new intolerance of religion; they suddenly stopped submitting petitions protesting church closures to the Standing Commission.[65] Meanwhile, the Commission tried to reregulate that process by proposing new legislation and suggesting that a quota of parish churches be set for every region in the country. Even the idea of very limited religious activity met with resistance in the context of political cannibalism. In 1938, the Standing Commission was disbanded, and control over religious organizations apparently fell totally into the hands of the secret police. The Standing Commission's proposed legal changes lingered on the agenda of policymakers for almost a year before the Orgburo finally torpedoed them in January 1939.[66]

Although news of renovationism at the local level between 1935 and 1941 is scarce, some information on the movement's fate in Kaluga and Leningrad is available.[67] By 1935, renovationism in Kaluga was a shadow of its former self. Only eight parishes remained out of the sixty-five reported eight years earlier (see Table 4.1). Four were located in the city of Kaluga; four others were scattered among the surrounding ten regions. These churches were served by an archbishop, six archpriests, one priest, and a deacon. Two additional clergy lived in the diocese but were not employed by any parish (*zashtatnye*).[68] Supporters of the patriarchal church exerted continuous pressure against renovationism. Believers asked about the differences between renovationism and the "old church." They wondered aloud, "Why do they say renovationists are red and lacking in divine grace and so forth?" Believers led by a monk disrupted renovationist church services with songs and advised parishioners to boycott renovationist sacraments. Old Believers joined in these attacks as they sought to gain control of a cathedral in Kaluga. Their priest reportedly held services in homes and in the cemetery that was ostensibly under renovationist control.[69]

Red priests in Kaluga defended themselves against these attacks by asserting their own canonical purity and questioning the Orthodoxy of their opposition. They based these claims on actions by the national councils of 1923 and 1925 that enlivened the church and liberated it from its errors. The old church did not really exist; it was only a group of disgruntled monks who refused to obey the decisions made by those "holy" councils. Those monks used "wild methods" against the true, renovated church. By their acts, those monks had destroyed Orthodox conciliarity and come close to heresy, thereby losing their claim to divine grace.[70]

Noticeably absent from the Kaluga files during these years is any attack on the political loyalty of the Tikhonites, although renovationist rhetoric otherwise echoed contemporary public discourse. Bishop Alexander Riabtsovskii wrote a plan for church work in Rybinsk for 1935 that was filled with the same self-criticism (*samokritika*) found in other parts of Soviet society. He included points on "responsibility . . . organizational work . . . mobilizing and deploying our forces in the battle with the opposing orientation." His plan stressed a classic Stalinist theme about the pivotal role of the preparation of cadres, which included the admission that "our cadres are extremely weak." The bishop also employed traditional Orthodox terminology. He spoke of the need for pastoral skills and greater spiritual knowledge in order to serve God in everything. Renovationist themes were obvious from the way Alexander stressed the importance of good sermons and the need for financial support for the diocese. Two months later, Bishop Nikolai Smirnov drew upon Alexander's ideas in a report on the state of renovationism in the town of Kaluga. Ironically, his appeal for greater unity and conciliar action came to naught after the diocesan administration followed the Holy Synod's example and dissolved itself on May 8, 1935.[71]

Renovationism in Leningrad after 1934 enjoyed a few years of official leniency, followed by a harsh crackdown. Mass expulsions of clergy from the city, the site of Kirov's assassination, began in March 1935. Leningrad officials began shutting down Orthodox parish churches in June. Between March 1931 and July 1937, sixty out of eighty-five Tikhonite churches were closed (71 percent). During the same period, 65 percent of renovationist churches were closed (seventeen out of twenty-six). However, 77 percent of Tikhonite clergy (265 out of 344) were expelled over those four years, as opposed to only 59 percent of their renovationist counterparts (62 out of 105).[72] At the height of the terror, differences in the treatment of the two groups by Leningrad officials vanished. Renovationist Metropolitan Nikolai Platonov left the city in September 1937 for a prolonged vacation, perhaps at the suggestion of the local state security officials. During his absence most of his clergy were arrested, and upon his return barely a dozen remained at liberty. In January 1938, Platonov renounced the church and began writing articles on atheism as a staff member at Leningrad's Museum for the History of Religion and Atheism (formerly Kazan Cathedral). By 1941, only two renovationist and thirteen Tikhonite churches remained open in the city and the surrounding region.[73]

A case from Moscow provides a glimpse into the process of terror against ordinary priests and lay activists. In September 1937, the secret police in Moscow arrested and interrogated a group of eight men on charges of intent to form an illegal underground church. Those arrested were both renovationists and Tikhonites, supposedly joined together by a common "reactionary" belief that both churches had "sold out" to Soviet power. The men were accused of plotting to organize a theological school that would prepare new priests to fight the Soviet government and establish a new church. Additional charges against individual members of this "conspiracy" included spreading rumors and supporting fascism. All were convicted under the political statute of Article 58. One of the supposed conspirators, Igor Drozhzhin, submitted a request for rehabilitation in 1955 in which he presented his account of that arrest. He explained that he had received theological education at the renovationist theological academy in Moscow in the 1920s and a graduate theological degree in 1929. From 1929–1932, he served as a priest in various Moscow churches. Arrested by the secret police for unspecified anti-Soviet activity in April 1932, Drozhzhin spent two years in a prison labor camp working on the White Sea-Baltic Canal and was released in 1934, a year before his sentence was completed. He claimed to have cut all ties with the church after this. In 1935–1937, he worked as a technical instructor in factories until his new arrest and subsequent imprisonment in the Gulag for ten years. Drozhzhin wrote in defense of his request for rehabilitation that he was convicted in 1932 only because he was a priest and in 1937 for being an active churchman as proven by the fact that he was a former priest. During his interrogation, his protests that he had severed all ties with the church after 1932 were ignored.[74]

Such was the fate of renovationism throughout Soviet Russia between 1937 and 1939. Many prominent renovationist leaders disappeared in 1937–1938; most were arrested and executed, including Alexander Boiarskii.[75] Metropolitans Alexander and Vitalii Vvedenskii remained free, although the former was criticized in the antireligious press for his amoral behavior and extravagant lifestyle. Writing in 1939, the atheistic publicist D. Diagilev lumped all churchmen together with counterrevolutionaries, Trotskyites, and Bukharinites. He pointedly included those who belonged to the renovationist movement in this broad assessment.[76]

Atheism had achieved a virtual monopoly in Soviet public life by 1940. Iaroslavskii congratulated atheistic activists in March 1941 on the success of their work. Petitions from Soviet citizens to open churches or organize new religious groups had become less frequent every day, he noted. And those who dared submit such requests acted as individuals—"kulaks, servants of cults, and former church activists"—not groups. In reality, this trend reflected fear of harsh reprisals by officials in the state security apparatus. The state encouraged written complaints to uncover wrongdoing by officials but clamped down on those who signed group petitions. Individuals acted alone out of fear of being labeled part of a conspiracy or an organized protest group.[77]

Nonetheless, a significant decline in active Orthodox parishes by 1940 provided a solid foundation for Iaroslavskii's praise of atheistic work. The combined total of active renovationist and Tikhonite churches in the USSR stood at 4,225 that year. That number included more than 3,000 in the country's western regions, newly acquired in 1939–1940.[78] In other words, only 1,200 Orthodox parishes—4.5 percent of the 26,800 reported in 1933—remained open. Vast stretches of the country were "churchless." In the RSFSR, no Orthodox churches functioned in twenty-five regions (*oblasti*); in twenty others, five or fewer parishes held services. In the official press, the idea of a "good Soviet priest" was dead.[79] Regrettably, the number of open Orthodox parishes cannot be broken down by affiliation with the renovationist or patriarchal churches. The percentage of functioning parishes within the USSR's pre-1939 boundaries that were loyal to renovationism may possibly have been significantly higher than in the early 1930s. Local authorities presumably continued to favor the pro-Soviet movement, despite official policy, and may have been more willing to allow renovationist churches to remain open. The absolute number of patriarchal parishes would still have been significantly higher due to the fact that all 3,000 additions in 1939–1940 were loyal to Metropolitan Sergii.

Last Rites

Ironically, the German invasion of the Soviet Union on June 22, 1941, and not the success of the Stalinist Revolution provided the final nail in renovationism's coffin. Sergii seized the initiative that very day by calling on all the faithful to rally to their country's defense. He soon began collecting funds for the war effort, ignoring the fact that his actions violated

Soviet law. The government responded by loosening restrictions on religious organizations and allowing church publications, more church services, and even the use of church buildings without proper registration. The national crisis overshadowed antireligious concerns, as did the fact that in the huge tracts of territory under German occupation, believers reopened churches by the thousands.[80] Leaders of other religious groups, including Alexander Vvedenskii, quickly followed Sergii's lead and organized their own efforts to aid in the country's defense. But Sergii had scored a coup by being the first national leader, political or religious, to speak on that Russian day of infamy.

Renovationism enjoyed a brief revival during the first two years of the war. Seven active bishops who had stayed out of Soviet prisons were joined by eight others; three who came out of retirement and five who were newly ordained. Alexander Vvedenskii took the reins of the church from Primate Vitalii Vvedenskii, who retired in August 1941.[81] Vitalii continued to serve in the renovationist hierarchy until March 1944, when he repented before Patriarch Aleksii Simanskii (r. 1945–1970) and was welcomed back into the patriarchal episcopate.[82] During the battle for Moscow in October 1941, leaders from both Orthodox factions were evacuated from the capital to the east and resettled temporarily in the town of Ulianovsk until 1943. At the urging of a general in the Ministry for State Security (MGB), Primate Alexander Vvedenskii placed newly ordained Bishop Sergii Larin in charge of the Moscow diocese.[83]

While in Ulianovsk, Vvedenskii worked to maintain the distinction between his church and the patriarchate. The primate realized that renovationism would never be the dominant trend within Russian Orthodoxy. He devised an alternate plan for becoming an ongoing movement like Old Believers, schismatics who broke with the patriarchal church in the middle of the seventeenth century.[84] In an effort to win backers among state officials and Soviet society as a whole, Vvedenskii pushed the renovationists to be more generous than the old churchmen in their support of the war effort. On Red Army Day in February 1943, he gave 500,000 rubles to the defense fund.[85] Days later, Metropolitan Sergii sent a letter to Stalin requesting permission for the patriarchal church to collect money that would be used for a tank column in honor of Prince Dmitrii Donskoi, the Muscovite leader who led the Russians in their first victory over the Mongols in 1370.[86] In dioceses across the Soviet Union, both Orthodox groups collected enormous sums of money for the nation's defense. In the Krasnodar region alone, patriarchal parishes gave 4.18 million rubles and renovationists 5.22 million as of July 1944.[87] Even in besieged Leningrad, the only functioning renovationist parish continued to receive special offerings for the army.[88]

In territory under German occupation, renovationists remained true to the Soviet government, in sharp contrast with the Tikhonites. Some supporters of the old church openly declared their disdain for Bolshevism and the Soviet system to the German officers in charge of religious affairs.[89] In the occupied Caucasus region, the German commandant of Piatigorsk prohibited the renovationists from engaging in religious services in August 1942 while granting such rights to the Tikhonites. The number of renovationist parishes in the Stavropol region dropped from eleven before the occupation on August 1, 1942, to only one during the six months of German rule. The number of Tikhonite churches for the same period climbed from 3 to 140. After the area was liberated, many parishes changed affiliation so that renovationists held fifty-one churches and those in the patriarchal camp dropped to ninety. Renovationists in the Orlov region suffered less discrimination from the Germans and were able to open ten parishes, compared to the eighty-six that were regained by the Tikhonites. A similar situation held in the Kalinin region, where renovationists increased their parish total from one to seven between 1941 and 1943, while the Tikhonites went from nine to forty churches during those same years of foreign occupation.[90]

The most active renovationists in occupied territory were found in the Krasnodar region, a longtime stronghold of the reform movement. In 1926, only 48 of the 501 functioning churches were loyal to the patriarchate; the rest were allied with the synod. Before the Germans arrived, four renovationist and three Tikhonite churches remained open. The occupation changed everything. Churches immediately began opening, and just as quickly the polemics between the two groups sharpened. Tikhonites denounced renovationists as pro-Soviet to German officials. Those officials ignored the charges and did not repress renovationism, although they relied mainly on the Tikhonite clergy for political support. Under the Nazis, the Tikhonites operated 100 parishes. The renovationists had ninety-two and a distinct advantage, because they had a bishop in the region who could ordain priests. After the liberation in the summer of 1943, the number of open churches in the region dropped to 143 because many clergy fled with the German army or lost the right to use public buildings.[91]

The Nazi invasion changed the regime's basis for political legitimacy, which forced a new alliance between communists and believers. The Bolshevik state was originally founded on ideological grounds and the promise of building a secular, socialist nation. After 1941, the Soviet government embraced "experiential legitimacy," which "stressed shared experiences rather than an ideological agenda—the state having led the nation, including its religious population, through the challenges of war."[92] The state found Sergii's ability to mobilize the majority of Orthodox believers within the Soviet Union useful in experiential legitimacy. Even open loyalty by renovationists in occupied territory could not sway the Soviet government to act in their favor.

Soviet government policy shifted from liquidating the church to controlling it from the center. Again, the patriarchate held greater promise for implementing that shift. By September 1943, a need for internal unity was supplemented by urgent foreign policy concerns. The Red Army wanted relief from the main brunt of the German forces, so Soviet political leaders searched for ways to speed the Western Allies' move for opening a second front in Europe. Stalin himself courted social and religious organizations in both the United States and Great Britain. He even engaged in personal correspondence with the Archbishop of Canterbury. British and American churches published special prayers on behalf of the Red Army and Russian people for use in church services. Anglican Church leaders requested permission to send a delegation to Moscow in the fall of 1943. Stalin approved this request on the eve of the Teheran Conference, which met in November and December 1943. The major problem, namely the need to have an official head of the Russian Orthodox Church to receive the Archbishop of York, was solved at the beginning of September.[93]

The famous meeting in September 1943 between Stalin and three senior metropolitans of the patriarchal church sealed the fate of renovationism. The schism itself was not discussed, but the new state policy in favor of the patriarchate was readily apparent. On September 3, Stalin met first with Malenkov and Lavrentii Beria, head of the secret police. They were joined by Georgii Karpov, a member of the state security apparatus who became the liaison between the government and Orthodox Church leaders for the next eighteen years. These men approved the creation of a Council for Russian Orthodox Church Affairs, which was headed by Karpov and was under the control of Sovnarkom.

That evening, Stalin and Karpov joined by Malenkov met with Metropolitans Sergii Stragorodskii, Aleksii Simanskii, and Nikolai Iarushevich to discuss the needs of the patriarchal church. Stalin referred to the numerous letters he had received from Soviet citizens, both believers and atheists, which had expressed positive opinions of church activities during the war. This, he indicated, was the reason he had called the meeting to discuss the needs of the hierarchs and their church. Nothing the bishops requested was refused them, although Stalin did not keep all his promises. They were given permission to hold an episcopal council to elect a new patriarch and synod, to open theological academies and seminaries, to publish a monthly journal, to organize candle factories and other enterprises, and to set up ecclesiastical executive bodies at both the region and local levels. When Sergii asked about the possibility of opening new churches in response to the many requests from clergy and laity, Stalin replied that the government would not oppose such actions. At the end of the meeting, the emboldened churchmen brought up the subject of imprisoned and exiled bishops and clergy. The General Secretary told them to present the information to Karpov in his capacity as the new head of the Council for Russian Orthodox Church Affairs.[94]

In effect, leaders in the Soviet government chose the patriarchal church to implement its new policy for regulating Orthodoxy. The war had placed an enormous strain on society; Orthodoxy provided many Soviet citizens with the means for coping with the stress that accompanied this national crisis. From the perspective of pragmatic politics, the patriarchal church was a better choice than renovationism for regulating the state's new religious program. Anthony Downs's analysis of the demise of organizations describes the death of renovationism. Downs writes that organizations ("bureaus") dissolve when they do not

> perform social functions of enough importance to make [its] members or clientele willing to sacrifice the resources necessary to maintain those functions. Such an inability can occur [when] . . . the functions remain important but some other organization performs them better. When the demise of a bureau . . . is caused by the capture of its functions by another organization, the bureau's members are sometimes transferred to the other organization.[95]

Such was the fate of renovationism; its commitment to Bolshevik ideals was less important than issues of practical politics. Red priests offered unconditional loyalty to Soviet ideals but could not rally the masses. The patriarchal church had broad popular support and showed unwavering patriotism during the war, at least in areas not under German occupation.

Advocates of renovationism immediately grasped the significance of their government's decision to allow the election of Sergii to be Patriarch of Moscow. Karpov assessed their reactions in a letter to Stalin and Molotov dated October 12, 1943. Some clergy and parishioners accepted their movement's lack of a future and had already begun to transfer to the Sergiite church. Other renovationists sought to preserve their organizational independence. Led by Alexander Vvedenskii, this group discussed the possibility of electing its own patriarch to maintain parity with the Sergiites. For his part, Patriarch Sergii refused to have any discussions with Vvedenskii but established conditions for receiving renovationist clergy into the patriarchal fold. Karpov closed with a proposal, to which Stalin and Molotov agreed:

> The renovationist movement earlier played a constructive role but in recent years has lost its significance and base of support. On this basis, and

taking into account the patriotic stance of the Sergiite church, the Council for Russian Orthodox Church Affairs has decided not to prevent the dissolution of the renovationist church and the transfer of renovationist clergy and parishes to the patriarchal, Sergiite church.[96]

Accordingly, Karpov sent secret instructions on October 16 to the heads of seventeen regions instructing them not to hinder the transfer of renovationist clergy, groups, and parishes to the patriarchate. He explicitly stated that the rules for such transfers had been established by Sergii and his diocesan bishops. From this memo, we can deduce that renovationist parishes were functioning at that time in Krasnodar, Ivanovo, Kalinin, Leningrad, Ulianovsk, Iaroslavl, Stavropol, Sverdlovsk, Moscow (city and province), Archangelsk, Tula, and five autonomous republics (Northern Ossetia, Kuban-Balkar, Chechen-Ingush, Dagestan, and Uzbek).[97]

The government's plans for a "merger" (*sliianie*) between renovationists and the patriarchate encountered opposition from both Orthodox camps and local authorities over the next three years. In October 1943 alone, three of the fifteen renovationist bishops petitioned the patriarchal synod for reception into its hierarchy. In two of these cases, Sergii raised questions about the actions and awareness of the renovationist leaders. The new patriarch made it clear that the basic sin of renovationism was not the loosening of marriage rules for clergy. Rather, it had taken corporate action against the holy church by luring away "lost sheep." Only after renovationist petitioners acknowledged that sin in word and deed could they be admitted into the ranks of the true Orthodox clergy.[98] The flow of clergy seeking admittance into the patriarchal ranks continued. Bishops Sergii Larin and Anatolii Sinitsyn were received in December as laymen because all their ordinations had been done by renovationist bishops. In both cases, the synod did not prohibit their future "Orthodox" ordination, and each man soon entered the patriarchal clergy. Within a year, Larin was the bishop of Odessa and Sinitsyn had become the senior archpriest in Alma-Ata. During the first half of 1944, all renovationist parish churches in Moscow except one came under patriarchal control. Seven other bishops, many clergy, and many parish churches (including the last one in Leningrad) reverted to the patriarchate. By August, Karpov reported that only 147 renovationist churches remained open in the USSR; 87 percent of them were located in two dioceses, Krasnodar (under Archbishop Vladimir Ivanov) and Stavropol (led by Metropolitan Vasilii Kozhin).[99]

This sudden influx forced Patriarch Sergii to devise a revised set of instructions that provided guidelines for accepting renovationist clergy and laity. Requirements that priests and bishops have valid ordinations and conduct acts of repentance were reaffirmed. They also had to renounce all renovationist honorific titles and promise to end all contact with the schismatics. However, the patriarch backed away from some of the harsher requirements of the earlier fight with renovationism. Repentance could be done in private under the direction of an Orthodox clergyman unless central church authorities decided that a public act was needed. Also, renovationist ordinations "performed by those not under a canonical cloud" would be recognized if the person so ordained repented before Easter 1944. The same deadline held for renovationist bishops ordained prior to April 1924, provided their consecration had been performed by at least one bishop having valid episcopal ordination prior to the schism. Such a cleric could even be taken back in episcopal rank if he either had not married or his wife had agreed to end the marriage and let him take monastic vows. Those "lacking the resolve" to end their noncanonical marriages were to be received only as parish clergy without any hope of entering the episcopacy. Similarly, parish clergy who married after ordination maintained their rank but lost the possibility of advancement within the priesthood provided they annulled their "illegal" marriages. Sergii did not, however, rescind the prohibition against remarried clergy. They could return to the patriarchal church only as laymen without any hope of church service except in the lowest clerical order of psalmist.[100]

This easing of rules by the patriarchate reflected the needs of both church and state. The patriarchal synod had full backing from the government and expected to emerge as the sole central authority for the Orthodox Church. So it could afford to show mercy. At the same time, the patriarchate faced a scarcity of clergy to staff reopened parishes and to run the dioceses. Sergii's bishops had problems finding priests for churches that had never closed. This shortage of clergy was compounded by the age and poor education of the candidates who were available.[101] The patriarchate saw properly supervised red priests as part of the solution to the problem of filling vacant posts. They would not agitate for a renovationist agenda, since most had long abandoned attempts to enact genuine church reforms. Vvedenskii himself commented in 1943 that the majority of clergy in the movement stayed because of their "family circumstances."[102] Soviet authorities desired to place loyal clergymen in patriarchal parishes and dioceses. Karpov's memo to Stalin in October 1943 specifically stated that renovationists should be absorbed into the Sergiite church.

Karpov became concerned when the initial rush to unite the two groups slowed by August 1944. He blamed Alexander Vvedenskii for opposing the government's decision and launched attacks on the primate's character in his reports to Stalin, Molotov, and Beria. Vvedenskii had tried several times to unite with the patriarchate, but both Patriarch Sergii and his successor Patriarch Aleksii refused to recognize his episcopal ordination because of his many marriages. Therefore, Vvedenskii began to work in opposition to the Soviet government's wishes—perhaps for the first time since 1917. He asked the Council for Russian Orthodox Church Affairs for permission to open new churches and appoint new bishops. When the Council refused, he tried to join forces with the Old Believers and Roman Catholics, to no avail. He even sought unsuccessfully to get his church placed under the jurisdiction of the new Sovnarkom body responsible for non-Orthodox religious bodies, the Council for Religious Cults. He compounded his failures with "provocative actions aimed at compromising the patriarchal Synod. He even expressed his dissatisfaction by saying, 'This is an escapade by the government' and 'this whole comedy is being staged for the West.'" In response, the Council for Russian Orthodox Church Affairs decided to speed up the process for liquidating renovationism. The main targets became the last two renovationist strongholds of Krasnodar and Stavropol.[103]

In reality, Vvedenskii was not the major obstacle to communist plans for the church. Despite state pressure and patriarchal incentives, some provincial renovationists fought to hold on to their parish churches. Six regions still had renovationist dioceses in March 1944 (Moscow, Rybinsk, Stavropol, Krasnodar, Irbit, and Arkhangelsk), and several others reported that scattered parishes were still resisting a merger with the patriarchate. The Council for Russian Orthodox Church Affairs acted directly to facilitate the transfer of isolated churches. In one such case, it decided that the only open Orthodox church in Vladimir, a renovationist parish, was not filling the religious needs of patriarchal believers. Similar decisions followed regarding parishes in Ordzhonikidze, Ivanov, Iaroslavl, and Molotov.[104]

A report on the status of Orthodoxy in the Udmurt ASSR showed the difficulties faced by a solitary renovationist parish. Officials from the republic told the Council for Russian Orthodox Church Affairs that only nine Orthodox parishes functioned there as of April 1944. The lone renovationist one was chastised for not engaging in any "patriotic work" (i.e., collecting funds for the war effort), and the parish priest explained that oversight as the result of his total lack of contact with his ecclesiastical superiors. The parish itself was healthy, serving over 1,500 parishioners in ten population centers. The same report praised the local patriarchal archbishop for his vigor in collecting funds for the army. By July, renovationist parishioners and their priest were ready to transfer allegiance to the patriarchate. The plaster interior of the church needed extensive repairs, and local authorities had threatened to halt services in the building until the work was completed. This appeared to have convinced all involved that they should switch allegiance to Patriarch Sergii.[105]

Not all isolated renovationists gave up so easily. The city soviet in Omsk reconsidered its decision to give a parish church to a group of

believers that were subsequently discovered to have renovationist leanings; it justified its change of heart by saying that the building was not in
good shape and was being used as a club. In Kazakhstan, a regional commissioner for the Council for Russian Orthodox Church Affairs reported
on renovationist clergy who were systematically and illegally conducting
religious ceremonies in private homes, in part because no renovationist
churches were open in Kazakhstan.[106] As late as July 1944, ninety-eight
renovationist parishes continued to function in the Ukraine, although a
move to unite them with the patriarchate was in the process.[107] On April 1,
1944, in eleven central regions (*oblasti*) of the RSFSR, 268 churches were
active under the patriarchal banner, compared to just 10 renovationist
ones. Three months later, the two groups had 300 and 9, respectively.[108]

In their two strongest dioceses, renovationists fought to maintain their
parishes even as the patriarchate and Council for Russian Orthodox
Church Affairs searched for ways to change their minds. Metropolitan
Vasilii Kozhin of Stavropol expressed the reasons he continued that struggle in a meeting with the Council's regional commissioner on January 17,
1944. In words intended for Karpov's ears, Kozhin said that he had dedicated twenty years to the cause of "eliminating Tikhonite reactionaries"
from the Orthodox Church. He added that under the Nazis, many Tikhonite parish councils had prayed for Hitler and later tried to cover their
acts with collections for the Red Army. Kozhin was personally insulted because Vvedenskii had not answered his letters or given instructions about
how to strengthen the movement in Stavropol. Nonetheless, the metropolitan could see nothing but harm coming from the old churchmen,
based on their previous opposition to collectivization and other policies of
the Soviet government.[109]

Under Kozhin's leadership, Stavropol remained a functioning renovationist diocese longer than any other, despite the continued loss of parishes
after September 1943. The fifty-one churches that recognized the metropolitan had dropped to forty-two by July 1944. Another twelve defected
shortly thereafter, helped by the willingness of local officials to expedite
their requests for a change in registration. Yet a few patriarchal parishes attempted to switch to Kozhin. When a village priest who was loyal to the
patriarchate ran off with the church's treasury, people were so unhappy
that they asked the renovationist metropolitan to send a replacement. In
another village, a parish that fired a mentally disturbed renovationist clergyman soon had two priests, one from each faction, competing for the va-
cancy. A third case revolved around Tikhonites who ran off a
renovationist priest, only to have their candidate chased off by pitchfork-
wielding opponents of the coup. In another village, a patriarchal priest

used deceptive and illegal methods to collect signatures for a petition to change the affiliation of a renovationist parish.[110]

Competition for parishes in Stavropol ended in February 1945, when Kozhin repented before the patriarchal synod and became an archpriest under the supervision of Archbishop Antonii Romanovskii, his former adversary. Kozhin relented after several meetings with Soviet officials. During a meeting on a train from Rostov, Kozhin reportedly responded to the transfer of his parishes to the patriachate by saying, "Of course I would not object, just as I would not have objected had I remained as leader of the patriarchal church in Stavropol. Renovationism's situation is unclear. I don't know what Vvedenskii is deciding about us. But if this will be in the interests of the government (that is, our transfer to the patriarchate), I am ready to do it today." By the end of 1944, Kozhin had begun negotiations with the patriarchal archbishop. Antonii promised Kozhin his choice of parish churches in the diocese or even the leadership of a diocese without a bishop. In January 1945, Kozhin sent a letter to Patriarch Aleksii explaining why he had become a renovationist. He attributed his actions to confusion over the canonical leadership in the church in the 1920s and even claimed that Patriarch Tikhon himself had advised Kozhin to remain in the movement for the sake of Orthodox unity in Stavropol. Kozhin indicated that neither he nor his wife of thirty-eight years had "compromised themselves in the eyes of social opinion," although she would live with their daughter after his return to the patriarchal church. Kozhin gave a different version of his actions to the regional commissioner of the Council for Russian Orthodox Church Affairs. He explained his letter to the patriarch as a necessity, not the truth. Kozhin's age, unwillingness to retire, and undying belief in Soviet power caused him to repent; he had not abandoned his renovationist ideals.[111]

The other two major renovationist dioceses also united with the patriarchate because of their ruling bishops. The strong renovationist contingent in Uzbekistan resisted patriarchal encroachment until their bishop, Sergii Larin, left for Moscow and submitted to the patriarch in 1944. They agreed to follow his lead under the condition that Patriarch Sergii continue to recognize Soviet power and allow their diocesan leaders to remain in place. The archbishop sent by Sergii to facilitate the transfer was sensitive to local concerns, so the process went smoothly.[112] By a similar route, eighty-one renovationist parishes in the Krasnodar region came under patriarchal control after the repentance and reordination of their archbishop, Vladimir Ivanov, on January 8, 1945.[113]

The patriarchate used more than pressure on bishops and appeals to self-interest to win over renovationist clergy. Old-church representatives in Krasnodar engaged in a campaign of personal correspondence with red priests. Archives of the Council for Russian Orthodox Church Affairs contain a letter from a Tikhonite priest, Daniel Gaidashev, to a renovationist named Fr. Alexander. Gaidashev complimented the renovationist priest for being "a good pastor of old, canonical ordination" and lamented the fact that the schism kept them from having cordial relations. Gaidashev urged Fr. Alexander to transfer to the patriarchate because it "will bring only good for you and your spiritual children." He ended by listing other renovationist clergy, friends of Fr. Alexander, who had already changed sides.[114] While the effectiveness of such personal contacts is difficult to judge, they convey a sense of pastoral care that was lacking in the machinations of bishops and politicians.

After the dioceses in Krasnodar and Stavropol transferred, St. Pimen's Church in Moscow became the sole remaining renovationist parish in the USSR. Vvedenskii's strong ties with the government and the security apparatus enabled him to control this parish until his death in July 1946. His position might have been strengthened by his considerable lay following, as evidenced by the throngs who attended Easter services at St. Pimen's. In 1945, approximately 8,000 participated in Pascal services, with young people comprising an estimated 40 percent of the total. Easter services in 1946 brought approximately 12,000 worshippers to that church.[115]

Supported by six clergy, which included two of his sons, Vvedenskii attempted to revive the movement. Several unemployed renovationist priests joined his efforts to rally believers in other parishes to their banner.[116] When that failed, he resumed his earlier quest for compromise with the patriarchate. He was shunned by those in attendance at the 1945 national church council that elected Aleksii as patriarch, and his first attempt to meet with Aleksii in June was blocked.[117] Aleksei Trushin, Moscow regional commissioner of the Council for Russian Orthodox Church Affairs, had a stormy meeting with the primate's alcoholic son, Aleksii Vvedenskii, on December 13, 1945. The drunken renovationist priest accused the patriarchate and the Council for Russian Orthodox Church Affairs of "interfering in our internal affairs and not giving us permission to restore our episcopate. If the primate should die, the Council will be most guilty and our parishioners will organize a demonstration so that everyone will know who harassed him. We will write a protest to Stalin and get our way."[118]

When even these threats were ignored, the elder Vvedenskii made another attempt to reconcile with Patriarch Aleksii by visiting his residence in March 1946. Aleksii refused to see Vvedenskii and hid in the garden. Vvedenskii caught a glimpse of the patriarch, followed him into the garden, and immediately presented his case. The renovationist metropolitan wanted to reunite with the church in his "present rank." The patriarch balked; not only was Vvedenskii's episcopal ordination invalid but he had also been married four times. Aleksii said that Vvedenskii might be received as an ordinary priest with the stipulation that he could never enter the altar area or serve the Eucharist. Vvedenskii asked if he could wear his miter and vestments, and Aleksii responded he could do so only at home or under other clothes. The patriarch fled into his house, leaving a stunned Vvedenskii to find his own way out.[119]

When Alexander Vvedenskii died on July 25, 1946, patriarchal loyalists immediately began to push for control of St. Pimen's Church. Both sides gathered signatures in support of their positions, but the government said that many collected by the prorenovationist faction were forged. The patriarchate succeeded in gaining the parish on October 12. When the new patriarchal clerical staff and believers took over the building, renovationist Metropolitan Filaret Iatsenko tried to block them. Trushin managed to prevent his interference. Shortly afterward, Ivan Popov, an unemployed renovationist priest working as a teacher in a school for the deaf, asked Trushin about the possibility of creating a new renovationist center at one of the unused churches in Moscow. Obviously, this was unacceptable to the Council for Russian Orthodox Church Affairs. In the first quarter of 1947, Trushin reported that six of the sixteen new priests received by the Moscow patriarchate were former renovationists. This number included the two sons of the late Primate Alexander Vvedenskii.[120]

Behind-the-scenes maneuvering by the Soviet government combined with renovationist acquiescence to the wishes of the state liquidated the visible Orthodox schism in 1946. Yet animosity between former renovationists and old churchmen remained. It had built up over a quarter of a century and could not be ended by fiat. Reports to the Council for Russian Orthodox Church Affairs for 1944–1946 include many examples of continuing hostility between the two groups even after they merged into a single organization. Bishops who had suffered under the Stalinist terror of the 1930s showed little mercy toward those whom they considered to have betrayed the faith. Clergy used the renovationist past of other priests against them. Laity opposed the appointment of former red priests to their parishes.

In Tambov, Bishop Luke Voino-Iasenetskii did not attempt to hide his contempt for former renovationists. Luke was both a monastic bishop and a famous surgeon who had received the Stalin Prize for his humanitarian work. His prominence provided some protection against reprisals. When he accepted a repentant renovationist into the patriarchal church in March 1944, Luke wrote his own rite for the occasion that called renovationism a "mortal sin" (*smertnyi grekh*) and praised Orthodox martyrs who were punished when they used violence against renovationists. At a meeting with a former renovationist priest, Luke rejected the argument that the patriarchal church had oppressed renovationism and said, "You renovationists felt expressions of the people's scorn, not oppression." He spoke of exiles, church closures, and transfers of parishes that had been instigated by renovationist clergy and also recited a personal example as proof that they were government agents. A renovationist priest had been expelled from his church. When parishioners searched the papers he left behind, they found a list of old-church clergy to be arrested; Bishop Luke's name was at the top of the list. Luke concluded that the majority of renovationist priests and bishops were filled with "cunning and lies" but admitted that a few individuals were highly principled. He mentioned Ioann Mirdov, the former renovationist metropolitan of Kirov, who was a socialist even before 1917. In Luke's words, "He [Ioann] finds that socialism and Christianity are compatible. He reads Lenin, Engels; he studies Karl Marx's *Capital*. I myself think it is impermissible to be interested in such things for long. It's better to study the Bible and the writings of the Fathers."[121]

Luke and like-minded patriarchal bishops did not limit their contempt for former renovationists to words. They actively sought to keep them from service in their dioceses. When priests asked Luke for parish appointments, the bishop granted only the requests of old-church clergy who had been arrested. During a trip to his former diocese in Tashkent, Luke refused to attend church services led by former renovationists. In Stavropol, Archbishop Antonii engaged in a struggle with Kozhin over control of the diocese and gave preferential treatment to clergy who had not been renovationist. Antonii replaced former renovationists with patriarchal priests in parishes in his diocese. Archbishop Manuil Lemeshevskii despised the former renovationist clergy in his new diocese in Chkalov region. He refused to give them permission to lead the Divine Liturgy and, in one case, even physically expelled an ex-renovationist priest from the altar.[122]

Parish clergy engaged in similar conflict that reflected the legacy of renovationist-Tikhonite struggle. In the Stalingrad region, a parish served by a priest from each camp was torn apart by their rivalry. Fr. A. P. Zaklinskii made allies with antirenovationist elements in the parish, while Fr. N. P. Popov claimed that Zaklinskii opposed his efforts to collect funds for patriotic work and the diocesan administration. The Council for Russian Orthodox Church Affairs commissioner in Tashkent attributed the continued antagonism between renovationist and Tikhonite clergy to disagreements over "income-producing parishes." Former renovationists could not obtain positions and wrote to their bishop with stories of impoverishment. In Kirgizia, the number of clergy who did not "remain pure from the sin of renovationism" was "miniscule" (in the words of an official from the Council for Russian Orthodox Church Affairs), and all churches had been closed before the war. Nonetheless, the few steadfast old-church clergy reportedly used their "sinless" status to rally believers against their new "colleagues."[123]

Ordinary Orthodox parishioners seemed to be the least forgiving of former red priests. They protested, for example, against the scandalous behavior of former renovationist bishop Dmitrii Lobanov, who became a parish priest in Kostroma after he repented before the patriarch in 1945. Lobanov's parishioners accused him of being drunk during the liturgy and keeping company with young women. He also supposedly headed a group of former renovationist clergy for the secret purpose of furthering the movement's ideals. In Tashkent, parishioners asked to have a single staff of clergy serve two churches in order to avoid having former renovationists as priests. Their requests were denied. These attacks may have contributed to one assessment by the Council for Russian Orthodox Church Affairs that former renovationist clergy continued in the pastorate due to age or lack of other options rather than out of great religious or ideological conviction.[124]

Anecdotal evidence from Soviet archives does not constitute proof that all patriarchal bishops, clergy, and parishioners displayed hostility toward all former renovationists. One must keep in mind that representatives of the Council for Russian Orthodox Church Affairs collected data that reflected the communist bias against religion. They focused on conflicts within Orthodoxy as a matter of course. Yet reports from the years 1922–1946 are unambiguous in showing the high level of antagonism between supporters and opponents of renovationism. Such acrimony would not have ended when the government forced the two groups to reunite.

Echoes of reactions to renovationism continue to be heard in the decades after 1946. In December 1950, the Council for Russian Orthodox Church Affairs burned 103 files of documents from the movement. These files had been delivered to its offices from Vvedenskii's apartment after his death. Karpov ordered their destruction without giving any reason for the act.[125] A letter to Communist Party chief Nikita Khrushchev from the end of 1956 showed that some still held the memory of Alexander Vvedenskii in high esteem. The letter recalled Vvedenskii's work of raising funds and morale during the war. It acknowledged that the late metropolitan "was a representative of religion; however, he did not preach blind and harmful faith but faith that teaches life and works for the good of the Motherland." The main point of the five people who wrote the letter was that Vvedenskii had left a widow and three young children behind who were in difficult financial straits ten years after his death. The signatories hoped that

Khrushchev would help the family as a gesture that the Soviet people would not forget the work of patriots such as Vvedenskii.[126]

Former renovationists never completely lost the stigmas of schism and heresy. For example, Andrei Rastorguev became a bishop in the movement in 1925 and rose to the rank of archbishop of Kaluga in the mid-1930s. He was convicted of tax fraud in either 1939 or 1941 (a common legal maneuver used against clergy by the Soviet government), was sent to a labor camp, and then was released soon after the war began. He returned to the renovationist episcopate in 1943 but shortly thereafter rejoined the patriarchal church. Because he was married, he lost his episcopal rank and was appointed as archpriest at Moscow's influential Sokolniki Church. In a conversation with Bishop Antonii on November 12, 1961, Rastorguev complained about the conduct of Archbishop Nikodim Rotov. The archpriest's comments were dismissed because "he had repented [of renovationism] but in spirit he had not changed and, therefore, he did not like Archbishop Nikodim and had a high opinion of himself."[127]

The controversial legacy of red priests continues long after the last of their comrades has died. A visit to Kalitnikov Cemetery in Moscow as recently as August 2000 found the grave of Alexander Vvedenskii, flanked by those of two of his sons, well-tended and decorated with flowers. People passing by stopped and showed respect for the metropolitan's memory by crossing themselves. Yet in a book on liturgical reform written over half a century after renovationism ended, Archpriest Nikolai Balashov notes that Russian Orthodox believers continue to associate "every change in [the church] . . . with 'renovationism,' that is, with schism, treachery, and betrayal."[128]

Red priests encountered hostility from every segment of society and watched their fortunes decline during a series of social upheavals that gripped Soviet Russia between 1929 and 1946. The failure of the renovationist vision for linking Orthodoxy and Soviet society became increasingly obvious as the movement declined after 1929. In the final analysis, neither believers nor secular policymakers accepted the idea of a Soviet Orthodox Church. Collectivization and the accompanying antireligious drive of the Stalinist Cultural Revolution disrupted renovationist parish life. A brief period of stabilization was soon followed by the Great Terror of the late 1930s, which decimated organized religion through waves of arrests and property seizures. Renovationist devotion to political loyalty and obedience was valuable to Soviet officials throughout the 1930s as they systematically closed churches while seeking to avoid violent protests by believers. In the end, however, the dynamics of terror allowed little distinction between red priests and clergy who were loyal to the memory of the late Patriarch Tikhon.

World War II opened unexpected possibilities for reviving organized religion in Soviet Russia. The great national crisis provided opportunities for all Orthodox believers to prove their loyalty and devotion to the Soviet state. Supporters of the patriarchal church had an advantage over renovationists: they combined political loyalty with an ability to rally the masses around Orthodox traditions of defending holy Russia. At the same time, isomorphic pressure transformed the government's ideal for a loyal church. The state applied its standard Stalinist organizational model to Orthodoxy. A unified, centralized, and hierarchical organization under close state supervision replaced fragmented and hostile Orthodox groups in September 1943. Independent renovationism became extraneous, and state officials facilitated the patriarchate's absorption of renovationist parishes and clergy by 1946, although differences between the two groups over Orthodoxy's place in Soviet society fed animosity for decades afterward. At its end, as at its beginning, the fate of Orthodox reformation was decided by state action.

CONCLUSION

RED PRIESTS SAW no inherent contradiction between radical socialism and Christianity. They consistently hoped to fuse the two, even during social upheaval, terror, and war. This attitude separated them from most Orthodox believers, lay or clergy, and caused them to be caught in the whirlwind of Russian revolutionary politics. The history of their movement reflects the complexities of a society that experienced a rapid succession of convulsions in the first half of the twentieth century. The story of red priests is therefore also complex. It is filled with tension between ideals and pragmatism, loyalty and betrayal, love and hatred, accommodation and manipulation.

The movement arose out of a drive for ecclesiastical reform at the end of the imperial era and grew into a cause for sweeping changes in the structure and purpose of the church. The earliest renovationists merged reform, revolutionary ideology, and Orthodox traditions. Russia's major political crises—the revolutions of 1905, February 1917, and October 1917—inspired attempts to involve the Russian Orthodox Church more closely with broad changes in society. These early attempts were all unsuccessful, but failure did not weaken the resolve of true believers for the cause of revolutionary Christian socialism. Their dedication to a vision for remaking the church grew as they awaited their next opportunity.

Determined that the Bolshevik Revolution would not bypass the church, a small group of champions of church reform took advantage of the opening offered by political crisis and famine in 1921–1922. They eagerly formed a secret alliance with the Bolsheviks to form the Living Church, which would be an alternative to the church headed by Patriarch Tikhon. Although they would soon be called heretics, traitors, and puppets of the Communists, founders of the Living Church acted out of a sincere belief that Orthodoxy was dying and could only be revived by linking the church with Bolshevik goals for Russian society. They readily accepted government help in a crusade to save their church from the dustbin of history. On alert for every opportunity, they boldly seized control of the church's central apparatus in May 1922, when Tikhon unexpectedly abdicated the patriarchate.

Zealous renovationists first tried to force dioceses and parishes to accept a radical program for religious change. The movement attracted support from parish clergy across Soviet Russia, thanks to proposals promising financial and administrative independence from both parishioners and bishops. The Living Church began imitating the successful Bolshevik Party by organizing parish clergy into a vanguard for church revolution. Revolutionary rhetoric and tactics became tightly linked. Living Churchmen formed "cells" in every diocese, and the national organization commissioned local plenipotentiaries to direct the work of renovating the church. Bishops and clergy who refused to acknowledge the authority of the new central ecclesiastical authorities were arrested or exiled by the local police.

Such tactics fit Bolshevik plans perfectly. The party wanted to neutralize any threat of organized counterrevolution from the Tikhonite church through a wholesale purge of the episcopacy. Bolshevik goals in fomenting church revolution also had an international component. The Politburo had deep concerns about a conspiracy between domestic Orthodox leaders and the actively hostile émigré church community. Renovationism promised to sever connections with the Russian Orthodox Church abroad. In abetting renovationism, the government showed that its first priority was pragmatic policy (disrupting the organizational unity of the Russian Orthodox Church) and not ideology (the mass conversion of believers into atheists).

Government cooperation led the renovationists to imagine that their goal of Bolshevik Christianity was attainable. They were wrong. Soviet leaders could never accept the formation of a new state church, and Orthodox believers rejected the very idea of red priests. The Communist Party's Antireligious Commission (ARK) assumed de facto control of Orthodox affairs in order to oversee the destruction of Tikhonite church leaders and to control internal divisions in the reformist camp that threatened to destroy the movement. ARK struggled, however, with local officials who formed alliances with renovationists and permitted them to act like a state church. Meanwhile, the overwhelming majority of laity still loyal to traditional Orthodoxy had no interest in either religious or cultural reformation; for them, renovationism was merely a Bolshevik-backed ploy for destroying the church from within.

Prospects for renovationist supremacy peaked at the national church council of May 1923. By that time, the party worried less about playing competing reformist groups against each other and more about furthering its main objective of destroying the Tikhonite church. Disorganization among Patriarch Tikhon's supporters rendered them nearly powerless, and the renovationists claimed control over nearly 70 percent of Orthodox parishes in the RSFSR. The national church council was a great success for renovationism and its state patrons. Controlled by the renovationists and influenced by the secret police, this council defrocked Tikhon and condemned his anti-Soviet policies for leading the church to the brink of ruin. Concurrently, it passed a limited church reform program aimed at balancing political demands of the state, social demands of the clergy, and religious demands of the peasantry. To these ends, the council proclaimed loyalty to the socialist revolution and the Bolshevik government. It adopted measures allowing the remarriage of priests and the ordination of married bishops. But it rejected radical church reform in favor of moderate changes that promised gradual adaptation to Soviet society, such as adopting the Gregorian calendar, allowing the liturgy to be chanted in the vernacular, and abolishing the patriarchate.

Accommodating renovationism to the Bolshevik state proved impossible after the church council ended. The state reassessed its position in light of potential threats from a strong reformed church and the international community that rallied around the imprisoned Patriarch Tikhon. Most important, the Bolsheviks never wanted either a unified or a state church, so they acted to curb growing renovationist power by freeing Tikhon from prison. The government discarded its earlier goal of the church's immediate destruction; instead, it pursued a divide-and-conquer strategy designed as a prophylactic measure to reduce Orthodox influence on Soviet society. State strategy was strengthened by popular reaction to renovationism. Even the limited changes advanced by the national church council proved too radical for the masses who defended Orthodox traditionalism and too tame for those already alienated from the church. Patriarch Tikhon became the rallying point for the defenders of quotidian Orthodoxy. Educated, socially ambitious Russians found little of appeal in Orthodox ideas, whether traditional or revolutionary. They abandoned the church in droves and joined the ranks of sectarians or the nominally nonreligious. Clergy generally preferred the renovationist approach but needed financial backing from the antireform laity to live. Many priests chose to ally themselves once again with the patriarchate, thereby accepting the Soviet assertion that religion and government must be separate.

Despite these setbacks, renovationists held to their guiding principle of combining Bolshevik and Orthodox truth. Enough support from clergy and government officials remained to allow the movement to continue until 1946. Renovationists responded to changes in their environment by gradually sacrificing reformist ideas to keep their organization alive. Survival hinged on balancing genuine political loyalty to the government with appeasement of Orthodox parishes by abandoning most church reforms. A more traditional ecclesiastical structure headed by a Holy Synod replaced the Bolshevik Party model. Reformers stopped insisting on adoption of the civil calendar and changes in the liturgy. Factional leaders who refused to accept the new order were expelled. At the diocesan level, collegial administrative bodies took the power formerly held by the much-feared Living Church plenipotentiaries. Yet appeasement proved to be a policy with limited appeal. Orthodox traditionalism could not attract those who had already abandoned the church, and limited renovationist reforms could not allay suspicions that red priests had sold out their faith to the godless Communists.

These developments pleased the government authorities in charge of church policy and proved useful to them during the religious NEP of 1923–1928. The party's highest organs entrusted Orthodox Church policy entirely to the Antireligious Commission, which manipulated Orthodox factionalism to consume the church's energies. Whenever Tikhon resisted government pressure to implement its will, state officials brandished the renovationist threat. The NEP era also witnessed the growth of "godless religion" based on revolutionary heroes and ethics. Renovationism could not compete with this new faith in the Soviet system that was so popular among the active younger elements of Russian society.

Government concessions—given in return for unswerving loyalty to the new Soviet order—played an important part in keeping the renovationist movement alive. Between 1922 and 1928, the state permitted the renovationists to conduct theological education, publish periodicals and brochures, hold regional and national gatherings, and speak in public. It also gave them control over most of the large urban cemeteries, the income from which kept the church financially solvent after the laity stopped paying renovationist clergy to conduct other liturgical services. Renovationists used the opportunities afforded them to attempt to enhance their legitimacy among believers. They trumpeted their connections with the Orthodox churches outside Russia in general and the Ecumenical Patriarch of Constantinople in particular. In the mid-1920s, the renovationist Holy Synod also supported the state's attacks on growing sectarian movements in the Soviet Union.

Still, renovationism remained the sickly child of Orthodoxy. Popular support dropped so much that by 1929 the Holy Synod controlled only 15 percent of Orthodox parishes in the country. As the Stalinist revolution gathered steam in the late 1920s, the range of activities permitted to the renovationists shrank. The number of publications declined rapidly, and the contents of those that remained were circumscribed. Other forms of contact with the general public were similarly curtailed. Renovationists were not happy with this turn of events and continued to hope for a strengthening of their position vis-à-vis Soviet society. They still envisioned a synthesis of Bolshevik and Christian ideas, united by the common goal of building a just society. The Bolsheviks, however, would not abandon their struggle against the "religious remnants of class-ridden society." Red clergymen dared not object too strenuously to the new restrictions for fear of seeming disloyal to the revolution. Although organized renovationism never relinquished its hope for ideological compromise between the church and state, many of its clergy succumbed to public pressure. They voluntarily defrocked themselves and renounced religion in a search for social acceptance and security. Simultaneously, by having condemned all renovationist ideas for reform and modernization, the patriarchal church remained impotent when confronted with the Bolshevik vision of a Communist, industrial utopia.

During the chaotic 1930s, the utility of promoting renovationist and other schisms as weapons in the government's ideological battle against the Orthodox faith diminished. The state effectively limited the church's influence within society through strict enforcement of the laws prohibiting public religious activity. Internally divided, the church could not organize an effective counterresponse. In effect, Orthodox believers found themselves trapped within their parish churches, outside which all religious activity was forbidden and inside which only purely cultic functions were allowed. Chaos followed collectivization, industrialization, and, finally, the political cannibalism that drove the Great Terror. Parish churches and clergy—even red priests—were easy pickings for authorities eager to prove their devotion to Stalinism.

Those who remained faithful to renovationist Orthodoxy tried to hold on to state support in the 1930s by assisting in the closing of patriarchal churches, which they still saw as the home base of the enemy. The Holy Synod stayed alert to shifting political winds. It once again imitated changes in its political environment in 1935 by abolishing itself after electing a "primate" to head the church. Even such deliberate acts of isomorphism did not enable renovationist clergy to avoid the terror of the late 1930s. Priests and lay activists of all religious persuasions stood out as obvious targets in a society obsessed with social conformity and rooting out "enemies of the people." This period brought wholesale closure of churches and arrests of clergy; few distinctions were made about which side of the renovationist/Tikhonite split they belonged to.

World War II completely changed state policy toward Orthodoxy. By the end of the war, the Russian Orthodox Church had been sovietized, and renovationism as an independent movement had ended. The Nazi invasion in 1941 provided Orthodox believers in both camps an opening to prove their loyalty and usefulness to the government. Metropolitan Sergii Stragorodskii acted quickly by calling on the Orthodox people to defend their motherland. He also began church-wide collections to be used in the national defense. Renovationists matched Sergii's moves with their own collections and proclamations. In some German-occupied areas, renovationist parishes reactivated in greater numbers than patriarchal ones, and conflict between the two groups flared up once again. Renovationists stayed loyal to the USSR even under occupation, and their Orthodox opponents denounced their pro-Soviet stance to the Germans. Reports of such activities did not sway the Soviet government's resolve to end the Orthodox schism in favor of the patriarchate. The writing on the wall was clear; government policy had turned toward a unified Orthodox Church headed by a loyal, compliant patriarch. Some renovationists struggled in vain for independence but in the end found this was not an option. The patriarchal church absorbed the remaining reformers, and decades-old hostility between old churchmen and red priests became part of the unified organization's internal life.

Renovationism's failure to merge Orthodox Christianity with a political system based on materialism and militant atheism should surprise no one. After all, the Bolsheviks intended to eliminate all religious symbols and practices from Soviet life. Party functionaries manipulated church reformers to increase conflicts within Orthodoxy while claiming to uphold the legal fiction of separation between church and state. The tenacity that renovationists displayed in defending their seemingly hopeless cause is surprising. They wanted to make their church the handmaiden of the Bolshevik state and refused to see their church as an organization with interests separate from those of that state. Red priests lived out their belief that modernity in politics and religion were inseparable.

Ironically, policies promoted by government leaders and red priests alike inspired the very type of religious devotion that both groups decried as backward, reactionary, and superstitious. By disowning traditional Orthodox beliefs in monasteries, relics, icons, and the liturgy—the very things that provided experiences of divine immanence—renovationists lost contact with ordinary believers who wanted those experiences. When renovationists rejected those expressions of devotion, they became permanently alienated from the Orthodox population whose support was vital for their survival.

The consequences of renovationism's failure have haunted the Russian Orthodox Church since 1946 in more ways than continued opposition to reform. Once they acquiesced to state control and rejected all programs for modernization, Russian Orthodox believers lost their ability to influence Soviet society. Russian society experienced a decisive break with its

Christian history and culture. The organized church could not resolve its most basic problem—defining its place and purpose in modern Russia. The failure of reform alienated ordinary Orthodox believers and reduced the importance of religious values in Soviet society. Believers continue to revile renovationism and, by extension, all proposals for reconciling Orthodoxy with post-Communist society and the modern world.

NOTES

Preface

1. Leading works on neoinstitutionalism are Walter W. Powell and Paul J. DiMaggio, eds., *The New Institutionalism in Organizational Analysis* (Chicago: University of Chicago Press, 1994), and W. Richard Scott and John W. Meyer and Associates, *Institutional Environments and Organizations: Structural Complexity and Individualism* (Thousand Oaks, Calif.: SAGE, 1994). A comprehensive overview of organizational theory is found in W. Richard Scott, *Organizations: Rational, Natural and Open Systems*, 4th ed. (Upper Saddle River, N.J.: Prentice Hall, 1998).

2. See Mark Chaves, *Ordaining Women: Culture and Conflict in Religious Organizations* (Cambridge, Mass., and London: Harvard University Press, 1997), and N. J. Demerath III et al., eds., *Sacred Companies: Organizational Aspects of Religion and Religious Aspects of Organizations* (Oxford: Oxford University Press, 1998).

3. The explanations of isomorphism and decoupling that follow are based on Scott and Meyer, *Institutional Environments*, 2–3.

4. Victoria Alexander, "Environmental Constraints and Organizational Strategies: Complexity, Conflict, and Coping in the Nonprofit Sector," in Walter W. Powell and Elisabeth Clemens, eds., *Private Action and the Public Good* (New Haven: Yale University Press, 1998).

5. Bishop Sergii (Larin), *Obnovlencheskii raskol*, 2 vols. (St. Petersburg Theological Academy Library, typescript, 1953–1959), 1: 1–4; and A. I. Kuznetsov, *Obnovlencheskii raskol v Russkoi Tserkvi*, 3 vols. (St. Petersburg Theological Academy Library, typescript, 1956–1959). Copies of both typewritten manuscripts are located in the libraries of the Moscow and St. Petersburg Theological Academies of the Russian Orthodox Church. See also A. A. Shishkin, *Sushchnost' i kriticheskaia otsenka "obnovlencheskogo" raskola russkoi pravoslavnoi tserkvi* (Kazan: Kazan University Press, 1970), A. Levitin and V. Shavrov, *Ocherki po istorii russkoi tserkovnoi smuti*, 3 vols. (Switzerland: Institut Glaube in der 2. Welt, 1977), A. Ch. Kozarzhevskii, "A. I. Vvedenskii i obnovlencheskii raskol v Moskve," *Vestnik Moskovskogo Universiteta, seriia 8*, no. 1 (1989): 54–66, Philip Walters, "The Renovationist Coup: Personalities and Programmes," in *Church, Nation and State in Russia and Ukraine*, edited by Geoffrey A. Hosking (London: Macmillan, in association with the School of Slavonic and East European Studies, University of London, 1991), 250–270, and M. V. Shkarovskii, *Obnovlencheskoe dvizhenie v Russkoi Pravoslavnoi Tserkvi XX veka* (Nestor: St. Petersburg, 1999).

1. The Path to Church Revolution

1. Gregory L. Freeze, "Rechristianization of Russia: The Church and Popular Religion, 1750–1850," *Studia Slavica Finlandensia* 7 (1990): 101–136.

2. Gregory L. Freeze, "Counter-reformation in Russian Orthodoxy: Popular Response to Religious Innovation, 1922–1925," *Slavic Review* 54, no. 2 (Summer 1995): 305–306.

3. Gregory L. Freeze, "Handmaiden of the State? The Church in Imperial Russia Reconsidered," *Journal of Ecclesiastical History* 36 (January 1985): 84–90.

4. See Freeze, "Handmaiden," J. H. M. Geekie, "Church and Politics in Russia, 1905–1917: A Study of the Political Behaviour of the Russian Orthodox Clergy in the Reign of Nicholas II" (Ph.D. dissertation, University of East Anglia, 1978), and Simon Dixon, "The Church's Social Role in St. Petersburg, 1880–1914," in *Church, Nation and State in Russia and Ukraine,* edited by Geoffrey A. Hosking (London: Macmillan, in association with the School of Slavonic and East European Studies, University of London, 1991), 167–192.

5. See B. V. Titlinov, *Pravitel'stvo imperatritsy Anny Ioannovny v ego otnosheniiakh k delam pravoslavnoi tserkvi* (Vilna: Tip Russkii pochin, 1905), and P. N. Miliukov, *Ocherki po istorii russkoi kul'tury,* 4 vols. (St. Petersburg: Tip. I. N. Skorokhodova, 1904–1909).

6. The concept of sovereignty and its role in organizational theory is found in Anthony Downs, *Inside Bureaucracy* (Boston: Little, Brown and Company, 1967), 44–46, and Peter B. Clark and James Q. Wilson, "Incentive Systems: A Theory of Organizations," *Administrative Science Quarterly* 6 (September 1961): 158.

7. B. V. Titlinov, *Tserkov' vo vremia revoliutsii* (Petrograd: Byloe, 1923), 3–7.

8. The state of the church at the end of the nineteenth century is summarized in Gregory Freeze, *The Parish Clergy in Nineteenth-Century Russia* (Princeton, N.J.: Princeton University Press, 1983), 450–466. See also John S. Curtiss, *Church and State in Russia: The Last Years of the Empire, 1900–1917* (New York: Columbia University Press, 1940), chaps. 5–6.

9. Quoted in F. Aurelio Palmieri, "The Russian Church and the Revolution," *Catholic World* 106 (February 1918): 661.

10. Freeze, "Handmaiden," 95–97.

11. Freeze, *Parish Clergy,* 458, 467.

12. Metropolitan Evlogii (Georgievskii), *Put' moei zhizni* (Paris: YMCA, 1947), 161–170; Freeze, "Handmaiden," 100. For analyses of the episcopal agenda, see John Meyendorff, "Russian Bishops and Church Reform in 1905," in *Russian Orthodoxy under the Old Regime,* edited by R. Nichols and T. Stavrou (Minneapolis: University of Minnesota Press, 1978), 170–182, and Gerhard Simon, "Church, State and Society," in *Russia Enters the Twentieth Century: 1894–1917,* edited by E. Oberlander et al. (London: Temple Smith, 1971), 199–235.

13. This process is described in Gregory L. Freeze, *The Russian Levites: Parish Clergy in the Eighteenth Century* (Cambridge, Mass.: Harvard University Press, 1977).

14. A vivid portrait of these difficulties is found in I. S. Belliustin, *Description of the Parish Clergy in Rural Russia: The Memoir of a Nineteenth-Century Parish Priest,* translated by and with an introductory essay by Gregory Freeze (Ithaca, N.Y.: Cornell University Press, 1985).

15. James W. Cunningham, *A Vanquished Hope: The Movement for Church Renewal in Russia, 1905–1906* (Crestwood, N.Y.: St. Vladimir's Seminary Press, 1981), 106.

16. Dixon, "The Church's Social Role," 167–169.

17. Paul R. Valliere, "Theological Liberalism and Church Reform in Imperial Russia," in Hosking, *Church, Nation and State,* 108.

18. Gregory L. Freeze, *The Parish Clergy in Nineteenth-Century Russia: Crisis, Reform, Counter-Reform* (Princeton, N.J.: Princeton University Press, 1983), 423.

19. A. Levitin and V. Shavrov, *Ocherki po istorii russkoi tserkovnoi smuti,* 3 vols. (Switzerland: Institut Glaube in der 2. Welt, 1977), 1: 4.

20. A detailed analysis of these responses is found in Cunningham, *A Vanquished Hope,* 134–204.

21. Granovskii's biography is found in Levitin and Shavrov, *Ocherki,* 1: 17–24.

22. Gruppa Peterburgskikh sviashchennikov, *K tserkovnomu soboru* (St. Petersburg, 1906).

23. Dimitry Pospielovsky, *The Russian Church and the Soviet Regime, 1917–1982,* 2 vols. (Crestwood, N.Y.: St. Vladimir's Seminary Press, 1984), 1: 47.

24. For a description of those protests, see Geekie, "Church and Politics," 285–287.

25. Quoted in Freeze, *Parish Clergy*, 471.

26. Quoted in Pospielovsky, *The Russian Church*, 1: 48–49.

27. See Abraham Ascher, *The Revolution of 1905: Russia in Disarray* (Stanford, Calif.: Stanford University Press, 1988).

28. Dixon, "The Church's Social Role," 212–213.

29. An agent is someone who is "capable of exerting some degree of control over the social relations in which one is enmeshed, which in turn implies the ability to transform those social relations to some degree." See William H. Sewell Jr., "A Theory of Structure: Duality, Agency, and Transformation," *American Journal of Sociology* 98 (1992): 21.

30. The Constitutional Democratic Party, known as the Kadets because of the initials of the party's name, was a party of liberal monarchists and republicans that was active between 1905 and 1917. The biographical notes on Vvedenskii are from Levitin and Shavrov, *Ocherki*, 1: 7–14.

31. In this period of Russian cultural revival, known as the Silver Age, ideas about religion, politics, and human progress were debated in the salons of St. Petersburg. That debate culminated in *Vekhi* [Signposts], a book that tied Russia's political liberation to its spiritual and cultural rebirth. For an overview of intellectual ferment in this period, see Donald W. Treadgold, *The West in Russia and China*, vol. 1: *Russia: 1472–1917* (Cambridge: Cambridge University Press, 1973; reprint, Boulder, Colo.: Westview Press, 1985), 223–239.

32. A. Ch. Kozarzhevskii, "A. I. Vvedenskii i obnovlencheskii raskol v Moskve," *Vestnik Moskovskogo Universiteta, seriia 8*, no. 1 (1989): 56.

33. While a student at the academy, he changed his surname from Segeniuk to the more elegantly Russian Boiarskii.

34. Levitin and Shavrov, *Ocherki*, 1: 14–16; Shkarovskii, *Obnovlencheskoe dvizhenie v Russkoi Pravoslavnoi Tserkvi XX veka* (Nestor: St. Petersburg, 1999), 94.

35. Georges Florovsky, *Puti russkogo bogosloviia* (Paris: YMCA, 1937), 470–475; Pospielovsky, *The Russian Church*, 1: 46–47.

36. Mark D. Steinberg, "Workers on the Cross: Religious Imagination in the Writings of Russian Workers, 1910–1924," *Russian Review* 53 (April 1994): 214.

37. A. V. Kartashev, "Revoliutsiia i Sobor 1917–1918 gg.," *Bogoslovskaia mysl'* (Paris) 4 (1942): 76.

38. Titlinov, *Tserkov' vo vremia revoliutsii*, 55–57.

39. A. I. Vvedenskii, *Tserkov' i gosudarstvo: Ocherk vzaimootnoshenii, 1918–1922 gg.* (Moscow, 1923), 31.

40. V. A. Alekseev, *Illiuzii i dogmy* (Moscow: Politizdat, 1991), 10.

41. Kartashev, "Revoliutsiia," 77.

42. Alekseev, *Illiuzii*, 14.

43. Kartashev, "Revoliutsiia," 76–84; Alekseev, *Illiuzii*, 13–15.

44. Levitin and Shavrov, *Ocherki*, 1: 26–27.

45. Alekseev, *Illiuzii*, 15.

46. Levitin and Shavrov, *Ocherki*, 1: 27–29.

47. Vvedenskii, *Tserkov' i gosudarstvo*, 31–32. In the 1920s, Vvedenskii used the Union's program to support his argument for "common goals of Christians and revolutionaries," based on wide support for those ideas in 1917 among the socialist parties, particularly the Socialist Revolutionaries. See Alekseev, *Illiuzii*, 16.

48. For a summary of the work of the Democratic State Conference and Preparliament, see Alexander Rabinowitch, *The Bolsheviks Come to Power: The Revolution of 1917 in Petrograd* (New York: Norton, 1976), 182–189.

49. Levitin and Shavrov, *Ocherki*, 1: 29–30.

50. Analysis of those elections and their significance is found in Oliver H. Radkey, *The Election to the Russian Constituent Assembly of 1917*, Harvard Historical Monographs 21 (Cambridge, Mass.: Harvard University Press, 1950).

51. E. S. Osipova, "Vremennoe pravitel'stvo i tserkov'," in *Tserkov' v istorii Rossii,* edited by Iu. Ia. Kogan (Moscow and Leningrad: Nauka, 1967), 317–319.

52. V. F. Zybkovets, *Natsionalizatsiia monastyrskikh imushchestv v Sovetskoi Rossii (1917–1921 gg.)* (Moscow: Nauka, 1975), 17.

53. Vvedenskii, *Tserkov' i gosudarstvo,* 34.

54. Vvedenskii, *Tserkov' i gosudarstvo,* 54–55.

55. For specifics, see L. I. Emeliakh, "Ateizm i antiklerikalizm narodnykh mass v 1917 g.," *Voprosy istorii religii i ateizma* (hereafter cited as *VIRA*) 5 (1958): 64–66, and D. A. Garkavenko, "Rost ateisticheskikh i antiklerikal'nykh nastroenii v armii i flote v 1917 godu," *VIRA* 8 (1960): 193–218.

56. Vvedenskii, *Tserkov' i gosudarstvo,* 51.

57. Alekseev, *Illiuzii,* 16–17.

58. Kartashev, "Revoliutsiia," 88.

59. Quoted in Alekseev, *Illiuzii,* 21–22.

60. William Fletcher, *The Russian Orthodox Church Underground* (Oxford: Oxford University Press, 1971), 34–35.

61. V. I. Lenin, *Collected Works,* 4th ed., 45 vols. (Moscow: Progress Publishers, 1961), 6: 30.

62. Lenin, *Collected Works,* 6: 404.

63. Quoted in V. D. Bonch-Bruevich, "Lenin o religii," *VIRA* 4 (1956): 11.

64. Bonch-Bruevich, "Lenin o religii," 12.

65. Quoted in Levitin and Shavrov, *Ocherki,* 1: 4. It is not clear where Lenin picked up the term "the new Orthodox movement," as it does not appear in other literature from the period.

66. RGASPI, f. 17, op. 60, d. 52, ll. 1–4.

67. Alekseev, *Illiuzii,* 23–26.

68. Catherine Evtuhov, "The Church in the Russian Revolution: Arguments for and against Restoring the Patriarchate at the Church Council of 1917–1918," *Slavic Review* 50, no. 3 (Fall 1991): 509–510.

69. Edward E. Roslof, "The Russian Orthodox Church and the Bolshevik Regime, 1917–1918" (M.A. thesis, University of Hawaii at Manoa, 1988), 54–58.

70. The Soviet view of Tikhon can be found in any pre-1988 work on the church, such as Shishkin, *Sushchnost' i kriticheskaia otsenka "obnovlencheskogo" raskola russkoi pravoslavnoi tserkvi* (Kazan': izd. Kazanskogo Universiteta, 1970). New biographies of Tikhon abound. One based on archival sources is M. I. Odintsov, "Zhrebii pastyria," Parts 1–4, *Nauka i religiia,* no. 1 (1989): 38–42; no. 4 (1989): 16–20; no. 5 (1989): 18–21; no. 6 (1989): 34–40. A popular, hagiographical study is M. Vostryshev, *Patriarkh Tikhon* (Moscow: Molodaia gvardiia, 1995). The official *vita,* written as part of the canonization process, is "The Life of Saint Tikhon, Patriarch of Moscow and All Russia," *Journal of the Moscow Patriarchate,* no. 4 (1990): 56–68. See also Edward E. Roslof, "Russian Orthodoxy and the Tragic Fate of Patriarch Tikhon (Bellavin)," in *The Human Tradition in Modern Russia,* edited by William B. Husband (Wilmington, Del.: Scholarly Resources, 2000), 77–91.

71. Quoted in Levitin and Shavrov, *Ocherki,* 1: 43.

72. Kartashev, "Revoliutsiia," 92.

73. Odintsov, "Zhrebii pastyria," no. 1: 40.

74. Levitin and Shavrov, *Ocherki,* 1: 50–51.

75. Vvedenskii, *Tserkov' i gosudarstvo,* 109–110.

76. Levitin and Shavrov, *Ocherki,* 1: 31–32. On John of Kronstadt's influence, see Nadieszda Kizenko, *A Prodigal Saint: Father John of Kronstadt and the Russian People* (University Park: : Pennsylvania State University Press, 2000).

77. Quoted in N. F. Platonov, "Pravoslavnaia tserkov' v 1917–1918 gg.," *Ezhegodnik Muzeia istorii religii i ateizma* 5 (1961): 216.

78. Levitin and Shavrov, *Ocherki*, 1: 46–48.

79. Alekseev, *Illiuzii*, 29.

80. Quoted in Alekseev, *Illiuzii*, 28.

81. Alekseev, *Illiuzii*, 35–37.

82. See the council's instructions of February 28 (o.s.), 1918, in Boleslaw Szczesniak, ed. and trans., *The Russian Revolution and Religion: A Collection of Documents concerning the Suppression of Religion by the Communists, 1917–1925* (Notre Dame, Ind.: University of Notre Dame Press, 1959), 37–39.

83. The complete text of these instructions is in P. V. Gidulianov and P. A. Krasikov, eds., *Otdelenie tserkvi ot gosudarstva*, 2nd ed. (Moscow: Iuridichesko, 1924), 363–370. M. V. Shkarovskii points out the difficulties the state had enforcing these instructions and others related to the separation of church and state in Petrograd in *Peterburgskaia eparkhiia v gody gonenii i utrat 1917–1945* (St. Petersburg: Liki Rossii, 1995), 25–43.

84. Lev Regel'son, *Tragediia russkoi tserkvi* (Paris: YMCA, 1977), 234–235.

85. Titlinov, *Tserkov' vo vremia revoliutsii*, 131–133.

86. The anathema is quoted in full in Paul B. Anderson, *People, Church and State in Modern Russia*, 2nd ed. (London: S.C.M.P., 1944), 53–55.

87. For example, they published the anathema with additions that criticized the Bolsheviks directly. See Odintsov, "Zhrebii pastyria," *Nauka i religiia*, no. 4 (1989): 16–17.

88. Printed in Regel'son, *Tragediia*, 234–235.

89. On February 1, 1918, the Soviet government officially adopted the Gregorian calendar. The Russian Orthodox Church refused to accept this change, as will be discussed in Chapter 4, although since the change in the civil calendar, church documents have been dated according to both the Julian and Gregorian calendars (in the twentieth century, the former lagged behind the latter by thirteen days).

90. Regel'son, *Tragediia*, 228–229.

91. Regel'son, *Tragediia*, 249.

92. Reprinted in "K istorii otdeleniia tserkvi ot gosudarstva i shkoly ot tserkvi v SSSR: Dokumenty i materialy," *VIRA* 5 (1958): 42–44.

93. These brochures are quoted at length in Levitin and Shavrov, *Ocherki*, 1: 32–36.

94. This section relies on archival research by V. A. Alekseev to describe politics and the church between 1918 and 1921. His ideas are supported by other sources.

95. Alekseev, *Illiuzii*, 56.

96. This explanation for Tikhon's actions is given in Alekseev, *Illiuzii*, 138–139.

97. Regel'son, *Tragediia*, 237.

98. Alekseev, *Illiuzii*, 57–59.

99. As described by Sheila Fitzpatrick, "The Civil War as a Formative Experience," in *Bolshevik Culture: Experiment and Order in the Russian Revolution*, edited by Abbott Gleason, Peter Kenez, and Richard Stites (Bloomington: Indiana University Press, 1985), 57–76.

100. Alekseev, *Illiuzii*, 100–104.

101. Varying estimates are found in William C. Emhardt, *Religion in Soviet Russia: Anarchy* (London: Mowbray, 1929), 29–30, and N. A. Krivova, *Vlast' i tserkov' v 1922–1925 gg.* (Moscow: AIRO-XX, 1997), 14–15. Evidence that a lower number of clergy was repressed under the Red Terror comes from the work of M. L. Beloglazov, who found only ten Orthodox clergymen brought before the Revolutionary Tribunal of Altai province for the six months following the reestablishment of Soviet power there in January 1920. M. L. Beloglazov, *Vzaimootnosheniia organov gosudarstvennoi vlasti i pravoslavnoi tserkvi na Altae (okt. 1917–1925 gg.)* (Avtoreferat, candidate's degree in history, Tomsk State University, 1992), 11.

102. Alekseev, *Illiuzii*, 62–66, 73–82 (on monastic property and relics), 91–93 (on Krasikov). Additional details on the relics campaign are found in Krivova, *Vlast'*, 15–16.

103. For Lenin's attitude toward the church's "provocations," see the comments by V. D. Bonch-Bruevich in M. M. Persits, ed., *Deiateli oktiabria o religii i tserkvi (Stat'i, rechi, besedy, vospominaniia)* (Moscow: Mysl, 1968), 14–24. Substantiating this source are Lenin's reactions to the various proclamations issued by Tikhon between 1918 and 1919, found in RGASPI, f. 5, op. 1, d. 120, ll. 1–15.

104. Lenin, *Collected Works*, 28: 181.

105. Michael J. Traina, "Lenin, Religion and the Russian Orthodox Church: An Analysis of Theory and Practice" (Ph.D. dissertation, Kent State University, 1970), 37, 188–202.

106. Steinberg, "Workers on the Cross," 237.

107. Alekseev, *Illiuzii*, 5–6.

108. RGASPI, f. 76, op. 3, d. 48, ll. 5–5 ob.

109. Alekseev, *Illiuzii*, 67–68, 140–168.

110. Szczesniak, *The Russian Revolution*, 50–53.

111. Szczesniak, *The Russian Revolution*, 49.

112. RGASPI, f. 17, op. 60, d. 52, l. 5.

113. Szczesniak, *The Russian Revolution*, 70–72.

114. Levitin and Shavrov, *Ocherki*, 1: 51–52. For a biography of Putiata, see Archbishop Manuil (Lemeshchevskii), *Katalog "Russkikh Arkhiereev Obnovlentsev,"* 3 vols. (unpublished manuscript, 1957), 1: 125–133.

115. Differing accounts of these events are given by *Vlast' Sovetov*, no. 11–12 (1922): 29, John S. Curtiss, *The Russian Church and the Soviet State, 1917–1950* (Boston: Little, Brown & Co., 1952), 102, Platonov, "Pravoslavnaia tserkov'," 229–230, and Shkarovskii, *Peterburgskaia eparkhiia*, 49–50.

116. RGASPI, f. 76, op. 3, d. 196, l. 3.

117. GARF, f. 353, op. 3, d. 795, ll. 1–12, 14. These documents leave no doubt of Krasnitskii's strongly held belief in radical socialism and church reforms.

118. Shkarovskii, *Peterburgskaia eparkhiia*, 37, 48; and *Obnovlencheskoe*, 96.

119. Levitin and Shavrov, *Ocherki*, 1: 54. This account dates from a 1943 conversation between Vvedenskii and Levitin. There is no contemporary record of such a conversation, although we do know that Vvedenskii represented Metropolitan Veniamin Kazanskii at a meeting with Zinoviev in September 1919. See Shkarovskii, *Obnovlencheskoe*, 12.

120. Alekseev, *Illiuzii*, 114–117.

121. Frances McCullagh, *A Prisoner of the Reds* (New York: E. P. Dutton, 1922), 263–265.

122. Levitin and Shavrov, *Ocherki*, 1: 52–53. Details of Trufanov's schism have yet to be uncovered. The Cheka report from December 1920 concluded that Trufanov, like Putiata, lacked the will to strike out against the church hierarchy. See RGASPI, f. 76, op. 3, d. 196, l. 3.

123. Curtiss, *The Russian Church*, 102.

124. Regel'son, *Tragediia*, 265.

125. GARF, f. 353, op. 6, d. 10, l. 228.

126. Regel'son, *Tragediia*, 269–270.

127. Alekseev, *Illiuzii*, 93–97.

128. RGASPI, f. 76, op. 3, d. 94, ll. 4–4 ob.

129. Curtiss, *The Russian Church*, 104–105; Szczesniak, *The Russian Revolution*, 56–57.

130. Alekseev, *Illiuzii*, 133–135.

131. Shkarovskii, *Obnovlencheskoe*, 94.

132. RGASPI, f. 76, op. 3, d. 196, ll. 2, 3.

133. RGASPI, f. 5, op. 1, d. 120, l. 10.

134. RGASPI, f. 2, op. 1, d. 18614, l. 1.

135. RGASPI, f. 5, op. 1, d. 120, ll. 12, 13.

136. Regel'son, *Tragediia*, 272–273; Alekseev, *Illiuzii*, 192–198.

137. Soon afterward, Egorov became ill and died. Platonov, "Pravoslavnaia tserkov'," 230–231; Shkarovskii, *Peterburgskaia eparkhiia*, 50.

138. Regel'son, *Tragediia*, 275–276.

139. TsGAIPD, f. 16, op. 9, d. 9121, ll. 10–13.

140. Szczesniak, *The Russian Revolution*, 57–58, 62–64.

141. Alekseev, *Illiuzii*, 169–175; Regel'son, *Tragediia*, 276–277; Szczesniak, *The Russian Revolution*, 58–62; Titlinov, *Tserkov' vo vremia revoliutsii*, 184.

142. Curtiss, *The Russian Church*, 9–10; Freeze, *Parish Clergy*, 233, 477–478.

2. Renovationists Come to Power

1. *Izvestiia*, March 15, 1922; N. A. Krivova, *Vlast' i tserkov' v 1922–1925 gg.* (Moscow: AIRO-XX, 1997), 32.

2. N. N. Pokrovskii and S. G. Petrov, eds. *Arkhivy Kremlia: Politbiuro i tserkov' 1922–1925 gg.*, 2 vols. (Moscow and Novosibirsk: Sibirskii khronograf and ROSSPEN, 1997–1998), 2: 5–6; V. A. Alekseev, *Illiuzii i dogmy* (Moscow: Politizdat, 1991), 198.

3. GARF, f. 1064, op. 1, d. 91, l. 64.

4. Lev Regel'son, *Tragediia russkoi tserkvi* (Paris: YMCA, 1977), 277.

5. GARF, f. 1064, op. 1, d. 6, l. 103 ob.

6. RGASPI, f. 5, op. 2, d. 296, l. 1. The telegram is reprinted in N. N. Pokrovskii and S. G. Petrov, *Arkhivy Kremlia: Politbiuro i tserkov' 1922–1925 gg.*, 2 vols. (Moscow and Novosibirsk, 1997–1998), *Kniga*, 2: 6.

7. GARF, f. 1235, op. 39, d. 11, l. 274.

8. John S. Curtiss, *The Russian Church and the Soviet State, 1917–1950* (Boston: Little, Brown & Co., 1952), 110–111.

9. See GARF, f. 1235, op. 39, d. 13, l. 12.

10. Pokrovskii and Petrov, *Arkhivy Kremlia*, 2: 15–18. See also O. Iu. Vasil'eva, "Iz'iatie tserkovnykh tsennostei b 1922 godu: nekotorie aspekty problemy," in *Religiia, obshchestvo i gosudarstvo v XX veke: Material konferentsii, Moskva, 22–25 oktiabria 1991 g.*, edited by Ia. N. Shchapov (Moscow: Institut istorii SSSR, AN SSSR, 1991), 57–62.

11. Alekseev, *Illiuzii*, 200.

12. Quoted in full in M. I. Odintsov, "Zhrebii pastyria," Part 3, *Nauka i religiia*, no. 5 (1990): 19–20.

13. Alekseev, *Illiuzii*, 202.

14. During the conference, Russian émigrés attacked the Soviet government's lack of good faith in keeping international agreements because of its poor policy on human rights. Alekseev, *Illiuzii*, 220.

15. Irinarkh Stratonov, *Russkaia tserkovnaia smuta, 1921–1931 gg.* (Berlin: Parabola, 1932), 46.

16. *Revoliutsiia i tserkov'*, no. 1–3 (1922): 24–26.

17. Alekseev, *Illiuzii*, 203–204.

18. A representative sample is found in Pokrovskii and Petrov, *Arkhivy Kremlia*, 2: 18–45.

19. Alekseev, *Illiuzii*, 218.

20. Alekseev, *Illiuzii*, 220–222. The papal mission left the country after the arrest of Catholic clergy in Petrograd at the beginning of 1923.

21. RGIA, f. 831, op. 1, d. 299, ll. 1–6. See also Curtiss, *The Russian Church*, 122–123.

22. RGASPI, f. 5, op. 2, d. 48, l. 10.

23. RGASPI, f. 17, op. 3, d. 280, ll. 5, 6, 19.

24. Pokrovskii and Petrov, *Arkhivy Kremlia*, 2: 45–50.

25. Quoted in full in Odintsov, "Zhrebii pastyria," Part 3, *Nauka i religiia*, no. 5 (1989): 20.

26. Alekseev, *Illiuzii*, 203.

27. RGASPI, f. 17, op. 3, d. 282, l. 2.

28. RGASPI, f. 5, op. 2, d. 48, l. 25. The Shuia incident was described at length in *Izvestiia* on March 28 in a front-page story. The telegram to Lenin and the published news account disagreed on details of the numbers killed and wounded.

29. The report from Petrograd, prepared by ROSTA, the Russian telegraph agency, is printed in Pokrovskii and Petrov, *Arkhivy Kremlia*, 2: 61–62.

30. Lenin's letter was finally printed in full in 1990. A *samizdat* copy, with several substantive errors, had appeared in the Russian émigré press two decades earlier. See Dmitri Pospielovsky, *The Russian Church and the Soviet Regime, 1917–1982*, 2 vols. (Crestwood, N.Y.: St. Vladimir's Seminary Press, 1984), 1: 94–96. The Central Committee Plenum of March 25 set the agenda for the congress but did not include the church question. See RGASPI, f. 17, op. 2, d. 77, and *Izvestiia TsK KPSS*, no. 4 (1990): 190–193, 195.

31. RGASPI, f. 17, op. 3, d. 283, ll. 1, 6, 7. Reprinted in *Izvestiia TsK KPSS*, no. 4 (1990): 194–195. A copy of the instructions sent by coded telegram on March 22 to the regional party committees can be found in TsGAIPD, f. 16, op. 1, d. 81, ll. 36, 36 ob.

32. RGASPI, f. 5, op. 2, d. 48, ll. 35–36.

33. Pospielovsky, *The Russian Church*, 1: 57. Archbishop Evdokim Meshcherskii of Nizhnii Novgorod later reported that he too met with the patriarch on March 25 and pointed out the need to renew the synod's mandate. The patriarch rejected advice on this occasion as well. See *Zhivaia tserkov'*, no. 8–9 (September 1–15, 1922): 7.

34. RGASPI, f. 17, op. 3, d. 284, ll. 4, 9.

35. RGASPI, f. 17, op. 60, d. 336, ll. 52, 75, 76, 81.

36. Krivova, *Vlast' i tserkov'*, 75.

37. From the GPU report on the seizure campaign for March 22, 1922. Pokrovskii and Petrov, *Arkhivy Kremlia*, 2: 83.

38. G. Shavel'skii, "Tserkov' i revoliutsiia," *Russkaia mysl'* (Paris), April 1922, 144 (quoted in Curtiss, *The Russian Church*, 114). See also Regel'son, *Tragediia*, 277.

39. RGASPI, f. 17, op. 3, d. 285, l. 13.

40. Quoted in Odintsov, "Zhrebii pastyria," Part 3, *Nauka i religiia*, no. 5 (1989): 20.

41. SOTsDNI, f. 27, op. 2, d. 832, ll. 61, 70.

42. Alekseev, *Illiuzii*, 212.

43. Curtiss, *The Russian Church*, 116–117.

44. *Izvestiia*, March 29, 1922, 2; March 30, 1922, 5.

45. GARF, f. 1066, op. 2, d. 299, l. 47.

46. The full text of Trotsky's proposal is included in Pokrovskii and Petrov, *Arkhivy Kremlia*, 1: 161–164.

47. Alekseev, *Illiuzii*, 218. Alekseev speculates that Trotsky's actions were driven in part by personal motives. In a March 24 article in *Izvestiia*, Trotsky called for an open battle with the reactionary forces in the Russian Orthodox Church. Two days later, in the same newspaper, Tikhon called Trotsky one of the main initiators of both the Civil War and the famine. The patriarch said Trotsky's ambitious expansion of the Red Army caused the impoverishment of the people, with the result that the church valuables in reality would support the army.

48. SOTsDNI, f. 27, op. 2, d. 832, l. 78.

49. Quoted in Odintsov, "Zhrebii pastyria," Part 3, *Nauka i religiia*, no. 5 (1989): 20.

50. The stenographic record of Tikhon's testimony is found in M. I. Vostryshev, *Bozhii izbrannik: Krestnyi put' sviatitelia Tikhona, Patriarkha Moskovskogo i vseia Rossii* (Moscow: Sovremennik, 1990), 152–190, and Prot. Vladimir Vorob'ev et al., eds., *Sledstvennoe delo*

patriarkha Tikhona. Sbornik dokumentov po materialam Tsentral'nogo arkhiva FSB RF (Moscow: Pamiatniki istoricheskoi mysli, 2000), 129–152.

51. This was the claim made in the indictment against Tikhon. He upheld the substance of these charges in his published statement of repentance in June 1923. See Curtiss, *The Russian Church*, 117.

52. RGASPI, f. 17, op. 3, d. 291, ll. 2, 3, 6.

53. Tuchkov's biography is given in Krivova, *Vlast' i tserkov'*, 83, and Damaskin (Orlovskii), *Mucheniki, ispovedniki i podvizhniki blagochestiia Rossiiskoi Pravoslavnoi Tserkvi XX stoletiia*, 2 vols. (Tver: Bulat, 1996), 2: 475–478.

54. Krivova, *Vlast' i tserkov'*, 138.

55. A. Levitin and V. Shavrov, *Ocherki po istorii russkoi tserkovnoi smuti*, 3 vols. (Switzerland: Institut Glaube in der 2. Welt, 1977), 1: 126–128.

56. Pokrovskii and Petrov, *Arkhivy Kremlia*, 2: 192–194.

57. GARF, f. 1064, op. 5, d. 194, l. 35. Although undated, the contents of this handwritten note indicate that it was written in late April or early May 1922.

58. RGASPI, f. 17, op. 112, d. 340, l. 56.

59. See Odintsov, "Zhrebii pastyria," *Nauka i religiia*, no. 5 (1989): 21. Nezhnyi claims that the patriarch was informed of these decisions on May 9; A. Nezhnyi, "Protokoly kremlevskikh mudretsov," *Ogonek*, nos. 31–33 (1992): 9.

60. *Izvestiia*, May 9, 1922.

61. Levitin and Shavrov, *Ocherki*, 1: 77.

62. Odintsov, "Zhrebii pastyria," Part 4, *Nauka i religiia*, no. 6 (1989): 34. Odintsov was unable to cite the source of his information on this meeting, although it apparently came from state security archives.

63. Krivova, *Vlast' i tserkov'*, 139.

64. See Levitin and Shavrov, *Ocherki*, 1: 77.

65. *Zhivaia tserkov'*, no. 1 (1922): 10.

66. Various accounts of this meeting exist. Both *Pravda* and *Izvestiia* described it on the first page of their May 17 editions. See also Vvedenskii, *Tserkov'*, 248–249, and Odintsov, "Zhrebii pastyria," Part 3, *Nauka i religiia*, no. 6 (1989): 35. Tikhon's letters are quoted in Regel'son, *Tragediia*, 286. The original of his letter to Kalinin is held in the state security archive and was done in Vvedenskii's handwriting but signed by the patriarch. Pokrovskii and Petrov, *Arkhivy Kremlia*, 2: 237.

67. Francis McCullagh, *The Bolshevik Persecution of Christianity* (London: E. P. Dutton, 1924), 38–40.

68. Reprinted in Regel'son, *Tragediia*, 287–288.

69. During 1922–1923, government leaders often referred to the renovationists publicly and privately as supporters of the "change of signposts" movement. *Vekhi* [Signposts] was written in 1907 by Nicholas Berdiaev, Sergei Bulgakov, and others in an attempt to apply liberal Christian ideas to Russian society. At the end of the Civil War in 1920, a new collection of essays appeared abroad, under the title *Smena vekh* [Change of Signposts]. The authors of this work supported Bolshevism as the only remaining force capable of holding lands in the former Russian empire together.

70. *Izvestiia TsK KPSS*, no. 4 (1990): 196–197. In a postscript to this letter, Trotsky berated the editors of *Pravda* and *Izvestiia* for ignoring historic church events while giving the minutest details of the Genoa Conference. On this point, Lenin scribbled "It is true! It is 1000 times true! Down with minute details!"

71. Regel'son, *Tragediia*, 288.

72. *Zhivaia tserkov'*, no. 2 (1922): 14. The appeal is reprinted in Regel'son, *Tragediia*, 288–289.

73. RGASPI, f. 17, op. 3, d. 293, ll. 4, 12.

74. *Vestnik Sv. Sinoda PRTs*, no. 6 (2) (1926): 14–15.

75. Levitin and Shavrov, *Ocherki*, 1: 119. This source also quotes at length from Krasotin's account but incorrectly cites the source. Tuchkov avoided publicity at all costs, which may explain his long tenure in the state security apparatus and peaceful death.

76. *Vestnik Sv. Synoda PRTs*, no. 2 (1925): 18.

77. Regel'son, *Tragediia*, 290–291. Regel'son notes that this correspondence between the VTsU and Antonin was unknown to Levitin and Shavrov, who mistakenly maintained that Antonin became head of the VTsU on his own initiative. See Levitin and Shavrov, *Ocherki*, 1: 88–90.

78. Levitin and Shavrov, *Ocherki*, 1: 90–92. Krasnitskii did not sign the undated letter inviting Antonin to head the VTsU, and the bishop was at the earliest meetings of that body. A logical explanation is that the invitation was issued while Krasnitskii was negotiating with Agafangel. If this was done without Krasnitskii's knowledge or prior consent, his reaction upon returning to Moscow is all the more understandable.

79. SOTsDNI, f. 27, op. 2, d. 832, l. 104.

80. Levitin and Shavrov, *Ocherki*, 1: 92.

81. *Zhivaia tserkov'*, no. 2 (May 23, 1922): 2–4.

82. *Zhivaia tserkov'*, no. 2 (May 23, 1922): 4–6.

83. RGASPI, f. 17, op. 3, d. 280, ll. 17–18; and d. 299, l. 6. In June, Trotsky submitted a written proposal in regard to Lvov, but this document is missing from the file of Politburo minutes in RGASPI.

84. *Zhivaia tserkov'*, no. 2 (May 23, 1922): 6–10. Quote from p. 10.

85. *Zhivaia tserkov'*, no. 2 (May 23, 1922): 12–13.

86. Levitin and Shavrov, *Ocherki*, 1: 98–99.

87. RGASPI, f. 17, op. 3, d. 294, ll. 9–10 (emphasis added).

88. *Zhivaia tserkov'*, no. 3 (June 15, 1922): 9.

89. This analysis of renovationism draws on the theoretic framework of Anthony Downs, *Inside Bureaucracy*, A RAND Corporation Research Study (Boston: Little, Brown and Co., 1967), 6.

90. Levitin and Shavrov, *Ocherki*, 1: 100–111.

91. *Zhivaia tserkov'*, no. 3 (June 15, 1922): 2. Curtiss mistakenly refers to the meeting of July 4 as the one that established the Living Church Group. See Curtiss, *The Russian Church*, 138.

92. *Zhivaia tserkov'*, no. 3 (June 15, 1922): 11–12.

93. RGASPI, f. 17, op. 112, d. 336, ll. 3, 46.

94. RGASPI, f. 17, op. 112, d. 340, ll. 2, 56. On June 12, the Orgburo referred the matter to the VTsIK Commission for Seizing Church Wealth. Finally, on August 17, it decided that the funds should come from the presidium of VTsIK, in effect funding the public attacks on Tikhon using money realized from sequestered church valuables. See RGASPI, f. 17, op. 112, d. 362, ll. 7, 273.

95. Provincial offices of the secret police produced daily reports on local activities and sent copies to Moscow. The GPU then compiled selections from these regional sources into a national report, which was distributed every day (except Sunday) in individually numbered copies to a short list of the nation's leaders. Pokrovskii discusses the value and limitations of these reports as historical sources in his introduction to Pokrovskii and Petrov, *Arkhivy Kremlia*, 1: 60–78.

96. RGASPI, f. 5, op. 1, d. 2633, ll. 23, 88, 113, 130.

97. SOTsDNI, f. 27, op. 2, d. 816, l. 13.

98. RGASPI, f. 5, op. 1, d. 2634, ll. 34, 35, 67, 81, 94.

99. RGASPI, f. 5, op. 1, d. 2635, ll. 7, 13, 17, 19, 40, 42, 43, 47, 91, 104, 122.

100. RGASPI, f. 5, op. 1, d. 2659, ll. 51, 51 ob.

101. Quoted in Levitin and Shavrov, *Ocherki*, 1: 153.

102. Pokrovskii and Petrov, *Arkhivy Kremlia*, 2: 307.

103. RGASPI, f. 17, op. 112, d. 337, ll. 3, 152.

104. Quoted in Levitin and Shavrov, *Ocherki*, 1: 94–95.

105. *Zhivaia tserkov'*, no. 3 (June 15, 1922): 1.

106. Levitin and Shavrov, *Ocherki*, 1: 95.

107. The Petrograd party organization had planned the trial of Veniamin and others even before Vvedenskii arrived, as evidenced by *gubkom* (provincial committee) protocols for May 11 and 23, 1922; TsGAIPD, f. 16, op. 1, d. 81, ll. 52, 54 ob.

108. *Zhivaia tserkov'*, no. 3 (June 15, 1922): 15. When Vvedenskii appeared in public after the incident, he wore a large bandage on his head. Some suspected that he used this attack to avoid testifying against his former mentor, Veniamin, and to gain sympathy for his own suffering. Later, he claimed that he had intended to defend the metropolitan in his testimony.

109. For an eyewitness account of the trial, see A. Valentinov, ed., *Chernaia kniga ("Shturm nebes")* (Paris: Izd. Russkago natsional'nago studencheskago ob"edineniia, 1925), 198–238.

110. Levitin and Shavrov, *Ocherki*, 1: 111–116.

111. GARF, f. 353, op. 6, d. 11, ll. 41, 52, 64, 65.

112. RGASPI, f. 17, op. 3, d. 303, ll. 4, 9.

113. Ioannikii (Fr. Ivan Chantsev) was the first bishop consecrated by the renovationists, but he took monastic vows just before taking office on June 3. *Zhivaia tserkov'*, no. 3 (June 15, 1922): 1, 10.

114. Levitin and Shavrov, *Ocherki*, 1: 142–143. Ioannikii's ties to renovationism appeared to have been much weaker. He did penance before Metropolitan Sergii Stragorodskii sometime in the late 1920s and served in the patriarchal church hierarchy until his death in 1933. Archibishop Manuil (Lemeshevskii), *Katalog "Russkikh Arkhiereev Obnovlentsev,"* 3 vols. (Library of the Patriarchal Holy Synod, Moscow, typescript, 1957), 1: 215.

115. *Zhivaia tserkov'*, no. 4–5 (July 1–15, 1922): 1.

116. *Zhivaia tserkov'*, no. 6–7 (August 1–15, 1922): 20.

117. Mikhail Pol'skii, *Novye mucheniki rossiiskie*, 3 vols. (Jordanville, N.Y.: Tip. I. Pochaevskago v "Sviato-Troitskam" monastyrie, 1957), 2: 107–108. Serafim also explained his break with the renovationist Holy Synod in 1928 as a result of his personally witnessing the intellectual and moral vacuum of its members.

118. Pokrovskii and Petrov, *Arkhivy Kremlia*, 2: 309.

119. Both documents are included in Levitin and Shavrov, *Ocherki*, 1: 120–124.

120. Levitin and Shavrov, *Ocherki*, 1: 124.

121. *Zhivaia tserkov'*, no. 4–5 (July 1–15, 1922): 23–24. The circular is undated. From the contents, it seems to have been issued in the second half of June.

122. *Zhivaia tserkov'*, no. 3 (June 15, 1922): 10.

123. *Zhivaia tserkov'*, no. 4–5 (July 1–15, 1922): 18–19.

124. *Zhivaia tserkov'*, no. 4–5 (July 1–15, 1922): 18–19.

125. *Zhivaia tserkov'*, no. 4–5 (July 1–15, 1922): 8–11; Levitin and Shavrov, *Ocherki*, 1: 97–98.

126. *Zhivaia tserkov'*, no. 6–7 (August 1–15, 1922): 13–14.

127. *Zhivaia tserkov'*, no. 4–5 (July 1–15, 1922): 23–24; and no. 6–7 (August 1–15, 1922): 22–23.

128. RGASPI, f. 5, op. 1, d. 2659, l. 61. These conclusions are consistent with other local GPU reports from late June through early August 1922. For example: SOTsDNI, f. 27, op. 2, d. 816, l. 91; RGASPI, f. 5, op. 1, d. 2636, ll. 82, 94, 108, 117, 133; d. 2637, l. 8, d. 2638, ll. 2, 75, 76, 87, 101; and d. 2639, ll. 2, 41, 44, 45, 47. See also the report from Tuchkov's office for July 15 to August 20 on the schism in the clergy reprinted in Pokrovskii and Petrov, *Arkhivy Kremlia*, 2: 311–332.

129. TsGA TASSR, f. 1172, op. 3, d. 31, ll. 1–2.

130. *Zhivaia tserkov'*, no. 6–7 (August 1–15, 1922): 15–16.
131. RGASPI, f. 5, op. 1, d. 2639, l. 44.
132. *Zhivaia tserkov'*, no. 6–7 (August 1–15, 1922): 3–4.

3. Ecclesiastical Civil War

1. *Zhivaia tserkov'*, no. 6–7 (August 1–15, 1922): 1–2.
2. *Zhivaia tserkov'*, no. 6–7 (August 1–15, 1922): 1–2.
3. RGASPI, f. 89, op. 4, d. 181, l. 56. Iaroslavskii thought the Living Church was a parody of the Bolsheviks and their slogan, "Workers of the world, unite!"
4. A detailed account of the Congress was given in *Zhivaia tserkov'*, no. 8–9 (September 1–15, 1922): 6–11. Tuchkov submitted reports on the Congress to high-ranking party and GPU officials. Two of his reports, covering events from August 3–11, are included in N. N. Pokrovskii and S. G. Petrov, *Arkhivy Kremlia: Politbiuro i tserkov' 1922–1925 gg.*, 2 vols. (Moscow and Novosibirsk: Sibirskii khronograf and ROSSPEN, 1997–1998), 1: 315–318. Minutes from the Congress apparently were never published.
5. According to A. Levitin and V. Shavrov, at the opening session, Krasnitskii asserted that the Congress represented only the white clergy and asked all the monks present to leave. A delegation from the Congress invited the monastic bishops to return for the plenary session that evening, but Antonin refused. See *Ocherki po istorii russkoi tserkovnoi smuti*, 3 vols. (Switzerland: Institut Glaube in der 2. Welt, 1977), 1: 160–162.
6. For the issues surrounding Tolstoi's excommunication, see Pål Kolstø, "A Mass for a Heretic? The Controversy over Lev Tolstoi's Burial," *Slavic Review* 60, no. 1 (Spring 2001): 75–95.
7. John S. Curtiss, *The Russian Church and the Soviet State, 1917–1950* (Boston: Little, Brown & Co., 1952), 141.
8. "K voprosu o reforme tserkovnogo iskusstva," *Zhivaia tserkov'*, no. 8–9 (September 1–15, 1922): 16–17.
9. "Neskol'ko slov v otvet V. L'vovu," *Zhivaia tserkov'*, no. 8–9 (September 1–15, 1922): 16–17.
10. Curtiss, *The Russian Church*, 124.
11. Levitin and Shavrov, *Ocherki*, 1: 129–130.
12. Lev Regel'son, *Tragediia russkoi tserkvi* (Paris: YMCA, 1977), 311–312.
13. GARF, f. 353, op. 6, d. 20, ll. 1–4.
14. GARF, f. 353, op. 6, d. 26, ll. 2–4 ob., 6–10.
15. RGASPI, f. 5, op. 1, d. 2640, ll. 2, 12, 15, 43, 66, 68, 70, 71, 72; and d. 2641, ll. 2, 11, 17, 18, 52, 68.
16. The League's charter was reprinted in full in several church periodicals at the time; for example, the Viatka diocese's *Slovo zhizni*, no. 2 (February 15, 1923): 4–6. It can also be found in Levitin and Shavrov, *Ocherki*, 1: 156–158.
17. *Trudy I Vserossiiskogo s"ezda ili sobora "Soiuza Tserkovnoe Vozrozhdenie"* (Moscow, 1925), 80.
18. Levitin and Shavrov, *Ocherki*, 1: 176–177.
19. See the VTsIK presidium's message to the regional executive committee of Rostov on the Don dated August 15, 1922, in Pokrovskii and Petrov, *Arkhivy Kremlia*, 2: 310–311.
20. Levitin and Shavrov, *Ocherki*, 1: 136–137. The article is reprinted in full.
21. *Zhivaia tserkov'*, no. 8–9 (September 1–15, 1922): 19. It appears that the Supreme Church Administration did not publicize all its decisions to "retire" bishops. Nafanail of Kharkov, for example, was not listed in the church news accounts of those removed.
22. RGASPI, f. 5, op. 1, d. 2641, ll. 68, 103, 110; Pokrovskii and Petrov, *Arkhivy Kremlia*, 1: 75.

23. RGASPI, f. 5, op. 1, d. 2643, ll. 22–23.

24. Levitin and Shavrov, *Ocherki*, 1: 180–181.

25. Ivan Tregubov, "Prelozhenie: 'Zhivaia tserkov' i 'Tserkovnoe Vozrozhdenie,'" in *K raskolu v Russkoi pravoslavnoi tserkvi*, by Ivan Bulatov (Vologda, 1922), 63–69. Sergii's statement against the Living Church was published in *Pravda* on September 23, 1922. That document and a request by Fedorov to convict Antonin at a church trial are included in Levitin and Shavrov, *Ocherki*, 1: 177–178, 181–182.

26. Levitin and Shavrov, *Ocherki*, 1: 178.

27. *Zhivaia tserkov'*, no. 11 (February 1, 1923): 20–21.

28. Levitin and Shavrov, *Ocherki*, 1: 212–215.

29. Levitin and Shavrov, *Ocherki*, 2: 31.

30. Levitin and Shavrov, *Ocherki*, 2: 33–39. This section includes the complete SO-DATs program.

31. GARF, f. 1064, f. 5, d. 193, ll. 48–49.

32. RGASPI, f. 5, op. 1, d. 2643, l. 76.

33. RGASPI, f. 17, op. 60, d. 158, l. 15.

34. Levitin and Shavrov, *Ocherki*, 1: 185.

35. *Zhivaia tserkov'*, no. 10 (October 1, 1922): 1.

36. *Drug pravoslavnogo naroda*, no. 4–5 (December 1922): 1–3.

37. Titlinov, *Novaia tserkov'*, 13–25. Although this booklet was published in 1923, the author finished writing it at the beginning of October, just as the Leftist Movement appeared (see the footnote on page 25).

38. *Zhivaia tserkov'*, no. 11 (February 1, 1923): 20–23.

39. RGASPI, f. 5, op. 1, d. 2646, l. 35.

40. Protests against this action quickly reached the VTsIK and Krasikov's desk at the Commissariat of Justice; GARF, f. 353, op. 6, d. 26, ll. 15–20.

41. RGASPI, f. 5, op. 1, d. 2659, l. 111.

42. A detailed description of the *Tikhonovshchina* is found in Chapter 5.

43. ARK's original name was "The Commission for Implementing the Separation of the Church from the State." Orgburo and Politburo minutes always referred to it as the Antireligious Commission. Details on its origins and membership are found in Pokrovskii and Petrov, *Arkhivy Kremlia*, 1: 83–85, 546–549.

44. RGASPI, f. 5, op. 2, d. 55, l. 229 (Report to the Politburo on ARK activities, December 12, 1922).

45. RGASPI, f. 17, op. 112, d. 367, l. 3. This Committee was also charged with beginning the publication of the magazine *Nauka i religiia* [Science and Religion].

46. RGASPI, f. 17, op. 112, d. 372, ll. 4, 19, 84–91.

47. RGASPI, f. 17, op. 112, d. 443a, l. 1.

48. RGASPI, f. 17, op. 112, d. 378, ll. 4, 61.

49. In his secret report of April 1924 to V. R. Menzhinskii, head of the GPU's Secret Department, Tuchkov wrote in 1924, "The quarrel among the renovationists arose mainly out of leadership claims in the church administration"; RGASPI, f. 17, op. 6, d. 509, l. 89.

50. RGASPI, f. 17, op. 112, d. 443a, l. 2.

51. RGASPI, f. 5, op. 2, d. 55, ll. 44–45 (Theses of Comrade Skvortsov-Stepanov on antireligious propaganda, undated but written between October 23 and 31, 1922).

52. RGASPI, f. 5, op. 2, d. 55, l. 43 (Report on the *Tikhonovshchina*, October 30, 1922).

53. RGASPI, f. 17, op. 112, d. 443a, ll. 3–3 ob. (Protocol of the ARK meeting on October 31, 1922).

54. RGASPI, f. 5, op. 2, d. 55, ll. 39.

55. Levitin and Shavrov, *Ocherki*, 1: 167–170.

56. RGASPI, f. 5, op. 2, d. 55, ll. 158–161; Pokrovskii and Petrov, *Arkhivy Kremlia*, 1: 352–353; Levitin and Shavrov, *Ocherki*, 2: 50–57.

57. Levitin and Shavrov, *Ocherki*, 2: 75–76.

58. *Sobornyi razum*, no. 1–2 (January–February 1923): 7, 21.

59. GARF, f. 353, op. 6, d. 20, ll. 56–59; M. V. Shkarovskii, *Peterburgskaia eparkhiia v gody gonenii i utrat 1917–1945* (St. Petersburg: Liki Rossii, 1995), 90–91.

60. Levitin and Shavrov, *Ocherki*, 2: 34; RGASPI, f. 5, op. 1, d. 2647, ll. 20, 49.

61. RGASPI, f. 5, op. 1, d. 2647, ll. 2, 21, 25.

62. SOTsDNI, f. 27, op. 2, d. 817, l. 7 ob. Similar accounts of renovationist impotence are found in ll. 11, 15–16.

63. See GPU summaries for the second half of November (RGASPI, f. 5, op. 1, d. 2648, ll. 16, 31, 42, 51, 84, 90) as well as detailed local reports from Saratov province for that period (SOTsDNI, f. 27, op. 2, d. 817, ll. 58, 79).

64. Fears of church-led counterrevolution subsided by the end of the year, but the government wanted to remove any possibility that the church might be able to lead or finance such a venture in the future. The VTsIK even announced an amnesty on November 23 for those who voluntarily turned in hidden church valuables; GARF, f. 353, op. 6, d. 6, l. 113.

65. RGASPI, f. 5, op. 2, d. 55, ll. 158–161 (ARK report to the Politburo on November 28, 1922); Pokrovskii and Petrov, *Arkhivy Kremlia*, 1: 349–354.

66. RGASPI, f. 5, op. 2, d. 55, l. 229 (ARK report to the Politburo on December 12, 1922); and f. 17, op. 112, d. 443a, ll. 18, 20 (Protocols for ARK meetings, December 5 and 19, 1922).

67. RGASPI, f. 5, op. 2, d. 55, l. 228; and f. 17, op. 112, d. 443a, ll. 18–21.

68. GARF, f. 5263, op. 1, d. 55, ll. 50–60; Pokrovskii and Petrov, *Arkhivy Kremlia*, 2: 322–323.

69. RGASPI, f. 5, op. 1, d. 2649, l. 4.

70. Although the details on this matter are not clear, the diocesan council seems to have been a pseudo-renovationist body. GARF, f. 353, op. 6, d. 10, ll. 228–231.

71. RGASPI, f. 17, op. 112, d. 443a, l. 23.

72. Pokrovskii and Petrov, *Arkhivy Kremlia*, 1: 350, 2: 341–342. An account of autocephalous activity in Petrograd is given by Shkarovskii, *Peterburgskaia eparkhiia*, 81–89. ARK made the decision to suppress Petrograd's autocephalous church leaders at its meeting on January 30, 1923 (see the protocol in RGASPI, f. 89, op. 4, d. 115, ll. 2, 2a).

73. *Vlast' sovetov*, no. 11–12 (1922): 80–81.

74. RGASPI, f. 5, op. 2, d. 55, ll. 158–161; Pokrovskii and Petrov, *Arkhivy Kremlia*, 1: 362.

75. For a discussion of the decline in the role of the Fifth Department of the Commissariat of Justice in church affairs, see M. I. Odintsov, "Gosudarstvo i tserkov': Istorii vzaimootnoshenii, 1917–1938 gg.," *Kul'tura i religiia*, no. 11 (1991): 26–27.

76. GARF, f. 353, op. 6, d. 20, l. 8.

77. The reasons for this change were not given in the protocol of the Orgburo's January 18 meeting, where the decision was made. Popov remained on ARK as vice-president. RGASPI, f. 17, op. 112, d. 405, l. 7.

78. Pokrovskii and Petrov, *Arkhivy Kremlia*, 1: 101–103.

79. *Slovo zhizni*, no. 2 (February 15, 1923): 7–8.

80. RGASPI, f. 89, op. 4, d. 180, ll. 3–4; Levitin and Shavrov, *Ocherki*, 1: 151–152.

81. GARF, f. 353, op. 6, d. 20, ll. 60, 62. This request was ignored because it lacked the 5-ruble tax stamp required for such petitions.

82. *Obnovlenie tserkvi*, no. 3–4 (January–February, 1923): 8.

83. *Tserkovnaia zaria*, no. 1 (September 15, 1922): 1; *Slovo zhizni*, no. 1 (January 5, 1923): 1–2.

84. TsGIAgM, f. 2303, op. 1, d. 4, l. 29; and d. 5, ll. 4, 4 ob., 14 ob., 18; GARF, f. 353, op. 6, d. 20, ll. 49–55.

85. Levitin and Shavrov, *Ocherki*, 1: 220–222.

86. *Sobornyi razum*, no. 2–3 (December 24/January 16, 1922–1923): 1–3.

87. Levitin and Shavrov, *Ocherki*, 1: 259. The authors noted that a large Soviet monument now stood on the spot formerly occupied by Nikol'skii's church.

88. RGASPI, f. 89, op. 4, d. 164, ll. 3–14. This twelve-page, top-secret report was produced in only five copies and distributed to Popov, Menzhinskii, Samsonov, Krasikov, and Iaroslavskii.

89. See RGASPI, f. 5, op. 1, d. 2650, ll. 32; d. 2651, ll. 19–20; d. 2652, l. 32, 43, 65; d. 2654, ll. 37, 63, 68; d. 2656, ll. 5, 13, 17, 31, 49, 59, 64.

90. RGASPI, f. 5, op. 1, d. 2655, ll. 4, 85.

91. See V. D. Krasnitskii, "Zhivaia tserkov' i bogobornyi ateizm," *Zhivaia tserkov'*, no. 11 (February 1, 1923): 4–5.

92. Documents collected by state security operatives during this long investigation, including transcripts of multiple secret police interrogations with Tikhon, are published in Prot. Vladimir Vorob'ev et al., eds., *Sledstvennoe delo patriarkha Tikhona. Sbornik dokumentov po materialam Tsentral'nogo arkhiva FSB RF* (Moscow: Pamiatniki istoricheskoi mysli, 2000).

93. RGASPI, f. 17, op. 112, d. 443a, ll. 10–11.

94. RGASPI, f. 17, op. 112, d. 393, l. 6.

95. RGASPI, f. 89, op. 4, d. 115, l. 2, 2a.

96. *Zhivaia tserkov'*, no. 11 (February 1, 1923): 2–4. See also Curtiss, *The Russian Church*, 154–155.

97. *Zhivaia tserkov'*, no. 11 (February 1, 1923): 5–7, 24.

98. RGASPI, f. 89, op. 4, d. 115, l. 3.

99. TsGA TASSR, f. 1172, op. 3, d. 408, ll. 3–11.

100. *Golos zhivoi very* (Tambov), no. 4–5 (February 25, 1923): 1–2.

101. RGASPI, f. 89, op. 4, d. 115, l. 6.

102. Pokrovskii and Petrov, *Arkhivy Kremlia*, 1: 364–365; RGASPI, f. 17, op. 3, d. 340, l. 3.

103. RGASPI, f. 89, op. 4, d. 115, l. 10.

104. RGASPI, f. 89, op. 4, d. 115, ll. 8–9.

105. RGASPI, f. 17, op. 112, d. 417, l. 129.

106. *Izvestiia*, March 13, 1923, 5. Reprinted in Levitin and Shavrov, *Ocherki*, 2: 66–69.

107. Levitin and Shavrov, *Ocherki*, 2: 46–50.

108. RGASPI, f. 17, op. 112, d. 443a, l. 35.

109. Valentinov, *Chernaia kniga*, 178–197, 239. See also Francis McCullagh, *The Bolshevik Persecution of Christianity* (London: E. P. Dutton, 1924), 213–247.

110. RGASPI, f. 89, op. 4, d. 115, ll. 11–12. This protocol also records a decision to deal with the reactionary Muslim clergy by assigning an agent named Peters to form a "renovationist" group among Muslim clerics.

111. Regel'son, *Tragediia*, 322.

112. RGASPI, f. 89, op. 4, d. 115, l. 13.

113. RGASPI, f. 17, op. 3, d. 347, ll. 1, 9; Pokrovskii and Petrov, *Arkhivy Kremlia*, 1: 263–267.

114. RGASPI, f. 17, op. 112, d. 417, ll. 5, 125.

115. M. I. Odintsov, "Zhrebii pastyria," Part 4, *Nauka i religiia*, no. 6 (1989): 36.

116. Pokrovskii and Petrov, *Arkhivy Kremlia*, 1: 92–93, 273–274.

117. RGASPI, f. 89, op. 4, d. 118, ll. 1–2.

118. V. A. Alekseev, *Illiuzii i dogmy* (Moscow: Politizdat, 1991), 245.

119. Levitin and Shavrov, *Ocherki*, 2: 22.

120. RGASPI, f. 5, op. 1, d. 2655, l. 76; Levitin and Shavrov, *Ocherki*, 2: 71–75.

121. Newspaper sources gave the total as 476, the number used by Curtiss in *The Russian Church*, 155. Alekseev asserts there were only 350 voting delegates and explains the discrepancy as confusion between the numbers of those invited to attend and those who showed up without such an invitation; *Illiuzii i dogmy*, 245.

122. RGASPI, f. 17, op. 6, d. 509, l. 89–90.

123. GARF, f. 5263, op. 1, d. 55, ll. 18–21.

124. *Deianiia II-go Vserossiiskogo Pomestnogo Sobora Pravoslavnoi tserkvi* (Moscow, 1923), 1–4.

125. Curtiss, *The Russian Church*, 157.

126. *Deianiia II*, 5–8.

127. *Deianiia II*, 8–9.

128. *Deianiia II*, 9–12. Vvedenskii was elevated to his new post on May 6. Levitin and Shavrov, *Ocherki*, 2: 125.

129. RGASPI, f. 89, op. 4, d. 115, l. 14.

130. Levitin and Shavrov, *Ocherki*, 2: 120–122. Tikhon's negative response to the council's decision was not officially acknowledged for many years.

131. RGASPI, f. 89, op. 4, d. 180, ll. 5–6.

132. RGASPI, f. 89, op. 4, d. 160, l. 3. A copy of Iaroslavskii's reply is not included in the file with this letter.

133. *Deianiia II*, 12–14.

134. Curtiss, *The Russian Church*, 158.

4. The Religious NEP

1. RGASPI, f. 89, op. 4, d. 9, l. 12.

2. William G. Rosenberg, "Introduction: NEP Russia as a 'Transitional' Society," in *Russia in the Era of NEP: Explorations in Soviet Society and Culture*, edited by Sheila Fitzpatrick, Alexander Rabinowitch, and Richard Stites (Bloomington and Indianapolis: Indiana University Press, 1991), 4.

3. The Earl of Ronaldshay, *The Life of Lord Curzon: Being the Authorized Biography of George Nathaniel, Marquess Curzon of Kedleston, K.G.*, 3 vols. (London: Ernest Benn, 1928), 3: 354–355.

4. Point 21 of Curzon's note is reprinted in full in Lev Regel'son, *Tragediia russkoi tserkv* (Paris: YMCA, 1977), 331.

5. Ronaldshay, *The Life of Curzon*, 355–356; Regel'son, *Tragediia*, 331–333. The Politburo's concern that a foreign invasion of Russia might result is evident in its deliberations during this period. See RGASPI, f. 17, op. 3, d. 351–359.

6. A. Levitin and V. Shavrov, *Ocherki po istorii russkoi tserkovnoi smuti*, 3 vols. (Switzerland: Institut Glaube in der 2. Welt, 1977), 2: 142–146.

7. RGASPI, f. 89, op. 4, d. 115, ll. 16–18, 20.

8. Émigré bishops were holding a council in Yugoslavia even as Iaroslavskii wrote this proposal. See Evlogii, *Put' moei zhizni* (Paris: YMCA Press, 1946), 606–607.

9. RGASPI, f. 17, op. 3, d. 360, l. 9. This proposal appeared in the ARK minutes of June 12 (RGASPI, f. 89, op. 4, d. 115, l. 24) and was approved by the Politburo two days later.

10. RGASPI, f. 17, op. 3, d. 360, l. 10.

11. R. Rossler, a German historian writing in the 1960s, expressed doubt about the long-accepted view that renovationism was weak and ineffective in the eyes of Soviet officials. He suspected that the government was being careful to ensure that the renovated church would not become more dangerous than the traditional one. However, Rossler dismissed the importance of the Curzon ultimatum in securing Tikhon's release. Lacking ac-

cess to archival records, historians were unable to penetrate the veil of secrecy that the Bolsheviks used to disguise their plans for Orthodoxy after Tikhon's release. Regel'son, *Tragediia*, 336.

12. RGASPI, f. 17, op. 6, d. 509, l. 91. This account is consistent with that given by M. I. Odintsov in "Zhrebii pastyria," Part 4, *Nauka i religiia*, no. 6 (1989): 37.

13. ARK was so pleased with this arrangement that it tried to expand it to other religious confessions. See RGASPI, f. 89, op. 4, d. 115, ll. 17, 24.

14. P. V. Gidulianov, *Tserkov' i gosudarstvo* (Moscow, 1924), 9–14. Partially reprinted in Regel'son, *Tragediia*, 334–335.

15. RGASPI, f. 89, op. 4, d. 115, l. 26.

16. An account of the events of that day is found in Levitin and Shavrov, *Ocherki*, 2: 146–157. However, the authors are in error in believing that Tikhon wrote his attack on renovationism after his release without any government supervision. The film on Tikhon was issued without ARK's approval. On July 19, 1923, ARK ordered the prints to be seized and began an investigation to discover who had approved its release. See RGASPI, f. 89, op. 4, d. 115, l. 35.

17. RGASPI, f. 89, op. 4, d. 115, l. 28. At this meeting, ARK also decided to review the cases of Tikhon's co-defendants and those previously exiled for activities related to the seizure campaign if those persons repented.

18. RGASPI, f. 76, op. 3, d. 306, ll. 161–162.

19. Two files in the archive of the patriarchal chancery are devoted to these letters. RGIA, f. 831, op. 1, d. 194 and 196.

20. V. A. Alekseev, *Illiuzii i dogmy* (Moscow: Politizdat, 1991), 251.

21. A chronicle of the two months following Tikhon's release is given by Levitin and Shavrov, *Ocherki*, 2: 156–170. Alekseev notes that "the reputation of being a renovationist long dogged [Sergii] because many bishops did not believe the sincerity of his repentance" (*Illiuzii*, 180).

22. RGASPI, f. 17, op. 6, d. 509, ll. 92–93.

23. RGASPI, f. 89, op. 4, d. 115, ll. 31–35. This new message attacking renovationism may never have been released. A copy of a possible text is found in Regel'son, *Tragediia*, 342–343.

24. Local officials continuously faced difficulties in understanding orders from the center. For an analysis and application to religion, see Sheila Fitzpatrick, *Everyday Stalinism: Ordinary Life in Extraordinary Times—Soviet Russia in the 1930s* (New York: Oxford, 1999), 26–27.

25. See M. I. Odintsov, "Gosudarstvo i tserkov': Istorii vzaimootnoshenii, 1917–1938 gg.," *Kul'tura i religiia*, no. 11 (1991): 27–30, and M. L. Beloglazov, *Vzaimootnosheniiaorganov gosudarstvennoi vlasti i pravoslavnoi tserkvi na Altae (okt. 1917–1925 gg.)* (Avtoreferat, candidate's degree in history, Tomsk State University, 1992), 15–16. A message to all local party committees from the Central Committee, sent out by the Politburo with Stalin's signature on August 16, 1923, ordered the strict observance of the laws on religion, a cessation of repressive measures against religious believers, and strict nonintervention in church affairs (RGASPI, f. 89, op. 4, d. 184, l. 1). An earlier draft of this message included a list of illegal practices used against the church; that list was deleted in the version Stalin signed. See Pokrovskii and Petrov, *Arkhivy Kremlia*, 1: 101–103, 408–418.

26. See documents on such cases in Armavir, Kaluga, Iaroslavl et al., in GARF, f. 5263, op. 1, d. 55, ll. 76, 102, 338, 354, 367.

27. On numerous occasions, Tuchkov and other party officials in charge of church affairs reprimanded local officials for not obeying the current rules on religious groups. See GARF, f. 353, op. 6, d. 26, ll. 42–43; f. 5263, op. 1, d. 55, ll. 272, 290, 320, 330. Michael Lipsky describes the process whereby local government workers acted as policymakers in *Street-Level Bureaucracy* (New York: Russell Sage Foundation, 1980).

28. Alekseev, *Illiuzii*, 251–252; Levitin and Shavrov, *Ocherki*, 2: 182–184.

29. RGASPI, f. 17, op. 112, d. 565a, ll. 47.

30. RGASPI, f. 17, op. 112, d. 565a, l. 52. The history of the 144-day *Manuilovshchina* in Petrograd is found in Levitin and Shavrov, *Ocherki*, 2: 217–244, and M. V. Shkarovskii, *Peterburgskaia eparkhiia v gody gonenii i utrat 1917–1945* (St. Petersburg: Liki Rossii, 1995), 96–103.

31. RGASPI, f. 89, op. 4, d. 115, l. 50; GARF, f. 353, op. 7, d. 6, ll. 17–18; and d. 17, l. 86.

32. RGASPI, f. 76, op. 3, d. 306, ll. 162.

33. For Tikhon's release as a miracle, see the letter to him from parishioners in Iaroslavl in RGIA, f. 831, op. 1, d. 194, l. 1, ff.

34. See Edward E. Roslof, "Calendar Reform of 1918," in *The Modern Encyclopedia of Religions in Russia and the Soviet Union*, Vol. 5 (Gulf Breeze, Fla.: Academic International Press, 1993), 5: 51–53.

35. RGASPI, f. 17, op. 112, d. 565a, l. 37.

36. GARF, f. 353, op. 7, d. 2, l. 16. On November 20, ARK charged Tuchkov with the task of implementing the calendar change by means of another message to the church from Tikhon; RGASPI, f. 17, op. 112, d. 565a, l. 43.

37. RGASPI, f. 17, op. 112, d. 565a, l. 48.

38. GARF, f. 353, op. 7, d. 16, l. 32; RGASPI, f. 17, op. 112, d. 565a, l. 53.

39. RGASPI, f. 17, op. 112, d. 775, ll. 11–12. At that same meeting, the GPU was told to investigate a statement by Tikhon to the VTsIK regarding the new-style calendar "in light of its clearly impermissible tone and counterrevolutionary character." The statement itself is not included in the file.

40. RGASPI, f. 17, op. 3, d. 488, l. 3; and d. 496, l. 7.

41. See RGASPI, f. 17, op. 112, d. 775, l. 44; and op. 113, d. 353, ll. 17, 24. For a discussion of popular opposition to the new-style calendar, see Gregory L. Freeze, "Counter-Reformation in Russian Orthodoxy: Popular Response to Religious Innovation, 1922–1925," *Slavic Review* 54, no. 2 (Summer 1995): 6–9.

42. RGASPI, f. 89, op. 4, d. 156, ll. 29–30.

43. RGASPI, f. 89, op. 4, d. 115, ll. 16–18.

44. Levitin and Shavrov, *Ocherki*, 2: 215.

45. Levitin and Shavrov, *Ocherki*, 2: 175–179.

46. Levitin and Shavrov did not know that ARK existed and attributed all these events to personal antagonisms between Tuchkov and various renovationist leaders (*Ocherki*, 2: 147).

47. GARF, f. 353, op. 7, d. 4, l. 82.

48. Levitin and Shavrov, *Ocherki*, 2: 161.

49. For the relationship between the decline in the significance of an organization's social function and its loss of social support, see Anthony Downs, *Inside Bureaucracy*, A RAND Corporation Research Study (Boston: Little, Brown and Company, 1967), 12–13.

50. N. F. Platonov, "Pravoslavnaia tserkov' v 1917–1918 gg.," *Ezhegodnik Muzeia istorii religii i ateizma* 5 (1961): 231.

51. This number includes both renovationist and Tikhonite parishes and comes from data collected by the NKVD RSFSR. See Odintsov, "Gosudarstvo," 36.

52. In his internal GPU report on his section's activities dated April 5, 1924, Tuchkov credited Tikhonites with control over 50 percent of parishes, renovationists with 35 percent, and autocephalous or wavering renovationists with 15 percent. He did not give additional statistics to back these conclusions, however, nor did he indicate whether he was referring only to the RSFSR. His conclusions are consistent with the general picture presented in Table 4.1. Pokrovskii and Petrov, *Arkhivy Kremlia*, 2: 419.

53. *Vestnik Sv. Sinoda*, no. 2 (15) (1927): 17. This accounting claimed 28,743 Orthodox parishes in Russia, giving renovationists 22 percent of the total.

54. Odintsov, "Gosudarstvo," 36.

55. RGASPI, f. 89, op. 4, d. 118, l. 5.

56. See Downs, *Inside Bureaucracy,* 11–12.

57. RGASPI, f. 17, op. 6, d. 509, ll. 92–93.

58. Levitin and Shavrov, *Ocherki,* 2: 179, 195–198. These authors assert that Evdokim hoped for reconciliation with Tikhon, but that seems unlikely in light of Tuchkov's desire to deepen the renovationist-Tikhonite split.

59. *Vestnik Sv. Sinoda,* no. 1 (September 18, 1923): 7–21. See also Levitin and Shavrov, *Ocherki,* 2: 198–205.

60. GARF, f. 5263, op. 1, d. 55, l. 155; RGASPI, f. 89, op. 4, d. 115, l. 32.

61. GARF, f. 353, op. 7, d. 17, l. 187; TsGAMO, f. 4570, op. 1, d. 2, ll. 139, 141.

62. Pokrovskii and Petrov, *Arkhivy Kremlia,* 1: 431–443. Quote on 433–434.

63. RGASPI, f. 89, op. 4, d. 115, l. 38.

64. Alekseev, *Illiuzii,* 262–263; Levitin and Shavrov, *Ocherki,* 3: 185–342. A significant portion of their third volume is devoted to Antonin's organization and his work for liturgical reform. He did not give up on the idea of church reform, despite his inability to attract a mass following even within Moscow. ARK acknowledged these limitations yet continued to grant his requests until 1925. See RGASPI, f. 17, op. 112, d. 565a, l. 62; d. 775, l. 25. Antonin may have had good personal connections within the party as Levitin and Shavrov suggest or, more likely, was seen by party officials as a powerful but uncontrollable church leader best kept isolated from other movements.

65. RGASPI, f. 89, op. 4, d. 115, l. 39.

66. RGASPI, f. 17, op. 6, d. 509, ll. 94–96.

67. RGASPI, f. 89, op. 4, d. 118, l. 5; Levitin and Shavrov, *Ocherki,* 2: 210–211.

68. This incident is recounted in several sources, including Levitin and Shavrov, *Ocherki,* 2: 264–277; and Regel'son, *Tragediia,* 356–361.

69. Regel'son, *Tragediia,* 387.

70. This meeting was recounted in *Vestnik Sv. Sinoda,* no. 7 (3) (1926): 5.

71. TsGAIPD, f. 16, op. 6, d. 6921, ll. 345–346.

72. According to one source, the GPU moved against Peter because he rejected Tuchkov's conditions for legalizing the patriarchal church's national administration during negotiations in November 1925. These conditions were said to have included a new declaration of church loyalty in addition to governmental control over Peter's selection and placement of bishops. See Regel'son, *Tragediia,* 389–390.

73. ARK decided Peter's fate on December 9, 1925, in the light of "concrete incriminating material" collected by the GPU that linked the metropolitan to anti-Soviet activity. The renovationists were not mentioned. See RGASPI, f. 17, op. 112, d. 775, l. 43. The official version of Peter's life after his arrest maintained that he was exiled to Siberia and died of natural causes. An account of his actual fate in Cheka prisons is given in Damaskin (Orlovskii), *Mucheniki, ispovedniki i podvizhniki blagochestiia rossiiskoi pravoslavnoi tserkvi XX stoletiia* (Tver: Bulat, 1996), 2: 342–366.

74. The text of the Holy Synod's statement is included in Levitin and Shavrov, *Ocherki,* 2: 205–208.

75. See *Vestnik Sv. Sinoda,* no. 1 (September 18, 1923): 1–3, 30.

76. *Vestnik Sv. Sinoda,* no. 1 (September 18, 1923): 3–4; Regel'son, *Tragediia,* 343, 349, 355.

77. Levitin and Shavrov, *Ocherki,* 2: 194.

78. RGASPI, f. 89, op. 4, d. 115, l. 49.

79. RGASPI, f. 17, op. 112, d. 775, ll. 3–4. Tikhon appears to have rejected that wording; the ban remained in effect until his death.

80. GARF, f. 5263, op. 1, d. 57, ll. 22–23.

81. *Vestnik Sv. Sinoda,* no. 1 (March 1925): 6–7.

82. Obnovlencheskaia tserkov', Leningradskaia gruppa, *Programma tserkovnykh obnovlentsev* (Leningrad, 1925[?]), 1–7.

83. A forceful exposition of this point is given by B. V. Titlinov, "Chto razdeliaet tserkov'," *Vestnik Sv. Sinoda*, no. 8–9 (3–4) (1926): 5–7.

84. *Vestnik Sv. Sinoda*, no. 6 (2) (1926): 30; and no. 7 (3) (1926): 3.

85. *Tserkovnaia zhizn'* (Vladimir), no. 1 (August 1924): 4–8; Levitin and Shavrov, *Ocherki*, 2: 313–334; Regel'son, *Tragediia*, 358–359.

86. See the Holy Synod's appeal immediately after Tikhon's death and Titlinov's commentary on Tikhon's "last testament" in *Vestnik Sv. Sinoda*, no. 2 (1925): 1–2; no. 3 (1925): 2–3. Evdokim's sudden departure from the national church scene just after Easter in 1925 was attributed to ill health. Levitin and Shavrov say that his mistakes in international affairs and disagreements with Vvedenskii were the real cause (*Ocherki*, 3: 67–70). ARK records from this period give no indication of state involvement in the change in renovationist leadership.

87. *Arkhangel'skii tserkovnyi golos*, no. 4–5 (June 11, 1926): 2–3.

88. See *Vestnik Sv. Sinoda*, no. 1 (March 1925): 9.

89. Unfortunately, we do not know what ARK expected out of the council. On June 27, 1925, it authorized the gathering and instructed Tuchkov to do "preparatory work" without further comment; RGASPI, f. 17, op. 112, d. 775, l. 38.

90. Titlinov's original comments are included in the official record (*deianiia*) of the Sobor, *Vestnik Sv. Sinoda*, no. 6 (2) (1926): 16–17.

91. Titlinov, "Chto razdeliaet tserkov'," *Vestnik Sv. Sinoda*, no. 8–9 (3–4) (1926): 5–7.

92. *Vestnik Sv. Sinoda*, no. 6 (2) (1926): 14–15, 18.

93. See the report explaining the decline in parishes loyal to the synod in *Vestnik Sv. Sinoda*, no. 2 (15) (1927): 17.

94. An account of positive reactions by renovationists in the months following the council is found in *Vestnik Sv. Sinoda*, no. 8–9 (3–4) (1926): 26–31. The plenary session of the Holy Synod in April 1926 examined the results of the council and found them mixed. The leaders decided that renovationism had grown more in quality than quantity; *Vestnik Sv. Sinoda*, no. 10 (6) (1926): 2–4.

95. This new title appeared on the masthead of *Vestnik Sv. Sinoda*, no. 1 (24) (1928).

96. ARK heard Tuchkov's recommendations on future Orthodox policy at its meeting of November 11, 1925, just one month after the council's close. A plan to divide Tikhonites and prosecute Metropolitan Peter contained no reference to a renovationist role; RGASPI, f. 17, op. 112, d. 775, ll. 39–41.

97. ARK voted to continue the delay of the trial on July 10 and August 5, 1923. On the second occasion, the commission found the threat of a trial necessary to ensure Tikhon's cooperation, even though an actual trial would give him an undesired "halo of a martyr." See RGASPI, f. 89, op. 4, d. 115, ll. 31, 39.

98. An overview of the controversy surrounding this document, including the full text and a discussion of its authenticity, is found in Regel'son, *Tragediia*, 368–375.

99. In September 1923, ARK pressed the patriarch to crush parish soviets and allow the remarriage of clergy in addition to accepting the new calendar. In return, Tikhon would have been allowed to publish his own periodical. RGASPI, f. 89, op. 4, d. 115, ll. 46–47.

100. For ARK's decisions, see RGASPI, f. 17, op. 112, d. 565a, ll. 47, 55, 58, 59 ob. *Izvestiia* announced the end of the investigation of Tikhon on March 22. See Regel'son, *Tragediia*, 353–355.

101. Regel'son, *Tragediia*, 355. The patriarch also accused the two leaders of spreading false rumors that he was negotiating with the pope to form a united church.

102. GARF, f. 5263, op. 1, d. 57, ll. 45–52, 85.

103. Metropolitan Kirill Smirnov of Kazan is credited with convincing Tikhon to cross Krasnitskii's name off the final membership list for the synod. Regel'son, *Tragediia*, 359–361. RGASPI, f. 17, op. 112, d. 775, ll. 1–2.

104. GARF, f. 5263, op. 1, d. 57, ll. 24–25. Another copy is found in RGASPI, f. 89, op. 4, d. 180, ll. 16–17.

105. Pokrovskii and Petrov, *Arkhivy Kremlia*, 1: 108–109; and 2: 451–453.

106. On April 24, 1926, ARK congratulated the GPU for splitting Tikhonites among supporters of Metropolitans Sergii and Agafangel plus those who followed the Temporary Supreme Church Soviet; RGASPI, f. 17, op. 113, d. 353, l. 9. For a history of these splits in the Russian church, see Pospielovsky, *The Russian Church*, 1: 70–72, 111–162.

107. ARK made all these concessions to Tikhonite groups, especially the one led by Sergii, after 1925. See RGASPI, f. 17, op. 113, d. 353, ll. 12, 49; d. 871, ll. 4–5, 7.

108. RGASPI, f. 17, op. 112, d. 775, ll. 26–28, 33–34, 36; op. 113, d. 353, ll. 7, 10; and d. 871, l. 24.

109. *Vestnik Sv. Sinoda*, no. 2 (15) (1927): 17.

110. *Pravoslavnyi tserkovnyi vestnik*, no. 1–2 (January 1, 1928): 7; Alekseev, *Illiuzii*, 181–183; Regel'son, *Tragediia*, 406, 430–434.

111. Historians connected with the Russian Orthodox Church continue to justify the modus vivendi chosen by Sergii for dealing with the Soviet government. A particularly vigorous defense was made on the seventy-fifth anniversary of the 1927 declaration by Hegumen Innokentii (Pavlov), "Metropolitan Sergii's Declaration and Today's Church," *Russian Studies in History* 32 (Fall 1993): 82–88.

112. RGASPI, f. 17, op. 112, d. 620, ll. 2, 18–23.

113. RGASPI, f. 17, op. 113, d. 353, l. 13.

114. RGASPI, f. 17, op. 3, d. 627, ll. 10–11.

115. RGASPI, f. 17, op. 113, d. 353, l. 40; and d. 871, l. 10.

116. RGASPI, f. 17, op. 112, d. 775, ll. 12–13, 18–21, 33–34; and op. 113, d. 353, ll. 15, 17.

5. Renovationism in the Parish

1. TsGAIPD, f. 16, op. 6, d. 6919, l. 283.

2. TsGAIPD, f. 16, op. 6, d. 6920, l. 121 (GPU summary report for August 1925).

3. The complaint that renovationists were motivated by greed is found repeatedly in parish petitions. For example, see the May 1923 statement from villagers in Tambov in the files of the Commissariat of Justice (GARF, f. 353, op. 6, d. 26, ll. 30–33).

4. GARF, f. 353, op. 7, d. 2, ll. 22–24.

5. RGASPI, f. 5, op. 1, d. 2643, l. 18 (GPU summary report on nationwide politics and economics for September 16–21, 1922).

6. M. V. Shkarovskii, *Peterburgskaia eparkhiia v gody gonenii i utrat 1917–1945* (St. Petersburg: Liki Rossii, 1995), 79.

7. For examples of such threats, see RGASPI, f. 5, op. 1, d. 2645, l. 71.

8. GARF, f. 353, op. 6, d. 21, ll. 208–211, 214–215, 216–220.

9. GARF, f. 353, op. 6, d. 27, ll. 4–5, 27–29, 33.

10. *Revoliutsiia i tserkov'*, no. 1–3 (1922): 6–9. Also, Lev Regel'son, *Tragediia russkoi tserkvi* (Paris: YMCA, 1977), 326.

11. GARF, f. 5263, op. 1, d. 55, ll. 70–74.

12. William Fletcher, *The Russian Orthodox Church Underground* (Oxford: Oxford University Press, 1971), 33.

13. See the April 1923 complaint by St. Nikolai Church of Khalmets, outside Moscow, to the Commissariat of Justice in GARF, f. 353, op. 6, d. 20, l. 61. Ironically, the parish had

to resubmit its petition because it had neglected to attach the appropriate governmental tax stamp.

14. GARF, f. 353, op. 6, d. 20, ll. 5–7.

15. GARF, f. 353, op. 6, d. 26, ll. 21–23. Petrograd government officials refused to act in response to the displaced parish council's complaints about this affair.

16. GARF, f. 353, op. 6, d. 26, ll. 11–13.

17. RGIA, f. 831, op. 1, d. 196, ll. 1, 4, 6, 11, 20, 24, 27.

18. RGIA, f. 831, op. 1, d. 245, ll. 10–14; TsGAIPD, f. 16, op. 5, d. 5911, l. 19 (letter from Zhemchuzin to Bishop Venedict, March 1924).

19. *Pravoslavnyi tserkovnyi vestnik* (Kazan), no. 4 (April 1, 1926): 7–9.

20. TsGIAgM, f. 2303, op. 1, d. 4, ll. 111 ob., 112. The parish council relieved Kotov of preaching duties for expressing these views but allowed him to continue serving the Eucharist. Kotov resigned in protest, and his supporters began calling members of the parish council red and agitating for their dismissal.

21. For example, see the December 1924 GPU report for Leningrad province in Ts-GAIPD, f. 16, op. 6, d. 6912, l. 70.

22. Michel d'Herbigny, "L'aspect religieux de Moscou en Octobre, 1925," *Orientalia Christiana Analecta* (Rome) V-3, no. 20 (June 1926): 210.

23. "Revoliutsiia i Tserkov'," *Sobornyi razum*, Petrograd, no. 1 (November 26, 1922): 2–3.

24. B. V. Titlinov, *Novaia tserkov'* (Petrograd-Moscow: tipografiia ar. L. Ia. Ganzburg, 1923), 51.

25. Quoted in A. I. Klibanov, "Sovremennoe sektantstvo v lipetskoi oblasti," *VIRA*, 10 (1962): 159.

26. This sentiment sometimes also extended to Sergii, as in another letter written in January 1928; Regel'son, *Tragediia*, 440–441, 447.

27. GARF, f. 353, op. 6, d. 20, ll. 35–36 (Petition from parishioners of the Valaam Monastery to the Commissariat of Justice, January 1923).

28. "O 'Zhivoi Tserkvi' v derevne," *Zhizn' i religiia*, no. 4 (December 15, 1922): 15.

29. *Drug pravoslavnogo naroda*, no. 3 (October 1922): 3–6.

30. George V. Zito, "Toward a Sociology of Heresy," *Sociological Analysis* 44 (no. 2 (1983): 123–130.

31. Popular opposition to specific points in the renovationist reformation, particularly to changes in the calendar and liturgy, is eloquently presented by Gregory L. Freeze in "Counter-reformation in Russian Orthodoxy: Popular Response to Religious Innovation, 1922–1925," *Slavic Review* 54, no. 2 (Summer 1995): 305–339.

32. Guy E. Swanson, *Religion and Regime: A Sociological Account of the Reformation* (Ann Arbor: University of Michigan Press, 1967), vii–viii.

33. As described by Helmut Altrichter in "Insoluble Conflicts: Village Life between Revolution and Collectivization," in *Russia in the Era of NEP: Explorations in Soviet Society and Culture*, edited by Sheila Fitzpatrick, Alexander Rabinowitch, and Richard Stites (Bloomington and Indianapolis: Indiana University Press, 1991), 195–202. Altrichter's assessment is supported by RGASPI, f. 17, op. 112, d. 775, l. 44; and op. 113, d. 353, ll. 17, 24 (ARK Protocols for December 9, 1925 and June 6 and December 11, 1926).

34. "Tikhonovskii krizis," *Piatigorskii eparkhial'nyi vestnik*, no. 1 (February 1, 1923): 18.

35. Altrichter, "Insoluble Conflicts," 192–209. See also the discussion of popular religion in Soviet Russia by Moshe Lewin in *Making of the Soviet System: Essays in the Social History of Interwar Russia* (New York: Pantheon, 1985), 57–71.

36. In Orthodox theological circles, immanence has been explained as the incarnation of divine energies, following the example of Christ. This line of thought has mystical connotations that were developed by Simeon the New Theologian (d. 1022) and Gregory Palamas (d. 1359), whose theology influenced Russian monasticism through the hesychastic

movement. See Jaroslav Pelikan, *The Christian Tradition: A History of the Development of Doctrine*, vol. 2: *The Spirit of Eastern Christianity (600–1700)* (Chicago: University of Chicago Press, 1974), 252–270. Accounts that illustrate popular Russian Orthodox understandings of this concept can be found in the biography of Anastasiia Logacheva (1809–1875) by Brenda Meehan in *Holy Women of Russia: The Lives of Five Orthodox Women Offer Spiritual Guidance for Today* (New York: HarperSanFrancisco, 1993), 41–60, and in devotional accounts, such as Jane Ellis, trans., *An Early Soviet Saint: The Life of Father Zachariah* (London: Mowbrays, 1976).

37. For example, the GPU reported that Orthodox peasants present at a meeting in Penza province on September 22, 1922, said they would be against renovationism if it changed the church service; RGASPI, f. 5, op. 1, d. 2644, l. 14.

38. Titlinov, *Novaia tserkov'*, 51; N. F. Platonov, "Pravoslavnaia tserkov' v 1917–1918 gg.," *Ezhegodnik Muzeia istorii religii i ateizma* 5 (1961): 254–259; Mikhail Pol'skii, *Novye mucheniki rossiiskie*, 3 vols. (Jordanville, N. Y.: Tip. I. Pochaevskago v "Sviato-Troitskam" monastyrie, 1957), 1: 105–106 and 2: 145–155; RGASPI, f. 5, op. 1, d. 2644, l. 97.

39. RGASPI, f. 5, op. 1, d. 2643, l. 52; and d. 2644, l. 26.

40. Regel'son, *Tragediia*, 313.

41. "Soobshcheniia s mest," *Zhizn' i religiia*, no. 1 (September 1, 1922): 8, 12–13.

42. "Khronika," *Zhizn' i religiia*, no. 3 (November 15, 1922): 11–12. The financial pressure on renovationism was reflected in the appeal for money at the end of this issue to enable the magazine to survive.

43. Gregory L. Freeze, *The Parish Clergy in Nineteenth-Century Russia: Crisis, Reform, Counter-Reform* (Princeton, N.J.: Princeton University Press, 1983), 454–455.

44. "Otzvuki zhizni," *Zhizn' i religiia*, no. 4 (December 15, 1922): 5.

45. These themes occur repeatedly in correspondence for 1923–1924 to Tikhon from believers and clergy. Their petitions, reports, and other documents are in the archives of the patriarchal chancery; RGIA, f. 831, op. 1, dd. 194, 196, 200, and 247.

46. Richard Stites, *Revolutionary Dreams: Utopian Vision and Experimental Life in the Russian Revolution* (New York: Oxford University Press, 1989), 121–122. A detailed account of parallels between Baptist and atheistic activism is presented in Heather Jean Coleman, "The Most Dangerous Sect: Baptists in Tsarist and Soviet Russia, 1902–1929" (Ph.D. dissertation, University of Illinois at Urbana-Champaign, 1998), 353–414.

47. Tuchkov's reports clearly valued popular disaffection with the Orthodox Church. For example, see his report from September 1923 in RGASPI, f. 89, op. 4, d. 118, l. 5.

48. Richard Stites, *Revolutionary Dreams: Utopian Vision and Experimental Life in the Russian Revolution* (New York: Oxford University Press, 1989), 101; John S. Curtiss, *The Russian Church and the Soviet State, 1917–1950* (Boston: Little, Brown & Co., 1952), 218.

49. V. A. Alekseev, *Illiuzii i dogmy* (Moscow: Politizdat, 1991), 264–268. The Central Committee investigated the party organizations in twenty-nine provinces of central Russia and was alarmed to discover that religious beliefs were still strong among party members; RGASPI, f. 17, op. 60, d. 52, ll. 1–4.

50. See the 1923 report for the Fifth Department of the Commissariat of Justice in *Revoliutsiia i tserkov'*, no. 1–2 (1924), cited in Regel'son, *Tragediia*, 349–350.

51. Sheila Fitzpatrick, "The Problem of Class Identity in NEP Society," in *Russia in the Era of NEP: Explorations in Soviet Society and Culture*, edited by Sheila Fitzpatrick, Alexander Rabinowitch, and Richard Stites (Bloomington and Indianapolis: Indiana University Press, 1991), 22, 26–27.

52. Iaroslavskii noted the synod's organizational advantage in a presentation to the Orgburo in December 1924 (RGASPI, f. 17, op. 112, d. 620, ll. 16–17).

53. TsGAIPD, f. 16, op. 6, d. 6924, l. 148 (GPU summary report for November 2–9, 1925).

54. RGASPI, f. 17, op. 112, d. 775, ll. 6–7.

55. See GARF, f. 353, op. 6, d. 26, ll. 42–48; and op. 7, d. 4, ll. 99, 235, 276; f. 5263, op. 1, d. 55, ll. 216, 296, 299, 320, 330, 341, 352–354.

56. GARF, f. 353, op. 6, d. 27, ll. 1–4, 229–230.

57. SOTsDNI, f. 27, op. 3, d. 146, ll. 71, 73 ob.; and d. 148, ll. 86, 88, 90, 92 (Provincial GPU political reports to Moscow for 1923). Archbishop Kornilii was a monastic with a long history of church service prior to the schism, which may have explained his charisma. See Archbishop Manuil (Lemeshevskii), *Katalog "Russkikh Arkhiereev Obnovlentsev,"* 3 vols. (Library of the Patriarchal Holy Synod, Moscow, typescript, 1957), 1: 239–241.

58. *Vestnik Sv. Sinoda*, no. 3–4 (26–27) (1928): 20. Nazarii subsequently joined the Gregorian schism; Manuil, *Katalog*, 2: 33.

59. The archbishop's personal charisma is evident in the periodical *Arkhangel'skii tserkovnyi golos*, no. 1 (December 21, 1925): 1–5, 15; no. 2–3 (February 11, 1926): 14; and no. 4–5 (June 11, 1926): 1. The periodical apparently ceased publication after his departure. Between 1925 and 1936, Mikhail served in ten different episcopal sees, despite a two-year return to the patriarchal church in 1929–1931; Manuil, *Katalog*, 2: 28–29.

60. These issues were addressed by the April 16–21, 1926, plenum of the Holy Synod; *Vestnik Sv. Sinoda*, no. 10 (6) (1926): 2–10.

61. TsGIAgM, f. 2303, op. 1, d. 21, ll. 74, 342, 381, 405, 599, 664 (Protocols from meetings of the renovationist diocesan council in Moscow, 1928).

62. TsGIAgM, f. 2303, op. 1, d. 20, ll. 251–252, 268, 305, 327. Zhuk's parish attempted to abandon renovationism in September 1927.

63. TsGIAgM, f. 2303, op. 1, d. 20, l. 330; and d. 21, l. 117.

64. TsGIAgM, f. 2303, op. 1, d. 18, ll. 113–114.

65. See the reaction to such a switch in June 1925 by a church in the Klin region; TsGIAgM, f. 2303, op. 1, d. 14, l. 11.

66. This information was included in a report to the synod's plenum of November 22, 1927, in *Vestnik Sv. Sinoda*, no. 2 (25) (1928): 3–8.

67. TsGIAgM, f. 2303, op. 1, d. 18, ll. 81–83. In this same document, diocesan clergy who had defected to the Tikhonites were dismissed as "passive to their pastoral duty," implying that they had compromised their principles for material security.

68. TsGIAgM, f. 2303, op. 1, d. 17, ll. 79, 80, 86, 88, 89–91, 94, 113–114, 118–119.

69. TsGIAgM, f. 2303, op. 1, d. 20, ll. 87, 94–96.

70. TsGIAgM, f. 2303, op. 1, d. 20, ll. 439–453.

71. On February 13, 1925, the Financial Department of the RSFSR refused a request by the Holy Synod to exempt its parishes from church taxes. The ruling indicated that such an exemption would be illegal because it would give the synod "a privileged position"; TsGIAgM, f. 2303, op. 1, d. 15, l. 106.

72. SOTsDNI, f. 27, op. 3, d. 147, l. 128 (Secret letter to the Saratov provincial party secretary from the corresponding secretary of the Kuznetskii region, July 1923). This situation continued through the fall and winter, according to later reports in d. 148, ll. 88, 92 (Saratov provincial GPU summary reports).

73. *Pravoslavnyi tserkovnyi vestnik*, no. 6 (December 1, 1925): 24.

74. TsGIAgM, f. 2303, op. 1, d. 15, l. 108 (Petition to the renovationist Holy Synod from Bogoliubskii Cathedral, February 1925).

75. Bishop Innokentii wrote to Tikhon in February 1924 with news of the effects of his assumption of his post in Stavropol. The believers in that city refused to attend churches controlled by synodal clergy and only relented after local clergy returned to the patriarchal fold; RGIA, f. 831, op. 1, d. 247, ll. 8–9.

76. Quoted in Levitin and Shavrov, *Ocherki*, 3: 48–49.

77. TsGIAgM, f. 2303, op. 1, d. 15, l. 277 (Petition to renovationist diocesan council, February 1925).

78. TsGIAgM, f. 2303, op. 1, d. 14, l. 5 (Petition to renovationist diocesan council, June 15, 1925).

79. See the analysis by Douglas R. Weiner in "'Razmychka?' Urban Unemployment and Peasant In-migration as Sources of Social Conflict," in *Russia in the Era of NEP: Explorations in Soviet Society and Culture*, edited by Sheila Fitzpatrick, Alexander Rabinowitch, and Richard Stites (Bloomington and Indianapolis: Indiana University Press, 1991), 144–155.

80. A vicious struggle for control of St. Nicholas Church in Moscow occurred when the former parish priest returned to his post after being unable to find secular work; TsGIAgM, f. 2303, op. 1, d. 14, ll. 6–9 (Request by Archpriest Leonid Bagretsov for a transfer to a new parish, June 15, 1925). Some renovationists voluntarily defrocked and took positions as antireligious activists. See Daniel Peris, "Commissars in Red Cassocks: Former Priests in the League of the Militant Godless," *Slavic Review* 54, no. 2 (Summer 1995): 350–351.

81. TsGIAgM, f. 2303, op. 1, d. 14, ll. 111–115 (Report from the parish council of Semenov Cemetery, August 22, 1925).

82. *Vse ispytyvaite khoroshego derzhites' (Likvidatsiia Kubanskoi Tikhonovshchiny)* (Krasnodar: Kubano-Chernomorskogo Eparkhial'nogo Upravleniia, 1926), 12.

83. TsGIAgM, f. 2303, op. 1, d. 15, ll. 193, 211–212, 227, 324, 326.

84. RGIA, f. 831, op. 1, d. 247, ll. 1–2. At a party meeting in Tatarstan in July 1926, the clergy who had privileges under the tsars were said to be Tikhonites, while "those formerly in subservient positions to that group" were labeled as renovationists; TsKhIDNIT, f. 15, op. 2, d. 172, l. 103.

85. TsGAIPD, f. 16, op. 6, d. 6917, l. 78 (GPU summary report for May 1–15, 1925).

86. *Pravoslavnyi tserkovnyi vestnik*, no. 6 (December 1, 1925): 22. The renovationists responded by caustically asking what would happen if they performed the liturgy together outside—would the Tikhonites need to douse the heavens with holy water?

87. *Vse ispytyvaite*, 5.

88. *Vestnik Sv. Sinoda*, no. 11 (7) (1926): 20–22.

6. Liquidation

1. Moshe Lewin, "Society, State, and Ideology during the First Five-Year Plan," in *Cultural Revolution in Russia, 1928–1931*, edited by Sheila Fitzpatrick (Bloomington and London: Indiana University Press, 1978), 41.

2. This statement was made by leading party theoretician Nikolai Bukharin during an address to the Second All-Russian Congress of the League of the Godless in June 1929. Quoted in M. I. Odintsov, "Purgatory," *Russian Studies in History* 32, no. 2 (Fall 1993): 61.

3. Odintsov, "Purgatory," 57.

4. For a description of this unsettled era, see Sheila Fitzpatrick, "Cultural Revolution as Class War," in *Cultural Revolution in Russia, 1928–1931* (Bloomington and London: Indiana University Press, 1978), 8–40.

5. Odintsov quotes at length from this still-classified report in "Purgatory," 58, and "Gosudarstvo i tserkov': Istorii vzaimootnoshenii, 1917–1938 gg.," *Kul'tura i religiia*, no. 11 (1991): 36.

6. For a detailed presentation of the Soviet view on religious activity, see Glennys J. Young, *Power and the Sacred in Revolutionary Russia: Religious Activists in the Village* (University Park: Pennsylvania State University Press, 1997).

7. N. N. Pokrovskii and S. G. Petrov, eds., *Arkhivy Kremlia: Politbiuro i tserkov' 1922–1925 gg.*, 2 vols. (Moscow and Novosibirsk: Sibirskii khronograf and ROSSPEN, 1997–1998): 2: 436–440.

8. Odintsov, "Gosudarstvo," 36–37.

9. Sheila Fitzpatrick, *Stalin's Peasants: Resistance and Survival in the Russian Village after Collectivization* (Oxford: Oxford University Press, 1994), 6, 28, 33–37, 212–214.

10. V. A. Alekseev, *Illiuzii i dogmy* (Moscow: Politizdat, 1991), 280–282, 293–295.

11. RGASPI, f. 17, op. 113, d. 871, l. 25; and f. 17, op. 3, d. 723, ll. 9–10.

12. Odintsov, "Purgatory," 57–59; and "Gosudarstvo," 38.

13. A history of this body is found in Arto Luukkanen, *The Religious Policy of the Stalinist State: A Case Study—The Central Standing Commission on Religious Questions, 1929–1938* (Helsinki: Suomen Historiallinen Seura, 1997).

14. Odintsov, "Purgatory," 60–61; Alekseev, *Illiuzii*, 291–292. For a history of the League, see Daniel Peris, *Storming the Heavens: The Soviet League of the Militant Godless* (Ithaca, N.Y.: Cornell University Press, 1998).

15. Studies of class war in various elements of Soviet society include Fitzpatrick, "Cultural Revolution as Class War," and Hiroaki Kuromiya, *Stalin's Industrial Revolution: Politics and Workers, 1928–1932* (Cambridge: Cambridge University Press, 1988).

16. RGASPI, f. 17, op. 113, d. 871, l. 33.

17. RGASPI, f. 17, op. 113, d. 737, l. 126.

18. RGASPI, f. 17, op. 113, d. 737, ll. 128–133. A subcommittee that examined the issue of closing churches concluded that 80 percent of the population were believers and that closures only helped "nepmen, kulaks, and priests."

19. Odintsov, "Purgatory," 62–63.

20. Odintsov, "Purgatory," 62.

21. See RGASPI, f. 17, op. 113, d. 871, ll. 27, 30, 41, 44, 47–49. Correspondence related to the closure of the St. Panteleon Chapel is also found in GARF, f. 5263, op. 1, d. 3, ll. 6–10. For reasons still unknown, the party's Central Committee dissolved the Antireligious Commission in November 1929. It is still unclear what body in the government or party took over ARK's policymaking functions. The Central Standing Commission on Religious Questions merely executed policy, as seen from its records in GARF, fond 5263. State security organs (OGPU and NKVD) most likely decided religious policy between 1929 and 1943.

22. The number of closures comes from Odintsov, "Purgatory," 62. The total number of functioning churches comes from a response to an inquiry by the Central Standing Commission on Religious Questions about buildings used for religious purposes between 1931 and 1933; GARF, f. 5263, op. 1, d. 32, l. 70.

23. TsKhIDNIT, f. 15, op. 2, d. 760, l. 17.

24. TsGA TASSR, f. 1172, op. 3, d. 1209, ll. 8, 11, 11 ob., 13–14, 19, 22.

25. Odintsov, "Purgatory," 62, 66.

26. The icon had become a bone of contention among Tikhonites, renovationists, and local officials as early as in 1927. The VTsIK decided the icon's fate in April 1929; its decision reflected the new antireligious stance of the government; GARF, f. 5263, op. 1, d. 3, ll. 70–87.

27. *Vestnik Sv. Sinoda*, no. 9–12 (42–45) (1929): 9–11.

28. A. Levitin and V. Shavrov, *Ocherki po istorii russkoi tserkovnoi smuti*, 3 vols. (Switzerland: Institut Glaube in der 2. Welt, 1977), 3: 369.

29. Such a portrait will come only with unrestricted access to archives of the former Soviet security ministries and the Moscow patriarchate—access that lies decades in the future.

30. John S. Curtiss, *The Russian Church and the Soviet State, 1917–1950* (Boston: Little, Brown & Co., 1952), 249–252; Peris, *Storming the Heavens*, 174–196.

31. Alekseev, *Illiuzii*, 314–315; Fitzpatrick, *Stalin's Peasants*, 6–7.

32. *Vestnik Sv. Sinoda*, no. 9–12 (42–45) (1929): 3.

33. *Zhurnal Moskovskoi Patriarkhii* (hereafter abbreviated ZhMP), no. 5 (1931): 2–3.

34. These interviews occurred in February 1930. See Curtiss, *The Russian Church*, 265–266.

35. *ZhMP*, no. 1 (1931): 3.

36. *ZhMP*, no. 7–8 (1932): 6, 7. Other instances relating to reception of renovationist clergy are found in *ZhMP*, no. 7–8 (1932): 4–5; no. 11–12 (1932): 5; no. 13 (1922): 2; no. 14–15 (1933): 5; no. 23–24 (1935): 2–3.

37. Alekseev suggests that Stalin preferred Sergii's faction in the mid-1920s for the same reason; *Illiuzii*, 280–281.

38. GARF, f. 5263, op. 1, d. 32, l. 66. Reprinted in Odintsov, "Purgatory," 64. According to this accounting, 46 percent of all Orthodox churches open before the Revolution had been closed by December 1, 1933.

39. These cases are found in the records for the Central Standing Commission on Religious Questions. GARF, f. 5263, op. 1, d. 1, ll. 13 ob., 19; d. 19, ll. 148–153; d. 21, ll. 196–199; d. 32, ll. 5, 49, 153; d. 34, ll. 15, 62; d. 39, ll. 34–35; d. 45, ll. 58–62, 95; d. 47, ll. 28, 72–73, 81, 93; d. 48, ll. 28–29; d. 182, ll. 7, 19, 39, 67–78; d. 588, ll. 5–7; d. 726, ll. 1–7; d. 989, ll. 99–110; d. 1122, ll. 1–19; d. 1149, l. 12; d. 1551, ll. 19–22.

40. GARF, f. 5263, op. 1, d. 19, ll. 140–141.

41. GARF, f. 5263, op. 1, d. 22, ll. 11, 12 ob.

42. The plan was published as a four-page brochure entitled *Rezoliutsiia sviashchennogo sinoda po doklady Osoboi Komissii "O prirode starotserkovnichestva i merakh tserkovnoi bor'by c nim" ot 19 sentiabria 1934 g*. A copy of this brochure is in GAKO, f. R-983, op. 1, d. 3, ll. 5–6. According to Levitin and Shavrov, the meeting at which the Holy Synod approved this plan was its last; *Ocherki*, 3: 358.

43. The presiding officer of the gathering closed the session by warning the representatives that the task of giving passports to clergy was very serious and that they must treat the instructions they received with the utmost secrecy. He threatened serious reprisals against anyone who revealed the contents of their discussions. M. V. Shkarovskii, *Peterburgskaia eparkhiia v gody gonenii i utrat 1917–1945* (St. Petersburg: Liki Rossii, 1995), 152. A history of the Josephite schism is given in Mikhail V. Shkarovskii, "The Russian Orthodox Church versus the State: The Josephite Movement, 1927–1940," *Slavic Review* 54, no. 2 (Summer 1995): 365–384.

44. *Vestnik Sv. Sinoda*, no. 5–6 (38–39) (1929): 17–19; and no. 9–12 (42–45) (1929): 4–5, 15–16.

45. Promoting members as a reward for their loyalty is a phenomenon common among organizations that are struggling for survival. See Anthony Downs, *Inside Bureaucracy*, A RAND Corporation Research Study (Boston: Little, Brown and Company, 1967), 18–20.

46. *Vestnik Sv. Sinoda*, no. 3–4 (46–47) (1930): 1–2. Vitalii and Alexander Vvedenskii were not related. The latter's comments on the election of the former are found in Levitin and Shavrov, *Ocherki*, 3: 372–373.

47. Curtiss, *The Russian Church*, 267.

48. TsGA TASSR, f. 1172, op. 3, d. 1209, ll. 25–27, 31–33, 36–37, 53 ob.

49. GARF, f. 5263, op. 1, d. 1473, ll. 23–29.

50. Curtiss, *The Russian Church*, 230–231, 272–273.

51. GARF, f. 5263, op. 1, d. 1152, l. 72.

52. These theses were adopted on November 15, 1931; TsGA TASSR, f. 1172, op. 3, d. 1209, l. 83.

53. Curtiss, *The Russian Church*, 262–264.

54. GARF, f. 5263, op. 1, d. 46, ll. 5–6, 17–19.

55. GAKO, f. R-983, op. 1, d. 3, ll. 3.

56. Krasikov's letter is dated October 1, 1935; GARF, f. 5263, op. 1, d. 39, l. 61.

57. GARF, f. 5263, op. 1, d. 32, ll. 1–2.

58. GARF, f. 5263, op. 1, d. 32, ll. 17–23.

59. Records of the Council for Russian Orthodox Church Affairs include many petitions from believers who asked to reopen parish churches. They often based their case on

the evidence that the church had never been officially closed and that they had maintained control of the building for years by keeping its keys. Eight cases from the Moscow area are listed in a report by A. A. Trushin for the first quarter of 1945; TsGAMO, f. 7383, op. 1, d. 5, ll. 2 ob.–3.

60. GARF, f. 5263, op. 1, d. 32, ll. 24–26.

61. Alekseev, *Illiuzii*, 332–333.

62. Levitin and Shavrov, *Ocherki*, 3: 344.

63. GARF, f. 5263, op. 1, d. 988, ll. 2–3. Krasikov expressed these sentiments in a letter to A. Petrovskii, the president of the Leningrad city soviet.

64. Odintsov, "Purgatory," 68.

65. Odintsov, "Purgatory," 68–69.

66. Odintsov, "Gosudarstvo," 62–63; RGASPI, f. 17, op. 114, d. 899, ll. 125–141.

67. Information on the church in Leningrad during the 1930s is found in works by Shkarovskii (who had access to municipal archives) and Levitin and Shavrov (who drew primarily on their personal experiences). For unknown reasons, documents from Kaluga's renovationist diocesan administration for 1931–1936 landed in the regional archive (GAKO, f. R-983). This file also includes a report from Rybinsk diocese for 1934–1935.

68. GAKO, f. R-983, op. 1, d. 6, ll. 1–2. This report indicated that one of the eight parishes had transferred to the patriarchate in 1935. The list for 1936, however, still includes eight parishes. GAKO, f. R-983, op. 1, d. 1, l. 13–13 ob.

69. See the correspondence between Archbishop Aleksander and his diocesan priests for February and March 1936 in GAKO, f. R-983, op. 1, d. 8, ll. 1–4.

70. GAKO, f. R-983, op. 1, d. 2, ll. 1–7.

71. GAKO, f. R-983, op. 1, d. 4, ll. 1–6; and d. 5, ll. 4–5, 15 ob.

72. Shkarovskii, *Peterburgskaia eparkhiia*, 149–150, 164.

73. Levitin and Shavrov, *Ocherki*, 3: 344–345; Shkarovskii, *Peterburgskaia eparkhiia*, 170.

74. Records from the investigation are in archives for the NKVD for Moscow and Moscow *oblast'* (GARF, f. 9035, op. 1, P-30285, ll. 42–161, 302–303). Transcripts of interrogation sessions clearly show that the supposed conspiracy existed only in the minds of the secret police. I was unable to search the whole collection for similar criminal cases involving renovationist clergy.

75. Levitin and Shavrov, *Ocherki*, 3: 362–365. After a decade of leading renovationism in Leningrad, Boiarskii became a bishop in 1933. At the time of his arrest in 1936, he was metropolitan of Ivanovo. He was executed by order of a three-man NKVD tribunal on September 9, 1937; M. V. Shkarovskii, *Obnovlencheskoe dvizhenie v russkoi pravoslavnoi tserkve XX veka* (Izd. Nestor: St. Petersburg, 1999), 94.

76. See Alekseev, *Illiuzii*, 261; Curtiss, *The Russian Church*, 285–286; and D. Diagilev, *Tserkovniki i sektanty na sluzhbe kontrrevoliutsii* (Cheliabinsk, 1939), 10.

77. M. I. Odintsov, *Religioznye organizatsii v SSSR nakanune i v gody Velikoi Otechestvennoi Voiny 1941–1945 gg.* (Moscow: Rossiiskaia Akademiia Gosudarstvennoi Sluzhby, 1995), 7; Fitzpatrick, *Stalin's Peasants*, 15. When state policy toward the Orthodox Church changed in 1943, thousands of petitions to open churches—including some with thousands of signatures—were submitted to the government. See T. A. Chumachenko, *Gosudarstvo, pravoslavnaia tserkov', veruiushchie. 1941–1961 gg.* (Moscow, AIRO-XX, 1999), 68–69.

78. O. Iu. Vasil'eva, "Russkaia pravoslavnaia tserkov' i Sovetskaia vlast' v 1917–1927 godakh," *Voprosy istorii*, no. 8 (1993): 54. Vasil'eva obtained these figures from GARF, f. 6991, op. 1, d. 1, l. 39. This file (*delo*) remains classified and therefore closed to foreign researchers.

79. Odintsov, "Purgatory," 71–72.

80. Odintsov, *Religioznye organizatsii*, 7–12. Odintsov provides important new material that supplements and corrects two older studies on the Russian church during the war; Har-

vey Fireside, *Icon and Swastika* (Cambridge, Mass.: Harvard University Press, 1971), and Wassilij Alexeev and Theofanis Stavrou, *The Great Revival* (Minneapolis: Burgess, 1976).

81. Levitin and Shavrov, *Ocherki*, 3: 378–379.

82. Archbishop Manuil (Lemeshevskii), *Katalog "Russkikh Arkhiereev Obnovlentsev,"* 3 vols. (Library of the Patriarchal Holy Synod, Moscow, typescript, 1957), 1: 111.

83. Levitin and Shavrov, *Ocherki*, 3: 383–386. As his later actions and career demonstrate, Larin obviously enjoyed the trust of Soviet state security.

84. Levitin and Shavrov, *Ocherki*, 3: 395.

85. RGASPI, f. 89, op. 4, d. 175, l. 8.

86. Alekseev, *Illiuzii*, 334–335.

87. GARF, f. 6991, op. 2, d. 17, ll. 12–13.

88. See the report on the activities of the Spaso-Preobrazhenskii Church during the first two years of the war; TsGA St. Peterburga, f. 4769, op. 3, d. 147, ll. 1–55.

89. See archival documents on the Orthodox in Belorussia from 1942, reprinted in A. M. Komarov, ed., *Dokumenty oblichiaut. Reaktsionnaia rol' religii i tserkvi na territorii Belorussii* (Minsk, 1964), 80–83, and Odintsov, *Religioznye organizatsii*, 39–43, 51–52.

90. GARF, f. 6991, op. 2, d. 13, ll. 96–103; d. 14, ll. 61–71; d. 16, ll. 91–92, 97.

91. GARF, f. 6991, op. 2, d. 14, l. 41.

92. Daniel Peris, "'God Is Now on Our Side': The Religious Revival on Unoccupied Soviet Territory during World War II," *Kritika* 1, no. 1 (Winter 2000): 98, 118.

93. Alekseev, *Illiuzii*, 336–346.

94. The accounts of these meetings are taken from Karpov's notes, included in GARF, f. 6991, op. 1, d. 1, ll. 1–10, as summarized by M. I. Odintsov in "Drugogo paza ne bylo . . ." *Nauka i religiia*, 1989, 2: 8–9.

95. Downs, *Inside Bureaucracy*, 22.

96. GARF, f. 6991, op. 1, d. 3, ll. 6–10. The file contains all three copies of Karpov's letter. Stalin returned his copy to Karpov with two notations written in red pencil: "I agree with you" and "This is correct" (ll. 7–8).

97. GARF, f. 6991, op. 1, d. 3, l. 11.

98. From the journals of the patriarchal synod, GARF, f. 6991, op. 2, d. 2a, ll. 9–10, 17–18, 20–24, 31–37.

99. GARF, f. 6991, op. 1, d. 3, ll. 137–138; and op. 2, d. 2a, ll. 40, 43, 44, 57, 66–68; Manuil, *Katalog*, 1: 61 and 2: 139.

100. GARF, f. 6991, op. 2, d. 2a, ll. 58–59.

101. On the shortage of patriarchal clergy, see protocols from the Council for Russian Orthodox Church Affairs in GARF, f. 6991, op. 2, d. 2, ll. 11–15. For examples of regional data on the age and education of clergy, see GARF, f. 6991, op. 1, d. 85, ll. 133–142 (for the Bashkir ASSR); op. 2, d. 12, l. 187 (for Gorkii); and TsGAMO, f. 7383, op. 1, d. 11, ll. 5, 5 ob. (for Moscow).

102. Levitin and Shavrov, *Ocherki*, 3: 381.

103. GARF, f. 6991, op. 1, d. 3, ll. 138–140; Levitin and Shavrov, *Ocherki*, 3: 397.

104. GARF, f. 6991, op. 2, d. 2, ll. 13 ob., 14 ob., 49–53; d. 4, l. 5 ob.

105. GARF, f. 6991, op. 2, d. 15, ll. 130–140.

106. GARF, f. 6991, op. 2, d. 35, ll. 3, 34–35.

107. GARF, f. 6991, op. 2, d. 16, ll. 109–111.

108. GARF, f. 6991, op. 2, d. 12, ll. 2–107.

109. GARF, f. 6991, op. 2, d. 16, l. 89.

110. GARF, f. 6991, op. 2, d. 14, ll. 81–88, 143–147; d. 16, ll. 87–92; d. 34a, ll. 1, 1 ob. Karpov personally visited both renovationist strongholds (Stavropol and Krasnodar) in February 1944; GARF, f. 6991, op. 2, d. 2, l. 38.

111. GARF, f. 6991, op. 1, d. 10, l. 33; and d. 12, ll. 103–110. Later in 1945, Kozhin became a monk and took the name Germogen. The next year, he became bishop of Kazan,

and in the last nine years of his life, he rose to the highest echelons of the patriarchal church. See Manuil, *Katalog*, 1: 91–93.

112. GARF, f. 6991, op. 2, d. 35, ll. 22–25.

113. GARF, f. 6991, op. 2, d. 14, ll. 41–53, 92–105; and d. 16, ll. 78–79. Ivanov took the monastic name Flavian as a patriarchal bishop and was sent back to the see of Krasnodar and the Kuban. Manuil, *Katalog*, 2: 173.

114. GARF, f. 6991, op. 2, d. 14, l. 57.

115. TsGAMO, f. 7383, op. 1, d. 5, l. 15; and d. 8, l. 17.

116. TsGAMO, f. 7383, op. 1, d. 11, ll. 10–11.

117. Levitin and Shavrov, *Ocherki*, 3: 405–416.

118. Trushin reported the event to Karpov in detail; TsGAMO, f. 7383, op. 1, d. 9, l. 6.

119. A record of this meeting is attached to the first page of the first volume of A. I. Kuznetsov's typewritten manuscript in the St. Petersburg Theological Academy Library (A. I. Kuznetsov, "Obnovlencheskii raskol v Russkoi Tserkvi," 3 vols. [typescript, 1956–1959]). Protopresbyter N. F. Kolchitskii, the patriarch's factotum, read Kuznetsov's history of the renovationist schism and added this recollection of Vvedenskii's final meeting with Aleksii.

120. TsGAMO, f. 7383, op. 1, d. 11, ll. 11, 11 ob., 66.

121. GARF, f. 6991, op. 1, d. 9, ll. 3–4.

122. GARF, f. 6991, op. 1, d. 9, l. 7; d. 12, l. 86; d. 45, ll. 15–17, 72–73; d. 49, l. 617; d. 90, l. 638.

123. GARF, f. 6991, op. 1, d. 12, ll. 15–16, 85–95; d. 52, ll. 216–218.

124. GARF, f. 6991, op. 1, d. 12, ll. 74–74 ob.; d. 61, l. 111–112; d. 84, ll. 9–17. For biographical data on Lobanov, see Manuil, *Katalog*, 1: 166.

125. GARF, f. 6991, op. 2, d. 82, ll. 1–3. The description of the files that were destroyed is intriguing in its brevity. One wonders if they were burned because they were unimportant or because they were too compromising.

126. Trushin was instructed to find the petitioners and tell them that the Council for Russian Orthodox Church Affairs could do nothing for the family; TsGAMO, f. 7383, op. 3, d. 17, ll. 3, 4, 4 ob. I thank Leonid Vaintraub for calling these documents to my attention.

127. A third clergyman present at that conversation reported what was said to Soviet officials; TsMAM, f. 3004, op. 2, d. 19, ll. 2, 9. Some biographical details for Rastorguev in this file conflict with Manuil, *Katalog*, 1: 66.

128. Prot. Nikolai Balashov, *Na puti k liturgicheskomu vozrozhdeniiu* (Moscow: Dukhovnaia Biblioteka, 2001), 6. The graves of the three Vvedenskii clergymen are located in a place of great honor, closest to the outside wall on the altar side of the cemetery church. Alexander's marker notes that he was a metropolitan. In personal conversation, women working in the church denied knowing that he is officially a schismatic and heretic in the opinion of Orthodox officials.

SELECTED BIBLIOGRAPHY

Archival Sources

Gosudarstvennyi arkhiv Kaluzhskoi oblasti (GAKO), Kaluga
    f. R-983   Posluzhnye i formuliarnye spiski sluzhitelem kul'ta, 1931–1936
Gosudarstvennyi arkhiv Rossiiskoi Federatsii (GARF), Moscow
    f. 353   Narodnyi kommissariat iustitsii, 1918–1925 gg.
    f. 1064   Tsentral'naia komissiia pomoshchi golodaiushchim pri VTsIK (Pomgol), 1921–1922 gg.
    f. 1235   Vserossiiskii tsentral'nyi ispolnitel'nyi komitet
    f. 5263   Komissiia po voprosam kul'tov, 1929–1938 gg.
    f. 6991   Sovet po delam russkoi pravoslavnoi tserkvi pri SM SSSR (1943–1960 gg.)
Rossiiskii gosudarstvennyi arkhiv sotsial'no-politicheskoi istorii (RGASPI), Moscow
    f. 5   Lenin
    f. 17   Tsentral'nyi komitet KPSS
    f. 76   F. E. Dzerzhinskii
    f. 89   E. M. Iaroslavskii
Rossiiskii gosudarstvennyi istoricheskii arkhiv (RGIA), St. Petersburg
    f. 831   Kantseliariia patriarkha Tikhona
Saratovskii oblastnoi tsentr dokumentatsii noveishei istorii (SOTsDNI), Saratov
    f. 27   Saratovskii Gubkom RKP(b)
Tsentr khraneniia i izucheniia dokumentov noveishei istorii Tatarstana (TsKhIDNIT), Kazan
    f. 15   Tatarskoi Obkom RKP(b) g. Kazan'
Tsentral'nyi gosudarstvennyi arkhiv istoriko-politicheskikh dokumentov (TsGAIPD), St. Petersburg
    f. 16   Petrogradskii/Leningradskii Gubkom RKP(b)
    f. 24   Leningradskii Obkom RKP(b)
Tsentral'nyi gosudarstvennyi arkhiv Moskovskoi oblasti (TsGAMO), Moscow
    f. 4570   Komissiia po voprosam kul'ta pri Moskovskom oblastnom Sovete RK i KD, 1917–1935 gg.
    f. 7383   Upolnomochnyi Soveta po delam RPTs pri SM SSSR po gor. Moskve i Moskovskoi oblasti, 1944–1961 gg.
Tsentral'nyi gosudarstvennyi arkhiv Tatarskoi ASSR (TsGA TASSR), Kazan
    f. 1172   Kazanskii eparkhial'nyi sovet, Kazanskoe eparkhial'noe upravlenie, Kazanskoe oblastnoe mitropolitskoe upravlenie (1915–1937 gg.)
Tsentral'nyi gosudarstvennyi istoricheskii arkhiv g. Moskvy (TsGIAgM), Moscow
    f. 2303   Moskovskoe eparkhial'noe upravlenie, 1914–1937 gg.
Tsentral'nyi munitsipal'nyi arkhiv goroda Moskvy (TsMAM), Moscow
    f. 3004   Upolnomochnyi SDP pri SM SSSR po g. Moskve (1943–1991)

Russian Periodicals

Antireligioznik
Arkhangel'skii tserkovnyi golos
Bezbozhnik
Drug pravoslavnogo naroda
Ezhegodnik Muzeia istorii religii i ateizma
Golos pravoslavnogo khristianina
Golos zhivoi tserkvi
Golos zhivoi very
Iaroslavskie eparkhial'nye vedomosti
Izvestiia
Izvestiia TsK KPSS
Khristianin
Nauka i religiia
Obnovlenie tserkvi
Piatigorskii eparkhial'nyi vestnik
Po stopam Khrista
Pravda
Pravoslavnyi tserkovnyi vestnik
Revoliutsiia i tserkov'
Russkaia mysl' (Paris)
Sibirskaia tserkov'
Slovo zhizni
Sobornyi razum
Tserkov' i zhizn'
Tserkovnaia zaria
Tserkovnaia zhizn'
Tserkovnoe obnovlenie
Tul'skii tserkovnyi vestnik
Ural'skie tserkovnye vedomosti
Vestnik Sviashchennogo Sinoda pravoslavnoi rossiiskoi tserkvi
Vlast' Sovetov
Voprosy istorii religii i ateizma
Za Khristom
Zhivaia tserkov'
Zhivaia tserkov' (Penza)
Zhizn' i religiia
Zhurnal Moskovskoi Patriarkhii

Published Primary Sources

Adamov, Dmitrii. *Politicheskoe obosnovanie tserkovnogo obnovlenchestva.* Voronezh, 1925.
Aivazov, I. G. *Obnovlentsy i starotserkovniki.* Moscow, 1909.
Antonin (Granovskii), Bishop. *Bozhestvennaia liturgiia, retsenzirovannaia po chinam drevn. liturgii.* Moscow, 1923.
Batalin, A. V. *Doklady o tserkovnoi zhizni.* Kaluga, 1927.
Beliaev, V. A. *Protiv kontrrevoliutsionnoi deiatel'nosti tserkovnikov.* Leningrad, 1939.
Belliustin, I. S. *Description of the Parish Clergy in Rural Russia: The Memoir of a Nineteenth-Century Parish Priest.* Translated and with an introductory essay by Gregory L. Freeze. Ithaca, N.Y.: Cornell University Press, 1985.

Bliakhin, P. A. *Kto i zachem stroit tserkvi.* Moscow, 1929.

Bogovoi, I. V. *Tserkovnaia revoliutsiia.* Arkhangel'sk, 1922.

Bonch-Bruevich, V. D. *"Zhivaia tserkov'" i proletariat.* 4th ed. Moscow: Molodaia gvardiia, 1929.

Bulatov, Ivan. *K raskolu v Russkoi pravoslavnoi tserkvi.* Vologda, 1922.

Chikin, I. *Kto takie tikhonovtsy i obnovlentsy i za kem itti?* Briansk, 1926.

Deianiia II-go Vserossiiskogo pomestnogo sobora pravoslavnoi tserkvi. Moscow, 1923.

d'Herbigny, Michel. "L'aspect religieux de Moscou en Octobre, 1925." *Orientalia Christiana Analecta* (Rome) V-3, no. 20 (June 1926): 185–279.

Diagilev, D. *Tserkovniki i sektanty na sluzhbe kontrrevoliutsii.* Cheliabinsk: Gubkom RKP, 1939.

Ellis, Jane, trans. *An Early Soviet Saint: The Life of Father Zachariah.* London: Mowbrays, 1976.

Evlogii (Georgievskii), Metropolitan. *Put' moei zhizni.* Paris: YMCA, 1947.

Gidulianov, P. V. *Tserkov' i gosudarstvo.* Moscow, 1924.

Gidulianov, P. V., and P. A. Krasikov, eds. *Otdelenie tserkvi ot gosudarstva.* 2nd ed. Moscow: Iuridicheskoe, 1924.

Gruppa Peterburgskikh sviashchennikov. *K tserkovnomu soboru.* St. Petersburg: Tipografiia M. Merkusheva, 1906.

Gubonin, M. E., ed. *Akty Sviateishego Tikhona, Patriarkha Moskovskogo i vseia Rossii, pozdneishie dokumenty i perepiska o kanonicheskom preemstve vysshei tserkovnoi vlasti. 1917–1943 gg.* Moscow: St. Tikhon's Orthodox Theological Institute, 1994.

Il'inskii, F. I. *Pravda tserkovnogo raskola.* Kozlov, 1924.

Kartashev, A. V. "Revoliutsiia i Sobor 1917–1918 gg." *Bogoslovskaia mysl'* (Paris) 4 (1942): 42–85.

Komarov, A. M., ed. *Dokumenty oblichaiut. Reaktsionnaia rol' religii i tserkvi na territorii Belorussii.* Minsk, 1964.

Krasikov, P. A. *Na tserkovnom fronte (1918–1922).* Moscow, 1923.

Levitin-Krasnov, A. E. *Likhie gody, 1925–1941.* Paris: YMCA, 1977.

Manuil (Lemeshevskii), Archbishop. *Katalog "Russkikh Arkhiereev Obnovlentsev."* 3 vols. Library of the Patriarchal Holy Synod, Moscow. Typescript, 1957.

———. *Die russischen orthodoxen Bischoefe von 1893 bis 1965.* 5 vols. Erlangen: Oikonomia, 1979–.

Materialy po obnovlecheskomu dvizheniiu. Polemika. St. Petersburg Theological Academy Library. Typescript. N.p., 1926[?].

McCullagh, Francis. *The Bolshevik Persecution of Christianity.* London: E. P. Dutton, 1924.

———. *A Prisoner of the Reds.* New York: E. P. Dutton, 1922.

Nikolai (Minin), Archbishop. *Vliianiia obnovlenchestva na religii v mirovom vselenskom masshtabe.* Semipalatinsk, 1926.

Nikolai (Tikhvinskii), Bishop. *Arkhipastyrskoe poslanie Usol'skogo i Solikamskogo episkopa Nikolaia k pastve Verkhne-Kamskogo okruga.* Usol'e, 1926.

Obnovlencheskaia tserkov', Leningradskaia gruppa. *Programma tserkovnykh obnovlentsev.* Leningrad, 1925[?].

Oleshchuk, F. N. *Kto stroit tserkvi v SSSR.* Moscow-Leningrad, 1929.

Palmieri, F. Aurelio. "The Russian Church and the Revolution." *Catholic World* 106 (February 1918): 661–670.

Persits, M. M., ed. *Deiateli oktiabria o religii i tserkvi (Stat'i, rechi, besedy, vospominaniia).* Moscow: Mysl, 1968.

Pokrovskii, N. N., and S. G. Petrov, eds. *Arkhivy Kremlia: Politbiuro i tserkov' 1922–1925 gg.* 2 vols. Moscow and Novosibirsk: Sibirskii khronograf and ROSSPEN, 1997–1998.

Pomestnyi sobor Russkoi pravoslavnoi tserkvi. *Deianiia II-go Vserossiiskogo Pomestnogo Sobora Pravoslavnoi tserkvi.* Moscow, 1923.

Rezoliutsiia sviashchennogo sinoda po doklady Osoboi Komissii "O prirode starotserkovnichestva i merakh tserkovnoi bor'by c nim" ot 19 sentiabria 1934 g. Moscow, 1934.

Stratonov, Irinarkh. *Russkaia tserkovnaia smuta, 1921–1931 gg.* Berlin: Parabola, 1932.

Szczesniak, Boleslaw, ed. and trans. *The Russian Revolution and Religion: A Collection of Documents concerning the Suppression of Religion by the Communists, 1917–1925.* Notre Dame, Ind.: University of Notre Dame Press, 1959.

Titlinov, B. V. *Novaia tserkov'.* Petrograd-Moscow: tipografiia ar. L. Ia. Ganzburg, 1923.

———. *Tserkov' vo vremia revoliutsii.* Petrograd: Byloe, 1923.

Trudy s"ezda predstavitelei dukhovenstva i mirian Smolenskoi eparkhii, 1–2 fev. 1928 g. Smolensk: izd. Smolenskogo eparkhial'nogo upravleniia, 1928.

Valentinov, A. A., ed. *Chernaia kniga ("Shturm nebes").* Paris: Izd. Russkago natsional'nago studencheskago ob"edineniia, 1925.

Vorob'ev, Prot. Vladimir et al., eds. *Sledstvennoe delo patriarkha Tikhona. Sbornik dokumentov po materialam Tsentral'nogo arkhiva FSB RF.* Moscow: Pamiatniki istoricheskoi mysli, 2000.

Vse ispytyvaite khoroshego derzhites' (Likvidatsiia Kubanskoi Tikhonovshchiny). Krasnodar: izd. Kubano-Chernomorskogo Eparkhial'nogo Upravleniia, 1926.

Vvedenskii, A. I. *Tserkov' i gosudarstvo: Ocherk vzaimootnoshenii tserkvi i gosudarstva v Rossii 1918–1922 g.* Moscow: Mospoligraf, 1923.

XX-letie otdeleniia tserkvi ot gosudarstva. Moscow, 1938.

Secondary Sources

Alekseev, V. A. *Illiuzii i dogmy.* Moscow: Politizdat, 1991.

Alexeev, Wassilij, and Theofanis Stavrou. *The Great Revival: The Russian Church under German Occupation.* Minneapolis, Minn.: Burgess, 1976.

Anderson, Paul B. *People, Church and State in Modern Russia.* 2nd ed. London: S.C.M.P., 1944.

Andreev, V. M. *Liberal'no-obnovlencheskoe dvizhenie v russkom pravoslavii nachala XX v. i ego ideologiia.* Avtoreferat, candidate's degree. Leningrad State University, 1971.

Ascher, Abraham. *The Revolution of 1905: Russia in Disarray.* Stanford, Calif.: Stanford University Press, 1988.

Balashov, Prot. Nikolai. *Na puti k liturgicheskomu vozrozhdeniiu.* Moscow: Dukhovnaia Biblioteka, 2001.

Bellah, Robert N. "Civil Religion in America." *Daedalus* 96 (Winter 1967): 1–21.

Beloglazov, M. L. *Vzaimootnosheniia organov gosudarstvennoi vlasti i pravoslavnoi tserkvi na Altae (okt. 1917–1925 gg.).* Avtoreferat, candidate's degree in history, Tomsk State University, 1992.

Berger, Peter L. *The Sacred Canopy: Elements of a Sociological Theory of Religion.* Garden City, N.Y.: Doubleday, 1967.

Bossy, John. *Christianity in the West, 1400–1700.* Oxford: Oxford University Press, 1985.

Chaves, Mark. *Ordaining Women: Culture and Conflict in Religious Organizations.* Cambridge, Mass., and London: Harvard University Press, 1997.

Christian, William A. Jr. *Local Religion in Sixteenth-Century Spain.* Princeton, N.J.: Princeton University Press, 1981.

Chumachenko, T. A. *Gosudarstvo, pravoslavnaia tserkov', veruiushchie. 1941–1961 gg.* Moscow: AIRO-XX, 1999.

Clark, Peter B., and James Q. Wilson. "Incentive Systems: A Theory of Organizations." *Administrative Science Quarterly* 6 (September 1961): 129–166.

Coleman, Heather Jean. "The Most Dangerous Sect: Baptists in Tsarist and Soviet Russia, 1902–1929." Ph.D. dissertation, University of Illinois at Urbana-Champaign, 1998.

Cunningham, James W. *A Vanquished Hope: The Movement for Church Renewal in Russia, 1905–1906*. Crestwood, N.Y.: St. Vladimir's Seminary Press, 1981.

Curtiss, John S. *Church and State in Russia: The Last Years of the Empire, 1900–1917*. New York: Columbia University Press, 1940.

———. *The Russian Church and the Soviet State, 1917–1950*. Boston: Little, Brown & Co., 1952.

Damaskin (Orlovskii). *Mucheniki, ispovedniki i podvizhniki blagochestiia rossiiskoi pravoslavnoi tserkvi XX stoletiia*. 2 vols. Tver: Bulat, 1992, 1996.

Davis, Nathaniel. *A Long Walk to Church: A Contemporary History of Russian Orthodoxy*. Boulder, Colo.: Westview Press, 1995.

Demerath, N. J. III et al., eds. *Sacred Companies: Organizational Aspects of Religion and Religious Aspects of Organizations*. Oxford: Oxford University Press, 1998.

Downs, Anthony. *Inside Bureaucracy*. A RAND Corporation Research Study. Boston: Little, Brown and Company, 1967.

Durkheim, Emile. *The Division of Labor in Society*. Translated by George Simpson. New York: Macmillan, 1933.

———. *The Elementary Forms of the Religious Life: A Study in Religious Sociology*. Translated by Joseph W. Swain. New York: Macmillan, 1915.

Emhardt, William C. *Religion in Soviet Russia: Anarchy*. London: Mowbray, 1929.

Evtuhov, Catherine. "The Church in the Russian Revolution: Arguments for and against Restoring the Patriarchate at the Church Council of 1917–1918." *Slavic Review* 50, no. 3 (Fall 1991): 497–511.

Fireside, Harvey. *Icon and Swastika: The Russian Orthodox Church under Nazi and Soviet Control*. Cambridge, Mass.: Harvard University Press, 1971.

Fitzpatrick, Sheila. *Cultural Revolution in Russia, 1928–1931*. Bloomington and London: Indiana University Press, 1978.

———. *Everyday Stalinism: Ordinary Life in Extraordinary Times—Soviet Russia in the 1930s*. New York: Oxford, 1999.

———. *Stalin's Peasants: Resistance and Survival in the Russian Village after Collectivization*. Oxford: Oxford University Press, 1994.

Fitzpatrick, Sheila, Alexander Rabinowitch, and Richard Stites, eds. *Russia in the Era of NEP: Explorations in Soviet Society and Culture*. Bloomington and Indianapolis: Indiana University Press, 1991.

Fletcher, William. *The Russian Orthodox Church Underground*. Oxford: Oxford University Press, 1971.

Florovsky, Georges. *Puti russkogo bogosloviia*. Paris: YMCA, 1937.

Freeze, Gregory L. "Counter-reformation in Russian Orthodoxy: Popular Response to Religious Innovation, 1922–1925." *Slavic Review* 54, no. 2 (Summer 1995): 305–339.

———. "Handmaiden of the State? The Church in Imperial Russia Reconsidered." *Journal of Ecclesiastical History* 36 (January 1985): 84–90.

———. *The Parish Clergy in Nineteenth-Century Russia: Crisis, Reform, Counter-Reform*. Princeton, N.J.: Princeton University Press, 1983.

———. "Rechristianization of Russia: The Church and Popular Religion, 1750–1850." *Studia Slavica Finlandensia* 7 (1990): 101–136.

———. *The Russian Levites: Parish Clergy in the Eighteenth Century*. Cambridge, Mass.: Harvard University Press, 1977.

Geekie, J. H. M. "Church and Politics in Russia, 1905–1917: A Study of the Political Behaviour of the Russian Orthodox Clergy in the Reign of Nicholas II." Ph.D. dissertation, University of East Anglia, 1978.

Gleason, Abbott, Peter Kenez, and Richard Stites, eds. *Bolshevik Culture: Experiment and Order in the Russian Revolution*. Bloomington: Indiana University Press, 1985.

Hosking, Geoffrey A., ed. *Church, Nation and State in Russia and Ukraine*. London: Macmillan, in association with the School of Slavonic and East European Studies, University of London, 1991.

Husband, William B. *"Godless Communists": Atheism and Society in Soviet Russia, 1917–1932*. DeKalb: Northern Illinois University Press, 2000.

———, ed. *The Human Tradition in Modern Russia*. Wilmington, Del.: Scholarly Resources, 2000.

Jacobs, James R., and Margaret C. Jacobs. "Anglican Origins in Modern Science." *Isis* 71 (1980): 251–267.

Kandidov, B. P. *Golod 1921 goda i tserkov'*. Moscow, 1932.

Kizenko, Nadieszda. *A Prodigal Saint: Father John of Kronstadt and the Russian People*. University Park: Pennsylvania State University Press, 2000.

Kolstø, Pål. "A Mass for a Heretic? The Controversy over Lev Tolstoi's Burial." *Slavic Review* 60, no. 1 (Spring 2001): 75–95.

Kozarzhevskii, A. Ch. "A. I. Vvedenskii i obnovlencheskii raskol v Moskve." *Vestnik Moskovskogo Universiteta, seriia 8*, no. 1 (1989): 54–66.

Krivova, N. A. *Vlast' i tserkov' v 1922–1925 gg*. Moscow: AIRO-XX, 1997.

Kuromiya, Hiroaki. *Stalin's Industrial Revolution: Politics and Workers, 1928–1932*. Cambridge: Cambridge University Press, 1988.

Kuznetsov, A. I. "Obnovlencheskii raskol v Russkoi Tserkvi." 3 vols. St. Petersburg Theological Academy Library. Typescript. 1956–1959.

Ladurie, Emmanuel Le Roy. *Montaillou: The Promised Land of Error*. New York: Random House, 1978.

Lenin, V. I. *Collected Works*. 4th ed. 45 vols. Moscow: Progress Publishers, 1960–1970.

Levitin, A., and V. Shavrov. *Ocherki po istorii russkoi tserkovnoi smuti*. 3 vols. Switzerland: Institut Glaube in der 2. Welt, 1977.

Lewin, Moshe. *Making of the Soviet System: Essays in the Social History of Interwar Russia*. New York: Pantheon, 1985.

Lipsky, Michael. *Street-Level Bureaucracy*. New York: Russell Sage Foundation, 1980.

Luckmann, Thomas. *The Invisible Religion: The Problem of Religion in Modern Society*. New York: Macmillan, 1967.

Luukkanen, Arto. *The Party of Disbelief: The Religious Policy of the Bolshevik Party, 1917–1929*. Helsinki: Suomen Historiallinen Seura, 1994.

———. *The Religious Policy of the Stalinist State: A Case Study—The Central Standing Commission on Religious Questions, 1929–1938*. Helsinki: Suomen Historiallinen Seura, 1997.

Majeska, George P. "The Living Church Movement in Soviet Russia." M.A. thesis, Indiana University, 1964.

Marx, Karl, and Friedrich Engels. *On Religion*. New York: Schocken Books, 1964.

Meehan, Brenda. *Holy Women of Russia: The Lives of Five Orthodox Women Offer Spiritual Guidance for Today*. New York: HarperSanFrancisco, 1993.

Meerson, Michael A. "The Renovationist Schisms in the Russian Orthodox Church." *Canadian-American Slavic Studies* 26, nos. 1–3 (1992): 293–314.

Melgounov, Sergey P. *The Red Terror in Russia*. London: J. M. Dent & Sons, 1926.

Meyendorff, John. "Russian Bishops and Church Reform in 1905." In *Russian Orthodoxy under the Old Regime*, edited by R. Nichols and T. Stavrou, 170–182. Minneapolis: University of Minnesota Press, 1978.

Miliukov, P. N. *Ocherki po istorii russkoi kul'tury*. 4 vols. St. Petersburg: Tip. I. N. Skorokhodova, 1904–1909.

Nezhnyi, A. "Protokoly kremlevskikh mudretsov." *Ogonek*, nos. 31–33 (1992): 8–11. (Translated in "Protocols from Meetings of the Kremlin Wise Men," *Russian Studies in History* 32, no. 2 [Fall 1993]: 89–104.)

Odintsov, M. I. "Drugogo raza ne bylo . . . " *Nauka i religiia*, no. 2 (1989): 8–9.

———. "Gosudarstvo i tserkov': Istorii vzaimootnoshenii, 1917–1938 gg." *Kul'tura i religiia*, no. 11 (1991): 1–64.

———. "Khozhdenie po mukam." Parts 1–5. *Nauka i religiia*, no. 5 (1990): 8–10; no. 6 (1990): 12–13; no. 7 (1990): 56–57; no. 8 (1990): 19–21; no. 7 (1991): 1–2. (Translated in M. I. Odintsov, "Purgatory," *Russian Studies in History* 32, no. 2 [Fall 1993]: 53–81.)

———. *Religioznye organizatsii v SSSR nakanune i v gody Velikoi Otechestvennoi Voiny 1941–1945 gg.* Moscow: Rossiiskaia Akademiia Gosudarstvennoi Sluzhby, 1995.

———. "Zhrebii pastyria." Parts 1–4. *Nauka i religiia*, no. 1 (1989): 38–42; no. 4 (1989): 16–20; no. 5 (1989): 18–21; no. 6 (1989): 34–40.

Osipova, E. S. "Vremennoe pravitel'stvo i tserkov'." In *Tserkov' v istorii Rossii*, edited by Iu. Ia. Kogan, 317–319. Moscow and Leningrad: Nauka, 1967.

Pelikan, Jaroslav. *The Christian Tradition: A History of the Development of Doctrine*. Vol. 2: *The Spirit of Eastern Christianity (600–1700)*. Chicago: University of Chicago Press, 1974.

Peris, Daniel. "Commissars in Red Cassocks: Former Priests in the League of the Militant Godless." *Slavic Review* 54, no. 2 (Summer 1995): 340–364.

———. "'God is Now on Our Side': The Religious Revival on Unoccupied Soviet Territory during World War II." *Kritika* 1, no. 1 (Winter 2000): 97–118.

———. *Storming the Heavens: The Soviet League of the Militant Godless*. Ithaca, N.Y.: Cornell University Press, 1998.

Platonov, N. F. "Pravoslavnaia tserkov' v 1917–1918 gg." *Ezhegodnik Muzeia istorii religii i ateizma* 5 (1961): 211–245.

Pol'skii, Mikhail. *Novye mucheniki rossiiskie*. 3 vols. Jordanville, N.Y.: Tip. I. Pochaevskago v "Sviato-Troitskam" monastyrie, 1957.

Pospielovsky, Dimitry. *The Russian Church and the Soviet Regime, 1917–1982*. 2 vols. Crestwood, N.Y.: St. Vladimir's Seminary Press, 1984.

Powell, Walter W., and Paul J. DiMaggio, eds. *The New Institutionalism in Organizational Analysis*. Chicago: University of Chicago Press, 1994.

Rabinowitch, Alexander. *The Bolsheviks Come to Power: The Revolution of 1917 in Petrograd*. New York: Norton, 1976.

Radkey, Oliver H. *Russia Goes to the Polls: The Election to the All-Russian Constituent Assembly, 1917*. Ithaca, N.Y.: Cornell University Press, 1990.

Regel'son, Lev. *Tragediia russkoi tserkvi*. Paris: YMCA, 1977.

Rittersporn, Gabor T. "Soviet Politics in the 1930s: Rehabilitating Society." *Studies in Comparative Communism* 19, no. 2 (Summer 1986): 105–128.

Ronaldshay, Earl of. *The Life of Lord Curzon: Being the Authorized Biography of George Nathaniel, Marquess Curzon of Kedleston, K.G.* 3 vols. London: Ernest Benn, 1928.

Rosenberg, William G., and Lewis H. Siegelbaum, eds. *Social Dimensions of Soviet Industrialization*. Bloomington: Indiana University Press, 1993.

Roslof, Edward E. "Calendar Reform of 1918." In *Modern Encyclopedia of Religions in Russia and the Soviet Union*, vol. 5, 51–53. Gulf Breeze, Fla.: Academic International Press, 1993.

———. "The Russian Orthodox Church and the Bolshevik Regime, 1917–1918." M.A. thesis, University of Hawaii at Manoa, 1988.

Scott, W. Richard. *Organizations: Rational, Natural and Open Systems*. 4th ed. Upper Saddle River, N.J.: Prentice Hall, 1998.

Scott, W. Richard, and John W. Meyer and Associates. *Institutional Environments and Organizations: Structural Complexity and Individualism*. Thousand Oaks, Calif.: SAGE, 1994.

Sergii (Larin), Bishop. *Obnovlencheskii raskol*. 2 vols. St. Petersburg Theological Academy Library. Typescript. 1953–1959.

Shiner, Larry. "The Concept of Secularization in Empirical Research." *Journal for the Scientific Study of Religion* 6 (Fall 1967): 207–220.

Shishkin, A. A. *Sushchnost' i kriticheskaia otsenka "obnovlencheskogo" raskola russkoi pravoslavnoi tserkvi.* Kazan: izd. Kazanskogo Universiteta, 1970.

Shkarovskii, M. V. *Obnovlencheskoe dvizhenie v russkoi pravoslavnoi tserkve XX veka.* Izd. Nestor: St. Petersburg, 1999.

———. *Peterburgskaia eparkhiia v gody gonenii i utrat 1917–1945.* St. Petersburg: Liki Rossii, 1995.

Sidorov, Dmitri A. "Orthodoxy, Difference, and Scale: The Evolving Geopolitics of Russian Orthodox Church(es) in the 20th Century." Ph.D. dissertation, University of Minnesota, 1998.

Simon, Gerhard. "Church, State and Society." In *Russia Enters the Twentieth Century: 1894–1917,* edited by E. Oberlander et al., 199–235. London: Temple Smith, 1971.

Steeves, Paul D. "Reevaluating Patriarch Tikhon." Paper presented at the annual meeting of the Southern Conference on Slavic Studies, Savannah, Georgia, March 1991.

Steinberg, Mark D. "Workers on the Cross: Religious Imagination in the Writings of Russian Workers, 1910–1924." *Russian Review* 53 (April 1994): 213–239.

Stites, Richard. *Revolutionary Dreams: Utopian Vision and Experimental Life in the Russian Revolution.* New York: Oxford University Press, 1989.

Swanson, Guy E. *The Birth of the Gods: The Origin of Primitive Beliefs.* Ann Arbor: University of Michigan Press, 1960.

———. *Religion and Regime: A Sociological Account of the Reformation.* Ann Arbor: University of Michigan Press, 1967.

Titlinov, B. V. *Pravitel'stvo imperatritsy Anny Ioannovny v ego otnosheniiakh k delam pravoslavnoi tserkvi.* Vilna: Tip Russkii pochin, 1905.

Traina, Michael J. "Lenin, Religion and the Russian Orthodox Church: An Analysis of Theory and Practice." Ph.D. dissertation, Kent State, 1970.

Treadgold, Donald W. *The West in Russia and China.* Vol. 1: *Russia: 1472–1917.* Cambridge: Cambridge University Press, 1973. Reprint, Boulder, Colo.: Westview Press, 1985.

Tsypin, Prot. Vladislav. *Istoriia Russkoi Tserkvi, 1917–1997.* Moscow: Spaso-Preobrazhenskii Valaam Monastery, 1997.

Vasil'eva, O. Iu. "Iz'iatie tserkovnykh tsennostei v 1922 godu: nekotorie aspekty problemy." In *Religiia, obshchestvo i gosudarstvo v XX veke: Material konferentsii, Moskva, 22–25 oktiabria 1991 g.,* edited by Ia. N. Shchapov, 57–62. Moscow: Institut istorii SSSR, AN SSSR, 1991.

———. "Russkaia pravoslavnaia tserkov' i Sovetskaia vlast' v 1917–1927 godakh." *Voprosy istorii,* no. 8 (1993): 40–54.

Vostryshev, M. I. *Bozhii izbrannik: Krestnyi put' Sviatitelia Tikhona, patriarkha Moskovskogo i vseia Rossiia.* Moscow: Sovremennik, 1990.

———. *Patriarkh Tikhon.* Moscow: Molodaia gvardiia, 1995.

Weber, Max. *From Max Weber: Essays in Sociology.* Edited and translated by H. H. Gerth and C. W. Mills. New York: Oxford University Press, 1958.

Young, Glennys J. *Power and the Sacred in Revolutionary Russia: Religious Activists in the Village.* University Park: Pennsylvania State University Press, 1997.

Zito, George V. "Toward a Sociology of Heresy." *Sociological Analysis* 44, no. 2 (1983): 123–130.

Zybkovets, V. F. *Natsionalizatsiia monastyrskikh imushchestv v Sovetskoi Rossii (1917–1921 gg.).* Moscow: Nauka, 1975.

INDEX

EDWARD E. ROSLOF is Associate Professor of Church History
at United Theological Seminary in Dayton, Ohio.
His research in Russian religious history concentrates on
the interaction between Orthodox Christianity and communism
in the twentieth century.